American Value

Migrants, Money, and Meaning in El Salvador and the United States

DAVID PEDERSEN

THE UNIVERSITY OF CHICAGO PRESS   CHICAGO AND LONDON

David Pedersen is associate professor of anthropology at the University of California, San Diego.

The University of Chicago Press, Chicago 60637
The University of Chicago Press, Ltd., London
© 2013 by The University of Chicago
All rights reserved. Published 2013.
Printed in the United States of America

22 21 20 19 18 17 16 15 14 13   1 2 3 4 5

ISBN-13: 978-0-226-65339-6 (cloth)
ISBN-13: 978-0-226-65340-2 (paper)
ISBN-13: 978-0-226-92277-5 (e-book)
ISBN-10: 0-226-65339-0 (cloth)
ISBN-10: 0-226-65340-4 (paper)
ISBN-10: 0-226-92277-4 (e-book)

Library of Congress Cataloging-in-Publication Data

Pedersen, David.
    American value : migrants, money, and meaning in El Salvador and the United States /
David Pedersen.
        pages. cm. — (Chicago studies in practices of meaning)
    ISBN 978-0-226-65339-6 (cloth : alk. paper) — ISBN 0-226-65339-0 (cloth : alk. paper) —
ISBN 978-0-226-65340-2 (pbk. : alk. paper) — ISBN 0-226-65340-4 (pbk. : alk. paper) —
ISBN 978-0-226-92277-5 (e-book) — ISBN 0-226-92277-4 (e-book)   1. Salvadorans—
United States—Economic conditions. 2. Salvadorans—United States—Social conditions.
3. Emigrant remittances—El Salvador. 4. Salvadorans—United States. 5. El Salvador—
Foreign relations—United States. 6. United States—Foreign relations—El Salvador.
I. Title. II. Series: Chicago studies in practices of meaning.
    E184.S15P444 2013
    305.868'7284073—dc23

                                                                    2012023405

♾ This paper meets the requirements of ANSI/NISO Z39.48-1992 (Permanence of Paper).

FOR JULIANNE AND CLARA

AND IN MEMORY OF FERNANDO CORONIL

Contents

List of Characters   xi

Preface   xvii

PROLOGUE

INTRODUCTION   3

ONE   A Roadmap for Remittances   28

PART I.

TWO   Brushing against the Golden Grain   55

THREE   Melting Fields of Snow   83

FOUR   The Intrusion of Uncomfortable Wars, *Illegals*,
and Remittances   116

PART II.

FIVE   The Wealth of Pueblos   147

SIX   Immigrant Entrepreneurship   167

PART III.

SEVEN   Welcome to Intipucá City   191

EIGHT   The World in a Park   209

FINALE

NINE   Options and Models for the Future   235

CONCLUSION   261

Acknowledgments   267

Notes   271

Bibliography   297

Index   301

Characters

Lo, I or you, Or woman, man or state, known or unknown. We seeming solid wealth, strength, beauty build. But really build eidolons. — Walt Whitman, 1876

VALUE—The eidolon that influences every character in this book. It "does not stalk around with a label describing what it is," but may be fleetingly grasped as the historical tendency across El Salvador and the United States for the most general qualities of human work capacity to take form as solid wealth: often strong or beautiful; always with a money-price.

SAMUEL HUNTINGTON—US political science professor who mentioned Intipucá in his 2004 book *Who Are We? The Challenges to America's National Identity*.

LARS SCHOULTZ—US professor of political science who referred to Intipucá in his 1992 essay, "Central America and the Politicalization of US Immigration Policy."

KAREN DEYOUNG and CHRIS DICKEY—Journalists who commented on Intipucá in their 1979 *Washington Post* article.

ALICIA, BEATRIZ, ISABEL—Three residents of Intipucá with no direct connection to the Washington, DC, area.

ROBIN LUBBOCK—US-based photographer and journalist who visited Intipucá in 1989.

ALFREDO CRISTIANI—President of El Salvador (1989–94). Owner of large cotton farm near Intipucá.

MARVIN CHÁVEZ—Intipucá resident who lived and worked in the DC area during the 1980s. Photographed by Lubbock during a return visit to the pueblo.

SIGFREDO CHÁVEZ—Father of Marvin Chávez and widely regarded as the first person from Intipucá to move to the Washington, DC, area.

LINDSEY GRUSON—*New York Times* journalist who wrote about Intipucá. Child of the late *Times* correspondent and columnist Flora Lewis and the paper's director and vice-chairman, Sydney Gruson.

CHARLES LANE—Author of 1989 magazine article about Intipucá and its history of migration to Washington, DC.

MANUEL—Intipucá resident who lived in DC during the 1980s, but returned in the middle 1990s to work as a farmer. Younger son of Miguel and a distant cousin of Marvin Chávez.

JHOON RHEE—Korean *taekwondo* master and founder of martial arts/self-defense training studios throughout the Washington, DC, area. Known for the advertising jingle with the refrain, "Nobody bothers me!"

WILLIAM WALKER—US Ambassador to El Salvador 1988–92; visited Intipucá in 1990.

GLORIA GRANDOLINI—World Bank economist and author of 1996 report on El Salvador that drew upon research conducted in Intipucá by Segundo Montes and Juan José García.

ELISABETH WOOD—US political scientist and expert on the war in El Salvador and its aftermath.

JUAN JOSÉ GARCÍA—Salvadoran sociologist who collaborated with Segundo Montes on research in Intipucá.

SEGUNDO MONTES—Jesuit priest and professor of political science and sociology at the University of Central America (UCA) in El Salvador who conducted research in Intipucá.

GABRIEL ESCOBAR—Author of two-part *Washington Post* article about Intipucá and surrounding area, published in 1993. Interviewed Sigfredo Chávez in Intipucá.

MANOLA FERNÁNDEZ—Cuban woman who lived in Mt. Pleasant neighborhood of Washington, DC, and helped many Intipucá residents settle in the area.

JUAN RIVAS—Owner of large farm in Intipucá. Grandfather of Sigfredo Chavez.

ROSA—Daughter of Juan Rivas and mother of Sigfredo Chávez.

PEDRO—Sigfredo's best friend from childhood.

REGELADO-DUEÑAS—Elite Salvadoran family that owned large farm adjacent to the Rivas farm. Members were early investors in Bain Capital, founded by US Republican presidential candidate (at this writing) Mitt Romney.

GENERAL SALVADOR CASTENADA CASTRO—President of El Salvador (1945–48) whose office ruled in favor of Intipucá in a land dispute with the town of Chirilagua.

GENERAL MAXIMILIANO HERNÁNDEZ MARTÍNEZ—Infamous dictator who ruled El Salvador between 1931 and 1944.

EL GRANO DE ORO—(The Golden Grain): Popular name for coffee in El Salvador.

MIGUEL—Intipucá resident who harvested coffee beans in Conchagua in the 1940s. Father of Manuel.

ARNOLDO SUTTER—Member of elite family in El Salvador and owner of sisal farm and production facility known as El Delirio.

GEORGE MCLAUGHLIN—DC resident who experienced the post-WWII recovery of the global coffee market through the sharp rise in cost of his favorite brand.

MILTON PETERSON—Successful real estate developer in northern Virginia.

LIEUTENANT COLONEL ÓSCAR OSORIO—Led El Salvador (1948–56) during the development of the cotton export sector.

MANLIO ARGUETA—Acclaimed Salvadoran author whose novel, *Un Día en La Vida* (One Day of Life) acutely captured the quotidian violence in rural El Salvador leading up to the 1980s war.

LUPE—Woman who is the central character in Argueta's novel.

DANIEL—Eldest son of Miguel and half-brother of Manuel. Worked on the Cristiani-owned cotton farm near Intipucá in the 1960s.

BENJAMÍN—Machine-shop owner whose business grew during the cotton export era.

ROBERTO—Man from a poorer family on the edge of Intipucá who lived and worked in Washington, DC, during the 1970s and 1980s and then returned to Intipucá to operate a successful sandwich and drink stand in the center of town.

JAIME—Cousin of Daniel who was threatened by Salvadoran national guard and moved to the DC area in the late 1970s.

GERALD HALPIN, RUDOLPH SEELEY, WILLIAM LEITH—Northern Virginia real estate developers.

JOHN T. HAZEL—Landowner and developer of Northern Virginia who worked together with Milton Peterson.

JOSEPH BRADDOCK, BERNARD DUNN, AND DANIEL MCDONALD—Founders of BDM International, a private defense contracting firm that completed a comprehensive evaluation of US military strategy in the Salvadoran war in 1987.

EARLE WILLIAMS—Directed BDM between 1972 and 1992.

CASPER WEINBERGER—US Secretary of Defense during the presidency of Ronald Reagan.

MAX MANWARING—Professor at the US Army Strategic Studies Institute who directed the BDM research and report.

JOSÉ NAPOLEÓN DUARTE—US-backed President of El Salvador between 1984 and 1989.

BILLY—Wealthy white cocaine user and distributor in the suburbs of Washington, DC. His parents were major business figures in the region.

RICHARD—Dominican man who sold cocaine to Marvin.

JORGE—Distributor of Coca-Cola products in the vicinity of Intipucá.

GUILLERMO—Young man employed by Jorge.

FERNANDO LEONZO, EBERTH TORRES, URSULO MÁRQUEZ, LIONEL SALINAS—Founders of an informal bank and money transfer service in Washington, DC, and Intipucá.

CHARLENE DREW JARVIS—Member of the Washington, DC, City Council representing Ward 4.

DANIEL GÓMEZ—Salvadoran man shot by Washington, DC, police officer Angela Jewell.

ARMANDO CALDERÓN SOL—Salvadoran president (1994–99) who visited Intipucá with his family in 1995.

OSCAR—Intipucá mayor at the time of Calderon Sol's visit. Worked as a young man on the farm owned by Ursulo Márquez.

HUGO SALINAS—Popular booster of Intipucá and its current Mayor. Son of Lionel Salinas.

JUAN DE DIOS BLANCO—Mayor of Intipucá during the visit of US Ambassador William Walker.

URSULO MÁRQUEZ—Father of Pedro, Sigfredo's best friend from childhood.

RAUL—Youngest son of Ursulo who owns farming and commercial businesses in Intipucá.

TOMMY—Hard-drinking Intipuqueño who moved to Washington, DC, in the 1990s.

JOHN KING—Catholic priest from Akron, Ohio, who ministered in Intipucá and surrounding region.

SONYA—Woman who lived in and cared for the Intipucá home owned by relatives of Benjamin. Mother of Manlio.

DAISY AND MANLIO—Young couple living near Intipucá. Manlio is the son of Sonya.

OMAR—Intipucá resident living in DC who was recruited by Marvin to help supply Billy's friends with cocaine.

MARÍA—Woman who worked for Omar at his restaurant in Intipucá. Moved to Virginia in late 1990s.

MÉLIDA—Wealthy landowner and business owner in Cuco, near Intipucá.

SANDRA—Woman from town near Intipucá who also worked for Omar.

PAUL WOLFOWITZ—US Deputy Secretary of Defense (2001–5) and major architect of the US invasion of Iraq.

JIM STEELE—Friend of Wolfowitz and veteran of US wars in Vietnam, El Salvador, and Iraq.

DKEMBE MUTOMBO—Former US professional basketball player from D. R. Congo introduced by President George W. Bush as an exemplary migrant entrepreneur at the 2007 State of the Union Address.

DILLIP RATHA—World Bank economist and proponent of remittance-based development and poverty reduction.

ELLIOTT BERG—University of Michigan economics professor credited with first proposing that World Bank and IMF loans be tied to structural adjustment policies.

MARK MOLLOCH-BROWN—University of Michigan graduate, political consultant, and director of UNDP when it funded a major report in 2005 on El Salvador's restructuring around migration and remittance circulation titled *A Look at the New "Us": The Impact of Migration.*

RAFAEL GALDÁMEZ—Salvadoran painter whose work was purchased by UNDP and reproduced on the cover of the 2005 Salvadoran report. The painting carried the image of a one-way road sign with the name Intipucá on it.

Preface

American Value seems a mildly enigmatic title, but I choose the phrase
because it describes in a single gesture the three main themes of the
book. Overall, this book is a historically inflected ethnography of El Salvador and its relations with the United States during the past fifty years, two
countries that share the hemisphere of the Americas, making them both
American in this sense of the term. The book looks especially at changes
in the dominant forms of value that have intertwined both countries up to
the present. By using value-form, I wish to signal that such expressions, especially various commodities, including money, exist in relation to a larger
social and historical content out of which they have been socially extruded
throughout both countries. In this way, to consider value in the Americas
as the book does means to look at how and why El Salvador has shifted
as a whole from being oriented around growing and exporting high-quality
coffee beans, especially to the United States, to being a country that now is
much defined by the circulation of over two billion US dollars annually remitted by more than one-quarter of its population that has migrated to live
and work in the United States. To consider American value also means to
inquire into how the United States has changed over the same period from
a country dominated by industrial manufacturing, especially with ferrous
metals in its heartland, to one now distinguished by the varied services, information, and high-tech goods produced in its coastal and southern cities.
American Value is about this hemispheric transformation of dominant value-
forms, the aggregate re-patterning of social relations that are their content
across El Salvador and the United States, and the qualities of meaning or
significance that are yielded from this relationship of form and content.

The title has a second implication. Since the lowest-wage jobs associated with the recent phase of urban service production in the United
States have tended to be filled by many of the Salvadoran migrants, it is

possible to view the past five decades as a reciprocal though unbalanced hemispheric affair. The de-industrialization of the United States has entailed a re-primarization of El Salvador as that country now effectively exports to the United States a new form of value: raw work capacity in people. Though not often thought of as something created in order to sell overseas, this personified work capacity has become the dominant commodity, like coffee in an earlier era, whose production, exchange, and consumption now directly undergird the national wealth of El Salvador. *American Value* refers to the appearance of this reality in El Salvador, where there is great significance and meaning in the US-bound migrant and their transfer of wealth from the United States back to El Salvador.

There is a third overtone to the title. The book explores this hemispheric restructuring of value formation through the lives of particular people in both countries, attending to their various feelings, actions, and habits in specific contexts. (See Character List.) The book also closely assays other meaningful forms, such as written and visual media, which have saturated the half-century across both countries. Drawing judiciously on insights taken from Marx's approach to capitalist value determination and also the semeiotic logic of Charles Peirce, the book traces how people and the objective expressions of their social world together have participated in shaping the overall hemispheric transformation, both as products and protagonists, especially through their tendency to present themselves and features of the transformation in certain ways, while occluding other qualities and connections. In particular, the book identifies how and why as a cumulative social outcome or tendency, rather than as their purely internal attribute, the dominant value forms across El Salvador and the United States gesture to and present only a limited feature of their content, usually some vague quotient of generalized human capacity. In this, they well hide the historical fullness of the human creative effort (as well as other earthly resources) that went into their formation, including often violent relations of domination, control, and exploitation that have characterized life in both countries. Within the many compelling expressions of wealth and progress across both countries lie those of social want and human desire. To delve into this hidden historical content, expressed in specific people and their relations, is the way that this book examines American value.

*   *   *

Among the most important contemporary instantiations of this tendency of occlusion, the book identifies an abiding constellation of representational forms derived from the lives of specific people in a small town in southeastern El Salvador called Intipucá and their family members and friends who have migrated to work for periods of time in the greater Washington, DC, metropolitan area. This composite expression that I call the Intipucá-DC Connection Story now circulates well beyond its immediate origins, contributing to a more general account of the contemporary moment that emphasizes entrepreneurial migrants and their money as the new source of progress and development, both for El Salvador and in US urban regions. In turn, this more general account that calls attention to capitalist entrepreneurship across both countries fits as a component part of a broader US foreign policy agenda in contexts worldwide, including Iraq and Afghanistan.

From specific vantages, especially in El Salvador, there is a palpable sense that although the new kinds of money, products, jobs, and idealized subjects have come to re-define daily life, there still is a durable (and barely endurable) long-term tendency whereby social life has been deeply constrained both as a result of and as a necessary precondition for the interhemispheric trafficking first of coffee and now migrant work capacity, services, and remittances. Inspired by this sensibility, the book hones a method of moving through the various expressions—the material and meaningful representational forms, legitimating doctrines, discursive categories, everyday practices, and patterns of social relations (over multiple decades across both countries)—in order to better discern the deep-set and lasting trends and tendencies amid the qualities of change and interaction. This method involves developing what I define as a realist semeiotic approach for the study of value formation. The impetus for this endeavor is to overcome several spatial, temporal, and conceptual distinctions that pervade existing scholarship, overly freezing, fragmenting, and in this way distorting our understanding of this capricious and uneven hemispheric historical transformation.

The result of this analysis, presented in nine chapters, is three-fold. First, it is both an explanation and a critique of how and why the various value forms, as well as this new narrative of migration, service work, and remittance-led development, have dissimulated their emergence out of more violent and long-term historical conditions across both countries, while also hiding their manner of contributing to the perpetuation of these same conditions, which are much at odds with their forward-looking story. Second, the book seeks to offer a fuller, more inclusive, and transdisciplinary account of these real conditions and social processes that have joined El Salvador and the United States, however unevenly and contingently, throughout the twentieth century. Third and in the process of the first two, the book amplifies other "stories" that have emerged in less regnant fashion, but that offer compelling alternatives to the dominant ones. Interweaving these stories as strands of argumentation, the book seeks to "transvalue" the dominant value forms. The introduction chapter that follows will examine in more detail what I mean with the term *stories*, their telling, and the process of transvaluation. It also further spells out the book's method and theoretical assumptions with regard to the realist semeiotic perspective on value determination, introduces some of the materials under consideration, and details my own position in relation to this project. Following this, chapter 1 directly situates and explains the larger significance of a widely circulating and well-known photo that captures both an expression of relative wealth in the foreground (a smiling man on the motorcycle) and that of want (the admiring onlookers) in the background, in Intipucá. Together, the introduction and chapter 1 provide the prologue for the rest of this book's undertaking.

PROLOGUE

Introduction

Isolating one wave is not easy, separating it from the wave immediately following, which seems to push it and at times overtakes it and sweeps it away; and it is no easier to separate the one wave from the preceding wave, which seems to drag it toward the shore, unless it turns against the following wave, as if to arrest it. — Italo Calvino, 1983

D espite its admonitory tone, this epigraph from Italo Calvino wonderfully isolates and arrests the central approach of this book in terms of its theory, method, and object of study. The challenge is how best to understand a particular form or expression, such as coffee, migrant remittances, or the concentration of published stories about the town of Intipucá and its ties to Washington, DC, in relation to a larger continuous process, the asymmetrical twentieth-century development of the hemisphere. Following Calvino, one must actively work to properly judge the small moment's appearance and effects in relation to the forces that are shaping it and that it reciprocally shapes, including those that may seem at first to be separate, working against it or not completely visible. Another lesson of Calvino's caution is that one must presuppose the larger process in some way before pressing out some of its constitutive features and qualities, all the while keeping the whole enterprise in motion. This book's preface was a first step. But the rest of the task is not easy and cannot be accomplished with fixed eyes from an immovable point on the shore.[1] It requires figuratively plunging in at various points and inquiring as if

swimming outward, downward, and backward, building up and reconstructing in the mind's eye what is happening while also being aware of
where oneself and the larger forces are heading. In this spirit, I now begin
with three plunges or dives whose results show the direction of this book.

First Dive: The Long Tale of 20 Percent

In 2004 Harvard University professor of political science Samuel P. Huntington wrote *Who Are We? The Challenges to America's National Identity*. Using "America" to denote specifically the United States, rather than
any other part of the hemisphere that shares this moniker, Huntington
argued that this country's national culture, which he defined as quintes-
sentially white, Anglo–northern European, English-speaking, Protestant,
and imbued with a deep-set reverence for individualism, was imperiled
by the recent decades of large-scale population migration from Latin
America, especially Mexico.[2] Though primarily an argument about a US
national essence as determined by its early settlers from England and later
northern Europe rather than about immigration, Huntington's book fed
directly into fierce public debate at the time about reforming US immigration laws, partially inspiring the restrictive House of Representatives
Bill (H.R. 4437) that criminalized undocumented migrants.[3] Huntington's
argument was echoed in statements made by armed US vigilante groups at
the Mexican border who called themselves "Minutemen."[4] More broadly,
Huntington's book, along with his earlier *Clash of Civilizations*, contributed to popular support for aggressively reasserting US sovereign authority in the aftermath of the 9/11/01 airplane hijackings and attacks on the
US Pentagon and the World Trade Center.[5] In this, it was a small but potent piece in the reordering of life on a planetary scale, marked by a crisis
in US dominance (and its allied Anglo-European states) and the possible
emergence of new configurations of power relations quite different from
historic twentieth-century or previous arrangements.[6]

In chapter 7 of *Who Are We?*, Huntington pointed out the increasingly well-documented phenomenon of *transnational* migrant communities, networks, or circuits, calling such migrant participants "ampersands"
since they appeared to integrate the lives and loyalties of their home
countries (predominantly Mexico and the countries of Central America
and the Caribbean) with communities of settlement in the United States.
Summarizing a central argument made in most of the scholarly literature

on this subject, Huntington explained that "historically migrants from a single locality in Country A tended to gather in a single locality in Country B. Now the people of both localities can be parts of a single transnational community."[7] Departing from the dominant perspective on transnational migration that has identified the formation of more tenuous and contradictory hybrids of "AB," Huntington then emphasized that "the community of origin is replicated in the United States."[8] To support this part of his argument, Huntington listed empirical evidence meant to show what he deemed a one-way imposition upon the United States. One main example was drawn from the Central American country of El Salvador, whose US migrant population currently represents about one-quarter of that country's total population and is the sixth-largest national/ethnic minority group in the United States. "In 1985, 20 percent of Intipucá, El Salvador, lived in the Washington, DC, neighborhood of Adams Morgan, with an organized club called Intipucá City that aided migrants from the town," wrote Huntington. In Huntington's nativist polemic, this Salvadoran town appeared to have "colonized" part of the US national capital city.

As the source of the Intipucá-DC example and its 20 percent measure, Huntington cited a book chapter written in 1992 by Lars Schoultz, also a political scientist (with a professorship at the University of North Carolina), well known for his comprehensive studies of US policy toward Latin America.[9] Schoultz's essay, "Central America and the Politicization of US Immigration Policy," appeared as a chapter in *Western Hemispheric Immigration and US Foreign Policy*, edited by Christopher Mitchell. In stark contrast to Huntington's deployment, Schoultz invoked the 20 percent measure as a historical effect, arguing that US military and political intervention in Central America had led to the increased migration from the region to the United States. As a consequence of US support for the Salvadoran military during the country's twelve-year civil war (1980–92), "Why would a Salvadoran from the small town of Intipucá *not* migrate to the Adams Morgan area of Washington, DC?" Schoultz asked provocatively.[10] "Twenty percent of Intipucans are already living in Adams–Morgan, and there is even a Club of Intipucá City at the corner of 18th Street and Florida Avenue, NW, one function of which is to provide information and funds for new arrivals," he continued.[11]

The basis of this well-traveled 20 percent measure turns out to be "A Profile of the Salvadoran Community, Washington, DC, 1981," written by the Washington, DC, Community Humanities Council.[12] The claim about 20 percent of the population of Intipucá living in Adams Morgan appeared on the first page of this report.[13] It seems that the 20 percent measure had been calculated from evidence in a 1979 front-page article in the *Washington Post* titled "The Long Journey to Find Work Here; One Came, then Many, as Intipucá Seeks Prosperity," written by Christopher Dickey and Karen DeYoung. This long article opens by referring to a popular myth-like tale:

> There is a story told over and over in the half-hidden world of Washington's illegal aliens. It's about a village in El Salvador called Intipucá, where there perhaps were only 5,000 people to begin with.
>
> One man came to Washington in 1966, so the story goes. He bought a car with the money he earned and sent home a picture of himself in it. The people in the village thought this looked like a good thing. Now there are more than 1,000 of them here.

One thousand out of five thousand is, indeed, 20 percent. Later in the article, the authors mention that "a *Washington Post* reporter who has written several articles about illegal aliens in the District of Columbia during the last year, repeatedly encountered people from Intipucá." Other than this indication, the article does not provide more sense of the immediate authors of the oft-told story, the context of its frequent telling, or any source for the numbers used in the article. Nevertheless, this 20 percent number has done a lot of work over a quarter-century, well beyond its origins in Intipucá and the District of Columbia proper.

Second Dive: The Intipucá-DC Connection Story

In 1988 I was living in Mount Pleasant, near the neighborhood called Adams Morgan, and often heard of Intipucá as the Salvadoran village that had a large number of residents living in the DC area.[14] I cannot recall exactly when or where I first learned this, but it was something that many people simply knew as a kind of neighborhood common sense. I eventually met specific *Intipuqueños* in Mount Pleasant (which is described in chapter 1), but well before this I had absorbed the general story of the town, its ties to DC neighborhoods, and a rough sense that DC had changed because of the migration. Mount Pleasant and Adams Morgan certainly were well known at the time for their large number of Salvadoran residents and small businesses. A decade after its front-page appearance in the *Washington Post*, the story of the town and its residents in DC was old news for many of us in the District.

In 1993, I visited Intipucá for the first time, returning again several more times in the 1990s for extended stays.[15] I have learned much about the town, including its 45-year history of migration to the DC area.[16] But I am hardly alone in these inquiries. In contrast to what one might assume about a small Salvadoran town, there is an immense and still growing collection of contemporary journalism about Intipucá and its DC ties, produced especially by Salvadoran and US radio, television, and newspaper reporters.[17] A number of popular Internet sites also carry information on the town. In addition, there is an array of aesthetic representations of the town, including paintings, photography, films, fiction, poetry, and music, produced by Salvadoran and US-based artists. Finally, similar to the way that Huntington invoked the town but usually without the negative evaluation with respect to its threat to a dominant US national creed, there is a nascent body of academic scholarship on Intipucá and DC that considers their connection to be an exemplary case of "transnationalism."[18]

Despite the variety of formats and relatively large number of authors across both countries, nearly all of this work focuses on the exclusive ties between the town and the DC area wrought by the decades of migration and the exchange of wealth and ways of life across both regions. This new set of connections usually is distinguished from a previous period when DC and Intipucá were fully separate, discrete, and quite different places. In this sense, all the work is more or less a sustained elaboration of the myth-like tale disclosed in the *Post* article of 1979: a large number of Intipucá residents have moved to live and work in the DC area; they left behind a modest agricultural and peasant-like background to become successful service workers and small-scale proprietors in the DC area, changing the city's ethnic landscape while also maintaining close ties with family and friends in the home town; the density of these ties together with hard work, investment savvy, and town cooperation has facilitated the transfer of wealth and modern US capitalist sensibilities back to the town, transforming Intipucá and distinguishing it from similar agricultural towns elsewhere in El Salvador. The 20 percent measure used by Huntington and Schoultz reflected and captured just one aspect of this composite story.

Though it appeared negatively in relation to US immigration debates by way of Huntington, this Intipucá-DC Connection Story, as I call it, also has been picked up in more forward-looking ways across both countries. In El Salvador, as migrant remittances replace agro-export earnings as the basis of national wealth, the Intipucá-DC Connection Story powerfully brings to life the heroic figure of the "migrant entrepreneur" who appears to lead the development of the country by leaving behind its agricultural past, moving to the United States, starting a successful business there, and transferring metropolitan wealth and acumen back to El Salvador, putting it to productive use in the hometown and, by extension, the home country.[19] As the accumulation of public representations attests and as I would argue on the basis of first-hand experience, Intipucá and DC together provide the most widely known example of such a relationship in El Salvador.[20] In the United States, as that country has become increasingly shaped by the influx of Latin American and Caribbean migrants and the overseas exodus of high-wage manufacturing jobs, this same figure (in contrast to Huntington's depiction) seems to substantiate the immigrant "American Dream," invigorating US cities with ethnic diversity and capitalist risk-taking while also acting as a new agent of US overseas development policy through their modernizing remittance transfer and home-town association organizing.[21] As the compendium of public accounts reflects, Intipucá's migrant entrepreneurs in DC provide compelling source material for this more general story of progress and passage into a new future. At the core of this model of modernity, in both its El Salvador and its US variant, there is great significance in the personage of the remitting migrant entrepreneur. The wealth of both countries appears to rest on this virtuous figure. The Intipucá-DC Connection Story, as it substantiates these broader national development models, points to the town and its ties to DC as archetype, a replicable model for the future of both countries.[22]

This broader El Salvador–United States transnational migrant entrepreneurship model, generalized from the Intipucá-DC Connection Story, is itself remarkably portable, informing other metamodels of the future in contexts worldwide.[23] It contributes substantively to remittance-based and "human capital"–oriented development strategies proffered by the United Nations (UN), International Monetary Fund (IMF), and World Bank elsewhere in Latin America, the Caribbean, Africa, and Asia. It also is a key feature in the appearance of El Salvador as a neoliberal success story: the place of a successful US-led counterinsurgency campaign (1980–92) that has given way to democratic nation-building and the consolidation of US-allied free-market capitalism. This larger "El Salvador Model" directly guides US counterinsurgency strategies in Iraq and Afghanistan and also US combat of narcotics trafficking and youth gangs worldwide.[24] By way of Huntington's book and these other doctrinal codifications, the

Intipucá-DC Connection Story has become a mainstream, practical, and effective building block for the future of El Salvador and the United States, the hemisphere of the Americas and beyond.

Third Dive: From Stories to Storytelling

One morning in April 1996, while I was living in Intipucá, I decided to walk out of the town along a rocky, dusty, unpaved roadway that ran south toward the Pacific Ocean. Not far into this venture, a woman about my age leaned out of the door of her home along the road and called to me. I walked up to the house where I saw three women standing together in the threshold. All at once they spoke to me in a spirited way, leaving me with a chance to reply only after a rapid staccato of statements:

"This isn't a rich town like they say."
"You need to be sure to talk to people like us out here."
"We're the ones who do not have any money."
"We've never been to Washington."
"No one sends us money [from DC]."
"You must tell our story, too."

"You must tell our story, *too*," she had said to me in Spanish that morning. This sentence came rushing back when I first saw mention of Intipucá in Huntington's book when it appeared in 2004. Throughout the late 1990s, I had spoken frequently with the three women and with many other people in the town, enough to craft an account of Intipucá's other 80 percent, I believe. But I take the women's choice of words that morning as an important insight. It has provoked me to think that the issue is not about choosing between separate stories, the increasingly dominant and widely circulating Intipucá-DC connection one or an alternative one about the town's other 80 percent. Rather, the challenge is to critically understand *storytelling* as a continuous, combined, and often imbalanced geohistorical process, yielding dominant stories like the Intipucá-DC connection one already sketched and less prominent stories such as those of the three people in the Intipucá doorway that morning.[25]

The three women I met that morning actually were linked to the wealthier DC-connected population of the town. They rented their dwelling from one member of this group while other household members found employment with DC-connected town residents. In this sense, part of the pronounced wealth of the DC-connected group in the town rested on everything done in this household to generate the monthly rent and produce the work capacities supplied by the residents. In this respect, the three women were part of the dominant story of the town, but remained invisible in it from the usual perspective of its telling. To shift about the perspective, level of focus, and spatiotemporal scale of analysis so as to include both stories, what they each referred to, and their achieved meanings, yields a fuller story of storytelling as uneven social and historical process, disclosing a dynamic relational hierarchy: the partiality of the big one and the way that its formation rests on but occludes what is in the small one. To tell this more inclusive story of storytelling changes both of the stories and their import, destabilizing the hierarchy and inviting further inquiry into the shared conditions of the stories' combined and uneven formation.

My encounter that morning in Intipucá, considered in relation to the town's appearance in books like Huntington's, sets the tone of this book and provides an initial line of questioning, no longer in the metaphorical realm of waves, water, and diving, but instead centered around the problematic of storytelling, broadly defined. Across El Salvador and the United States, how and why have certain dominant, but highly partial, accounts of life formed and circulated, hiding the fuller history from which they emerged, including other stories that are completely at odds with theirs? How and why does the continued circulation of dominant stories hide the way that they contribute to perpetuating conditions that actually contradict their accounts? To answer these questions now in a very cursory way helps to illustrate the book's approach. After we work through the questions with some examples, however provisionally, it then becomes possible to examine some of the more basic theoretical issues that inform this book and its analysis.

Social Abstraction and Relational Hierarchy

A preliminary answer to how the big Intipucá-DC connection story took form is that an aggregate process of social abstraction occurred, whereby the concrete fullness of the town and all its complex generative relations across the hemisphere, including but not limited to its Washington, DC, ties, became compressed into a complex of modular accounts.[26] On the surface, these accounts are not wrong, just highly exclusionary, as the three women well knew and told me that morning. Exactly this process of representational narrowing is what this book considers in a variety of contexts across several decades in El Salvador and the United States. To further clarify what it means to study such narrowing, I now offer what should be understood as one preliminary "pass" at how such an instance of social abstraction occurred. I return to this example in greater detail in chapter 2.

At the beginning of the twentieth century, much of daily life across El Salvador was closely tied to the production and export of coffee beans.[27] The often coerced mixing of human effort with other natural resources in the soil and sky yielded not just this primary agricultural commodity, but also a deep patterning of intersubjective outlooks and orientations, not the least toward the little bean itself. In El Salvador, coffee was *el Grano de Oro* [the Golden Grain] because of the new wealth and sense of progress that it seemed to deliver, at least to some parts of the country. How did it come to tell such a widely consumed story in El Salvador?

As an export in the twentieth century, the beans left their immediate origins in the highlands of El Salvador to be consumed again in the production of new manufactured goods and their "manufacturers"—the abilities of both people and machines—especially in cities across the middle of the United States. Coffee breaks (and spills) marked day and night, work and leisure, saturating the everyday sensibilities of production and reproduction in the United States.[28] Earnings from coffee returned to El Salvador in the form of electrical motors, lights, telephones, radios, cars, and countless other hard-currency accoutrements of modern life imported largely from the United States, all of which shaped the outlooks and capacities of the state and its citizenry, influencing not only memories and desires, but also measures of gross national product (GNP) and the country's position on scales of "development" worldwide. From this perspective, the primary export of coffee appeared to directly equal national wealth, yielding or at least promising progress and passage to a modern future. This was the story reflected in its magisterial title, the Golden Grain.

Intipucá developed as a small part of this overall productive system as a group of *mestizo* families owned and operated relatively large farms in the region organized around relations of sharecropping and land tenancy. They produced corn along with other grains, livestock, and dairy products. This surplus food production contributed to sustaining the seasonal workforce employed on the coffee *fincas* in upland areas near the town.[29] Overall, the Intipucá landowners were a relatively well-off group within El Salvador's rural southeastern "tortilla basket" that played a crucial role in supporting and reproducing the coffee export system through its production of basic foodstuffs.

For most people in Intipucá, it felt as if the town were completely separate from and outside of the wealth and progress delivered by the Golden Grain in metropolitan centers like the capital city, San Salvador. The landowners in Intipucá played on, and were played on by, this sense of separation and inequality, even as their substantial wealth relative to landless coffee-laborers was predicated on the coffee system. The dominant "story" in the town, though not uncontested, was one emphasizing the rural commonality of landowners and their workers in contradistinction to the metropolitan coffee elite and their trappings of wealth. Indeed, this became one strategy of maintaining labor relations in the countryside. At a national level this contributed as well to the popular understanding that the country was neatly divided between a small urban coffee elite and a large impoverished rural peasantry.

In the late 1960s when young men and women from the Intipucá landowning families first traveled to Washington, DC, they worked in service jobs even as they also founded small businesses in the area, effectively expanding and deepening the kinds of capitalist ventures that they had been a part of in the pueblo. Later, with the influx of poorer Salvadoran migrants fleeing the 1980s civil war and settling in DC, the already established Intipucá business class in DC gained new co-ethnic consumers and workers. In this context, they continued the habit of emphasizing a shared rural agricultural background with their new employees and clients.[30]

Since at least the 1979 *Post* article, this Intipucá business class that extended across the town and throughout the DC area has adeptly represented the town to those who inquired into it, emphasizing the venerable tale of humble rural origins. This sense that everyone in Intipucá shared a relatively modest pastoral existence was accurate relative to wealthier metropolitan areas in El Salvador and in the United States. But to live off ground rents in the region was quite different from being a seasonal coffee-worker or tenant farmer. Even if migrants did disclose their land-owning status and experience of being skilled bosses of a workforce in El Salvador, most US-based journalists and social scientists have tended to fit their accounts into a dominant rags-to-riches "American Dream" narrative framework or, more recently, the successful "transnational migrant entrepreneur" variant.

Causal Powers

Answering "why" dominant stories have appeared through a process of social abstraction that hides a fuller account of the relational hierarchies of which they are a part is more complicated than answering the "how" form of the question (addressed above). It is a slightly loaded question as well, since part of the answer already has been disclosed. As I have mentioned, the tendency of emphasizing a rural subaltern status among Intipucá elite was accurate in relation to metropolitan centers in El Salvador and to Washington, DC, in the United States, yet it hid their relatively dominant position in the countryside and among Salvadoran migrants in DC. Similarly, the US "immigrant success story" was a descriptive schema predicated on understanding El Salvador as completely separate and other from the United States—a nonrelational and absolute hierarchy. (Chapter 2 examines this schema in detail.)

It would seem that all these accounts could be explained simply by the perspective and relative agency of their most immediate authors: town elite and their interaction with similarly belief-laden journalists and social scientists. This book asks whether there might be something else behind or within this process of social abstraction that is more or less "out there" and operating with causal efficacy, but not reducible either to the actions of specific individuals or to a purely ideational system. The answer lies in the issue of storytelling as an uneven historical process that my encounter with the three women that morning brought to the fore and also in this book's understanding of "value" as a particular manner or tendency of storytelling.

Storytelling as the Interaction of Stories, Their Objects, and Their Meaning

To make the shift from choosing between different stories to enquiring into the overall process of storytelling, however imbalanced, this book draws loosely on the logic of semeiotic or "sign-action" developed by Charles S. Peirce. Indeed, my use of the term *story* is meant as a palatable proxy for the more generic but also slightly technical term of *sign*. Following such a semeiotic approach, it becomes possible to account not just for the stories, but also for the specific objects, people, and practices that the stories gesture to, resemble in some way, or stand for, as well as those entities that tell, re-tell, and make sense of the stories, whether a person or another story, broadly defined.[31] Together, as a continuous three-fold relational process, *storytelling* is the manner through which (1) stories present (2) their objects, including other stories, in particular ways so as to generate (3) another more developed "story" in the sense of a quality of meaning. This more developed story then re-presents the object so as to generate yet another story in what is a continuous and potentially infinite process.

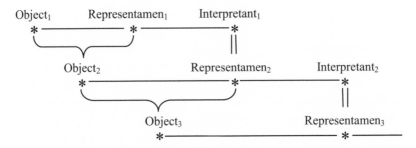

FIGURE 1. A model of semeiosis. Reprinted from Kelly A. Parker, *The Continuity of Peirce's Thought* (Nashville: Vanderbilt University Press, 1998), 148, with permission of the publisher.

In slightly more technical language, any sort of sign (S)—Peirce called this the Representamen—represents an object (O) so that the object can then determine another sign. This more developed sign is what Peirce called the interpretant (I). The interpretant, in turn, represents the same object in a more developed way to yet another sign (S_2). Metaphorically, the process is like passing something, though the entity passed carries aspects and qualities of all its previous bearers and their acts of passing it, which get stuffed into it with each pass, tendentiously reproducing it, developing it, or radically changing it. Following Peirce's triadic logic, (S) and (O) "pass" each other to (I). (S) and (O) together then form the new object (O_2), that (I), becoming a new co-passer of sorts (S_2), then extends to the new (I) called (I_2), and so on infinitely.

Without getting lost in a relational string of inflected letters, there are several key points we can take from this framework. First, any sign (S) represents its object (O) only partially, pulling out and capturing some aspects while neglecting others. At any moment when the process is grasped, the object of the sign is what it is at that moment of appropriation by the sign, not all that it is or possibly could be, nor necessarily all that it was in any previous sign relationship. In other words, objects are always partial and immediate to the context of their being pulled out and presented by a sign. Peirce actually called this the "immediate object" of a sign and distinguished this from the "dynamical object"—the real object as it could be fully known. Also in the action of signs, any subsequent interpretation may provide more or less information about the object than a previous one. The whole from which the most immediate object is pulled out in each successive representation contains aspects of the previous representation and therefore is ever so slightly different. In this sense semeiosis is inherently historical and "fateful."[32] It is potentially an infinite process and there is always the possibility of growth and development. Another implication of this modality is that semeiosis does not sit still as a discrete frozen sign. Its built-in "motivation" is to generate an interpretant.[33]

As some readers may notice, I have avoided using the term "discourse" in this introduction since it often is understood to mean a discrete batch of "words" or a "text," which then is distinguished from and contrasted with that to which it refers, often "nondiscursive" entities. By following Peirce's semeiotic logic I hope to avoid such a separation between words and their world. In this sense I also understand semeiosis as a simultaneously material and meaningful representational process, not a discrete, individual, and static sign.[34]

Reversing the order of the opening account of Huntington and the three women in Intipucá helps clarify my understanding of storytelling-*qua*-process as semeiotic or sign-action. At its time and place of figuratively jumping in as a sign, the 1979 *Washington Post* article presented as its most immediate object a vague group of people in DC regularly telling a story that emphasized some features of the town of Intipucá and its relations with Washington, DC. Obviously, this object of the *Post* article was much more, but these qualities were not picked up by the story (and may not have been known by the reporter). With continued inquiry it might be possible to get to this group of people in a more concrete way. Nevertheless, the telling of the story by this group as practical action and process was turned into a "thing" and figuratively passed by the newspaper account to the reader and, in this process, deftly linked with the two numerical measures. This quantitative piece of the story was pulled out in the subsequent accounts I considered, completely leaving out any reference to its formative conditions. Refashioned as a fraction of one hundred to indicate relative proportions of a quantity, it was passed by the account on the first page of the DC Community Humanities Council report to would-be interpreters. One was Schoultz, who pulled out and passed the percentage in his essay so as to yield a different kind of meaning. The Huntington book passed the same percentage measure (by way of Schoultz), so as to produce a meaning quite different from both Schoultz and Schoultz's sources. Although the percentage as a story itself made other appearances, it was Huntington's use of it that became aggregated into another object that appeared in (was "passed" by) various nativist claims and assertions of US national sovereignty, which themselves could be followed, at least in principle, into subsequent policies and political practices.

My own story tracing all of these works and citations had as its object this twenty-five year interchaining of stories, which it presented so as to highlight the attenuated presence of Intipucá and DC in all the stories. Juxtaposed with my other story of the three residents' stories that morning in Intipucá, we are left with a story about the telling of stories, their objects, and their meanings, understood both as a generative historical process that is as much meaningful as material and as a variety of congealed moments (stories or signs) within such a continuous course. My analysis jumped in on just one phase or, better, one phrase in this process.

Value as Representational Tendency

To identify a specific representational tendency that dominates over others, I draw on Marx's conceptualization of capitalist "value." Using the commodity as the point from which to dive into the world of capitalist relation, Marx proceeded to press out two opposing qualities or aspects of it, "use-value" and "exchange-value." He then moved outward and backward from this initial distinction to explore how, in the moment of capitalist exchange, distinct commodities and their formative histories are brought into or "reduced" to equivalence. Marx parsed this relational moment to show that it stands for another relationship: "a common element of identical magnitude exists in two different things."[35] From this juncture, he then explored how this common element is an objectification of the most abstract dimensions of the human capacity ("labor-power") that went into creating the commodities. Marx called this common element or substance "value."

In other words, when anything becomes a commodity, it essentially takes on and participates in a tendency of representation that is socially and historically specific to the capitalist relations in which it is produced and circulates. As a manner of storytelling, at any moment of exchange, a commodity presents as its most immediate object only the most general or abstract quality of human work capacity that went into it, so as to generate its meaning, another more developed story, its money-price.[36] In this sense, it is a "value form." This abstract entity or quotient of human capacity, whether accurately measurable or not, is much like the object "Intipucá's 20 percent" in the *Washington Post*, Schoultz, and Huntington stories. It may never be found and immediately perceived or measured as an actual object in the world, but the various stories could not be what they are without having it as such. Commodities gesture to a similarly oblique immediate object when they tell their story as things to be bought and sold.

This tendency is not wholly internal to the commodity, but rather it is a systemic propensity and outcome of capitalist relations—a "social product," as Marx put it famously:

> When we bring the products of our labor into relation with each other as values, it is not because we see in these articles the material receptacles of homogeneous human labor. Quite the contrary: whenever, by an exchange, we equate as values our different products, by that very act we also equate as human labor, the different kinds of labor expended upon them. We are not aware of this, nevertheless we do it. Value, therefore, does not stalk around with a label describing what it is. It is value rather that converts every product into a social hieroglyphic. Later on we try to decipher the hieroglyphic, to get behind the secret [that is] as much a social product as language.

Commodities do not always tell this story where the object of money-price is some agglomeration of the most abstract dimensions of labor-power—coffee is much more than just what it costs—but as commodities they nevertheless have to tell this story in order to be able to tell any other kind of story. Otherwise, they would not be commodities. Wealth is their dominant story; value is this amorphous object re-presented in the process.

Given this real representational tendency, the fuller personal, intersubjective, and also context-specific dimensions of human life (as well as other earthly resources) that went into the formation of the commodities completely disappear when viewed from the vantage of their price in the market.[37] Thus, at any moment of exchange, a radical historical dissimulation occurs. To the extent that money price is the dominant story, it regularly drowns out other stories—both what was necessary for its formation and also what may contradict its story or even lie relatively exterior to it. But these stories are never gone. They constantly press at the dominant tale of wealth, always threatening to expand the content of its object, drawing from a host of potential and actual qualities, and in this way changing the story's meaning—*transvaluing* it. This is the real story of storytelling behind the Intipucá-DC connection story.

When the three women spoke of having their story included, they effectively were asking for a fuller account of what had produced the wealth of the pueblo, including the opposite of the dominant wealth story, their relative deprivation as renters and workers for the DC-connected town elite. This more encompassing story of imbalanced storytelling is one that discloses the tendency of valuation within the objects of wealth. As the women seemed to know, to dwell in the dominant story of money-price divorced from the overall process of storytelling is to confuse wealth with value.[38]

Marx posed the value relationship as one of a specific manner of representation to be explained. "Why is labor represented by the value of its product and labor time by the magnitude of that value?" he famously asked in *Capital*, defining the study's critical goal.[39] Transposing Marx's analysis of value as representational tendency into Peirce's terms, it becomes possible to view any commodity as a triadic sign-in-development. The critical line of questioning then can proceed this way: What is the dynamical object of a commodity as sign in the instance when its immediate object is its value? How did this immediate object (value) become determined or shaped out of a concrete dynamical object, the full history of people, and all the aspects of their effort that went into making it? How does this history lie occluded in the moment of exchange, making the commodity "a social hieroglyphic," as Marx called it? Capitalist value determination as a real semeiotic process is the (immediate) objectification of the abstract dimensions of labor-power.

As I did with the mention of Intipucá in the Huntington book, I will take up the coffee example again to illustrate briefly what I mean by value as real representational tendency. Coffee first told its highly partial tale in El Salvador when coffee workers received a wage for their harvesting efforts. This money gestured hazily to some kind of general effort put out by all the workers, what they and others called *trabajo* (work) without any further specification. In a US commodities market coffee again told its all-purpose story, referring in a similarly vague way to the most general qualities of human effort that went into its production back in El Salvador. At both moments, the concrete qualities of effort, including, for example, the individual beans and the full person (represented by a specific name) whose hands had touched them in a particular way, was effaced. And again, when the hard currency obtained for the coffee in the US markets was used to purchase US goods for export back to El Salvador, these new imports yet more deeply hid the concrete historical efforts of the coffee laborers (not to mention the productive capacities and efforts of US factory laborers, which were marshaled in part with the aid of their consumption of Salvadoran coffee). By the time coffee told its story of being the Golden Grain, it effectively hid the harsh conditions on which this story was premised. Intipucá land-owners and their tenant farmers as well were hidden in the story. To include this story in the story would radically transfigure the value form, making the Golden Grain more like its opposite.

This rough account of coffee entailed a process of social abstraction similar to that of the Intipucá-DC Connection Story congealing and hiding its fuller formative conditions in the town. The difference, however, is that the representational tendency of commodities like coffee is a requirement of the capitalist relations that have enveloped El Salvador and the United States for several centuries. To the extent that accounts of Intipucá and DC, such as the *Post* newspaper stories, feature as their objects new commodities and forms of wealth (such as the reference to the first migrant's new car purchased in DC), they participate in this systemic tendency, simultaneously as contributor and as outcome. By telling this story of storytelling, it becomes possible to better appreciate not only the dominant representational tendency, but also its tenuous predication on, yet constant hiding of, other stories that go against it. To critically disclose the overall process helps to amplify these other stories, not as separate and external to the dominant one, but as immanent, within and constantly pressing at it.[40] This is the shift from stories to storytelling, from signs to semeiotic, from objects of wealth to value as representational proclivity that lies at the heart of this book and its method.

I would like to return to the wave-water metaphor to re-emphasize some implications of this perspective on value, which then sets the ground for a more detailed discussion of what is necessarily presupposed by this framework. Following the epigraph taken from Calvino, any form of value is not moving about atomistically, separate from the larger whole from which it has emerged and which it reciprocally shapes. Instead it is a momentary instantiation or coagulation out of an open, dynamic, and interactive process. In exactly this circulatory manner, value makes its appearance in varied form as commodities, including the quotient of human capacity bought, sold, and used in the production of other commodities, and as money, whether in wages, prices, rents, or interest.[41] As objects, these appear together with their human subjects, each as a coagulation of the other.[42] Following on this, value formation as a representational tendency also is richly historical. In this sense, every form, like a wave, emerges from its antecedent whole and in turn ever so slightly shapes the conditions of any subsequent formation.[43] Finally, though it is a durable proclivity within whatever social and historical whole is under consideration, this always is a provisional account amidst what is otherwise geographically and historically quite dynamic, open, and interactive. I take this to be the implication of Calvino's slightly baleful comment that I explore in more detail below.[44]

Open Holism: The Book's Reality

Pursuing together these initial how and why questions in a much more sustained and substantial way leads to the swift realization that what constitutes the Intipucá-DC connection story as an ensemble of interconnected
three-way signs—the actual written and spoken and visual accounts,
the people and other objects presented by them, and the audiences and
achieved meanings—is a relatively small, though important, individuated
expression that participates in a much larger open-ended hemispheric process. Arriving at a full and inclusive sense of this aggregate process is this
book's ultimate goal. This larger development or course, as I mentioned
in the preface, is El Salvador's transformation over the past fifty years
from a country largely oriented around exporting washed green *Arabica*
coffee beans, especially to the United States, to one that currently is much
defined by the circulation of remittances sent from Salvadorans working
in the United States. It includes as well the United States' transformation over the same half century from a country dominated by industrial
manufacturing, to one now much defined by production of services and
high-tech goods. As I have mentioned, the Intipucá-DC connection story
is both a product of and a player in this overall transformation, but as one
should now expect, there is much more to the story.

Moving between larger process (El Salvador and the United States
over the past half-century) and smaller moment (for example, a 1979 empirical measure of Intipucá's population in a DC neighborhood) and then
back out to a more fully explored larger part by uncovering what went
into the measure and also what it contributed to, is not a typical method
of analysis. The more conventional approach would be to work through a
number of separate and discrete parts, assembling them in a particular order so as to yield a complete and finite set, often with some sort of built-in
logic of separate cause and effect. Much of the scholarly literature on the
countries of Central America and their relations with the United States
reflects this arrangement. What is of particular interest is the manner of
distinguishing and dividing up the separate parts, since there is remarkable continuity in this, despite the variety of disciplinary perspectives and
topics of research.

The first of these is the recurring inclination to distinguish neatly
between two spatial scales of analysis, reflected in the popular dyads of
macro/micro, fragment/totality, and local/global. Scholars have tended

to privilege one scale as their primary field of analysis or to posit one in distinction to the other, as in the framework of "the local" being either in contradistinction to or a manifestation of a larger scale, often "the national" or "the global."[45] With respect to Central America–United States relations, the smaller scale often is posited in the isthmus, while the United States is understood as the larger one.[46] One important variation on this is the body of work on "transnational" phenomena, which are understood to occur within, at, and beyond the scale of the nation.[47]

Often intersecting with the dyadic spatial framework is the common temporal partition of past/present/future, with the disciplines of the social sciences tending to take up the present and historians doing the past. (The future, however delimited, has been relatively less emphasized in scholarship, though this was not always the case.) The past and present distinction also has tended to be distinguished by separate diachronic and synchronic approaches, again divided between historians emphasizing diachrony and social scientists pursuing the synchronic. Although the dichotomous approach to spatial scale has been unsettled by research that adopts a "transnational" perspective, this temporal split has remained largely assumed within that literature. The limitation of the subset of work on transnational population movement or migration (indeed, of most "migration studies") is that often save for another variable, all else besides migrants is held constant and fixed, and never similarly understood to be "trans-" or in spatiotemporal process, conceived of at any scale.

Across the spatial and temporal categorical framings, much work also invokes the well-liked and seemingly inescapable conceptual triad of political/economic/sociocultural and its dyadic variant of political-economic/sociocultural.[48] This latter distinction is reproduced in scholarship that distinguishes sharply between deeds and words, behaviors and thoughts, matter and meaning, even base and superstructure.[49] One "ideal type" example of how these three kinds of distinctions appear in scholarship is the typical format of beginning with the global or macro, political-economic, and historical past ("context") followed by analysis of the local cultural ("text") in its present, focusing separately on its material and/or meaningful dimensions. It is not possible to review all the recent work, but even a cursory review shows variants of this structure of rhetorical parsing to be dominant.

The problem is not that any one categorical perspective is true/false and subject to empirical test. Rather, it is that rigid and unexamined distinctions can lead to the error that the contents or objects of analysis are fundamentally different in kind. The risk is that vigorous and continuous relational processes become calcified into motionless and separate things, as if, borrowing from the Calvino epigraph, one had actually isolated and held still a wave. Difference of facet becomes hierarchy of type, yielding competing ideologies of inquisition (institutionalized in strong form as academic disciplines) where one object is opposed to another as if it were ontologically distinct and even ultimately determinate.

The alternative approach of this book that I call "open holism" involves presupposing that the real world under consideration is an infinite spatio-temporal continuum.[50] In other words, it has parts, but no ultimate parts. In principle, any individuated part, anywhere and any-when, can be divided infinitely. This book also presupposes that with open-ended collective and full inquiry, any part could be expanded so that all that shapes it is the infinite whole of which it is a product. This means that the continuum or open whole is expressed, however partially, through any of its individuated parts. Parts are partial, but moving outward and backward through all that shaped a part at any moment would lead, through inquiry without limit, to the infinite whole. Metaphorically this is similar to Calvino's comment on the relationship of waves to their larger bodies of water, except that the oceans are presupposed as infinite.

The main corollary of this approach to part as individuation out of an "open whole" is the recognition that anything—a form like money or coffee beans, a discursive category such as "migrant entrepreneur," a doctrine like that of "remittance-led development" as codified by the IMF or World Bank, a place like Intipucá or Washington, DC, a specific person there, a set of practical habits such as sending remittances, and a durable pattern of social relations such as Salvadoran low-wage service work in the United States or remittances in El Salvador—is necessarily the congealed figure of its own geohistorical formation and development. In this respect, all of these entities—forms, categories, doctrines, practices, institutions, social relations—continually produce the world in which they circulate and, reciprocally, are the congealed expression of that world. To begin with the assumption that such individuated parts all are the congealed expressions of the other implies a fluid, internally related, dynamic, and interactive framework that assumes relational movement, development, and transformation. It is the appearance of stasis and durability, like the twenty-five year presence of the Intipucá-DC Connection Story, that invites critical explanation.

What I call "open holism" is not a typical presupposition about the reality of the world that often is made explicitly in the mainstream of the social sciences. Nevertheless beginning with the work of mathematician Georg Cantor in the late nineteenth century on set theory and including such varied figures as Charles S. Peirce, Jorge Luis Borges, Henri Lefebvre, Jacques Derrida, and Alain Badiou, infinitude has been given its due.[51] Such a notion of infinite whole and individuated parts is a necessary presupposition about the real world examined by this book. At any moment of its analysis (in any chapter), the book essentially grasps just some of the relations of the various individuated parts that define the contours of whatever portion of the open whole is under consideration. In the case of this book, the largest scale is roughly a half-century across El Salvador and the United States. As I have suggested, these relations, as they become more discernible, help illuminate the durable tendencies of the provisionally bounded whole under study. They define its directionality, making it a dynamic and interactive system going somewhere, not random chaos. In this respect, the book hypothesizes about such tendencies (Peirce called this *abduction*) and seeks after them as real entities understood to have causal powers, the potential capacity to make other things happen. This is the realism presupposed by this book.

"Pulling Out": The Book's Object and Method

How can one seek after real tendencies within an open continuum of relations? The book's method is predicated on pulling out or abstracting specific qualities and dimensions according to various criteria. Peirce called this *prescinding*, and it may be distinguished from a way of working that assumes a closed set of discrete and separate entities and then seeks after constant conjunctures of events, as in "whenever A, then B." The challenging aspect of this former method is that the terms of delimiting must be consciously and constantly specified, rather than assumed. As I mentioned earlier, specific academic disciplines often naturalize these terms or criteria, so that to properly follow them is to correctly do and to be a person of such a discipline.

Rather than assuming the dominant spatial, temporal, and conceptual distinctions that I described, this book self-consciously modulates its "pulling out" according to several different criteria that do not correspond necessarily with a specific disciplinary home. First, it "prescinds" according to a variety of geohistorical loci, levels of focus, and spatiotemporal scopes or scales of analysis. This means changing up the vantage points or perspectives, the phenomena considered, and the geohistorical reach of analysis. As the opening story showed, Samuel Huntington's locus, focus, and scope of analysis was quite different from that of the three women in the doorway, though both sought to generate an account of the same thing—Intipucá. By strict definitions of disciplinary foundationalism, one would need to be at least an anthropologist and political scientist to make the introductory story that I did. Obviously in practice one must remain a little undisciplined or at least multidisciplined.

A second set of criteria that defines the book's method of pulling out involves distinguishing qualitatively among moments of open *possibility* or potentiality, which then may give way to specific instantiations in their "here-and-now" *actuality*, which in turn may yield the characteristic of *generality*. For example, a coffee bean or a Salvadoran migrant in DC potentially could be many things. When this potentiality becomes defined by a price or as a quotient of work capacity exchanged for the promise of a wage at any particular moment, the entities become commodities in their actuality. When this manner of definition and its associated practices comes to dominate in any spatiotemporal field, we enter the realm of generality as in a tendency or proclivity. But within generality lie potentiality and actuality. The other qualities of coffee beans or human work capacity not fully represented in domains dominated by money-price are potentials that may be actualized, even generalized, relative to the commodity's dominant story. When this happens, the dominant story is destabilized and coffee or a person's work capacities come to mean much more—or much less—than their price.

Finally, the most important feature of this introduction's opening story and also the short account of coffee is what I identify as the process of "transvaluation." When the beans referred to the modern wealth they appeared to generate, they were "The Golden Grain." But when I showed how they also much less visibly gestured to the harsh conditions of their production in highlands outside of Intipucá, they were the Golden Grain's opposite. This capacity for the same form or sign to shift or expand its immediate object and therefore its meaning is what I call "transvaluation." It lies at the heart of this book, both as the process studied and as the book's critical technique.

The Book's Shape

This multiplex approach toward pulling out according to various criteria further implies that one must work retroductively—guessing, hypothesizing, moving spatially backward and temporally outward, abstracting according to the criteria listed, provisionally reconstructing and empirically checking—in order to move carefully toward the identification of general tendencies internally related to any phenomenon in its actuality as well as its countless potentialities. The Huntington book versus three Intipucá women prologue was an illustration of this kind of approach, a small first step of retroduction. It began with a particular form or expression and then worked outward and backward to discern more of its occluded contradictory historical content. It is not that Intipucá and DC caused Huntington's book. Rather, that book contains the history of Intipucá and DC as part of the shaping conditions of its formation, but only certain aspects of the town and ties to DC are perceivable, at least from the 2004 book-reader perspective. Each chapter in this book now follows a similar procedure, figuratively plunging into a specific expression, understood as a more or less unified concentration of forms, categories, or practices, and then working geographically outward and historically backward.

It would be impossible to reach the whole that gives rise to all the individuated parts in this book. However, there are some forms that have some unexpected and also exceptionally invisible and contradictory determinants. On the basis of a mixture of judgment, evidence, and research capacities, in each chapter the book endeavors to bring some, but obviously not all, of these into view. The choice of what to trace out is guided by the kind of transvaluation that I seek to foment. At points along the way relatively dominant forms will become destabilized—even radically transformed—in the process of the book's narrative unfolding. To anticipate this, it is helpful to briefly map in advance the book's organizational logic, by parts and chapters.

In tandem with this introduction so as to fashion a kind of two-part **Prologue**, chapter 1, "A Roadmap for Remittances," focuses on the period of the late 1970s to the early 1990s, predominantly in and from the vantage of El Salvador, though with one significant sojourn to Washington, DC, and the United States more generally. The logic of the chapter is that of a combined timeline and spatial map with considered focus on four key moments, each defined by a particular visual representation. The chapter highlights one indexical moment, the third in the series of four, when a key part of the Intipucá-DC Connection Story congealed as both product and protagonist in the aggregate transformation of migrant remittances into interest-bearing capital in El Salvador. The chapter shows how this third moment was internally related to the other three stops on the timeline/map. This extruded sign is part of a semeiotic concentration that, once discerned, serves as the practical jumping-off point for the subsequent three chapters (2–4) of the book.

Part I (chapters 2–4) works across the largest spatiotemporal scale, multiply shifting its locus and focus across both El Salvador and the United States throughout the twentieth century. All three chapters may be read together as a multidecade history of El Salvador and its relations with the United States (figuratively like Calvino's "ocean") and also as a combined explanation and critique of how and why the Intipucá-DC Connection Story congealed in wave-like fashion out of this larger history.

Chapter 2, "Brushing against the Golden Grain" begins with one subfeature derived from the key third moment identified in chapter 1. This subfeature is a specific person (related to someone from chapter 1), whose life and ability to recount features of it in particular ways rests on but also hides the larger history of coffee production and export that has interwoven El Salvador and the United States since the early twentieth century. This person's narrative account emphasizes a switch-like before/after moment of transition, which is accurate from the perspective of his immediate lifetime and experiences. However, as it becomes better anchored in the larger and more concealed historical conditions of its formation, the account takes on a slightly different significance.

Chapter 3, "Melting Fields of Snow," begins with two other stories, one of which tightly reverberates with the opening story of chapter 2 and the other that resonates with what was concealed in that story. In this way, each may be understood as abstracted from the whole of chapter 2, together setting the point of departure for this next chapter. "Melting Fields of Snow" moves outward and backward from these two accounts, gradually filling in more of their shared content. In the process, what seemed like two distinct stories become merely different perspectives of the same whole—the rise of cotton production in El Salvador out of the earlier coffee era and the development of suburbia in the United States. These two larger processes then are shown to be related in surprising ways, including early migration between El Salvador and the United States beginning in the 1960s.

Chapter 4, "The Intrusion of Uncomfortable Wars, *Illegals*, and Remittances" closely examines the decade of the 1980s, when the cotton and coffee export system in El Salvador collapsed amidst more than a decade of civil war and a fundamentally new relationship emerged as direct US government aid and the millions of dollars sent home by Salvadorans living and working in the United States became the dominant source of national wealth. As chapter 1 directly introduced via its "third moment," chapter 4 returns to the historical juncture at which the Intipucá-DC Connection Story began to take form.

Part II of the book (chapters 5–6) shifts from the scale and focus of Part I to move closely into the more immediate geographical and historical conditions that yielded the Intipucá-DC Connection Story yet remained relatively invisible amidst its growing circulation. Chapter 5, "The Wealth of Pueblos," moves through the appearance of wealth in Intipucá and among Intipuqueños in DC to identify some of the quotidian relations of domination and exploitation upon which it rests and the surplus of human life that presses at the wealth forms. Chapter 6, "Immigrant Entrepreneurship," places these everyday patterns within a slightly broader context, linking them especially with financial and political transformations that unfolded in Washington, DC, and across the Americas during the 1980s.

Part III (chapters 7–8) moves via a yet closer focus on Intipucá and DC to the most recent context of El Salvador–United States relations. Chapter 7, "Welcome to Intipucá City," focuses on the way that the former president of El Salvador (1994–99), Armando Calderón Sol, attempted to link a national project of governance with the particularities of the pueblo and its ties to Washington, DC. Chapter 8, "The World in a Park," examines the lives of people who live and work at the margins of Intipucá, barely represented in the dominant models, yet necessary for their formation.

The **Finale** comprises a substantial chapter (9) that shifts the analysis to a different scale, and a conclusion that offers a concise wrap-up and provisional finish to the study conducted by this book. Chapter 9, "Options and Models for the Future," marks a distinct widening of perspective and a shift toward critically viewing the near future from the perspective of what has been covered in chapters 1–8. It connects the counterinsurgency principles that the US government has followed in Iraq and in other contexts worldwide with actual 1980s wartime fighting around Intipucá. It also places the town of Intipucá and its ties to DC in relation to the rise of an overall model of remittance-led development being adopted by governments, international organizations, and nongovernmental organizations (NGOs) worldwide amidst what is widely regarded as a deep crisis in "neoliberal globalization." In the conclusion, I offer some reflections on the ground covered by this book and suggest where things figuratively stand in 2010 as the story necessarily stops, at least for now.

CHAPTER ONE

A Roadmap for Remittances

Dip the pitcher into the water enough and it finally breaks. — Popular saying in El Salvador

The common expression chosen as the epigraph for this chapter may be heard in Spanish with slight variation throughout the hemisphere of the Americas.[1] I took note of it in El Salvador and in the Washington, DC, area and have come to understand it to be as much a warning about overuse as an expression about how, as something grows in quantity, it may at some point undergo a qualitative transformation.[2] In the case of the pitcher and water, there is a dipping tipping-point, so to speak. On the basis of cumulative repetition, what once was a container becomes something fundamentally different, a smattering of fragments contained within what used to be the object of its transport. The pitcher parable achieves its rhetorical resonance because it brings together two different temporal moments or states of being within a single continuous process. This is not quite the same logic as distinguishing between *either* one condition *or* another and setting apart cause from effect.

Just such a process of quantity-to-quality transformation occurred between the late 1970s and early 1990s in El Salvador as the country became increasingly oriented around remittances, the quotient of US dollars circulating in the country sent mostly by Salvadorans living and working in the United States. Starting as a barely recognized trickle near the onset of the war, migrant remittances became the centerpiece of a completely reorganized society and productive system by the middle 1990s. Quite literally, remittances had changed from small wads of well-worn US dollars used to store and exchange wealth in El Salvador into something more sublime: interest-bearing capital, that is, money that appeared to make more money. By following this quantity-to-quality transformation as a kind of 15-year road trip, it is possible to grasp a key transformative moment in the larger jointly asymmetrical development of El Salvador and the United States over the past fifty years.

It is beyond the scope of this chapter to arrive at the full capital-m "Measure" of the transformation of remittance money from means of exchange and wealth storage into interest-bearing capital in El Salvador—the absolute and complete before, after, and infinitesimally small point of transition.[3] Instead, this chapter covers just a few key points in the transformation, figuratively as if following a road, but with a concern for some rest stops. In this sense, the chapter is a specific and necessarily limited roadmap, not the fullness of the complete route and journey. Despite the partiality of its account—shaped by the particular perspective, level of acuity, and scalar reach that it assumes—the four stopping-off points on the map do complement and overlap each other in a way that yield a rough composite or amalgam of the overall transformation or, more figuratively, the whole road trip. The subsequent eight chapters of this book may be read as other kinds of maps that enrich and expand the rendering offered in this chapter.

The first and second stop-overs in this chapter are two photographs taken in 1989 by a journalist visiting El Salvador. The second photograph, in particular, introduces the way that the town called Intipucá began to be socially pulled out as a kind of representative model of and player in the overall transformation, internal to it, yet also congealing out of it in particular ways. This is perhaps the closest that this roadmap gets to marking a point of transition in the journey, where remittances appear to shift from a minor side effect to the defining feature of El Salvador's future. The next stop is a set of important numerical measures of money derived mostly from official Salvadoran government reports and presented in the form of two charts, compiled in 1995. The last layover in this journey is a document published by the World Bank a year later in 1996. As the chapter unfolds, these four sojourns on the route put Intipucá on the map, so to speak, and illustrate the larger, ongoing process of transformation in which it is embedded.

First Stop: Pictures at an Election

In spring 1989, a British photojournalist named Robin Lubbock traveled
to El Salvador to chronicle developments in the conflict between a coalition of popular revolutionary organizations called the *Frente Farabundo
Martí para la Liberacion Nacional* (FMLN; Farabundo Martí National
Liberation Front) and the heavily US-backed government of José Napoleon Duarte of the Partido Demócrata Cristiano (PDC; Democratic
Christian Party). "I went to cover the [Salvadoran Presidential and munic-
ipal] elections. A lot was happening. I ended up staying for three years,"
Robin recalled slightly more than a decade later.[4]

Among the happenings of early 1989 was that the FMLN offered—for
the first time in the history of the conflict—to support and participate in
government-held elections if they would be slightly delayed. The *Frente*
followed this gesture with the announcement that they would suspend all
direct attacks on US personnel and installations in El Salvador because of
the "positive response" to their election proposal that they had received
from members of the new George H. W. Bush presidential administration in the United States. In turn, the Bush administration sent an important message back in the form of Vice President Dan Quayle, who made
a highly publicized visit to El Salvador and requested that the military
high command investigate the September 1988 "San Sebastian massacre"
where soldiers of the Fifth Brigade's *Batallón Jiboa* had murdered ten
civilian farmers. The new US administration appeared to be testing the
Salvadoran military's capacity to curb forms of wartime violence and also
signaling that future aid and support could be conditioned in part by the
outcome of the investigation.[5]

Alfredo Cristiani, the Salvadoran presidential candidate of the rightist
Alianza Republicana Nacionalista (ARENA) party bested Duarte in the
national election (March 19), receiving just over 53 percent of the popular
vote. In the end, the FMLN did not participate. Despite the conservative
roots of ARENA, the new Salvadoran leader rhetorically carved out a
fresh position on the war. At his June inauguration Cristiani announced
that his new administration would consider beginning peace talks with the
FMLN without a prior cessation of hostilities. "We will dedicate all our
efforts to the conquest of a permanent peace that does not exclude any
Salvadoran," Cristiani said. "We are ready to initiate dialogue with the
guerrilla immediately." Though critics decried this offer as empty talk,

FIGURE 2. Robin Lubbock's photograph of presidential candidate Alfredo Cristiani address-ing an ARENA rally in Sensuntepeque, February 19, 1989. Used with permission of the photographer.

the words themselves were both real and new. The previous Duarte gov-ernment, as well as its main patron, the US presidential administration of Ronald Reagan (1981–89), had desired complete evisceration of the FMLN.

Cristiani's use of the word "we" at his inauguration presented himself, the elected government, and the party that dominated it (ARENA) in a particularly unified way for his audience. Indeed, this momentary triangu-lation granted the whole gesture its authority. Yet Cristiani would not have been in the position to make this exact statement were it not for a more complex history that lay somewhat submerged in the utterance. Lubbock captured a moment in this larger history when he photographed Cristiani campaigning before the 1989 election.

Cristiani had been active in ARENA since 1984, working especially to broaden its base of support among poorer and middle classes and to re-duce the party's public identification with its founder Robert D'Aubuisson, a US-trained military officer, widely believed to have organized right-wing paramilitary "death squads" in El Salvador. Cristiani had received a de-gree in business administration from Georgetown University in Washing-ton, DC, and publicly admired the neoliberal economic policies of Chile implemented throughout the 1970s and 1980s. He represented a faction of elite business interests in El Salvador, whose members not only were connected to the agro-export sector, but also maintained holdings in industry and commerce. In contrast to oligarchic land-owning families more narrowly tied to the agro-export sector, especially coffee, this group of more diversified capitalists had profited during the war through their ties to the remittance-driven commercial sector. Though the war was hardly resolved by 1989, the gesture toward meeting with the FMLN signaled a desire to end the conflict via a political solution rather than continue what already was recognized as a three-year military stalemate.[6] Arguably, part of the motivation came from business concerns.[7]

This understanding that negotiating the right kind of end to the war would auger well for the Cristiani-led faction came in part from their experience of being courted and supported directly by officials in the US State Department to the tune of $100 million. A primary vehicle for this bolstering was the organization known as FUSADES, founded and funded by the US Agency for International Development (USAID) in 1983 to generate proscriptive policy research and also to directly fund financial liberalization and the privatization of state sectors in El Salvador. From the perspective of the last two stopping points in this chapter's narrative journey, the charts and the World Bank Report, it will become more clear how the Cristiani government followed this agenda almost to the letter. In 1998, the ascendance of the FUSADES-backed Cristiani faction to political office in El Salvador nevertheless signaled an important realignment of social forces in El Salvador.[8] It also represented a shift in the United States as the State Department appeared to have wrested control of United States–El Salvador policy from hard-liners in the Pentagon and in the previous Reagan presidency.[9] Lubbock's photograph of Cristiani's campaigning, as much as the new president's utterance of "we," figuratively was the tip of a wave amidst an incipient sea-change in El Salvador.

Second Stop: The Wealth of Pueblos

Along with covering events that revolved around the national elections and unfolded in the capital city of San Salvador, Robin Lubbock ventured to other locales around the country. Among his stops was the *pueblo* (small town) of Intipucá in the Department of La Unión, located about eighteen miles south of the large eastern city of San Miguel. Like many pueblos in the region, it had lost a significant part of its population because of wartime migration to the United States. However, the first *Intipuqueños* (natives of Intipucá) who traveled to live and work in the United States actually had begun to do so in the late 1960s. Building on initial patterns and contacts established by these residents who had settled in the Washington, DC, metropolitan region, almost all of the town's expatriates went to the DC area over the ensuing decades.

At the time of Robin's visit, Intipucá had concluded its annual festival to celebrate the patron saint of the town, San Nicolas Tolentíno. In the later years of the 1980s, the region around Intipucá was relatively free of military conflict and Intipuqueños residing in DC and its Maryland and Virginia suburbs were able to return for the celebration. Coinciding with the national elections, the pueblo's municipal elections followed on the heels of the festival. This sequence tended to favor the incumbent mayor since he usually could link himself and his administration with both the celebration and the return *en masse* of DC-based Intipuqueños, whose visit yielded a brief but substantial influx of US dollars.

Amidst the postcelebratory climate in the pueblo, Robin took pictures and casually spoke with many long-time residents as well as the recent visitors from DC. One of his many black-and-white photographs, the second image considered by this chapter, features a smiling young man straddling his Kawasaki Ninja motorcycle outside of the town pool hall. "He was a great guy. I really enjoyed meeting him. He showed me around and told me all about the pueblo," recalled Robin, referring to the subject on the motorcycle. "It was an interesting place. All the houses looked nice and people seemed reasonably well off. I shot at least a whole roll [of film]," Robin told me years later.

On July 18, 1989, the *New York Times* printed one of Lubbock's compelling snapshots as part of a short article about Intipucá. The text highlighted the relative wealth of the pueblo in comparison with nearby areas and attributed this to the significant amount of money sent back by residents who had settled in the Washington, DC, area. According to the article, more than 15,000 people in the DC area claimed ties to Intipucá and they remitted over $150,000 each month to family and friends in the town. A brief description beneath Robin's photograph identified the motorcycle rider by name and implied that he stood for this more general feature of the pueblo: "Marvin Chávez on his motorcycle in Intipucá, El Salvador, a rural town made wealthy by millions of dollars sent home by residents who emigrated to Washington, DC. Mr. Chávez's father was among the

MAP 1. El Salvador with Intipucá (lower right) at about 13° 11′ 18″ N latitude and 88° 3′ 11″ E longitude.

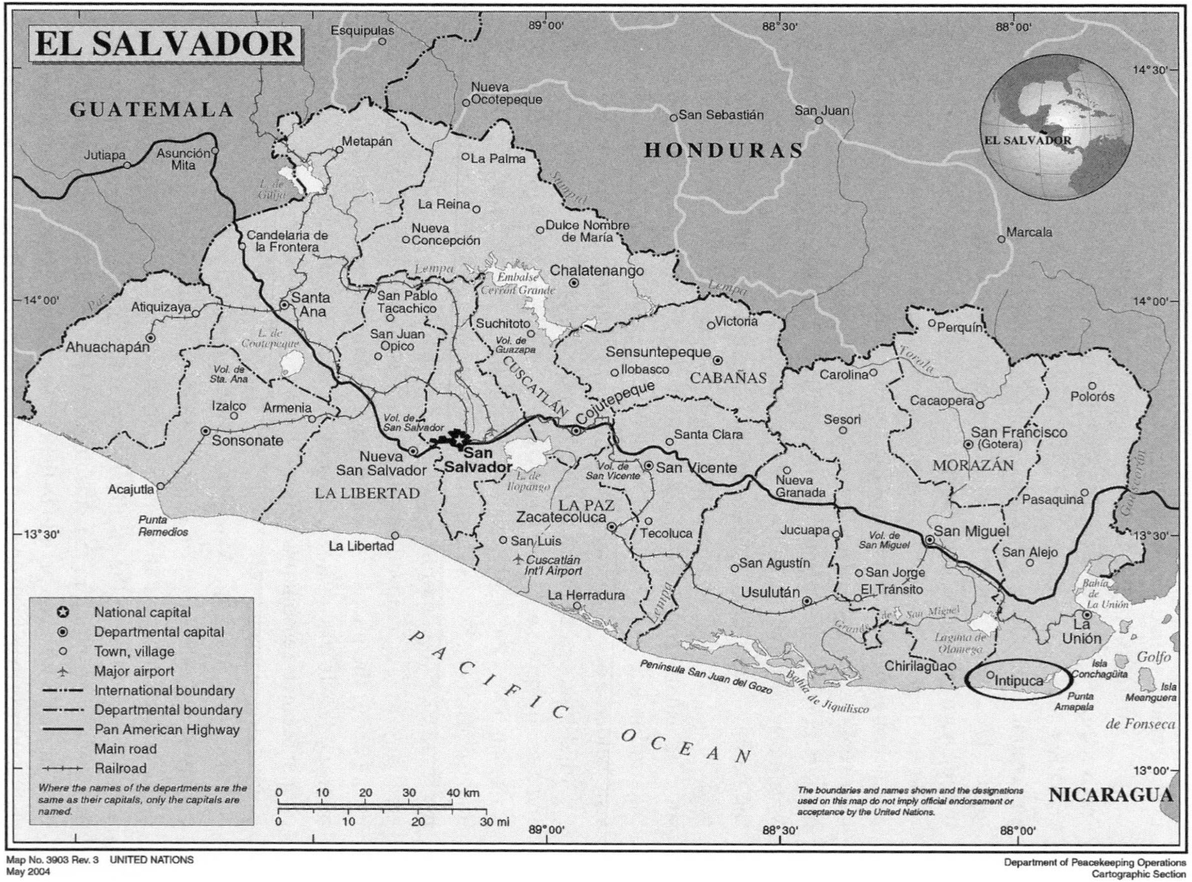

FIGURE 3. One of Robin Lubbock's many Intipucá photographs.

first emigrants." [10] The picture, its caption, and the accompanying essay by staff writer Lindsey Gruson appeared under the title "Emigrants Feather Their Old Nests with Dollars" in the international section of the paper, comprising one the newspaper's periodic "Journal" features—in this instance, Intipucá Journal.[11]

As the Cristiani photograph reflected via both the FUSADES support and the class fraction he represented, US government money formed one unheralded source of Salvadoran national wealth throughout the 1980s. Nearly $1 billion annually sent back to the country by Salvadorans who were living and working in major cities like Washington, DC, in the United States provided another. This second and equally unprecedented font stimulated steady levels of commercial and financial activity, including in rural areas like Intipucá. Lubbock's photographic image of the town and its reproduction in Gruson's article caught a portion of this whole, illuminating some meaningful features of it. Though not definite, the promising political events during the first half of 1989 coupled with the *Times* article about the relative wealth and tranquility in one small Salvadoran town did seem to hint at a new future for El Salvador different from the years of violent conflict.

THE NEW YORK TIMES, TUESDAY, JULY 18, 1989   K

Intipucá Journal

Emigrants Feather Their Old Nest With Dollars

By LINDSEY GRUSON
Special to The New York Times

INTIPUCA, El Salvador — This is probably the country's richest town, a pastel oasis of plenty with more in common with an exclusive United States suburb than a destitute and devastated land.

Television antennas adorn rows of concrete houses, freshly painted in peach, lime and purple. In a country where a parcel of land often makes the difference between starvation and survival, these homes boast of almost wasteful wealth — front yards with well-tended flower gardens.

"We used to be so poor we had to fish for crabs by sticking our arms in the ocean, but now everybody is going around in coats and ties," said Domitila Blanco, who owns and runs a grocery store. Like most houses in the town, her shop has many of the luxuries of modern living, including a television, videocassette recorder and stereo with tower speakers.

Emigration Is the Source

The source of all this wealth, as well as of growing resentment, is emigration, legal and illegal. In the last 20 years, an estimated 15,000 Intipuqueños have moved to Washington or its suburbs. There are now three times as many Intipucá natives living around the United States capital as there are residents of this town.

"If a family has five children and they're not married, they're all there," said Maximiliano Arias, who spent 15 months in Washington in the late 1980's before becoming homesick and returning.

The exodus from Intipucá began two decades ago with a trickle of emigration in which relatives and neighbors followed those already established around Washington. It turned into a flood after the civil war hit home in the 1960's.

The emigrants have sent home millions of dollars earned working in the restaurants of Washington and on its construction sites. That money probably has made Intipuqueños this country's wealthiest rural residents and has remade the town, 110 miles southwest of San Salvador. It paid to pave the streets, install four-inch curbs, build a school, commission the side of the peach-colored exterior of the Roman Catholic church — nothing less, in short, than to transform a poverty-stricken backwater into a Salvadoran center of wealth and conspicuous consumption.

Paradoxically, that is in large part due to the decade-old civil war, which so far has killed 70,000 people and displaced more than one in 10 Salvadorans, many of whom have fled to the United States. Three years ago, the Urban Institute, a Washington-based research group, estimated that 500,000 to 850,000 of the five million

The New York Times/Robin Lubbock

Marvin Chávez on his motorcycle in Intipucá, El Salvador, a rural town made wealthy by millions of dollars sent home by residents who emigrated to Washington. Mr. Chávez's father was among the first emigrants.

Salvadorans were living in the United States. More recent estimates put the number even higher.

The exodus from Intipucá started in the late 1960's, before the civil war, when Sigifrido Chávez, a 28-year-old bank clerk, broke up with his wife. A friend advised him to go the United States, which at the time was generous with visas, find a job and forget about the failed marriage. He did. Word of his good fortune quickly spread through the town. His brother soon followed, as did many neighbors.

The trickle of emigrants turned into a flood after Sept. 24, 1983, when about 300 guerrillas attacked the town and killed 10 soldiers and 4 civilians suspected of collaborating with the army. By the next day, when army reinforcements drove out the insurgents, the town's collective psyche was deeply scarred. Thousands of frightened residents fled, joining refugees from nationwide repression and innumerable other battles throughout the country.

Those expatriates are a major factor in keeping this country afloat. American officials estimate that they send home $350 million a year. That has made Salvadorans working in the United States the second or third largest source of hard currency. The United States Government sends $533 million a year in military and economic aid, accounting for more than half the annual budget. Coffee ex-

ports have been the second largest source of income in recent years. But a series of storms last year, which resulted in a disastrous harvest, combined with plummeting international prices, is expected to bring a sharp drop in coffee earnings.

Mr. Arias, the director of a committee that decides how to spend money raised for the town, estimates that Intipuqueños working in Washington send their families here $100,000 a month.

The infusion of dollars has probably made Washington the pre-eminent power both here and throughout the country. Immigration changes in the United States last year, which cracked down on employers hiring illegal aliens, has cut the flow of emigrants and has had a greater effect on Intipucá than any recent decision by the Salvadoran Government. Local residents say it is now much more difficult for new emigrants to get into the United States.

Culture Is Affected Too

The American involvement — interference in the view of many critics — extends far beyond political and military matters. It increasingly pervades the country's culture.

The American influence has provoked rising nationalism throughout this dependent society and an increasingly virulent debate over United States aid. A large segment believes that American concerns

over human rights violations have handicapped the army. Many still call the land-redistribution program, imposed eight years ago to tarnish the lure of leftist revolution and break the dominating power of the oligarchy, "U.S.-imposed socialism."

In large part, that criticism grows out of the deepening economic crisis and the continued concentration of wealth in the hands of an elite. Despite the infusion of billions of dollars in aid and remittances from the United States in the last decade, the average Salvadoran's real income has dropped by a third in that period. Most now live in worse conditions than at the beginning of the war. Fewer rural residents have safe drinking water and a greater percentage of their children die.

Dissatisfaction is growing even among Intipuqueños. Many note that the influx of money is an incentive against working and that many residents do little but wait for their checks. They say the "free" dollars are perverting cherished values and breaking up many families.

Mrs. Blanco said she scolded her daughter when she returned home for a visit this year and began praising life in America in front of the other children. "I hold her to stop talking and putting ideas about the U.S. into their heads," she recalled. "I don't want to lose them. When I die, they can leave. I'll never let them go as long as I live."

FIGURE 4. *New York Times* article with Lubbock's photograph.

Like other Journal features in the *New York Times*, Gruson's piece gained its significance by seeming to discover the unexpected. The expression on Marvin's face, his expensive new motorcycle, and the admiring and perhaps desirous looks of his colleagues coupled with the story of the town and the relative wealth of its residents living in DC and in Intipucá starkly contrasted with reports of the violence of the Salvadoran conflict and the experiences of people both in the country and as migrant workers scattered across the United States. In 1989, this visual and textual composition was both product and protagonist in the transfiguration of value across both countries. It gets as near to a formal marker of the tipping point as anything in its here-and-now actuality. In its manner of expression, it serves as the crux of the overall transformation covered in this book.

Yet, as a marker, it is hardly a discrete or original entity. Only two months before the *Times* appeared, a similar but much more detailed account of Intipucá appeared in the Washington, DC, magazine *Regardie's*, written by Charles Lane, the Central America correspondent for the US magazine *Newsweek*. Lane and Gruson had been in El Salvador at the same time, sharing informal membership in the pool of reporters covering the war for foreign publications. US reporters regularly received by fax a news digest produced by staff at the US embassy in El Salvador. It usually contained copies of all recent news publications on the war. I believe it is likely that Gruson read Lane's article and from it derived his idea for a story, built around a meeting he had with Sigfredo Chávez in the pueblo.

*　*　*

During the summer of 1989, I read and clipped the *Times* article about Intipucá with its picture of the fellow on the motorcycle when I was living in the northwest DC neighborhood called Mount Pleasant and working several miles away in Dupont Circle.[12] With its reference to the ample income earned by hard-working Intipuqueños in DC, the article ran against my own sense of the challenges faced by thousands of Salvadorans, especially young adults from the eastern part of the country, who had fled the war and come to live without any legal documentation in Mount Pleasant and other adjacent neighborhoods, taking low-wage service and construction jobs throughout the DC area. The story also stood apart from numerous reckonings of DC's urban poverty, contemporary studies of its so-called underclass, and its complex history of racial and class division. Beyond the specificity of the Salvadoran war, the apparent resources and serenity of Intipucá also contrasted with much reporting and popular debate about the devastating effects of the public debt crisis that had rippled across Latin America and the Caribbean during "the lost decade" of the 1980s. At the time it seemed anomalous and hardly representative of life in El Salvador or Washington, DC.

When I read the article, I did not know that my basement room in a rented house was less than a mile from where Marvin lived in the neighborhood and only two blocks away from his father's house. Although I had not met either Marvin or Sigfredo at the time, I was familiar with

Intipucá, as were many people in the neighborhood. I also knew one former resident, whom I shall call Manuel. He had arrived in DC in 1984, traveling clandestinely through Mexico and the US Southwest. We occasionally played billiards together in the basement of a nearby church that served as an after-school recreation center for Salvadoran youths. At this time, Manuel was working without legal papers as a house painter, and he lived with his sister and several other Salvadorans in a small apartment in the neighborhood. He told me of his hometown and encouraged me to visit, despite the ongoing war and—unlike the example of Marvin displayed in the newspaper story—his despondent judgment that he could never return. From Manuel's perspective in DC, the *Times* article was similarly aberrant.

Interlude: Roadblock and Clearing

Back in San Salvador the nascent reciprocity suggested by the various political gesticulations of 1989 dissolved back into tumultuous conflict: Most of the army personnel responsible for the San Sebastian killings avoided prosecution; paramilitary forces loyal to the Salvadoran government bombed the Federación Nacional Sindical de Trabajadores Salvadoreños (FENASTRAS) union headquarters in San Salvador, killing nine people; and in November the FMLN launched a large-scale assault and occupied major cities throughout the country, including upper-class neighborhoods in San Salvador. The Salvadoran military retaliated with aerial bombing and heavy strafing in San Salvador and in the city of San Miguel, to the north of Intipucá. In anger and frustration, one internal faction of the armed forces orchestrated the assassination of six Jesuit professors, their housekeeper, and her daughter at the University of Central America in San Salvador.[13] Even as peace talks between the FMLN and the Cristiani government had at last begun in Mexico City, military actors in the conflict continued to attempt to shape the direction of the conflict and the terms of its possible resolution.

Then came a resounding message from Washington, DC, that echoed throughout the hemisphere. In December, US forces invaded neighboring Panama. The rapid assault included attacks on neighborhoods in Panama City and led to the eventual capture of the country's leader, a military general named Manuel Noriega, whom the Carter and Reagan administration previously had supported. This aggressive unilateral action by the new Bush government sent a powerful message to countries, leaders, and especially all military forces throughout the Isthmus and Caribbean Basin. This resonant reminder of the ultimate arbiter of force in the region was made at the same moment that the Cold War was ending, and with it, the dominant security paradigm that had defined the American hemisphere (north and south) for forty years. From the perspective of a CIA agent who was working near San Miguel at the time, "Everything was cracking up: the Cold War ended, the FMLN leaders left the mountains and headed for the city, we didn't have anything to do."[14] It was this "cracking up," as the agent (known to some in Intipucá) had glossed the end of the Cold War moment, that further moved the war toward a negotiated settlement by 1992.

Out of the Picture

In April 1993, I visited Intipucá, flying to El Salvador on the Central American airline TACA (popularly known to be well staffed by recently unemployed Salvadoran Air Force pilots), which just had secured landing rights at Dulles International Airport in Northern Virginia. Quite unexpectedly I met my old acquaintance Manuel in the town pool hall. He had, in fact, returned and, again in contrast to the image presented of town residents in the Gruson article, seemed quite happy to give up wage labor in DC to work his family's modest plot of land in the nearby *cantón* (small territorial division) known as Chichipate, growing corn and grazing several dairy cattle. "I was never meant to live in Washington. In my heart, I am a Salvadoran farmer and worker," he stated with emphatic pride when we reminisced about late-1980s Mount Pleasant. "It was not a good place for me—even with the pool table," he said with a smile.

The following summer I again traveled to Intipucá to see Manuel and his mother and father, help him on the farm, and learn more about everyday life in the pueblo. During this second visit I met Marvin and learned that he and Manuel were distant cousins, since Manuel's father and Marvin's grandmother were both from one of the oldest Spanish-surname families in the pueblo. Although I often asked Manuel and Marvin to tell me about Intipucá, we usually found ourselves sharing our experiences during the 1980s in the DC area. In contrast to Manuel, Marvin had arrived in Mount Pleasant in 1980, traveling by airplane and carrying a legal visa. He attended a public high school in northwest DC and within several years he obtained US citizenship. Marvin and I learned that we had eaten at the same McDonald's restaurants in the area, gone to the same movie theaters and public swimming pools, and watched many of the same television shows. One day we spontaneously repeated in English the dialogue from the well-known commercial for "Jhoon Rhee Self De-fense," a popular martial arts studio located in the DC area: "Nobody bothers me!" "Nobody bothers me, either!" was the refrain.[15]

Perhaps stimulated by this unplanned exchange, Marvin then warmly recalled his Ninja motorcycle and his frequent visits to the pueblo through-out the war. However, he spoke of Robin Lubbock's picture and its ap-pearance in the *New York Times* article with surprising indifference. "I remember him. I showed him around the pueblo. He seemed like a nice guy. . . . I was here [in Intipucá] visiting my grandmother when that [pic-ture and article] came out. My cousin called me and said, 'Marvin, you're in the newspaper!' but I never actually saw it. I think that my mother has a copy."

The article and picture did not seem important to Marvin when we talked in 1994, nor could they be generalized to adequately represent Manuel's starkly different experiences in DC and subsequent return to the pueblo. If Manuel had an "Intipucá Journal," it would be more wanting and would feature the difficulties of traveling to DC and working without legal documentation, his inability to save enough money to send home to his parents, his bouts of melancholy and heavy drinking, and the later ir-repressible joy of returning permanently to the pueblo to become a small-scale farmer who owned land and cattle rather than a motorcycle.

One of Many Expressions of Wealth and Progress

Lubbock's photograph and Gruson's text form an important part of a still growing collection of news stories about Intipucá that has helped to pro-pel particular aspects of the pueblo into the public spotlight in both El Salvador and the United States. Since 1979, when reporters from the DC regional newspaper, the *Washington Post*, reported on the town (mention-ing Marvin's father), there have been at least 40 substantial articles about Intipucá published in Salvadoran, Latin American, US, and European newspapers and magazines. US and Salvadoran television networks also have produced short reports on the town and its ties to DC. For example, in January 2003, Public Radio International, a collaboration between WGBH in Boston and the BBC in London, produced a six-minute audio report on the town.[16] The story highlighted the circulation of US dollars in Intipucá and, rather than characterize the pueblo as an anomaly like Gruson's account did almost fifteen years earlier, the report emphasized the importance of Intipucá and its ties to DC as an exemplary and potentially replicable model of town-based remittance-led development successfully administered by a private organization based in DC and Intipucá.

Despite important differences that tend to correspond with the time of the story and the national origins of the media source, there are several similarities across the various journalistic representations of the town. All accounts tend to emphasize Intipucá's relatively new ties to the Washington, DC, area and describe how two otherwise different and discrete places became linked through patterns of migration, communication, and money circulation. The accounts also comment extensively on evidence of the town's wealth in comparison with other towns in the region, which typically includes observations about the particular commodities present in everyday life. Often, the news stories note the prevalence of English-language idioms and everyday speech in the town. Finally, the news stories usually include interviews with selected residents and emphasize their hard work and investment savvy, which has yielded the immediately perceivable wealth of the town. As a whole the accounts present evidence of a kind of entrepreneurial and consumer class that diligently works in the United States, but "develops" the hometown through the market activities of remittance transfer, travel, and commodity sales and purchases. This image of small-scale transnational private development stands in contrast to the still resonating twentieth-century history of large-scale state-led programs of national development in El Salvador and throughout Latin America.[17]

Not surprisingly, the town of Intipucá has attracted the attention of academic researchers from El Salvador and the United States. Two Salvadoran social scientists have authored important books on the pueblo and its unique ties to DC.[18] Besides myself, at least two US-trained social scientists have visited there to interview residents.[19] Since the 1990s, references to the town have appeared in documents produced by NGOs as well as international agencies like the International Bank for Reconstruction and Development (World Bank) and the International Monetary Fund (IMF). In the United States, policymakers, analysts, and social scientists have cited Intipucá as an exemplary case study of immigrant entrepreneurship, remittance-led development, and transnational "hometown association"–building.[20]

Intipucá also has served as an important political stage for both US and Salvadoran officials. In 1991 the US Ambassador to El Salvador,

William Walker, visited the town, calling it an example of the future of El Salvador and its new relations with the United States. He was followed by several Washington, DC, politicians and community leaders later in the year who attempted to ameliorate tensions in the DC Salvadoran community by stressing the warm ties between the city and the pueblo. In July 1995 Salvadoran President Armando Calderón Sol of the ARENA party (1994–1999) visited the pueblo after meeting with US President Clinton in Washington, DC, and delivered a speech in the center of town, commending the efforts of Intipuqueños who (much like in Gruson's narrative) worked hard in the United States, sacrificing for the betterment of their family, their pueblo, and the nation of El Salvador.

Intipucá continues to emerge in everyday Salvadoran talk, especially since January 2001 when the government of President Francisco Flores, also of ARENA, passed laws to allow US dollars to circulate alongside the Salvadoran colón as an equivalent national currency, replacing it completely in all bank accounts as well as public and private financial operations. Proponents and critics alike of the neoliberal "dollarization" policy understand it as a direct outcome of the steady influx of US dollar remittances.[21] In his highly critical commentary on the dollarization policy, a professor at the private Universidad Tecnologica in San Salvador upbraided supporters for their use of the rhetorical claim: "Look at Intipucá where they've been using dollars without any problem for years."[22] In March 2001, shortly after the new dollarization plan went into effect, several Salvadoran friends of mine living in the capital city—one of whom has received prestigious scholarships and an advanced degree in economics from a major US university—jokingly called national dollarization "the Intipucanization of El Salvador."[23]

Intipucá also has appeared in other creative works. US-based painter David Amoroso, known for his bright acrylic style, completed a series of images after visiting the town. One of them, *Intipucá III*, appeared as the cover image of the book *A Latino National Conversation: Prospectus and Introductory Readings,* published by the Great Books Foundation in 2001. In 1995 Salvadoran-born writer Mario Bencastro, who currently resides in Northern Virginia, wrote *Odisea del Norte* (Odyssey to the North), incorporating actual published newspaper articles on Salvadoran migrants in DC and imagined details of their lives in El Salvador and the DC area as well as their difficult treks through Mexico and the US Southwest. Early in this innovative polyvocal form of *testimonio*, a character named Calixto walks through the neighborhood of Mount Pleasant and down to the adjacent neighborhood of Adams Morgan. Eventually Calixto comes to stand in front of a McDonald's restaurant on the corner of 18th Street and Columbia Road, NW, and asks a friend whether he knows of any job opportunities. At this moment in the conversation, the fictive character in Bencastro's book recalls his hometown of Intipucá and all the people, including his family, who live there and rely upon the remittances that he and other Intipuqueños send them from Washington, DC.

Like the photograph of Marvin and the way that it appeared as evidence of broader claims about Intipucá made by Gruson in the accompanying *Times* article, aspects of Intipucá's recent and particular history of ties to DC through migration, trade, communication, and remittance transfer are being abstracted and objectified in a way that is yielding highly general models of reality. As a framework of understanding, the Intipucá-DC model beautifully holds still and presents in a simple way all the most important and immediate causes of the new migration and remittance circulation. It also statically exhibits some of the most significant and desirable outcomes of this transformation. Bringing together cause and effect within a neatly functioning entity, the model may be held out not only as a predictor, but also as something that can be replicated and applied so as to bring into being such a desired future elsewhere.

In form, the model is a constellation of signs that present aspects of Intipucá and Washington, DC, El Salvador and the United States, in certain ways so as to create particular meanings for an interpretive audience. It is not patently wrong or false, nor does it suffer terminally from all that it cannot account for or explain. As a kind of parable or analogue, it is convincing in its various aesthetic, ethical, and logical dimensions. As an exemplary model it is proving useful for influencing productive activities, crafting subjective memories and desires. To the extent that a newspaper story, a work of fiction, or a casual street-corner or dinner-table discussion carrying a reference to the town actually contributes to the practical shaping of life's possibilities in the pueblo, throughout El Salvador or in the United States, the model effectively has been pulled out so that it can react back upon its own origins as a powerful external entity.

Third Stop: Foreign Exchange Inflows and Gross Domestic Product (GDP)

The third point on the remittance roadmap comes in the form of calculations presented six years after Lubbock's photos (1995), by Elizabeth Wood, a highly regarded comparative political scientist and expert on the Salvadoran civil war period and its aftermath.[24] The first chart disaggregates Salvadoran gross domestic product (GDP) to show the relative contributions of three major sectors: agriculture, manufacturing, and commercial activity. The second chart shows the rapid growth of two new sources of US dollars flowing into El Salvador, direct US government expenditure and migrant remittances, along with a decline in the returns yielded from agro-exports (coffee, cotton, and sugar).

Taken together, these charts provide one empirical rendering of what was happening in El Salvador over the period of the late 1970s into the early 1990s. Migrant remittances as well as direct US government expenditure in the country were growing throughout the period while agroexport earnings tapered. Though not shown in these charts, the growth in remittances partially reflected the fact that Salvadoran migration to the United States was increasing as well. Export agriculture, especially cotton production, had dropped off during the war years while commercial activity had increased, driven by the influx of the remittance dollars. [25]

Like any visual image, the chart gestures to and holds still for the sensemaking audience particular features of a larger continuous process. The

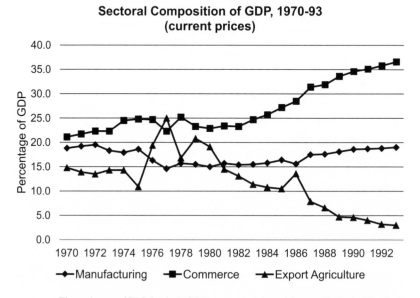

FIGURE 5. The make-up of El Salvador's GDP, 1970–93. Adapted from table 8.1 in Elizabeth J. Wood, "Agrarian Social Relations and Democratization: The Negotiated Resolution of the Civil War in El Salvador" (PhD diss., Stanford University, 1995).

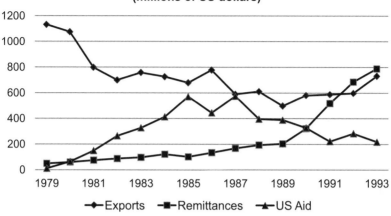

FIGURE 6. Immediate sources of US dollar inflows to El Salvador, 1979–93. Adapted from table 8.4 in Elizabeth J. Wood, "Agrarian Social Relations and Democratization: The Negotiated Resolution of the Civil War in El Salvador" (PhD diss., Stanford University, 1995).

immediate objects presented in these charts are aggregate quotients of money within El Salvador, officially tallied and published by the Salvadoran Central Reserve Bank (BCR) at regular intervals. The empirical veracity of these two charts rests in part on the not immediately perceivable practices of accounting that yielded these numbers.[26] Without pursuing the full intricacies of this, it is possible to appreciate that measuring foreign exchange inflows involves recording stocks of money at various moments over a period (usually within an official banking system) in order to yield the measure of a flow. Similarly, GDP accounts rest on tallying money amounts that correspond with the market worth of all the final goods and services produced within a country. Though there are different ways to calculate GDP and there has been significant debate about what the number means with respect to the quality of social life within a country, it is useful in this context because it offers a relatively closed set of inputs and outputs. When GDP is compared over time, it becomes possible to chart overall growth and decline as well as to gauge the proportional contributions of various "sectors" in this activity. Thus, according to Wood, across the period of the 1970s up through the early 1990s in El Salvador, the portion of GDP contributed by agricultural production dropped significantly from 13 percent in 1977 to under 5 percent in early 1990s. Over roughly the same period, the commercial sector in El Salvador expanded its con-tribution to GDP from 20 percent to over 36 percent.[27]

The charts are meaningful also because these money amounts ges-ture in some way to the activities that yielded the multitude of deposits, transfers, and exchanges. At first glance, this simply is a sum of practices: people and institutional actors conducting the various transaction activi-ties. The larger significance and authority of the charts, however, rests on the understanding that the money measures bear some relationship to the composite of other activities that lead up to this actual transaction activity. The challenge, however, is that these money quotients can hardly gesture to the full conditions of their formation. The relative size of the numbers is simply a quantitative reflection of how much exchanging and depositing actually was happening, not a full judgment of its significance for anyone, why it occurred or with what consequences. The numbers point to their existence as prices paid for specific commodities and as wages—or por-tions of wages—for work effort bought. In this, they signal only the most general quality of human effort that went into all these entities (see the introduction). The rest is history, so to speak, since much of social life still cannot be referred to by its price, even if these activities contributed in some way to buying and selling other things with prices.[28]

Like the introductory account of the three women in Intipucá in rela-tion to Samuel Huntington's account of the town, there is much that is necessary for—but that lies systematically unrepresented in—dominant measures like foreign exchange inflows and GDP. Part of the charts' con-tent is carried in the photographic images of Robin Lubbock. In this sense, he captured different angles and perspectives of the same overall process of remittances becoming interest-bearing capital in El Salvador. They now should be understood as enriching supplements rather than alternatives to the two charts above.

Last Stop: The Roadmap

In 1996, while I was living for the year in Intipucá, the World Bank released its "country study" of El Salvador, subtitled *Meeting the Challenge of Glob-alization*. The detailed 85-page report profiled the national economy and recent political history and stated that the Salvadoran government should swiftly craft and enact new policies that would reform state institutions and encourage "outward-oriented private-sector growth" so that all of El

Salvador could take advantage of the opportunities presented by "globalization." The report described six policy areas in its overview chapter, "A Road Map for El Salvador," and developed each domain through five subsequent comprehensive chapters: (1) "Enhancing Macroeconomic Stability," (2) "Improving Labor and Infrastructure," (3) "Modernizing the Legal and Regulatory Framework," (4) "Facilitating Trade and Technological Diffusion," and (5) "Strengthening the Financial Sector."[29]

The first chapter on macroeconomic stability argued that the government should focus on policies designed to improve the fiscal performance of the state. Also, it should control inflation and interest rates, keep the exchange rate stable, and increase and broaden the range of export commodities. At the center of these three issues is an acknowledgment by the bank report that a fundamental change had occurred in the nature of the Salvadoran economy as a result of "high foreign exchange inflows," particularly the money remitted by Salvadorans living and working in the United States. According to the bank report, "Worker remittances have increased faster than any other inflow and currently represent approximately 70 percent of total exchange flows, while official transfers represent about 20 percent."[30] This was deemed a significant restructuring that should be considered a long-term change in the Salvadoran economy and its relation to the world. By using the category "gross domestic product" (GDP) within which to agglomerate and measure the remittances, the money was rhetorically and in practice "domesticated" into the Salvadoran national economy.[31]

In its analysis, the report profiled the two kinds of inflows, investments and remittances, and introduced an important conceptual model for understanding how both affect the Salvadoran economy. Countries that experience a "Dutch disease" phenomenon—an export boom and an influx of foreign exchange (like Holland did during its discovery and exploitation of North Sea oil reserves in the 1970s)—tend to experience conditions of inflation and a drop in the worth of their domestic currency, a rise in the circulation of foreign consumer products, and a limiting or retarding effect on the development of other productive sectors in the country. Viewed as a short-term affliction, "Dutch disease" is rare for large diversified economies like those in the United States and Europe and hence constitutes something like an acute 24-hour flu. As Fernando Coronil pointed out in his examination of the model as it has been used to understand Venezuela's petroleum export sector, for countries like El Salvador that have exported only a handful of primary commodities since colonial times and have relied on the foreign exchange garnered from their sale for purchasing all the accoutrements of modern life, "Dutch disease" constitutes a chronic state of being.[32] By invoking the model, the report highlights the newness of this transformation understood as an unprecedented flow of wealth to the national doorsteps of El Salvador.

The report establishes the newness and uniqueness of the remittance flow through two important claims: (1) the flow is long-term and structural, and (2) people in El Salvador use remittances to purchase mostly non-tradable consumer goods. The first claim is indeed just that and there is no reference to any supporting evidence: "As long as emigrant workers remain in the US, and the US economy continues growing, remittances will continue. However, they should not increase much beyond current levels, remaining at 8–10 percent GDP."[33]

The second claim regarding the use of the remittance monies is substantiated by reference to a report written by the policy research center FUSADES (*Fundacion Salvadoreña para el Desarollo Economico y Social*) founded in 1983, as I have mentioned, with support from the US Agency for International Development and known for its steady production of neoliberal-oriented policy reports and its support for the Cristiani-led faction of the ARENA party. The FUSADES report referred to by the Bank report is the *Economic and Social Bulletin* of January 1994 called "Salvadoran Emigration and Its Economic and Social Impact."[34] The report is short and contains four sections. In the third section, "Economic and Social Impact of the Emigrations," the authors refer to "studies completed by CEPAL" (the Economic Commission for Latin America and the Caribbean or ECLA in its English acronym) that indicate, according to the FUSADES authors, that remittances are principally used for "family consumption."

There is no more reference information for the CEPAL reports, but it seems likely that the FUSADES authors have in mind a report issued on June 19, 1991, that was based on research conducted by Salvadoran sociologist, Juan José García, who served as a consultant to the Commission. The report is called "El Salvador: International Remittances and Family Economics" and draws upon a wealth of survey research, interviews, and a review of government documents conducted by the author.[35] The report analyzes the social and economic impact of the remittances on daily life among poorer urban and rural sectors of Salvadoran society and suggests several ways to more effectively channel and concentrate the remittances at a local level to increase people's productivity and thereby improve living conditions.

Segundo Montes

Salvadoreños refugiados en los Estados Unidos

El Salvador 1987

Instituto de investigaciones
Universidad Centroamericana
José Simeón Cañas
San Salvador 1987

FIGURE 7. The cover of Montes' book with picture of road sign pointing to Intipucá.

García has had a distinguished research career in El Salvador and abroad (he was a visiting professor at Swarthmore College in 1992–93) and was among the researchers who worked with Jesuit priest and sociologist Segundo Montes during the 1980s in his groundbreaking research on Salvadoran migration and remittances. Montes was among those professors murdered by Salvadoran military forces in 1989, and García has remained one of the most active scholars working in the tradition of

Montes and pursuing lines of inquiry that were developed and advanced from the 1980s research. Among Montes and García's best-known collaborative work was a study that included a brief survey and case study of Intipucá and was published first in El Salvador and later in the United States.[36]

Crossroads

In the World Bank document, the "roadmap" for El Salvador leads through Intipucá and DC, even though the pueblo and its residents abroad are not well marked. Through a multilayered process of abstraction, aspects of life in the town and in DC have been pulled out and generalized, first by Montes then by way of Garcia's document, only to be stretched by FUSADES so as to stand for the general use of remittances for "family consumption" in El Salvador. Intipucá also helps provide the basis for the report's argument in the last chapter that the Salvadoran government should institute policies that would "deepen" the formal financial sector, bringing more people into relations with private banks and thereby capturing remittance flows before or on their way to other points of exchange, where they are used to purchase end-use consumer items. If a bank can show that its access to remittances is "long-term and structural," as the World Bank report claimed it was, this flow of wealth could be "securitized," bought and sold profitably as a financial instrument. At this juncture, remittances had become fully defined as interest-bearing capital. The Cristiani faction, through its control of the privatized financial sector in the aftermath of the war, would directly benefit from these World Bank recommendations on how El Salvador should participate in "globalization." For this new model of national development, the bank report had abstracted from Intipucá and DC to argue that El Salvador can best participate in globalization by using remittance flows to produce a more profitable financial sector.

The goal of this chapter was not to provide the complete story of El Salvador's shift from agro-exports to remittances as a central source of national wealth, but rather to highlight how the simple increase of remittance dollars over more than a decade formed an integral part of this systemic reorganization. Remittances were at once cause and effect. Using the notion of quantity-to-quality transformation, like grains of sand slowly turning into a specific mountain, this relationship was brought into relief. This approach and method of analysis is meant to emphasize a holistic and processural transformation, not simply two temporal moments, before and after, determined by a completely external cause, as if tripping an on/off switch.

The second goal of the chapter was to point out prominently the presence of the town of Intipucá in this process of change. This meant showing the town's "enmodelment" and also some of what was hidden or muffled in the process, such as the figure of Manuel. The argument is that this town with its ties to Washington, DC, is not contingent to the overall transformation but is an integral feature or outcome as well as participant in it. This is so both because the town really exists in El Salvador and also because of the way it has become larger than life through the many partial representations of it—themselves, like the town's attenuated presence in the World Bank report, active participants, even agents, in the overall transformation.

Chapter 2 begins explicitly with a part of this dominant Intipucá story that was at the center of Lindsey Gruson's article in the *New York Times* about the town—the figure of Sigfredo Chávez, the father of the man on the motorcycle. Following a method that now should be more recognizable to the reader, the chapter moves from this point of entry into the larger world of twentieth-century coffee production, consumption, and circulation unevenly entwining El Salvador and the United States, Intipucá and Washington, DC, well before the time of the war, Salvadoran migration, and growing remittance circulation. Following this larger scope of analysis other "causes of causes" come into relief, not otherwise visible at the scale of the Salvadoran nation-state between the late 1970s and the early 1990s. Logically, the content covered in this first chapter is internal to that of chapter 2, neither its temporal precursor nor its descendent.

PART I

Brushing history against the brain, [our] task is to examine what has been recorded and uncover what has been silenced, bringing to light possible histories. — Fernando Coronil, 2011

The three chapters that follow all open with a focus on words written and uttered in the 1980s and 1990s about El Salvador, especially the town named Intipucá. Recorded and transmitted from one source to another, these descriptors join the larger constellation held still under the designation Intipucá-DC Connection Story, itself a constituting part of the more general and widely circulating model-like tale of El Salvador's progressive reorganization around migration and remittances. The chapters begin with these words, understanding them as intimations or signals of other concepts or notions, which themselves have been socially pressed out of a much larger interactive and dynamical reality. Inquiring into this process of expressive transmission yields a historical account or, more properly, a composite *history* in the conventional sense of the term. In tracing out and telling this history, however, the chapters follow a less conventional approach, signaled by the epigraph from Venezuelan-born anthropologist Fernando Coronil's assonant ad-lib on Walter Benjamin's seventh of eighteen "Theses on the Concept of History." Benjamin's famous criticism of mainstream German historiography is built around a notion of oppositional co-inclusion, illustrated when he forcefully writes:

There is no document of civilization which is not at the same time a document of barbarism. And just as such a document is never free of barbarism, so barbarism taints the manner in which it was transmitted from one hand to another. The historical materialist therefore dissociates himself from this process of transmission as far as possible. He regards it as his task to brush history against the grain.

That documents or any social phenomena could be composed of opposing qualities or be the co-instantiation of them is not a habitual way of working in the mainstream of the humanistic and social scientific disciplines, which for the most part are informed by the under-labor of formal logic and mathematics.

Coronil's riff on Benjamin makes clear that there is a quality of relative discontinuity between subjects and objects, would-be critics and what comprises their accounts. While Benjamin emphasizes the capacities and more so the responsibilities of "historical materialists," Coronil's phrase seems to underline the brute actuality of the world as it forces itself upon cognition.[1] While "brushing against" is the operation, the truth of the matter (its epistemic authority) lies neither wholly in immediate perception nor wholly in seamless collective thought.

Taking the perspective on the co-inclusion of opposites to heart, part I examines the historical processes through which the keywords have come to present their most immediate objects, which themselves had been abstracted from a larger open whole. Moving into this historical content shows the way that the words represent things in certain ways and not in others, leaving this larger content as the open domain of "possible histories." By illuminating these possibilities alongside the many actualities and generalities that work to silence them, the original words become transvalued, destabilized by their own contradictory content.

CHAPTER TWO

Brushing against the Golden Grain

Intipucá owes both its progress and its predicament to the migration, which began when . . . a field hand ended up in Mount Pleasant and inadvertently blazed a path to the "gold mine," as Washington has come to be known.[1] — Gabriel Escobar

Before, we were *malformado* (malformed, poorly educated); now we are civilized. People have respect for each other. There is money, nice houses, roads, water, electricity.
— Sigfredo Chávez

This chapter begins with two epigraphs. The first is the written words of Gabriel Escobar, a DC-based journalist who was born in Bogotá, Colombia, and migrated with his family to New York City in 1964. The second is the spoken observations of Sigfredo Chávez, the resident of Intipucá described in Gruson's *New York Times* essay, who had migrated to the United States two years after Escobar in 1966. Escobar visited and wrote about Intipucá in the 1990s several years before Sigfredo and I spoke there in person about it. Despite these different contexts and their respective backgrounds, both Escobar and Chávez described a dramatic transformation of life in the town, which they organized rhetorically around a notion of historical "progress" and the arrival of widely recognized metrics of "civilization."

The three defining terms, "civilization," "progress," and "predicament," present specific objects to their would-be interpreters. Sigfredo specified some of this when he mentioned money, houses, roads, water, electricity, and manners of comportment and social interaction, glossed as "respect." Although Sigfredo described Intipucá's figurative arrival at a more desirable place and time, Escobar was less sanguine, suggesting that along with "progress" comes a "predicament." Elsewhere in his article, Escobar pointed out that although Intipucá and other towns like it in southeastern El Salvador appeared relatively flush with consumer goods and the kinds of local infrastructure that Sigfredo referred to, at the edge of such municipalities the residents confronted deteriorated public roads, bridges, and public services. The region around Intipucá struggled with limited electrical capacity, inadequate sources and supplies of potable water, and occasional shortages of fuel and basic foodstuffs. Escobar highlighted the contradiction that while many people had refrigerators, televisions, and VCRs, they often could not use them for lack of sufficient amperage.

Both Escobar's and Sigfredo's accounts suggest that from the perspective of the pueblo in the 1990s, there has been a relatively rapid and dramatic transformation. By noting Intipucá's "predicament," however, Escobar broadened the scope of his story. He identified not only the contradictory intersection of Intipucá with its immediate periphery, but also the collision of the past and present in El Salvador, by way of fuzzy TV screens, exhausted automobile shock-absorbers, and the rising cost of red beans. Expanding further the geographical and historical scope of analysis in order to understand more of what is contained in Sigfredo's utterance of "civilization" and Escobar's categories of "progress" and "predicament," this chapter asks, what are some of the most important and necessary determinants upon which the narratives rest and which lie dissimulated within them? Just as silver mined in the New World under Spanish dominion later created the possibility for English industrial expansion, the "gold mine" of Washington, DC, as well as "civilization," "progress " and the "predicament" of Intipucá, all rest on another kind of gold: El Grano de Oro (the Golden Grain), what Salvadorans have called coffee since the late nineteenth century. The potent bean structurally mixed with and invaded daily life across both countries between the 1930s and 1950s, providing the shared grounds of later migration and remittance transfer as well as the outpouring of accounts much like and including Escobar's and Sigfredo's above, even as the sun, rain, soil, and beans together with aspects of the lives of thousands of people who helped produce coffee dissolved into and became invisible in these stories.

After an overview of coffee in El Salvador before this history and then beginning to rub against it, the chapter considers in detail the words and experiences of Sigfredo and the way that he described the pueblo's "escape" from underdevelopment in eastern El Salvador. The chapter explores his autobiographical account, situating it within a broader history of the pueblo. It traces how the pueblo was integrated into the Salvadoran nation through the circulation of money, especially during the 1930s and 1940s. This money, together with people who left the pueblo to work on coffee *fincas* (farms), linked the town not only with areas of production elsewhere in El Salvador but also to parts of the United States where most of the coffee beans were imported, roasted, and ground after World War II. In spite of its appearance throughout the twentieth century as a relatively isolated pueblo without the trappings of "civilization," by the late 1940s Intipucá was wrapped up in a complex array of coffee, labor, and money circuits that extended across El Salvador and to the United States.

After moving outward and backward from Sigfredo's account in 1996 to this more circuitous geographical and historical perspective, the chapter considers two important crises in 1948 when competing class fractions in both countries struggled and coalesced in separate attempts to alter some aspects of the coffee circuit and to control the forms of wealth that it generated. In El Salvador the struggle took the form of a coup d'état, while in the United States there was a less dramatic but equally significant shift in the relative power of US capitalist and state military factions. These two events rippled across the circuit during the early 1950s, directly affecting the lives of Intipuqueños like Sigfredo as well as residents in DC and its suburbs, significantly shaping the conditions within which people orchestrated their daily lives across both places. The chapter concludes by tracing how Sigfredo's narrative rests upon but also dissimulates this broader transnational coffee circuit. Finally, the chapter argues that the trappings of wealth and the ways of life that define "civilization," as well as their absence and their opposite, have arisen together in a pooled and patchy process.

Overview of the Context of Sigfredo's Appearance as Author and Agent

Among El Salvador's most important literary figures, Francisco Gavidia was born in the eastern city of San Miguel in 1863 as this notoriously hot and humid region of El Salvador slipped into relative decline with the demise of the Central American indigo trade.[2] Like Cuba's José Martí and Nicaragua's Rubén Darío, Gavidia wrote prodigiously; his writings placed

El Salvador amidst the powerful currents of literary modernism.[3] During his long life of nine decades he wrote fiction and a work of nonfiction important at the time, *Historia Moderna de El Salvador*, published in 1917. Through all his work he explored immediately perceivable changes in El Salvador as the country left behind the last vestiges of that colonial-era export crop, the source of blue dye for North American and European textile industries, to become one of the most productive coffee growing nations in the world.[4] By the twentieth century El Salvador's washed green arabica bean exports were second only to those of Colombia in their quality and in the price that they garnered on the New York Coffee and Sugar Exchange.[5] Throughout most of the twentieth century, these coffee export earnings purchased El Salvador's future, even if the price fluctuated and many of the accoutrements of progress arrived cloaked in European garb, such as the Italian architecture of Salvador's great theatrical stage in the western city of Santa Ana.

By the middle of the century, measures of the modern in El Salvador tended to come from the United States in the form of manufactured commodities imported and paid for with the hard currency earned from selling almost all of each year's coffee harvest to several US roasting companies. Gavidia's hometown, San Miguel, and the surrounding countryside beneath the volcano Chaparrastique remained places largely devoted to domestic food production and to the recovery and reproduction of the abilities of the many thousands of people who worked part of each year in the central highland regions of Occidente (western El Salvador) tending the coffee plants and harvesting their ripe cherries. In spite of the consistent labors of these people and a brief boom in cotton production for export during the 1950s and 1960s around San Miguel, the trappings of civilization—money, houses, roads, respect, as Sigfredo called them in the opening passage—appeared to be relatively less present and widely available in the Oriente (eastern El Salvador) during most of the twentieth century. They were perceivable elsewhere in Santa Ana, in the capital city of San Salvador, and in other metropolitan centers throughout the world.

At the edge of the twenty-first century, Gavidia's San Miguel, known as the "Pearl of the Oriente," and its nearby departments came alive again, flush with indicators of progress obtained from selling not primary agricultural crops but abstracted and objectified efforts and capacities of Salvadorans working in the United States. As in times past, the majority of this labor force hails from the Oriente, but unlike those in the previous century, these people currently provide far more US dollars each year (by sending home to their friends and family and also by spending in the context of return visits) than the total amount of foreign currency generated by the still active Salvadoran coffee trade.

One perspective on this transformation may be found in 1996 in the front room of Sigfredo Chávez's home on a tree-lined road popularly known as Los Laureles in Intipucá, just 28 miles south of Don Gavidia's birthplace.[6] At this time and place, Sigfredo delivered the statement excerpted at the beginning of the chapter as part of a long personal account and analysis of changes in the town that he had experienced. As I have mentioned, he told of a simple conjuncture where "civilization" arrived in the pueblo as the result of the movement of Intipuqueños to the Washington, DC, area, their hard work there, and their transfer of money back to the town. He defined civilization as the presence of specific objects such as money, houses, and roads, and of subjective habits, especially *respeto* (respect), which he defined as a quality of deferential regard for others. He also stressed that the arrival of these things was the outcome of a chain of events that he helped initiate in 1966.

First Level of Authorship

Like many Intipucá homes in the late 1990s, Sigfredo's front door was answered by a young woman servant who had grown up in one of the small settlements on the outskirts of the pueblo. The *muchacha* (young woman servant; literally girl) Maria was from Santa Juliana, a worker settlement adjacent to land owned by the Hernández family of Intipucá south of the pueblo. The front door led into a tile-floored sitting room with wooden and wicker-seated chairs and couch facing a large varnished wood shelf and cabinet ensemble along one wall. On one shelf sat a television set and videocassette player/recorder. On the other shelves Sigfredo had displayed color photographs of his children from his second marriage: his daughter was smartly dressed in her US Marine uniform and his son was pictured in a US high school photograph. Sigfredo explained that his son lived in New York, and although his daughter currently resided in Maryland, she had lived for some time in California where she received military training "in communication and computers." Sigfredo's older son, from his first marriage, was Marvin, who was living at that time in the pueblo. Sigfredo kept no picture of him on display in his house and frequently was critical of his lifestyle and work habits. From this tranquil locus Sigfredo talked about his hometown of Intipucá and its 30-year history (at that time) of ties to the DC area.[7] Like the published writings and popular discussion

of the town, he offered evidence of a strong contrast between a past that
lacked the congealed habits of civilization and a present inundated with
them. Sigfredo compared the years he spent growing up in the pueblo with
the important changes that had come about as a result of his initial move
to DC in 1966–67 and his subsequent visits for extended periods, which
formed part of the general movement of Intipuqueños to the DC area
over the ensuing decades. In a well-spoken and nearly rehearsed manner,
Sigfredo recounted his decisions and actions, presenting himself as an important historical agent of this broader shift.

> In 1966, I went to the United States. I was the first from here. I was working in
> San Miguel and making 120 colónes a month. My friend Luis had gone to Los
> Angeles and he told me that it was easy to get a visa. I went to the [US] Consul-
> ate in San Salvador. At that time it was just a little room with a desk—no more.
> It is not like that now. At that time only the very rich Salvadorans and business
> people traveled to the United States. They gave me a five-year visa!

Sigfredo smiled broadly. To obtain a visa in 1996 from the US Consulate
was considerably more difficult and the legal document usually restricted
one's travel to a period much shorter than five years. Sigfredo noted the
different situation and stressed the work habits of fellow Intipuqueños,
anticipating and countering tenets of anti-immigrant rhetoric that he had
directly faced and that dominated political debate in the United States and
also El Salvador during the second half of the 1990s.

> At that time it was easy to get social security in the US and residency. We always
> were trying to do it well and legalize our status in the US. Gradually there was
> an exodus from Intipucá. People worked hard and with their sweat they were
> able to send money back to Intipucá, build their houses, and bring up others
> from the family. I was making $75 a week as a bus boy. Back then you could get
> 2.5 colónes for one dollar.[8]

In our conversation, Sigfredo described a series of encounters that led
to his arrival in Washington, DC. He explained the decisive moments that
brought him to a particular neighborhood in DC and suggested how they
solidified into a regular travel route for others.

> The secretary in the Mayor's office here in Intipucá was Cesar Matamoro. He was
> from San Miguel. His daughter was living in Washington, DC. She was a teacher,
> but was making very little money. He was the one who told me about DC. In Mi-

ami, in the airport, I met a Puerto Rican woman and she told me the best place to find work was in one area of Washington, DC, called Mount Pleasant. When I landed in Washington, I met a taxi driver who spoke Spanish. He knew Mount Pleasant and he took me to the house of Manola Fernández. Her family was from Spain but she had grown up in Cuba. She had a house in Mount Pleasant. . . . She helped me find work, gave me a table, a bed. I paid 30, 40 dollars a month for rent. I loved her like my second mother. She died a year ago or so. After 11 months working as a dishwasher I came back and told everyone in Intipucá that you could make good money in Washington, DC, and live with Manola in her house.

At this moment in our conversation, Sigfredo jumped up and retrieved a collection of more than 100 photographs from an adjacent room. They had been taken over at least a 20-year period in Intipucá, in DC, and on several car trips back and forth via Mexico. He showed me a well-worn picture of himself standing next to a red Ford Mustang, taken by a coworker outside a building in Northern Virginia. "I bought this car up there. Pedro was jealous!"[9] Sigfredo then showed me a series of photographs of himself as a young boy in Intipucá. "My family was the first to have a camera in the pueblo," he explained. "Look at the old houses! There was mud everywhere, no good roads, no electricity. . . . Compare that to now!" In one photograph, Sigfredo and his childhood friend Pedro stood holding pistols. "We are playing cowboys here. We were friends with *la Guardia* (National Guard) so we could carry guns without problems," he explained.

Sigfredo's account includes a series of assumptions about the causal efficacy of certain things, including himself. Sigfredo appeared as an autonomous individual who orchestrated his travel to DC and his return to Intipucá in a way that stimulated later migration, which in turn brought about the passage to civilization. According to this generalized narrative, by dint of agency, initiative, and hard work, Intipuqueños in DC and El Salvador made a particular world for themselves defined by the positive measures of "civilization" in the pueblo. As a closed indexical system, indicators of wealth, especially "money, nice homes, water, lights," as well as other commodities, together with particular styles of social interaction—"respect"— all combined to point toward the abstract thing called civilization.

Conditions behind Authorship: Intersection of Land and Race

In the winter of 1993, the *Washington Post* staff writer Gabriel Escobar traveled to Intipucá and met Sigfredo Chávez, whom he later described in his two-part series of articles as a "field hand." This description was accurate from the perspective of a journalist and other newspaper readers in a US city like Washington, DC, but in the pueblo Sigfredo had never been employed on the farm under this title. He was regarded by most people not as a farm worker, but as among the most privileged men in the pueblo. His family owned a large parcel of land and he, together with his parents and brothers, helped to manage it, facilitating the many kinds of productive labor carried out by a group of tenant farmers and laborers who lived and worked on the property.[10] The family, including Sigfredo, accumulated great wealth on the basis of relations of ownership that placed them in a unique position regarding the territory and all else that comprised the *hacienda* (farm), the workers' various efforts, and the cash markets for their products in San Miguel.

The hacienda had been acquired by Sigfredo's grandfather Juan Bautista Rivas in the late nineteenth century. The large farm dominated the cantón of Chichipate that pertained to the municipio of Intipucá and extended up the side of La Panela, or more properly Montaña Panela, a small hill that rose over 700 meters above sea level on the north side of the pueblo.[11] On its western flank, the farm bordered land owned by the Regelado family, who were famous for their vast coffee plantations in western El Salvador. In comparison to the Regelados, Juan Rivas was a modest farmer, but among pueblo dwellers he was a considered a large-scale proprietor. To the east, the hacienda abutted a series of farms owned by other Intipucá families, especially members of the Gallo family, who frequently changed or hid their family name to avoid its unsavory connotation of being "a screaming rooster."

Members of these older land-owning families in the town often stressed their Spanish colonial ancestry and distinguished themselves from people with indigenous backgrounds. The way that they recounted the history of the pueblo reflected this understanding. In the late seventeenth century, British pirates based on the island of Meanguera in the Gulf of Fonseca between El Salvador and Nicaragua periodically attacked the pueblo and other towns along the coast. According to popular accounts, in 1683 the pueblo was looted and completely destroyed by pirates, though by 1689 the town had been rebuilt higher up on the hillside, out of the range of ship cannons.[12] Sigfredo's mother, whom I shall call "Rosa," was born in 1901. She explained to me that by the time that she was a young child, the pueblo had moved back down the mountain to its present location.[13] At that time, the concentrated houses and buildings that made up the "new" pueblo belonged almost exclusively to land-owning families in the area.[14] Rosa separated herself from other residents nearby through a particular recollection of the early twentieth century. "I remember Indios walking up from the ocean carrying baskets of fish on their heads and speaking a language that I could not understand."

For Rosa to use the term *indio* in the late 1990s when we talked sheds light on the complicated intersection of race and class in El Salvador during the twentieth century. According to historical accounts that draw upon metropolitan sources, the term *indio* tended to become a less salient social category in El Salvador after La Matanza of 1931–32, replaced especially by "communist," a term broadly used to refer to rural peasantry involved in any form of organizing and protest.[15] Indeed, most analyses of the famous revolt and subsequent violent government-led reprisal have emphasized its class origins.

Earlier in the century a highly moralized racial hierarchy dominated Salvadoran society. In 1914 the government published a large multilingual account of "modern El Salvador," describing the country as one of the many new modern nation-states that were emerging throughout Central America. Despite its universalistic aspirations, the book contained a careful description and hierarchy of "races in El Salvador" that moved from Anglo-Europeans to fair-skinned Salvadorans to Mestizos to Indians, finally concluding with "the lowliest members of society, the small number of very dark-skinned Negroes in El Salvador." Throughout the 1920s, the Salvadoran military kept records of each soldier that offered detailed phenotypic descriptions based on skin color, shape of nose, type of hair (straight, curly), and whether the person had been born as a "legitimate" child with a mother and father.[16]

The term *indio* is relationally fluid and much alive throughout contemporary El Salvador. From the perspective of a farm owner like Rosa, who was not of the same social origins as families such as the Regelados but who was a significant landowner in the pueblo, the term *indio* marked an important line of distinction that remained salient for her. In our discussion in 1996 Rosa used several words that her grandson Marvin and I could not understand. "Those are Indian words," Marvin explained to me with a smile.[17] In 1996 when a university-educated small-business owner from San Salvador visited the pueblo, he referred to Marvin as "one of those indios that David knows in the pueblo."

The workers on the farm that Rosa would later inherit from her father lived on the hillside in a small conglomeration of grass huts near a large fresh-water spring on the mountainside, a rare and important natural re-source at such altitude. This settlement grew throughout the twentieth century and came to be known as Caulotio, as people from Honduras and regions to the north of Intipucá in the Department of Morazán moved to the area to rent land, sharecrop, and find work on the farm. During this period there was significant north-south population migration between these eastern Departments.[18] According to Sigfredo, his grandfather Juan Rivas *tuvo problemas* (had problems) with the mayor of Intipucá and was obligated to leave the farm to live for a period in San Francisco Gotera in Morazán, where he began to study to become a pharmacist. He eventually returned to Intipucá and the family continued to maintain contact with families in Gotera, much like the workers on the farm and other residents of Intipucá.

During the early years of his life in the 1950s, Sigfredo obtained some rudimentary education available in Intipucá. General schooling was of-fered by one teacher in the pueblo, but a succession of grade levels did not exist at that time. By the time he was 12, Sigfredo was able to live with family friends in Gotera and attend a private primary school, paid for with colónes earned from the sale of the corn that Rosa received as "rent" from the tenant farmers in Caulotio. Sigfredo's closest friends, such as Pedro and the children of other land-owning families in the pueblo, traveled to the departmental capital cities of La Union and San Miguel to obtain similar private schooling, paid for with colónes that were obtained through similar productive relations with sharecroppers and employees who worked their land.

In 1996 Caulotio's present-day dwellers recalled that Juan Rivas was thought to have been a decent fellow who much of the time lived in a mod-est house in the settlement with his workers and frequently labored with them on the farm. Rosa was also generally respected during her tenure as overseer of the farm, but the contemporary residents of Caulotio recalled that her demand for one-quarter of their total corn production during the 1960s was unfairly high.

Throughout his period, some of the tenant farmers had clandestinely organized ways to hide their production from Rosa. They strongly con-demned her for the prosecution of a farm worker for cutting down large trees and selling them to a carpenter in the nearby town of Tierra Blanca. The man was evicted from the farm and served a brief jail term in La Union. Currently he and his family live in a small adobe house at the side of the road adjacent to the main entrance to Intipucá. The families who still lived in Caulotio reserved their harshest words for Sigfredo who had managed the farm throughout the 1970s. "He is two-faced!" was one frequent refrain. More circumspectly, residents mentioned that he had periodically made them work at gunpoint during harvest time, keeping all of the corn produced and rewarding them with only one nightly meal.

Contained in the title "field hand" that identified Sigfredo in a particular way for the *Post* readership was a longer history of relations and interactions that conditioned his outlook and capacities as well as his travel and work in DC throughout the late 1960s and early 1970s. Sigfredo was born into a privileged position within a regional agrarian productive system and became highly skilled at accumulating wealth from the efforts of tenant farmers who lived on a relatively large piece of property owned by his family. Despite his modest background and life in rural El Salvador, he was among the best-educated and most experienced managers and landowning capitalists in the pueblo at the time that he traveled to DC. He was imbued with a sense of Eurocentric "whiteness" that was part of Salvadoran national history and was also the habitual mode through which his family and friends had distinguished themselves in the pueblo.

Tensions within the Conditions of Authorship

Although sharp social distinctions between landowners and workers could be marked to some extent with the racial category of indio, there were also significant divisions among landowners that were characterized in terms of town residence and political allegiance. Throughout the twentieth century families like Sigfredo's began to construct more substantial houses out of wood, and later brick, as well as to develop limited municipal infrastructure and public spaces. By the 1940s, the pueblo was informally run by several *caciques* (chiefs or political bosses), as they were remembered. These were men who were the major farm-owners in the region and who donated land that became public property. Officially there was an elected mayor, and he usually came from among this relatively small group of landowning families.

Occasionally there were internal disputes, such as when Juan Rivas left Intipucá for San Francisco Gotera, as well as a more dramatic instance when one of the richest town residents, who had donated the land for the central park and later the town school, paid for the assassination of the mayor, a member of another prominent family in the town. During

1944 and 1945, this mayor had presided over a drawn-out quarrel with the nearby town of Chirilagua about the location of boundary markers between the towns. This conflict was part of a long history of divisions and rivalries between the two towns, but it was significant because it was resolved through the direct intervention of the national government, after formal complaints from both town mayors circulated as far as the office of the new president, General Salvador Castañeda Castro, who ruled from 1945 until his ouster in the 1948.[19]

The local boundary struggle played itself out between the bureaucratic labyrinth of San Salvador and the farms of Intipucá and Chirilagua. After the Interior Ministry sent a surveyor to determine the official political borders, which also reflected the division between the two departments, San Miguel and La Union, Chirilagua claimed that the new border markers had been moved by someone in Intipucá. Ultimately, Intipucá was forced to cede a large portion of property to Chirilagua and this contributed to the Mayor's loss of support among some landowners in the pueblo. Though there seems to be no documentary evidence of a connection, a decade later he was murdered and many people still believe that this was connected with the loss of land to Chirilagua.

Money as a Fundamental Precondition

A recurring sign or indicator of the present that Sigfredo called "civilization" and that many of the newspaper articles also chronicled was the money that circulated in new ways in the pueblo. It was a complex form that referred to specific objects in ways so as to create particular kinds of interpretable meanings. As Sigfredo noted, the exchangeability of US dollars earned in DC with colónes in Intipucá formed part of the conditions that made migration and work abroad seem "worth it." In the hands of someone like Sigfredo in the pueblo, his US dollars that could be translated into colónes seemed to be a radically new feature of daily life.

When Sigfredo was born to Rosa in 1938, the family was receiving colónes from the sale of harvested and dried corn that they transported to the city of San Miguel. It was an arduous trip that took two days. The first half of the journey involved travel by mule to the shores of Lake Olomega where they would transport the corn by boat across the lake to the town also called Olomega. In Olomega they would take the train (the International Railway of Central America that linked El Salvador with

Guatemala) to San Miguel and then make their way to warehouses near the station where buyers would purchase their bags of corn. In exchange they would receive coins and notes issued by the new *Banco Central de Reserva* (BCR or Central Reserve Bank) of El Salvador.

The BCR had been founded in 1934 as part of a general transformation of the Salvadoran state under the dictatorship of General Maximiliano Hernández Martínez, who ruled infamously for twelve years (1932–44). While ostensibly "stabilizing" the country in the context of a worldwide depression and a significant drop in both the price and demand for arabica coffee beans, Martínez decreed laws that transferred the powers of an emergent private financial sector to his nascent military state, a shift that also tended to favor relatively the coffee-export interests in the country. Through the new laws, especially the Ley Moratoria, the dictatorship temporarily suspended all debts payable in Salvadoran colónes and reduced the interest rates on these loans charged by the major private banks.[20] In addition, the law halted foreclosures on land mortgages that had dramatically increased with the fall of the European and US coffee export markets. The creation of the BCR allowed the state to further direct national monetary and fiscal policy and to usurp the power of the private banks that had until this time also issued their own money in colón denominations. With its founding, the BCR became the sole issuer of national currency and the regulator of the country's international gold exchange. Through these mechanisms it could intervene in ways that served to "fix" the worth of the national currency at 2.5 colónes to the US dollar. This was the same cardinal relationship that Sigfredo recalled from his first trip to DC and figured in his calculations and exchanges when he returned a year later.

On January 7, 1947, when Sigfredo was nine years old, the BCR issued new one-colón paper notes that became available throughout the country: The bill was delicately engraved and printed in large quantities by the preeminent US printing and engraving firm at the time, the American Bank Note Company (ABNC), many years later consolidated as part of the American Banknote Corporation.[21] The one-colón banknote was printed on "melamine," a type of paper developed during the early 1940s by ABNC together with American Cyanamid Company and Crane & Co., a US paper manufacturer. The tough paper could withstand vigorous folding and rubbing and retained much of its strength when exposed to moisture. This was a desirable feature for the bill's circulation in the hands of farm owners like Rosa, Sigfredo, and the San Miguel merchants, because

FIGURE 8. One-colon note issued in 1947.

less rugged paper notes deteriorated more rapidly during the annual rainy season in El Salvador.

The note featured a particular graphical layout and set of images that would help distinguish it from others in and outside of El Salvador, including especially forged copies. As a whole, the bill referred to and presented a kind of object for interpretation in a particular way to its user. In its materiality, the note told a complex story and attempted to stand for many things at once. The front of the bill was dominated by the image of a man tilling a field with a wooden plow pulled by an ox. Immediately next to the farm worker was a large coffee bush, and the whole image of pastoral productivity was framed in elaborate scrollwork.

These were familiar images that stood for everyday practices in a particular way, yet as a whole, the note referred to the complex abstraction that composed "Salvadoran national wealth," and these three concrete terms themselves were generalized from a historical ensemble of quotidian practices. The image of the farmer tilling the land on the front of the currency accurately reflected part of the story of wealth during the 1940s and this was a dominant activity throughout the country, though one cannot glean from the image whether this "farm-hand" actually owns the land or the product of his labors and we cannot find the origin of the plow. The image of the peasant farmer was consistent with a general policy of attempting to regain limited legitimacy among rural laboring classes after the *Matanza* (slaughter or massacre) of 1931–32. The tranquil image of a hard-working farmer was a gesture toward making these classes take on particular orientations and ways of life. In this way they could become part of a national civil society that would be represented by and be capable of interacting with its government. In the background, coffee trees stood for another part of the story of national wealth that I have already suggested.

Coffee as a Condition of Authorship

Among many popular phrases for coffee in El Salvador there are two, "Golden Grain" and "Gift of God," that when juxtaposed leave the little bean stranded somewhere between heaven and earth, dwelling between the spiritual and the material world. Indeed, this is the proper place for understanding the "cherries," as they are called when freshly picked, because they contain huge amounts of stored-up energy from the sun and also are a product of the efforts of people who worked to plant, tend, and harvest coffee plants, not to mention those who processed, roasted, ground, bought, sold, and finally made into a drink. Together this exceedingly complex array of social and natural relations endowed the bean with great power. By printing money with a specific image, a peasant farm worker, that was abstracted from the long journey from bean to cup, the Salvadoran state simplified the coffee and money circuits upon which it and El Salvador more generally were based.

In the 1940s, the source of national wealth appeared to be the hard work of small-scale farmers. Not directly shown by the notes, however, was the way that money allowed other kinds of social efforts and capacities to be turned into a thing that could be extracted, accumulated, and held by others. In this way, the state-issued notes, even as they appeared to represent a part of El Salvador's rural working population in a particular way, also occluded many other kinds of labor and the circuitous processes of exploitation upon which the great wealth of a relatively small group of Salvadorans rested.

Another part of the coffee and money circuit was the "natural" resources that combined with labor to yield the coffee bean. In El Salvador, this was the zone of wet subtropical forest located between 600 and 1,500 meters above sea level that stretched across El Salvador and received on average more than 2 meters of rainfall each year, mostly between April and October. These volcanic slopes offered about 6,000 square kilometers of territory with a mineral-rich blend of soil, clay, and sand.

Besides land, water, and sunlight, growing coffee required a seasonal work force of tens of thousands of people to weed and pick the beans between October and January each year. A smaller number of regular workers tended the plants throughout the year, moving along steep slopes amidst a tapestry of shade trees and coffee plants. For 8 months out of the year the fincas expelled most of their workers, and as a result, the regions of El Salvador not devoted to coffee growing emerged as the sites where people reproduced their capacity to work during the harvest. In the area around Intipucá, people cultivated corn, beans, rice, and sorghum, harvested a variety of tropical fruits, and raised pigs, cows, chickens, and an occasional duck. Intipuqueños lived within an hour's walk of the Pacific Ocean with a large river delta and several tidal estuaries, all of which provided abundant seafood. Across the south and east of El Salvador, the ocean, rivers, streams, lakes, and broad lowland plains combined to form a "tortilla basket" of sorts, feeding, clothing, and housing the huge coffee workforce. As an aggregate, El Salvador's national productive activity was compressed onto the face of the bill as the bimodal interaction and mutual reinforcement of coffee fincas and small- to medium-size farming sectors. Invisible was the landless seasonal laborer.

As the colón note circulated in El Salvador, it appeared to contain a portion of this combined product, and ostensibly the exchange of national currency served to distribute or concentrate wealth within the country. The image on the bill tells a highly static and delimited story. To follow the money's movement in relation to people like the peasant farmer and things like the coffee plant helps to fill out the story of Salvadoran national wealth and show both separations and connections with the United States—and even Washington, DC—well before Sigfredo first ventured to live and work abroad.

Following the Golden Grain

When Sigfredo's mother Rosa was in her late twenties, a cousin of hers had a child whom I shall call Miguel. Growing up in Intipucá, Miguel had the nickname Forolo, the name of a flat-bladed cutting tool, because he had a reputation for being especially adept at fighting with his machete.

Miguel lived in Intipucá with his family but, like many people throughout the region, he had to leave and work on coffee plantations during the harvest in order to earn income for the family. In 1944, while his uncle was serving as mayor and he was 15, he traveled east on the cobblestone road toward La Union, walking and getting rides on carts for several days until he arrived at the small town of Conchagua, high on a mountainside overlooking La Union. Conchagua was famous in the region for its ample supply of fresh water that flowed into the town from a large spring and poured out of a fountain featuring carved stone lions.[22] The lion fountain, known throughout the region, stood across from a large Catholic church and together they designated the center of the small village.

Between 1944 and 1948, Miguel traveled to the town to work harvesting coffee and also to tend and pick red beans grown at a similar altitude. The task required some patience and care because branches and existing buds had to be protected from damage while the other ripe cherries were removed quickly by hand. Usually each bush would be picked twice over the course of a harvest, since berries could become ripe within three months. During the coffee harvest Miguel lived in a palm leaf hut on the mountainside above the pueblo and received food twice a day—thick corn tortillas, beans, and salt along with a cup of boiled coffee with ample sugar. Like most people, he occasionally supplemented this ration with an avocado or boiled egg acquired elsewhere.[23] Along with his daily food ration, Miguel received about ten colónes for a week of picking berries. At that time, according to Miguel, one colón could be exchanged for a reasonably large fish caught nearby in the Pacific Ocean.

Each year during the harvest, Conchagua celebrated its patron saint with a large festival and dance in the town center. With his newly earned colónes, Miguel ventured down with fellow workers to attend the dance, paying a small fee to gain entrance. "The girls were so beautiful in this town. We danced and danced all night," Miguel recalled fifty years later. "Did you see the fountain? Water came out of the lions' mouths!" After the harvest, he returned to Intipucá and brought the rest of his earnings back to a small wooden house where he lived with his sister and mother. Years later he inherited a small piece of land near the cantón of Tierra Blanca and was able to raise several cows and grow corn, passing each day much like the image on the face of the one-colón note. Though he never said this, in some ways the note held out an ideal to which he and many others aspired.

Each day the cherries that Miguel and many other young men and children collected were taken by truck to a processing center near La Union where they were hulled, washed, and packed for shipping through the night and into the next day. In the 1940s, most of these processing plants were owned by members of the largest coffee land–owning families. These plants converted ripe cherries into green coffee by means of the "wet process": removing the pulp and mucilage with water, followed by a drying phase, after which the dried husk would be taken off by hand, usually by women who were paid by the amount of husk residue collected each day.[24] Most large processing centers in El Salvador employed this method although it took twice the amount of labor needed for the "dry process": letting the berries dry in the sun before removing pulp and husk in one step.

Products Contributing to Coffee Wealth

During the 1940s, the large sacks for the coffee were woven from fiber derived from the maguey plant (sisal) that was farmed on lower terrain throughout the region. Like Caulotio that began as a workers' settlement, other small cantóns were formed by families who found semiregular work on large maguey farms to the north of Intipucá.[25] Transforming maguey into fiber for cordage was a relatively simple though arduous process. Besides regular weeding and occasional pruning of the plant as it grew, the bulk of the work involved hacking large stalks off the cactus-like plants and transporting them to a central place where they could be mashed and soaked in order to separate the tough fiber from the softer plant tissue. The fibers were hung to dry in the sun before being twisted into cordage suitable for weaving fiber for sacks large enough to hold about 150 pounds (69 kilograms) of processed coffee beans. The fiber was also used to make inexpensive hammocks.

Five decades later, a man born near El Delirio around the time that Miguel was picking coffee in Conchagua boasted of his capacity to harvest and process the maguey plant, something he had done since childhood, but also acknowledged its relational "toughness" and capacity to best the efforts of the laborer. "Maguey is tough! You need to work hard and have tough arms and hands for this work. Look at me *[flexes his arms]*. Maguey hurts you!" he said, proudly showing off the many tiny scars on his hands and arms.

Also during the 1990s, the current owner of the sisal farm visited El Delirio to supervise local surveying in preparation for widening the stretch of the Littoral that passed the settlement. A member of the Sutler family of San Miguel and San Salvador, he was excited to resume production on the farm because sisal bags were in greater demand; they retained the flavor of the highest-quality coffee beans better than plastic bags, and the high-end gourmet coffee market was expanding during the 1990s, especially in US urban regions. "Martínez [the General who ruled El Salvador from

1932 to 1944] was brilliant," he explained to me. "He was criticized for not importing machinery, but he kept this country alive and everyone working with that policy. It was very smart."[26]

The State as Author of Coffee Wealth

Martínez was the singular leader who appeared to deliver to El Salvador a form of salvation in the context of a worldwide crisis in coffee during the 1930s up to his downfall in 1944. His "smartness" was mostly the result of a tense series of relations and exchanges that appeared to transform the arduous practices associated with growing and harvesting arabica coffee beans into glamorous representations of national wealth. As I have mentioned, part of this drama involved the passage of the Ley Moratoria and formation of the BCR that made the Salvadoran state a more direct and leading agent of the national economy. Two years earlier in 1932, Martínez had founded the quasi–state-led mortgage bank specifically oriented toward the coffee sector, El Banco Hipotecario de El Salvador. Members of the Asociación Cafetalera, a consortium of the most prominent coffee growers that had formed in 1929 at the onset of worldwide crisis, owned 75 per cent of the stock in the new bank and they led it to directly compete with the other major private banks that had served as domestic credit sources. By the late 1930s the bank owned subsidiary operations in marketing and the warehousing of agricultural goods, especially coffee.[27] In 1942, two years before Miguel went to work for him, the owner of the finca in Conchagua together with other members of the Association and those represented on the board of Hipotecario, founded the Compaña Salvadoreño del Café, a consortium that sold over 10 percent of all Salvadoran coffee abroad.

Martínez helped to consolidate and expand the power of an elite tied to coffee production and processing relative to nascent commercial, industrial, and financial sectors. By controlling the colón–US dollar exchange rate through the BCR, collecting a substantial duty on all coffee exported, and fixing this amount in relation to the market price of coffee, Martínez was able to extract a steady and significant portion of surplus coffee value and make himself appear as sole author of national "stability," "order," and "progress." Martínez accomplished this especially through the establishment of state monopolies in mail, telegraph, and telephone services and radio broadcasting in El Salvador.

By the late 1940s about 90 percent of El Salvador's foreign exchange came from earnings derived from coffee export. Changes in market prices or production costs rippled through society, especially affecting the expanding public sector. Ever since the 1930s, the Salvadoran state had levied a flexible tax on coffee exports that could be shifted according to the market price garnered on the New York Exchange. Over a five-year period in the late 1950s, UN researchers visited over one thousand coffee plantations in El Salvador and made important quantitative estimates that otherwise remained unrecorded by most planters, comparing these data with other public accounting estimates. According to the report, "the proportion of total fiscal income represented by the state export tax increased from 7 percent in 1945 to 20 percent in 1950, afterwards rising to 30 per cent in both 1954 and 55." As foreign exchange revenue climbed, so did the capacity to import foreign goods, the bulk of which also came from the United States in the two decades after WWII. Through duties levied on these imports, the Salvadoran state captured another third of its income, so that by the late 1950s, at least two-thirds of the official government budget was directly tied to the coffee production and trade circuit.[28] Through taxing commodities leaving and entering El Salvador, the Salvadoran state acted much like a landlord, extracting a toll from the traffic of goods and services across its territory.

Coffee beyond El Salvador

Although Conchagua was hardly at the heart of the coffee-growing areas to the west, it was quite near the port of Cutuco, several miles to the east of La Union. More than half of all coffee in El Salvador traveled to Cutuco on the train line that traversed the country (the same that Rosa used to transport corn to San Miguel) and was shipped out from there. La Unión and Cutuco are hot and humid with long mud flats that stretch out into the Gulf of Fonseca. On a clear day Nicaragua can be seen to the east as well as the Island of Meanguera, where the English pirates once congregated. In Cutuco, the Compaña or any of the other private Salvadoran exporters would purchase and consolidate lots of about 250 bags of coffee that were of uniform quality, mix them, and arrange for their sale abroad. By the end of the 1940s, over 90 percent of all washed green coffee beans from El Salvador were shipped to US ports, especially New York. Typically a Salvadoran exporter would monitor the international market price for coffee on the New York and London exchanges and deal directly with a US roasting company that would purchase the coffee from the exporter when it arrived (the "spot" market) or for delivery at a certain time (the "shipment" market). Usually, the US importer would pay with a letter of credit in US dollars drawn upon its US bank. Many of the Salvadoran export companies, including the Compaña, maintained small offices in New York, but overall they were represented in the United States by the Pan-American Coffee Bureau, also based in New York. The Bureau served as a kind of public relations firm for "promoting the consumption of coffee and fostering good will between the coffee-producing countries and consumers."[29]

Since 1940 under Martínez, Salvadoran (indeed, all Latin American) trade in coffee with the United States had been governed by the Inter American Coffee Agreement (IACA). According to the agreement, which was partially stimulated by the loss of the European coffee market with the onset of WWII, the US market was more or less evenly shared among the major national coffee producers and exporters of Latin America. Miguel's relatively small contribution to Salvador's exported coffee likely was sold on the New York exchange, where most of Salvador's coffee was purchased by about six US-based roasting companies that dominated coffee sales in the United States, including General Foods, Folgers, Hills Bros., Standard Brands, and A&P.[30] Each company blended, roasted, and ground the various beans that they purchased, crafting its own taste that often was regionally specific. For example, Wilkins Coffee of Washington, DC, produced a distinctive blend familiar to most residents throughout the twentieth century.[31]

The many companies like Wilkins Coffee that were concerned with commercial coffee roasting and distribution in the United States were members of the National Coffee Association and also the Joint Coffee Publicity Committee.[32] The two coffee associations, to the extent that they represented all roasters, constituted a small part of an emergent bloc of capitalists in the United States that gradually began to dominate the US state during WWII. This fraction included industries, such as coffee roasting, that relied on primary commodity imports and also were capital intensive. This group also included investment banks and some large commercial banks that invested abroad. Though quite diverse and often in competition, all of these kinds of business shared a general orientation toward promoting conditions that facilitated expanded international trade.[33]

The gradual dominance of the US state by this group of capitalists and the eventual reversing of many New Deal–era policies began in 1940 when

Roosevelt invited Henry Stimson to become US Secretary of War. Stimson had been Secretary of State under Republican President Hoover and was a senior member of the Wall Street law firm Winthrop, Stimson, Putnam & Roberts. Roosevelt also appointed the Republican Frank Knox, the editor of the world-renowned *Chicago Daily News*, to the office of Secretary of the Navy. These two men recruited other conservative allies from both parties to positions in government and as directors of new international institutions at the end of the war, drawing from a network of connections across US finance and corporate law. Dean Atchison, James Forestall, W. Averill Harriman, John J. McCloy, William Draper, and Paul Nitz became well known in the decades after WWII in the context of the Cold War. In many ways this group of corporate internationalists and their allies significantly shaped the postwar world.[34] They were committed to a path of recovery for Europe that insured a climate favorable to their investments and trade activities and that subverted the interests of nascent left/liberal governmental coalitions and popular socialist movements in Europe.

In the broadest terms, this capitalist bloc that included coffee importers and roasters in the United States shared interests that were similar to those of Salvadoran coffee growers, since all were committed to the general expansion of markets for exports. By extension, Sigfredo and Rosa as commercial corn growers who sold in San Miguel, the tenant-farmer families who picked the corn on their farm, Miguel who picked coffee after 1945, and the managers and distributors of Wilkins Coffee in DC were all part of a transnational circuit of production and exchange. Their habits of daily life and the forms of wealth that they trafficked in were quite different yet internally related as part of a larger social whole.

During WWII, Brazil and Colombia had destroyed vast stretches of coffee plantings and accumulated stocks of beans as the world market shrank. As worldwide demand for coffee rose with European recovery, the price of coffee shot upward. In Washington, DC, a man named George McLaughlin, a 39-year-old native of the city who was about five years younger than Rosa, complained that the price of his favorite brand of coffee, Borden's, which contained a portion of coffee grown in El Salvador, had risen dramatically.

> I am a retired Government clerk on an annuity, and on the first of the month I received my notice and my payment and went over to the branch bank where I deposit. I think it was probably half past 8 or 9. I deposited the check, and then I walked over to the Safeway store. My purpose in going in was to buy a dozen

eggs. But after I got there, well, I thought I had better buy some coffee, and I went over to the place where—it is a self-service store on Fifteenth Street near M. I went over to the place where I knew the coffee was and started to reach down for the coffee. There was a fellow working down there; he was squatted down or something, and I said, "What are you doing?" He said, "I am raising the price of coffee." I said, "Good. Give me a Borden's." And he was working on one, and he gave me one of these tins of Borden's. "What are you raising it to?" He said, "51 cents." He handed me this . . . showing that the price was marked up from 42 cents to 51 cents.[35]

The coffee boom and the struggle to take part in it across the United States and El Salvador provided the interlinked conditions for two important shifts which have had lasting effects on relations between both countries and especially quotidian conditions across Intipucá and DC.

US State Transformation and the Consequences for Washington, DC

As I have mentioned, the international capitalist bloc, including the coffee interests, supported the development of the Marshall Plan to stimulate European recovery. They also tended to ally themselves with other interests to support the position put forward by the US Army that Europe's future security should be guaranteed by large-scale deployment of US troops and additional ground forces that would remain on constant alert in the United States. To support this effort, the US Army and Navy called for the passage of "universal service" laws that would obligate every eligible US man to serve for a period in the military.[36]

As Congressional voting on the relevant bills neared, a series of complex and secret negotiations transpired. At the last minute, the votes reflected a significant realignment of power in the United States. The US Air Force had defected from the other armed forces and quietly allied itself with Taft-led isolationist Republicans and a sector of domestic capitalists in direct opposition to the alliance of the internationalist capitalist bloc (Wall Street and multinational corporations) and the rest of the US military that wanted stability in Europe via the development of ground military forces.[37]

The outcome of this power shift was a gradual increase in defense spending oriented toward aerospace research and development. The

Midwestern national capitalists were short-term bedfellows for the growing aerospace sector, because production shifted toward the southwestern United States and along both ocean coasts where new airplane and
electronics factories and later missile testing and production sites were
built.[38]

After Henry Stimson became US Secretary of War in 1944, his young
assistant, an engineer named Thomas Meloy, purchased a small aerospace
company. In 1952 Meloy located its new headquarters in suburban Falls
Church, Virginia, at that time barely more than a tapestry of cow pas-
tures and dairy farms to the south of DC across the Potomac River. He
called his firm Melpar, which was derived from his name and that of Joseph Parks, his business associate who died two years later. In 1951, the
firm was bought by the Westinghouse Air Brake Company for $1 million.
Meloy remained its president and board chairman well into the 1960s. Fed
by generous contracts in the early years of aerospace growth when the US
Air Force secured support for developing the first US intercontinental
ballistic missiles, Melpar was the largest industrial employer in the Washington area during its existence, peaking at 6,000 workers.[39]

Melpar set the pace; in the decades after WWII the counties of Northern Virginia attracted the headquarters of a host of high-tech military
and aerospace companies. The arrival of well-financed aerospace firms
and their use of land developed by speculators in the region combined
in a powerful way to broadcast a particular story about the DC suburbs.
Developing such land meant transforming territory into something that
contained wealth and could be resold for a profit, as well as used for its
intrinsic qualities. Milton Peterson, a successful developer in Northern
Virginia during the 1980s, reflected on the early years and explained, "The
demander of space is like a voter. Developers, what do they build? They
build what they think they can sell. So they're saying, You, voter or consumer, what do you want, what would you pay for, okay?"[40] But the product, in order to circulate so as to yield a profit and become capital, had to
be backed by a promise of the future. Peterson explained how Melpar held
out this promise, breaking from the present and holding out a new future
temporally and spatially freed from other times and places.

> The ultimate, okay, is Melpar. Melpar was the flag, the lawn, and set back from
> the road, but the big thing was to have a brick front. Why was brick a big thing?
> Because everything else anybody had seen was shitty old aluminum or steel!
> You build with what you think the people want and that then [1952] was Melpar.

Trying to be the antithesis of the city. Total antithesis. Curvilinear as opposed to rectilinear. See, the whole thing in sales and marketing is making people feel good about themselves.[41]

In the District proper, the patterns of development followed a less genteel line than in Virginia. "Slum clearance" and "urban renewal" provided the theme around which a conservative alliance gathered: high-ranking military officers who resided in the DC area after WWII, the DC Board of Trade, and the Real Estate Board, and their collective assemblage of city banks, building associations, title and insurance companies, as well as a group of conservative southern politicians, especially Sen. Theodore Bilbo of Mississippi, who controlled the District committees in Congress. This group generally opposed federal redevelopment plans, which they saw as a continuation of New Deal–era public spending, and instead pushed for a project of private investment, backed by city enforcement of residential zoning and sanitary codes. One federally funded project was carried out in southeast DC, but elsewhere, a nascent form of "gentrification" pushed out black working-class residents while driving up rents in the downtown area.[42]

Eleanor Dulles, a member of the liberal-minded postwar elite who was a member of the National Committee on Segregation in the Nation's Capital and who supported federal redevelopment plans, purchased what was once an "alleyway" populated by African Americans and took part in fixing up and selling it at great profit.[43] Gradually, as the suburbs continued to attract investment, people in downtown areas were compressed into devalued regions that would later provide the kind of low-rent housing that Sigfredo was able to obtain in the late 1960s. Northern Virginia, where Melpar was located, offered employment in an expanding low-wage service sector.

Salvadoran State Transformation and the Consequences for Eastern El Salvador and Intipucá

Nine months after the US Air Force "victory" in the US Congress, a group of younger Salvadoran military officers took over the Salvadoran government of Castañeda Castro, forcing him to relinquish the office of president. Within the year, the new government of Lieutenant Colonel Oscar Osorio began to pursue policies that would make the state a more active participant in the development of productive enterprises other than the coffee trade. They promoted countrywide education reforms and restructured the electoral process, creating a new civil servant class of municipal-level teachers and administrators that complemented the longer history of military presence in rural areas. These changes brought pueblos like Intipucá into more direct contact with the capital city, San Salvador. Cesar Matamoros, Sigfredo's friend who encouraged him to go to DC and work, traveled to the pueblo as part of this new civil servant class. By reaching directly to the countryside, through a seemingly coherent project of infrastructure development and limited social and political reforms, the Salvadoran state attempted to expand and deepen its legitimacy while also capturing a larger portion of coffee revenue.[44]

On January 14, 1949, the military issued its first copy of a new glossy magazine, *Boletín del Ejército*, that circulated widely throughout the cities and rural areas, especially because of the modest expansions in public education. The first issue focused on the three themes that were said to guide the 1948 revolutionary government: *maestros* (teachers), *arboles* (trees, nature), and Guttenberg (printing press, information).[45] Throughout the 1950s the magazine regularly appeared, always leading with an article that described public support and expenditure for education and "cultural events," such as a national symphony orchestra. The magazine frequently included a short passage quoted from either George Washington or Benjamin Franklin, followed by a column on astronomy and one on logic, *Cursos Logica*. The magazine promoted a paradoxical definition of national rationality with articles that inveighed against the "false religion of materialism" and "the bad religion of communism," while calling for a renewed but vaguely defined "spiritualism" in El Salvador.

The magazine also reflected the harder edge of military rule in El Salvador but tinged with the spirit of reform. One issue published on February 23, 1951, announced new laws in the "campaign against delinquency" that called for the complete disarming (firearms) of rural populations. Despite the legal ruling, local relations such as those among Sigfredo, Pedro, and the National Guard stationed in Intipucá made it possible for more elite town members (local land-owners) to keep their guns. The article in the magazine also announced a policy that farmers carrying machetes were forbidden to walk or gather in groups larger than three people. In the April 20, 1951, issue there was a long article discussing a recent revolt on a hacienda that was quelled by military force. The article actually blamed the hacienda owners and the *patrones* (overseers, foremen) for not properly taking care of the needs of the workers, rather than attributing it to innate criminality, generalized habits of violence, or the result of communist organizing.

Within a year of the coup, the Osorio government announced the formation of the Comisión Ejecutiva Hidroeléctrica del Rio Lempa CEL (Lempa River Hydroelectric Executive Commission), which was explicitly organized in the spirit of the "Tennessee Valley Authority" and the rural electrification programs of the Roosevelt Administration in the 1930s. US New Deal–inspired politics were weakened after WWII in the United States by the interests of the corporate internationalists, but they provided a compelling model of state-led development in El Salvador. By June 1951, the Salvadoran state presented itself as the singular progenitor of the hydroelectric dam on the Lempa River. This was announced in the *Boletín* and also through a thick official document that celebrated the "National Program of Electrification." Mixed within the image of the government ushering the modern into El Salvador, the dam and power plant were heavily financed by a loan in US dollars from the World Bank. Much of this money paid for the Chicago-based Harza Engineering Company to serve as a consultant to CEL in the construction of the dam.[46]

In 1954, the Salvadoran government obtained a second loan from the World Bank to begin a massive road-building project along what was known as Salvador's "Littoral," the low-lying Pacific coastal region along the central and eastern half of El Salvador. The road replaced the stone tracks followed by Miguel in 1944 when he picked coffee in Conchagua. It ran from La Union to Intipucá to the corner of El Delirio, where an extension across the low-lying swampy region linked it to San Miguel. From Delirio, the road reached the central city of Usulután and continued to San Salvador and then to the border with Guatemala.[47]

Conclusion: What Lies behind the Capacity to Appear as Agent and Author

From the perspective of Sigfredo's front room, Intipucá had changed considerably since 1966, the year in which he first moved to DC. But these changes were the complex outcome of a longer history and broader geography of interaction. As much as he and other residents appeared to bring "civilization" to Intipucá, they were also actors who stood on the shoulders of the coffee circuit that had always brought civilization and its opposite together, in ways that linked Intipucá and DC well before the period of migration. The subtle power shift within the US government that helped the Air Force win the "war on the Potomac" and the more dramatic coup in El Salvador, both in 1948, helped to determine new patterns of state spending and activity in both countries. Both upheavals may be understood together as part of state-led interventions into the loosely configured circuit of international capitalists who shared an interest in maintaining conditions conducive to producing, selling, buying, and using primary agricultural products. In El Salvador, the military state made a play to increase its relative power and legitimacy by capturing a part of the coffee wealth and shifting it into infrastructure and the development of cotton, as well as the promotion of limited industry. In the United States, the Air Force allied itself with domestic capitalists concentrated in the Midwest and helped to shift state expenditure toward new high-tech aerospace development in southern and coastal cities.

Both of these diversions of the circuit had effects at various spatial scales. The Littoral road allowed Rosa to sell corn more easily and in larger quantities in San Miguel, increasing the wealth of the family and the resources available for Sigfredo's early education and training. With the expansion of the public sector in El Salvador, Sigfredo encountered other well-educated civil servants from the capital, from whom he learned of the possibility to travel and work in the United States. The relation between downtown DC and the Northern Virginia suburbs changed as a result of new federal spending patterns in the United States, creating the conditions for cheap housing downtown and wage work in the suburbs. The production of coffee across El Salvador and the United States in the decade after WWII yielded the uneven concentration of wealth and "civilization" across both countries. This chapter has shown some of the connections and social content that necessarily appeared as formally separate and static entities. The next chapter continues this method of analysis, exploring how a circuit of cotton grew out of the coffee circuit, forming the necessary preconditions for the emergence of the migrant labor-power and remittance circuit later in the 1980s, even as these connections were occluded through the establishment of the strong distinction among culture, politics, and economics.

CHAPTER THREE

Melting Fields of Snow

War is a mere continuation of politics by other means. — Carl von Clausewitz, 1832

War is a continuation of politics by other means and politics is only about economics quintessentialized. — Roque Dalton, 1974[1]

Culture, the arts—poetry, literature, music, dance—are a continuation of politics by other means. — Eladio, 1993[2]

This chapter begins with a brief exploration of two dominant understandings of El Salvador produced at the end of the 1970s. From this vantage point, the chapter moves backward and outward, tracing some of the concrete social threads that are contained and also hidden in a complex knotted fashion throughout both accounts. The chapter examines the rise of cotton production and trade associated with new patterns of money circulation between the 1950s and the 1970s across the southern and eastern regions of El Salvador. Over the same period, increased US defense spending, especially after the success of the Cuban Revolution in 1959, shaped the world of cotton production in El Salvador and the development of DC and its Northern Virginia suburbs. This chapter illuminates forms of violence across this circuit and shows how "economic" immiseration, "political" violence, and "cultural" domination are internally related, rather than different entities or processes of kind. The chapter argues that the shared structuring of violence across the circuit is contained within the very different empirical experiences of people and the dominant understandings that circulate in both countries.

Establishing a Relationship between Violence and Migration

San Miguel is not only the birthplace of Francisco Gavidia but also the early home of Salvadoran author Manlio Argueta, well known for his 1979 novel *Un Dia en la Vida* (One Day of Life). Constructed as an intricate and poetic *testimonio* (testimonial narrative) featuring the voice of a woman named Lupe, Argueta's short book explores the insidious expansion of military violence and death squad terror during the 1970s in response to the work of Jesuit priests and labor organizers in El Salvador's northern Department of Chaletenango. Argueta's novel was significant at the time of its publication not only because it critically examined aspects of government repression in the countryside (including the presence of US "special forces" advisors), but also because it drew upon folk tales, myths, and linguistic nuance to explore the everyday practices of those whose labor-power had made El Salvador's century of coffee-led development possible.

If Francisco Gavidia, the great turn-of-the-century Salvadoran modernist author, explored the formal appearance of metropolitan wealth and its meaning for the emergent Salvadoran nation-state, then arguably Argueta should be known for imaginatively examining much of its brutal content and everyday meaning for rural coffee laborers later in the century. Argueta's characters with their colloquial expressions, wry sense of humor, and ever-changing sense of themselves in the face of quotidian forms of domination provided a significant contrast to pastoral images of peasant passivity, such as the narrow two-dimensional iconography of the 1948 colón note in chapter 2. As interpreters and critics have suggested, Argueta's writings at that time and *Un Dia* in particular formed part of an aesthetic turn in Salvadoran literature away from a European-inspired urban modernism to a more Central American focus on personal accounts of the daily life and labors of rural populations.[3]

The same year that *Un Dia* was published in El Salvador (and was banned by the government, obligating Manlio to flee the country), Salvadoran migrants were "discovered" in the United States by two *Washington Post* journalists, Christopher Dickey and Karen DeYoung. Their three-part series of articles was among the first popular accounts of Salvadoran migration to the United States and appeared on the front page of the newspaper. The authors described Salvadorans as "illegal aliens" and "economic migrants" who had left severe poverty and unemployment and traveled to the DC metropolitan region to find work and earn higher wages. Echoing yet modifying the twentieth-century trope of the "American Dream," the article described how they succeeded by dint of hard work and sacrifice in the United States and were able to send home a portion of their earnings to help those who remained in the country. Two more articles by Dickey and DeYoung followed in early May. These articles were cited along with US immigration and census data in the first scholarly studies of Salvadoran migration to the United States written by US authors.

Though obviously quite different literary forms with distinct modes of establishing meaning and a sense of veracity among readers, Argueta's novel and the *Post* articles both offered focused accounts of daily life amidst broader transformations during the 1970s. Considered together at the end of that decade, they contribute aspects and partial pieces to a broader perspective linking exploitative systems of agricultural production, collective organization, and state violence in El Salvador, migration and work in US cities, and the transfer of remittances back to El Salvador via tightly woven social connections across both places that only during the late 1980s came to be understood and debated as features of an interrelated whole. In 1979 such a "transnational" world of people, products, and money was less easy to immediately perceive. Manlio's fictive account of peasant organizing and state-led violence drew upon real events that later became widely documented and understood. However, his testimonial contained no mention of the growing exodus of people and wealth from El Salvador across social classes, including people who fled Chaletenango, an exodus in which he also participated after his book was banned. The *Washington Post* article series, like other US-centered accounts of Salvadoran migration that appeared in the late 1970s, focused on the new population movement and the phenomenon of remittance transfer, linking both with low wages and unemployment in rural El Salvador and the availability of jobs in US cities like DC. In the *Post* article, the only reference to the Salvadoran government was that "it gave people nothing" and that it suspected priests in the area of "promoting communist subversion." Unlike in Argueta's novel, there was no discussion of the violently repressive *Guardia* (National Guard) or the activities of "death squads."

The partiality of each account may be understood as a reflection of the distinct locations of their respective authors as they were caught up in events that were outrunning the available categories and interpretive frames through which they might be conceptualized. El Salvador was in crisis and rapidly moving toward civil war as the military government and its largely export-led model of development were failing to provide or even appear able to promise a viable way of life for much of the population. People from all social classes were moving themselves and their wealth out of the country at increasing magnitudes. Over the same decade major US cities were undergoing "de-industrialization" even as they absorbed unprecedented numbers of Salvadorans as well as other people from Central America, Mexico, and the Caribbean into their burgeoning low-wage service sectors. At the time, however, there were no popular accounts that linked these two transformations as part of a larger hemispheric shift.

Argueta's novel subtly captured human aspects of change in one part of El Salvador, especially some of the violent relations through which rural coffee-laborers were formed as subjects. Argueta wrote with sensitivity to (and great hope in) the ways that people, though deeply shaped by increasingly brutal encounters, could influence and alter their historical conditions. The *Post* articles highlighted new kinds of one-way movement of people and money that linked El Salvador and the United States, emphasizing the agency of subjects and their capacity to contribute to broader transformative social projects in the United States as hard workers or in El Salvador as generous remitters. Dickey and DeYoung's articles lacked *Un Dia*'s quality of relational interaction and sensitivity to the mutual determination of people and their world. Instead the authors posited more internally stable and discrete subjects and objective realms where human agents rationally acted in the face of either/or logical propositions. At the risk of simplistic comparison, Argueta confined a dynamic story within a mildly fetishized Salvadoran nation, while the *Post* journalists examined empirically new international connections even as they also reproduced the individual and the nation as discrete and internally coherent entities. While Argueta focused on a dynamic and hierarchal world of human actors, the *Post* writers implicitly separated the spheres of the economic and the political (people were "economic migrants") and reproduced the image of an atomistic equilibrium-seeking world composed of discrete "push" and "pull" factors.

In *Un Dia* and the *Post* articles, individual people and nations, the spheres of the economic, political, and cultural, and the conditions of violence, war, and peace appear as separate and discrete entities or states of being. The challenge is not just to point out either the tenuousness or partiality of the book and the news accounts by comparing them internally as I have done in a preliminary way above. The task of this chapter is also to explore how and why such accounts and others like them tended to dominate, rising to the surface over other possible understandings and tendencies. This involves moving between the forms and discursive categories contained in the documents and the actions, practices, social relations, and structures that comprised their broader geohistorical conditions of possibility. This is as much a problem of historical agency, power, and causality as one of knowledge, truth, and representation. To some of the social content and meaning of these forms I now turn.

The Social Relations of Cotton Production Contained in the Literary Representations

Near the middle of Manlio Argueta's novel, the character of Lupe describes traveling as a young girl from Chalate to work in the cotton fields along the Pacific coast of El Salvador. As she helped weed and pick the plants with her parents, she would idly think about her world, her fear of heavy rainstorms that she thought might carry her away, and the painful memories of watching children in her pueblo die from malnutrition and untreated infections. In her testimony Lupe recalled how as she worked, she created explanatory tales that put her at ease.

> When I was a little bigger, all of us would go to the coast to pick cotton. . . . My teacher used to say that sea water goes up, in vapors. And then that same water falls as rain. . . . In other words, the water rises to the sky by means of invisible rivers, and that's why huge showers of rain fall in the winter. . . . I love the vapor of water, taking into account that it is the river in which spirits navigate, the river in which angels who are children float. My father would tell me that one should believe in these things, because that's the only way that life has meaning.[4]

Lupe imagined a world in which children, including herself, would not be lost in death, but instead would linger safely in the world. As she ages in Argueta's novel, Lupe's desire to overcome fears and the love she has for her father continue to orient her—what she calls "the little light of hope that lives in you, maybe . . . like the light of a candle it is"[5]—even as her childhood imaginings fail to make sensible the violent murders and deaths that she witnesses throughout her life.

Argueta's manner of presenting her fictive testimony filled with reflections on the surrounding world is often difficult to parse or synthesize. In this abbreviated passage and throughout the book, Argueta seems to explore changes in the way that "life has meaning," as Lupe's father put it, because it is the constant interplay between people and their world, each changing in relation to the other, partially arbitrated by the human capacity to establish and act upon reasonable and desirable "would-be's," as well as to let go of them, but also mediated by objects that can directly intrude upon habits of understanding and action, making other things happen.

Like the fictive character Lupe who is middle-aged at the time that Argueta presents her words in the late 1970s, a nonfictive and much-alive man whom I shall call Daniel, the eldest son of Miguel (the man who harvested coffee in chapter 2), was able to look back upon a period of his youth when he too worked in the cotton fields near Intipucá: "Hijhhhhuej. . . . *Everyone* did it! Before [the migration to DC], cotton is what made this pueblo. Ask anyone. Every day we left before the sun came up and returned in the dark. Around here [motioning with his arm] was like a giant field of snow that went on forever."[6]

Between the 1950s and early 1970s, Daniel and many other people in the region labored on large farms in the area, including the vast expanse of land owned by the wealthy Cristiani-Burkhardt family of San Salvador whose hacienda, San Ramón, abutted the much smaller Gallo family farms and extended eastward toward Conchagua and La Unión.[7] Daniel traveled the same road that his father had used in his coffee-picking days, although now it was paved and well traversed by new trucks and automobiles. Daniel continued to describe the significant changes that germinated out of the cotton fields in those three decades: "Cotton was the first thing that gave people money. I could earn four colónes for a day of picking cotton at San Ramón. Younger kids, fifteen, sixteen years old, earned one colón in one day. Before cotton everyone just lived off the ocean and the corn that we planted."[8]

Like Argueta's account of Lupe's childhood memories, Daniel's reflections were creative interpretations and recollections of an immediate world. In his brief statements, he tended to emphasize the agency of cotton and its capacity to re-make life in Intipucá, to "give" people money for the first time. As he said, cotton bulked so large as to blanket much of Oriente with the feeling of a permanent presence that "went on forever."

Hacienda owners throughout El Salvador had grown cotton in small quantities since the 1860s, shipping bales to buyers in New York when the prices rose, but cotton never approached the importance of coffee as an export crop. With the gradual recovery of European and Asian, especially Japanese, textile production after WWII, the worldwide demand for all grades of cotton grew and market prices rose dramatically. The powerful pesticide DDT, developed in 1939, combined with the new roads, bridges, and rural electrification from the late 1940s in El Salvador, helped make possible the transformation of the southern and eastern lowlands of the country into productive cotton-growing zones.

As Daniel and others in the pueblo were picking cotton for a wage, families that owned arable land around Intipucá began to convert their fields from corn to cotton. Despite the size of Rosa's hacienda, much of the land slopped steeply upward from the pueblo, making it difficult to use for cotton growing. Other flatter territory in the region rapidly changed from green to white and there was a dramatic drop in land devoted to corn production; the majority of that land was converted to cotton between the 1950s and 1970s.[9]

The families from Intipucá who were growing cotton obtained all their "inputs," save human work capacity, through the government cooperative called El Papalón, located in San Miguel. The Papalón center included ginning and bailing equipment as a well as places for families to relax, including a swimming pool, basketball courts, and a soccer field. The names on the Papalón membership roster included all the oldest Intipucá landowning families: Arias, Chávez, Blanco, Lazo (whose land was contained in the municipio of Chirilagua even though they tended to associate with Intipucá), and a group that had recently arrived in the area, the Villatoros. The Villatoro group consisted of three brothers who had moved with their young families from San Francisco Gotera, the town where Rosa's father had studied pharmacy and where Sigfredo lived while attending high school during the late 1950s.[10]

As I have described in chapter 2, the decades of the 1950s and 1960s were a time of rapid change in Oriente. New roads, bridges, and sources of power contributed to the construction of small factories. Processed cottonseed oil, cotton textiles, clothing, and shoes were domestically produced and available. An increasing number of imported automobiles traveled the new highways. People in the region trafficked in money and goods with an intensity not seen since the days of colonial indigo. San Miguel grew as an important commercial and industrial center tied to the cotton system, and generally became more integrated with its outlying pueblos, such as Intipucá. State-led development projects, partially funded by the United States, helped to integrate the eastern part of El Salvador, creating a nascent "middle class" connected to expanded financial and commercial activity. Overall, there was a dramatic monetarization of the countryside as sharecroppers were displaced and any would-be land user was charged a fee in colónes.[11]

Despite the reformist tone of the Salvadoran government after 1948, there were constant internal tensions and divisions among military and oligarchic factions. On October 26, 1960, a group of reformist military officers took over the government, ousting Colonel José Mariá Lemus who had been elected in a fraudulent contest in 1956. Within a year, a counter-coup of more conservative officers took back the government with tacit approval from officials in the United States government. This new government, headed by Colonel Julio Rivera, embraced the newly elected US president John F. Kennedy, and within several months the US president announced his new "Alliance for Progress" with Central American leaders. The Alliance was formed in the wake of the Cuban revolution, shortly before the failed Bay of Pigs invasion.

With guidance from the US CIA, Rivera organized the Salvadoran National Security Association or ANSESAL that in turn organized a large-scale rural and urban network of informants and paramilitary groups known as ORDEN. Annual US financial and military aid increased from about $1 million at the end of the Eisenhower administration to over $17 million year under the Kennedy administration.[12] Besides aiding the Salvadoran state's capacity to control and dominate the countryside, the Alliance also yielded real changes in rural productive life. In Intipucá, one of the three Villatoro brothers became the first in the town to be proficient at artificial insemination. This allowed regions not suitable for cotton or corn to become devoted to cattle grazing for beef and milk products, especially dry cheese that did not require refrigeration.

Along with the money came US Peace Corps volunteers and missionaries, including several who worked in the region near Intipucá. "The US government really gave us something back then, unlike today," recalled one Intipucá merchant much later in the 1990s. "We used to get free clothing every year—not any more, now we have to buy it." In 1964, the Catholic Diocese of Cleveland, Ohio, organized its mission to El Salvador and sent several priests and nuns to the city of La Unión. Among their first projects was the refurbishment of the Catholic Church in Conchagua, paid

for with a large grant from a family in Cleveland. In 1965, missionaries arrived in the town of Chirilagua adjacent to Intipucá and worked throughout the region.

The complex relations that intertwined the cotton co-op, particular factions of the Salvadoran state, and their allies in the US state all helped
yield a more integrated system through which both people and things were
produced. In the early 1960s, a young woman from Intipucá whose father
sold cotton at the co-op met a young man in San Miguel. They soon married and had a son, whom I will call Benjamín. The man had moved to
the city to take part in the cotton boom and opened a small repair shop
where he specialized in fixing mechanized farm equipment. Gradually he
expanded his business, acquiring a large piece of commercial property
at the outskirts of San Miguel where the Pan-American highway entered
the city. In the process of repairing cotton gins, trucks, tractors, plows, and
occasionally parts of airplanes that were used for spraying fertilizer
and pesticides on the cotton fields, he found that he could more quickly
and profitably fabricate replacement parts than order them from suppliers abroad. In a highly particular way, this man took part in the process
of "import substitution industrialization" (ISI) and became a self-taught
Salvadoran machinist. He cleverly built his own lathes and presses and
also acquired specialized milling equipment from the United States. According to Benjamín, who remembered growing up in the 1960s and 1970s
and frequently swimming in the pool at Papalón, "My father enjoyed talking with the growers and he used to say that cotton is the greatest thing to
have happened to him and to El Salvador. He always used to laugh and
say, 'It will last forever.'"

In the pueblo of Intipucá, cotton production yielded new money relations on the basis of rent and wages. This "cotton-money" circulated
in the town in ways that produced commercial activities and particular
people who engaged in them. One entrepreneur in the town opened a
small bordello in his newly built wooden house, charging a modest fee to
clients. At that time, a young boy whom I will call Roberto, whose family
was extremely poor and lived near the Pacific Ocean, liked to venture to
Intipucá and peek through the cracks in the walls of the house. One evening, he was discovered by one of the visitors who jabbed a stick through
the hole in the wall, hitting Roberto in the face. The stick missed his eye,
but caught on his nose and tore his right nostril. Roberto healed without
problem and eventually moved to the DC area in the early 1970s where he
worked as a cook. Years later Sigfredo's son Marvin often joked about the

curious scar on Roberto's nose and how he had received the injury, calling him "Peeping Roberto." In a highly abstracted manner, cotton itself had scratched his nose, as much as Roberto sought to amuse himself amidst changes that cotton had brought to the pueblo.

At this time, several of Sigfredo's childhood friends who were accumulating wealth by growing cotton and renting their land to growers pooled their earnings and purchased a large diesel generator. They brought it to Intipucá and strung up a limited system of electrical wiring and lighting among houses in the center of the pueblo, charging a modest fee for this new service. Although national electrification had not yet extended to Intipucá, these local entrepreneurs took advantage of the expanding money economy and tried to capture a small fee from those who wished to have electric power. In multiple ways, cotton seemed to promise new opportunities and habits of life for many people in the town.

Contradictions of Cotton Production

In 1996, Daniel recalled the cotton era while sitting under a tree near a large patch of watermelons that he had planted. "I say that it looked like a giant field of snow because I once saw snow in Washington, DC. It was horrible and I left! [*laughs*]." Daniel paused and reflected on his current situation. "I like it here [and now] because it is *tranquilo*," he said, comparing at that moment Intipucá in the late 1990s with Washington, DC, at least a decade earlier.[13]

"What about in the time of cotton?" I asked.

"There were many, many problems," he softly replied, hinting at the contradictions amidst the apparent permanence of cotton's reach. At that moment, however, Daniel changed the direction of our conversation, shifting back to a focus on the pleasures of being a watermelon and corn farmer in Intipucá in 1996. "Let's eat one," he offered, brandishing his steel machete in the late afternoon sun.

Just more than thirty years before our snack, in 1965, the US Congress reversed the policies through which it protected its southern cotton growers, especially in Texas, and released its accumulated stocks on the world market. In short order, the market price of cotton plummeted and Salvadoran growers had trouble securing additional financing. Some landowners tentatively began to convert their land back to other crops, especially corn, while others tried to further reduce production costs so they might remain moderately profitable in the face of overall declines in the international market. The many people who had been displaced during the expansion of cotton growing since the 1950s either lost work opportunities or earned less for their labors in this period of contraction. Salvadoran military forces more directly intervened in people's lives in increasingly unregulated fashion. Besides conflicts among growers and harvesters, there were also conflicts among more elite factions in the area, stimulated in part by how they were unevenly affected by the cotton decline.

In the middle of the 1960s, a member of the National Guard stationed in the pueblo raped and killed a young girl in the town. At this time Sigfredo's friend Pedro was the mayor of Intipucá. He also controlled the switch for the generator and each night it was his responsibility to turn off the town power supply. One evening, just after Pedro shut down the generator, a group of townspeople stormed the Guard headquarters and killed the guardsman with their machetes. The next day the Guard seized Pedro and took him away. He barely escaped his own execution and hid in a nearby town for several months. Pedro continues to suspect that one of the Villatoro brothers suggested to the Guard that he may have known of the attack and coordinated the power shutdown accordingly.

In spite of the drop in price for cotton after 1965, state development plans steamed ahead in Oriente, kept alive by borrowing and concentrated efforts to keep production costs, especially wages, as low as possible. In 1967 the Salvadoran government completed construction of the Cuscatlán Bridge, better linking the eastern and central cotton regions with the rest of the country. At this time Central America had become the third largest regional producer of cotton in the world, after the United States and Egypt. The arrival of state-owned electrical service in 1967 would put out of business the private diesel generator consortium and, in anticipation of their losses, they immediately began to petition the government to buy back their generator. Official letters rich with the language of "serving the development of the patria" were passed back and forth between Intipucá and several government offices in San Salvador. Consistently the government refused to buy or compensate them for the generator, and eventually the owners sold it to another family in the pueblo.

At this conflicted time Sigfredo, who had been working as an accountant at a bank in San Miguel, returned from his year in DC with tales and pictured proof of having purchased a new car. Within the year a group of six people, including several women from the pueblo, traveled to DC, following the route and contacts established by Sigfredo. They all found work in hotels and restaurants and lived in the rooming house run by Manola, the Cuban woman. Within several years, Benjamín's mother separated from her husband and left for DC. The mother of "Peeping Roberto" left, as did Daniel's stepsisters, the daughters of Miguel. When this initial exodus from Intipucá began, the Salvadoran state was completing two decades of sustained infrastructure development through central and eastern El Salvador, under the rhetoric of modernization and national security.

The Social Content of the Newspaper Account

The first of the 1979 *Post* articles that I considered at the beginning of the chapter began by incanting a myth-like tale of origins gleaned from the authors' research in DC:

> There is a story told over and over in the half-hidden world of Washington's illegal aliens. It's about a village in El Salvador called Intipucá, where there perhaps were only 5,000 people to begin with. "One man came to Washington in 1966," so the story goes. "He bought a car with the money he earned and sent home a picture of himself in it. The people in the village thought this looked like a good thing. Now there are more than 1,000 of them here [Washington, DC].

When I spoke with Sigfredo in 1996 at his house in Intipucá, he showed me the infamous and well-worn picture along with many others. With the growing crisis in cotton, everyday strife and uncertainty increased among workers and in relation to their employers, but there was also heightened conflict among competing landowners. Sigfredo's new clothes and car seemed appealing. These things had been obtained by a man who shared no more resources or advantages than other people of his generation whose parents had owned moderate-sized farms since the turn of the century and who had become wealthier with the cotton boom. What cannot be inferred from the picture nor from the way it was invoked in the *Post* article is the complicated history of events between when the photo was taken in the late 1960s and just over a decade later, when "there [were] more than 1,000" Intipuqueños in the DC area.

The *Post* account suggests a simple conjuncture of events and assumes that the "1,000 of them" (people from Intipucá) constituted a relatively homogeneous group, all actively deciding to follow the almost natural and eternal pull of new consumer items, wages, and jobs and the push of not being able to get a job in Intipucá. Concealed within this deft thirteen-year summary of change, however, was a much more complicated and tumultuous history where many people faced exceedingly difficult dilemmas and were obligated to act in ways that were hardly of their choosing.

In Argueta's fictive testimonial, Lupe refers to aspects of a massacre of demonstrators in downtown San Salvador and a series of attacks on people and clergy throughout the capital that actually did occur, shortly after Carlos Romero was elected president of El Salvador on February 20, 1977. Conservative business interests who had previously opposed land reforms had heavily financed his campaign.[14] Lupe also mentions that soldiers occupied a town in the Department of Chaletenango, 60 miles north of San Salvador. At the time of the book's writing, Manlio was probably aware that in the town of Aguilares, approximately fifty people were killed and three priests were arrested and forced to leave the country.[15] This region of Chaletenango in particular was a part of El Salvador where Jesuit priests, drawing upon the tenets of a more liberal Catholic theology, had been organizing peasants together with the Christian Federation of Salvadoran Peasants (FECCAS). The military directly threatened all Jesuit priests in the country, and a paramilitary "death squad" linked to the military and oligarchic backers, the "White Warriors Union," demanded that fifty priests leave the country or face "execution."[16]

On November 25, 1977, Romero announced the passage of the Law of the Defense and Guarantee of Public Order. The new legislation gave military forces increased legal authority to use arbitrary arrest and detention against anyone deemed to be a "subversive." With the passage of the law, the military broadened its rural strategy to target not only peasant labor organizations and priests, but also high school and university students who were deemed to be sympathetic to or directly involved in the rise of popular protest across the country.

At this time a distant cousin of Daniel, whom I shall call Jaime, had heard from someone in the local Guard unit stationed in Intipucá that an associate of his from the eastern campus of the National University in San Miguel had named him as a "communist" to government authorities. "It was just because I had gone to the university," he explained later in 1993. "But I had to leave or they would have killed me. That's what they were doing then. That's why many of us left, just because we were students." This period of direct threats from the Guard on a heightened, almost

nation-wide, scale existed within and in contrast to another pattern of relations where frequently a group of town residents maintained alliances
with the local authorities, although these sometimes collapsed in the wake
of factional conflict, as in the experience of Pedro.

Another member of this relatively privileged group of people in Intipucá was Marvin, the son of Sigfredo and a distant cousin of Daniel
through his grandmother Rosa. Marvin was a precocious child with a
strong sense of himself at an early age. He was relatively short and famous
for running around the town carrying a wooden stick that he waved at
people in a mock threatening fashion. Residents began to call him "Caveman," and this nickname stuck with him throughout his life.

During the 1970s Marvin was among a small number of children who,
after completing primary school in the pueblo, traveled by bus to San
Miguel to attend a private high school. In Intipucá, he and his friends were
often teased and picked on by the children of poorer residents who did not
attend school. Marvin wore a uniform with dark pants and a white shirt
with the emblem of the school sewn on the breast pocket. In his wallet he
carried a small card that identified him as a student of the school and allowed him access to its modest library. During the week, rather than make
the slow bus trip each way, he would stay over with cousins who lived in
the city.

Early in the morning as he would arrive by bus or be waiting with
friends in front of the school, members of the Guard would walk by and
order all of them to put their hands in the air or against the wall of the
school. Members of the Guard would yell at them and accuse them of being "communists," "subversives," and "terrorists." Frequently the guards
would threaten to kill them. These attempts to scare the school children,
especially boys, increased during the period of the Public Order Law,
and several school-aged children were murdered by the Guardia over the
course of the year. Marvin began to discuss with his family the possibility
of leaving El Salvador. His father and mother were estranged, but each
lived in a small apartment in the DC neighborhood of Mount Pleasant.
Marvin's father frequently returned to Intipucá during the winter to look
after the large farm. If Marvin were to leave, it was agreed that he would
live with his mother in DC.

As the Guard increased its threats and daily forms of terror in the eastern part of El Salvador, and people like Marvin contemplated leaving,
some residents took advantage of the climate of shifting alliances to strike
back against perceived wrongs in the countryside. Occasionally someone

could harness the violence of the Guard by fingering another person. The only recourse was to attempt to bribe the guards or to flee the area and live clandestinely elsewhere in El Salvador or outside of the country. Adjacent to the mayor's office, the Guard used a small room for interrogation and, according to people who spoke about the period in 1996, for torture.

During this time in the popular seaside town of Cuco, the son of the man who had purchased the old diesel generator and owned huge tracts of land in the region, was threatened several times by armed workers on the farm. Explaining these events years later, he employed the category "guerrillas," although officially war had not broken out in the 1970s. It is more likely that they were people who were retaliating for the abuses they had suffered while working on his father's farm and were not part of the People's Revolutionary Army (ERP), which had begun to organize in these rural areas at the time.

One day a group of farm workers on the hacienda in Cuco emerged from the underbrush along the road and shot at his car as he approached the town. He crashed off the road and as they approached his car, he lay still. As they were upon him and about to shoot him, he shot and killed four of the men with an Uzi machine gun that he had recently acquired.[17]

In 1979 he decided that it was too dangerous to stay in Cuco and made plans to leave for Los Angeles, California. He carefully stored his machine gun with his relatives at the farm and took most of his savings out of the bank in San Miguel. He traveled across Mexico and clandestinely entered the United States. He used his savings to start a small construction company in Hollywood. Out of fear that other Salvadorans from Cuco in the United States might know him, he avoided hiring Salvadorans and employed only Mexicans.[18] Almost twenty years later he returned to visit the farm and invest money in new buildings in the town, planning to build a restaurant and bordello. He had recently met a young woman from another part of El Salvador and they had hastily agreed to marry each other, although he was legally married to several other women in the area. She had arrived that evening with him, ostensibly the first night after their marriage, and he confided to me that she would likely be working in his new restaurant after he returned to the United States later in the month, although she had not been aware of these plans. During this visit he carried his old Uzi machine gun with him in his pick-up truck; he had recently escaped yet another attempt on his life when someone tried to drive him off the road while he was riding his motorcycle. "I'll get them. I know who they are," he said.[19]

The contradictions of the state-led cotton system, the military forces recruited to enforce it, and the displacement of share-croppers who were forced to work in the cotton fields produced more violence in the region. In one instance, a group of cotton-workers attacked a foreman, stuffed his clothing with cotton to give him the appearance of having breasts and a large butt, and then hacked him with their machetes and hung his dead body from a tree by the main road where it remained for several days. Cotton, by displacing small-scale farmers, disrupted a powerful definition of maleness in the countryside. The attackers symbolically inverted the process by feminizing the foreman before murdering him.

Redistributing National Wealth

Throughout El Salvador during the late 1970s, adversarial groups used kidnappings and the threat of death as a way to alter the meaning of people, objects, and their relations, transforming human life into an exchange-value. To kidnap meant that someone's life could be placed on "the market" and a price for its exchange could be determined and demanded by the seller as ransom. The effect of such a transaction was to redistribute wealth in the country among this new configuration of buyers and sellers. Changing the meaning of objects in this market also altered the subjects involved in the transaction. It was an expensive and dangerous time of transactions. Many people, as the ultimate proprietors of themselves, tried to withhold themselves from the market by hiring military protection or leaving the country.

In highly publicized "transactions" on May 14, 1978, Ernesto Sol Meza and Luis Méndez Novoa were kidnapped by one of the armed guerilla factions, the Popular Liberation Front (FPL). Sol Meza was released for $4 million and Méndez Novoa for $100,000. Another faction, the National Resistance (RN) began a systematic campaign three days later, kidnapping a Japanese industrialist, Fugio Matsumoto, and demanding money and the release of several Salvadoran political prisoners. When the government and his family balked, he was executed and his body turned up later in October. Earlier in August, the RN captured a Swedish executive, Schel Bjork, and demanded the publication of their manifesto in international papers. Throughout November and December, the RN kidnapped executives working for Phillips Corporation, two British bankers, and another Japanese businessman. In January 1979, the RN kidnapped Ernesto

Liebes, president of Salvador's largest coffee exporting firm. His family missed the deadline for paying the ransom and he was found dead. During this violent rush to the market of life and money, the RN amassed about $36 million, in a sense appropriating surplus value that had been accumulated at other times and places.[20] Scholars have also suggested that various kidnapping rings were operated by the military as a way to extract wealth from the business elite in El Salvador. Another faction in the market was the elite themselves who tried to buy protection. In one case, former Army captain Mena Sandoval met with a group of people who composed an informal military investigation team funded by the owners of Banco Cuscatlán. In his capacity he learned that some kidnappings were indeed carried out by the Salvadoran military.[21] On a smaller scale, people, sometimes as members of guerilla factions, made direct threats on land-owning elites. In Intipucá, one of the Villatoro brothers was threatened regularly. Since he was friends with an army colonel at the military barracks in La Union, he made arrangements for his family to move to the base for most of the late 1970s and 1980s.

Between 1977 and 1979, there was a massive change in the meaning of human life and property in rural El Salvador. In a sense, various social groups were struggling to fix particular meanings within a complex web of power. One consequence was that people like Jaime, the man in Cuco, the Villatoro brother in Intipucá, and many others removed themselves and loved ones to safer places where their lives could not be forcibly exchanged or destroyed. The massive departure of Salvadorans during this period and the arrival of many of them in the United States were not yet formally documented in El Salvador, but were gradually noticed by US social workers, clergy, and some journalists in the United States. In El Salvador and in the United States, it was the increasing violence and movement toward outright civil war, albeit one presented within the framework of the Cold War as a conflict between communism and democratic capitalism, that made front-page news.

The Coup

As Salvadorans were leaving and violent confrontations in the cities and countryside were increasing, in San Salvador a coalition of civilians and younger military officers overthrew the government of General Romero on October 15, 1979. Using the language of reform and restoration of order, they attempted to capture the diminishing wealth of the nation through the power of the state and to use it in a way that would augment their political power and legitimacy as leaders of El Salvador. On the day of the coup, the junta, dominated by the group of young reformist military officers, released the "Proclamation of the Armed Forces of the Republic of El Salvador, 15 October 1979." In it they listed four points that were argued as justification of their take-over. They concluded this first section with a striking universal claim that "on the basis of the Right of Insurrection that all peoples have when governments fail to uphold the law, we depose the Government of General Carlos Humberto Romero and will immediately form a Revolutionary Junta."

The Proclamation continued with a four-point Emergency Program. The third of these points was called "Adopt Measures Conducive to an Equitable Distribution of National Wealth, Increasing at the same time the Gross National Product" and included five major provisions, two especially that would lead to specific policy changes: "Creating a solid basis for initiating a process of Agrarian Reform; Furnishing greater economic opportunities for the population by means of reforms in finance, the tax system, and foreign trade."

The junta secured $5 million in aid from the Carter administration and began to implement three structural reforms. The Carter money was routed through the Central Reserve Bank, and this allowed the revolutionary junta to begin a process of taking over the control of the major lands and capitals in El Salvador. Wrapped in the language of reform, it was a national power play, akin to the many smaller acts of appropriation of people, money, and land that had been stepped up in the countryside and city.

On December 20, 1979, the Junta passed Decree 75, which called for the nationalization of the coffee export trade through the establishment of the Instituto Nacional del Café (INCAFE), through which the government would manage the export business. The key to the new government monopoly was that it would sell the coffee at the international price in US dollars. However, INCAFE paid the landowners and producers in the domestic currency, at a rate that was one-half to one-fourth of the international price. This skimming off of a portion of coffee wealth appeared in the national records as a foreign-exchange surplus.[22]

On March 6, 1980, the junta issued the Agrarian Reform Decrees 153 and 154, which called for a three-phase government take-over of the largest private lands in the country. The first phase included territories larger than 500 hectares (approximately 1,235 acres). Within the next 24 hours troops occupied these properties around the country and secured them for the government. Among the properties affected by the reform was the large farm outside of Intipucá owned by Rosa, the mother of Sigfredo Chávez and grandmother of Marvin. More formally, it was known as the small cantón of Caulotio in the middle of Rosa's property. With the land reform, the sharecroppers of Caulotio received small plots of land, their houses, as well as some equipment and money to help them organize their newly acquired small farms. In 1996 the people that I spoke with in the town agreed that the agrarian reform was the most important event that changed their lives and they praised the United States as much as the Salvadoran government for it. Years after the reform, most people equated their relative prosperity with the benevolence of foreign countries, especially the United States.

Shortly after Marvin's grandmother lost large portions of her hacienda, the military and conservative factions struck back via a death squad that would link assassinations of people with the social memory of the Matanza by calling themselves the Max Hernández Brigade. Two kinds of killings became powerfully significant in El Salvador: those of students and those of priests, especially Jesuits.

One morning on the road connecting San Miguel with the farm towns to its south, such as Intipucá, Cuco, and Chirilagua, people happened upon a row of murdered students laid across the road. Residents who found them remarked that they were obviously wealthy students from the city, perhaps even San Salvador, judging by their fine clothing and healthy look. The pile of bodies blocked the road that connected the southern coast with San Miguel and ran in front of the San Miguel campus of the National University. Marvin, when he heard of the bodies, knew that it was the method of some combination of the army, the Guard, and the death squads and that it was meant as a message specifically for students on their way to San Miguel. Within the year Marvin left for Washington, DC, flying by plane with a legal visa to visit the United States.

Marvin was the relatively well-educated and skilled child of a major regional land-owning family, but they were not coffee growers or a family connected with the most powerful ones in San Salvador. Marvin had grown up on a farm that specialized in dairy and grain products for selling in a regional market that included the city of San Miguel. Such a farm provided food for internal consumption when the best lands were devoted to export crops in this part of El Salvador. In a sense, with Marvin's flight, coffee money that paid for the death squads and also the portion appropriated by the state was marshaled to attack the basis of large-scale dairy and grain production in the country. In this violent competition of capitals, Rosa lost her grandson, her farm laborers, and a portion of her productive land. In the race for the spoils of the nation, factious capitals were destroying what was left even as a new source of money was on the rise—and not flowing into the pockets of the coffee elite nor those of the state.[23]

Automatically White

When I spoke with Sigfredo in 1996, he showed me the infamous picture of his red Mustang along with many others. The picture of the car, however, sparked a specific line of commentary. Sigfredo immediately began to make stark comparisons among social groups in the pueblo and in DC, gradually creating a hierarchy that placed "whites" and aspiring Salvadorans like himself near the top and "blacks" and rural Salvadoran campesinos (peasant farmers) who lived outside the pueblo near the bottom. He justified part of this static evaluative schema with stories of his experiences with African American coworkers in the DC area and linked these experiences with a contemporary interpretation of the life of his daughter, who had recently graduated from high school in Washington, DC.

During one of his early visits to DC in 1970, Sigfredo worked as a janitor in a Northern Virginia office building. He narrowly escaped a lunchtime assault by black coworkers using hammers and pipes because another worker from Puerto Rico intervened by warning Sigfredo in Spanish and then imploring the four attackers to stop after they had demolished Sigfredo's red Mustang car.

> For that I don't like blacks. I never want to see them. . . . My children are friends with blacks and do not know any whites. My daughter is a best friend with a black, "Aicha." That name makes me crazy. It is really a problem. It makes me ill and gives me a pain in my shoulder here. She says that the whites discriminate against her, but the blacks do not. The whites are better, more educated, more civilized and decent people, I tell her. Blacks are bad people.

In a series of abrupt statements Sigfredo then brought together his family history, migration from Intipucá to DC, and transformations in the pueblo and his notions of racial difference and hierarchy:

> We are not white. We are a mix, Spanish and Indian. You are automatically white. Before the migration we lived from growing corn and rice. Rosa [Sig-

fredo's mother] rented the land to the campesinos. We weren't campesinos; we
lived in the pueblo. There is a big difference. When we [Intipuqueños] went
to DC, we were the intruders. You were the first to make that country, but we
are all human. We respected the whites. They [blacks] have no respect. They
remember slavery and that is why they are sick, are bad.

With the exception of the last sentence that acknowledged the lingering
effects and presence of the past, Sigfredo's comments about Intipucá, his
work experiences in DC, his daughter's friends, and his distinctions among
campesinos, town-dwellers, Salvadorans, blacks, and whites all contributed to the figurative creation of a rigid framework within which there
were distinct grades of civility and morality. Potentially a social group or
entity might be able to move between levels, but the levels themselves
were assumed to be marked and defined by self-evident criteria.[24]

Sigfredo's characterization of people and their supposed natures and
self-contained moralities can be understood by looking more carefully at
events between the late 1960s when Sigfredo moved to DC and throughout the 1970s as more Intipuqueños migrated. Into what kind of world
were relatively skilled managers and commercial capitalists like Sigfredo
thrown, and why did they have such violent interactions with DC's African
American population at that time?

Another L. A.

The growth of US government social service and defense-related programs contributed to a surge in federal employment; the federal civilian
work force of metropolitan Washington, DC, rose from 239,873 in 1960
to 327,364 in 1970. This increase in public employment was accompanied
by even greater expansion in the private sector of the Washington, DC,
economy. This expansion, however, was centered in the suburbs of Maryland and Virginia. Indeed, the growth of the suburbs in the 1960s, from
1.99 million in 1960 to 2.86 million by 1970, includes the uninterrupted
flight of over 140,000 white residents from the city. Throughout the 1960s
the African American population of the District grew steadily; by 1970,
almost three-fourths of Washington, DC, comprised African Americans.
This demographic pattern, combined with the containment of the black
population within the District, was related to deepening unemployment
for downtown African American residents and the persistent shortage of
manual workers in the suburbs.

By the middle 1960s, it was clear that jobs and private investment were moving to the Maryland and Virginia suburbs. The working class neighborhoods of downtown Washington, DC, became increasingly isolated. Late summer and early fall of 1965 also marked a turning point for public uprisings in the district, or at least for media coverage of events. Large-scale confrontations between groups of young people and police occurred at several public locations in the District.

On August 5, 1965, an outdoor carnival held at 1st and K Streets, NW, erupted into a huge free-for-all as cash boxes were looted and police were attacked with rocks and bottles. According to a District policeman, "It was raining rocks. . . . We did the best we could. The minute we got there we realized it would be impossible to make even one arrest without touching off a full-scale riot." Police Lt. Clarence A. Chaney, on special assignment at the 2nd Precinct, described the police objective: "We had to disperse the people. Arrests would have incited them even more." According to one newspaper account the next day, "Police officials said today most of the spectators and carnival workers involved were Negroes and there were no apparent racial causes for the disorder. Police said the trouble followed the failure of a featured vocalist [Jackie Wilson] to appear in a tent musical show featuring girl dancers."[25]

In a later report carried by the *Washington Post*, a slightly different story emerged:

Paul Miller, a private security agent working for Miller Bros. Amusements of Tampa, Florida, said that the trouble began when a concession stand operator caught a youth "trying to steal a teddy bear." Miller said a private policeman from the Universal Detective Agency was followed by an angry crowd as he escorted the youth from the grounds. The private policeman, George Smith of 1408 Harvard St., NW, was struck by a rock as he led the youth to a crowded sidewalk outside the premises. The carnival is located just east of a construction site, which quickly turned into an ammunition dump as scores of youths seized lumber and rocks and turned on the dozen private policemen.[26]

The city eventually closed down the carnival, further eradicating from the city open spaces where protest could occur. Rather than a random outbreak of undirected violence, this event, the *Post* account hinted, was an organized attack against police. Again, various events triggered an outbreak, but the targets of attack ultimately were police and property.

On September 8, 1965, African American residents of the neighborhood of Mount Pleasant, near 14th Street and Park Road, NW, clashed with local police. The series of events was a graphic illustration of how a spontaneous confrontation gradually took on an articulated political meaning, changing the consciousness of those involved. As four youths, aged 12 through 16, played football in a short alleyway off of Park Road, NW, two DC police intervened and attempted to take the four juveniles to the local precinct for questioning. As their ball hit the hood of a parked car, the owner, Ronald Smallwood, came outside to answer police questions. "I told them I was going to go back inside and watch TV," Smallwood said. "I knew those kids. One of them was my brother-in-law. I didn't want to press no charges. They didn't hurt the car anyway."[27]

As Officers Trolia and Spiker were calling for a patrol wagon from the corner call box, a white motorcycle patrolman, Pvt. Walter G. Rourke, joined them. About the same time, Michael Norman, 21, an African American soldier from Andrews Air Force Base, walked up to the police and was pushed back by one of the officers. Norman swung a quick punch and Rourke's nose erupted with blood. Both police jumped on Norman as a crowd gathered. Norman's younger cousin arrived and joined in, trying to free his relative.

According to an account published in the *Washington Post*:

> As the crowd pressed around the fray, a police wagon and cruiser pulled up, and the four juveniles plus Norman were taken away. Norman and Officer Rourke were treated for minor injuries.[28] Norman was subsequently charged with assaulting an officer, as was his juvenile cousin. The crowd subsided and there was a lull as residents along Park Road grumbled among themselves about past incidents. And they grumbled as never before, about the policemen in No. 10.[29]

Six months later, at the assault trial of the airman, Officer Trolia added a detail that the *Post* reporter had evidently missed. As the crowd of 200 to 250 residents "were closing in on us," Trolia recalled, "one woman shouted 'Let's make this another Los Angeles. Let's jump them now!'"[30] The visible echoes of the Watts Rebellion earlier in 1965 clearly permeated the consciousness of some DC residents. There was more than "grumbling" in Washington, DC.

As news of the arrests spread through the neighborhood, people poured into the streets and began to march on the local precinct office. In a report made several days later by Inspector Raymond S. Pyles, commander of DC's "Tactical Division"—informally known as the "Riot Squad"—the crowd dispersed quietly after the police wagon left with the four youths and Airman Norman. Pyles said that the march on the station house that followed about two hours later "was incited by a woman who wandered through the neighborhood calling for a demonstration."[31]

The *Washington Post* account continued:

> Police are silent on what happened in the precinct station. They say they must await results from the official investigation. Negro eyewitnesses, however, say that about 25 persons crowded into the small foyer of the station, while more than 100 milled about outside. This was about 8:30 p.m. Ellen Norman, an aunt of the arrested airman, was extremely upset as she sought information in the foyer, according to Smallwood and other witnesses. [Smallwood was the owner of the car that deflected an errant football pass.] When she attempted to enter an interrogation room where Norman was held, an officer warned her to get back. "She got all excited," Smallwood said. "'I ain't doing nothing. Leave me alone,' she said. Then the cop rushed over at her, twisted her arm and hit her in the stomach." The crowd rushed forward angrily, trying to "pull the cop off the woman," witnesses said. A fire extinguisher was knocked over in the tumult and discharged wildly all over the room.[32]

At this point the executive secretary of the local NAACP chapter, Edward Hailes, along with Inspector Kratochvil of the precinct, calmed the crowd by offering to hear individual complaints. Hailes announced that the NAACP would conduct its own investigation of the case. Over the course of the next year a police investigation followed as well as a grand jury investigation. The incident became highly politicized. The issue of police behavior received regular attention in local papers. Several local business groups entered into the debate surrounding the police department's handling of the situation. Led by John L. C. Sullivan, a coal company executive, the business groups defended the policemen.

What began as a confrontation between four kids playing football and two DC "riot squad" officers began to symbolize larger social fissures in the District. Contestation over the use of public space took on deeply political meanings. The *Washington, DC, Afro American*, in an editorial column, expressed in words what had formed in the minds of residents as they gathered that evening in early September:

> The citizens in some of the ghettos in this city have lost confidence in the fairness of the police. They regard them not as friends, but as sworn enemies whose primary task in life is to make things as miserable for a black man as possible. They know better than to complain. They realize their complaints will fall on

deaf ears. And so, they take the insults and the mistreatment, and deep down inside of them a bitter corrosive hate grows and grows. The white businessmen, who live in comfortable and clean suburbs, may be unaware of this feeling, but it is there, and it will never go away until the police who work in these areas realize they are dealing with human beings, and not with a group of faceless blobs who have no rights, who have no voice.[33]

Lest El Salvador and downtown DC appear as conflict- and crisis-ridden environments compared to the rest of the world, I would like to shift outward to the Northern Virginia suburbs, where other kinds of struggles ensued.

West of Washington, DC

Throughout the 1960s, Gerald T. Halpin, a Virginia native, purchased land from farm owners in Northern Virginia, concentrated especially around the dusty intersection of Routes 7 and 123 in Fairfax County.[34] Halpin had become familiar with the region while working for Atlantic Research Corporation (ARC), a military high-tech firm like Melpar that had moved to the region in the late 1950s to be closer to the national military command, control, and communication center at the Pentagon, and to influence and remain abreast of the Congressional appropriation process.

In 1962, together with Rudolph G. Seeley, another man with experience in the DC area land markets, Halpin formed first the West Group and later the Westgate Corporation.[35] Together they acquired over 600 acres of land on both sides of Route 123 in Fairfax, paying as little as 8 cents per square foot. Seeley was married to a member of the Ulfelder family, operators of a 200-acre farm in the region since 1925. Mixing kin relations with the supposed objectivity of market exchange, the Westgate Corporation acquired the Ulfelder farm and established its headquarters in the 1870-vintage main house on the property.[36] Reflecting on that time, their company name, and the way they had gambled on a predictable future, Halpin explained, "The highway system here was going to be better than anywhere. This was the west entrance to Washington. This was the west gate to Washington!"[37]

In 1969 William T. Leith, Chairman of the Board of Peoples Life Insurance Company in Washington, DC, arranged to merge his company with the much larger Capital Holding Corporation of Louisville, Kentucky.[38]

Together they formed Plicom Investments, and by the next year had assembled $5 million to invest in a new real estate development project organized by Halpin and Seeley.[39] That year Halpin and Seeley had formed Westpark Associates, a general partnership that included all of the old Westgate partners along with Leith's Plicom Investments Inc. Together, they sought to develop 300 acres north of the latest addition to the DC metropolitan highway system, the National Capital Beltway or Interstate 495, built in 1968 as part a project of national security that provided a highway 14 miles from the center of DC, a sufficient radius to escape a nuclear bomb attack. The Westpark property was bounded by route 123 on the east and the new Dulles Airport Access Road on the north.

Westpark Associates drew on sums of money accumulated from the sale of a future to people in DC and Kentucky—the promise of a money payment in case of death from an unpredictable event—now moved back into the present as land and buildings in Northern Virginia. Yet this money was loaned as credit against another kind of future—the conditions that would allow the built space to generate rents or sale prices that would offset and hopefully exceed the costs of developing the land. After the Fairfax County government solicited a master plan for the development of the whole region (known as Tysons Corner), Westgate took part in the transformation of a pool of accumulated Kentucky and DC insurance premiums into physical structures in Northern Virginia.[40]

In order to obtain credit money for the present, the conditions of possibility for the future accumulation of value from people and from land had to be predictable. Those who gambled on the future with money from the future sought assurance and backing by some system of authority. In Northern Virginia such authority lay with the municipal state and its ability to "zone" property for particular kinds of long-term use. The gleaming new office buildings that came to define Northern Virginia later in the 1980s contained a human struggle over determining and fixing both the meaning of the land and the people who would work and live there, not only in the present but in the future as well. Such struggles over zoning, to which we now turn, were dramas of domination and control, rather than smoothly functioning "growth machines" in the gardens of Northern Virginia.

Tilling the Future in Virginia Land

John Tilman Hazel was a Virginia native who returned there after completing law school at Harvard University in 1957.[41] Til, as he was popularly known, founded a law firm in 1966 and gained notoriety that year when he successfully defended a well-known US government official against federal bribery and racketeering charges in connection with the zoning of Fairfax County. He began to specialize in zoning cases, and in 1968 his law firm led the legal battle in Virginia for zoning changes that cleared neighborhoods and communities for the construction of the Beltway. As he transformed the legal meaning of land around the DC perimeter, like Halpin, he bought up parcels adjacent to the future road. In the 1970s he joined with Milton Peterson, a tall man of Swedish descent, and formed the Hazel/Peterson Company.[42]

In 1968, as the Beltway was nearing completion, a Minneapolis-based computer company, Control Data Corporation (CDC), purchased a 53-acre industrial site at the new centrally located intersection of the Beltway, the Dulles Airport access road, Dolly Madison Boulevard, and Lewinsville Road.[43] They attempted to get this potentially valuable piece of land in the area of McLean, Virginia, rezoned for a "campus-like" complex that would house offices for its growing computer business. CDC desired "industrial zoning" that would allow large high-tech corporations to locate production facilities in the region, but they encountered many critics in the nearby residential communities, led by the McLean Citizens Association, who wanted all new industry confined to the other (south) side of the Dulles Airport road. CDC agreed to a number of restrictions on how its site could be developed, but by 1974 they abandoned their original plans in favor of a project calling for more conventional office buildings to be leased to other corporations. In an effort to stretch the range of use for the land, CDC attempted to claim that the restrictions it had originally accepted should no longer apply. The county zoning administrator and the Board of Zoning Appeals upheld the original ruling in favor of the residents and CDC was stuck with a grassy field surrounded by the noise of growing automobile traffic and declining profits.[44] Within the same year, after being fined in connection with a bribery scandal and suffering a stockholder revolt, they placed their piece of Beltway property up for sale.[45]

Hazel/Peterson Co. purchased the property for what at that time was considered a bargain price: $3,750,000. They bought not only the 53-acre CDC site but also two tiny parcels adjacent to it that combined to form less than two acres. Hazel/Peterson immediately applied for industrial zoning for the two small lots, pursuing a clever strategy to get a county recommendation that would support industrial zoning for the two small parcels, but with none of the restrictions on development that were attached to the CDC site. In principle, they would then be able to take the

CDC case to court and argue that, if the restrictions did not apply to the two small parcels, then they should not apply to the larger site. As Hazel well knew, Virginia courts had ruled (in suits brought by Hazel) that adjacent landowners must receive equal treatment.

The county recommended more restrictive industrial zoning than Hazel had sought, but it did not rule that the 17 conditions set on the CDC land should apply to the two acres adjacent to it. The Citizens Association that had objected to Control Data's development plans received the rough message of Hazel's legal triumph: If they continued to balk at the development plans, they might soon share their McLean neighborhood with the smells of a paper mill or an oil refinery should Hazel take them to court and win. The Association also learned that although the county supported the 17 restrictions on the CDC land, it had no clear plan to enforce them. With victor's grace, Til and Milt granted several concessions, among them agreeing to leave an extensive strip of undeveloped land or "greenbelt" around the former CDC property. Entering the 1980s, the two developers were poised to build commercial structures with up to 900,000 square feet of useable and exchangeable space—200,000 more than CDC would have been permitted!

Bypassing Fate with Absolute Faith

During the 1970s, Hazel and Peterson acquired 1,700 acres of land in the central part of Fairfax County.[46] The region was not well connected with roads to the more densely settled regions to the east, but as Peterson had said, "It is partly ego. If you have patient money and you have a vision, you can be ahead of the market."[47] Hazel had put it a different way, but it suggested that one's relationship to the future (if one had "patient money") determined the possibility of transforming land into capital. "You've got to have absolute faith in the future," was Hazel's favorite refrain.[48]

For Hazel, a first step in turning uncontrollable fate into absolute faith in the future involved connecting one's land to other regions so as to alter the conditions of possible use. Since the 1960s and the imagined but never built "outer Beltway" that would extend westward into the state, politicians, developers, and citizens groups had debated the construction of the "Springfield Bypass" that would extend from Route 123 at Fairfax Station to Route 1 at Lockheed Boulevard. In 1975, the plan appeared for the first time as part of the Fairfax County's planning program and was called Fairfax County's "top priority" by major politicians in the region.

During late summer of 1978, the Republican Governor of Virginia, John N. Dalton, who had been a roommate and friend of Hazel's at Harvard University in the 1950s, flew in a helicopter with John F. Herrity, the chair of the Fairfax County Board of supervisors, and Waverly L. Brittle, a state highway official. They traversed the proposed bypass route from the air. Shortly before they left, the Governor gave a press conference where he emphasized that the bypass "is a major priority in the Northern Virginia area."[49]

With the governor publicly joining the bypass boosters, the project gained greater political urgency. By the fall, the County Board, led by Herrity, planned to meet with members of the US Federal Highways Administration to suggest that a federal requirement that multiple studies be developed and considered would dramatically slow the project. Board Supervisor Martha V. Pennino outlined the Board's objective: "We want to make it very clear to the federal government where we think that road should go."[50]

To hasten the arrival of a particular kind of future, Milton Peterson made an unorthodox offer to the Fairfax county government via his attorney, Til Hazel. They offered the municipal government roughly 90 acres for a fraction of what the government had already agreed to pay for another parcel of land just south of Peterson's parcel. The county sought to build a new more expansive government center to replace its tight quarters in Fairfax City and supervisors had budgeted $5.5 million to purchase the "Smith-Carney" tract of land between Lee Highway and I-66. Peterson offered his land for $7,000 an acre, but built into the offer was the provision that the significant savings realized by the government would have to be used to begin construction of the Springfield Bypass.[51]

In December 1978, Pennino introduced a board motion to have a citizens committee study the Peterson and Hazel offer. Within three months they recommended to the County government that the offer be rejected. Michael Horwatt, chair of the citizen's group, said that only 50 acres of the 158-acre site were rated good for the development of the governmental center. A county soil scientist rated the other 108 acres marginal, poor, or unsuitable. On March 23, a majority of Fairfax County supervisors rejected the offer on the basis of this report. Members of the county government who had been pitted against Hazel in previous legal actions were wary of the offer. "I think that it would give the county a bad image if we accepted the land," said one member, who admitted that he was "delighted" that the committee had recommended rejecting the offer. Supervisor Marie B. Travesky, of the Springfield district that included Hazel and

Peterson's land, suggested that not rejecting the offer would have allowed Hazel to force a rezoning of his land around the bypass, likely increasing its value. Hazel tried to present the offer in worth terms as well. "I am talking about $600,000 rather than $5.5 million."[52]

By the spring of 1979, officials at the US Federal Highway Administration announced that they would not fund the construction of the bypass in Virginia. Melvin J. Deale, an assistant division administrator at the FHA's office in Richmond, Virginia, explained, "There's just not that much federal funds for non-interstate projects coming to Virginia."[53] According to Deale, although the state usually would receive about $180 million annually from the FHA, about $130 million had already been allotted to interstate projects under way. The bypass would be classified as intra-state and therefore would be eligible for only limited funds. At most, according to Deale, about $4 million could be obtained for the road each fiscal year. "It would take 20 to 25 years to fund the road federally," he said.[54]

William B. Wrench, a resident of Fairfax and representative from Northern Virginia on the State Highway Commission, the powerful and prestigious body that reviewed and allotted federal funds to Virginia, noted that the 13 counties of Virginia only received $26 million annually in road funds. "We can't build the road with the funds that are available. We will have to find a new mechanism for funding."[55] Wrench coveted his position (he had been appointed by Gov. Dalton) and was a strong supporter of the bypass. He was among those who frequently suggested that Fairfax County could borrow against the future by selling bonds.

Against the bypass proponents was an informal alliance of "citizens groups" from the area near where the bypass would cut between routes 123 and 50. They found representation on the county board from Supervisor Audry Moore, who frequently argued that the bypass would accelerate development in the region and would benefit developers and large landowners rather than residential homeowners and renters. She was frequently critical of Hazel, who at one moment in frustrated response to her shouted, "It's not going to affect my developments one whit."[56]

In June 1979, the Fairfax County Board of Supervisors entertained a complex debate that reflected the growing power struggle around the bypass. With opposition from Audry Moore as well as John F. Herrity, the chair of the Board, the Board passed a resolution that would delay the bypass plans in order to cede authority to the Virginia Department of Highways to make the final decision on the actual alignment of the highway.[57] This would allow the Department to arbitrate between the Board plan and two competing ones offered by the alliance of citizens groups and the Department's consultants.

Although a bureaucratic matter, this shift in authority brought to the surface some of the competing interests behind the highway. Throughout the rest of April and May, a series of public hearings was held and the various factions debated the three proposed plans. Citizens groups took an active role and some argued against all of the plans. They also competed with developers over how to zone most of the property adjacent to the proposed bypass, much of it owned by Hazel and Peterson. This struggle expressed itself discursively at various hearings as competing groups invoked a strangely antiseptic and arcane language to describe what was largely a struggle over not only the physical, but also the moral geography of Northern Virginia. From the perspective of the developers, "zoning" was "the factor that limits the amount of money that can be made from the site." Similarly, "proffers" and "public amenities" were terms interpreted to mean strictures or stipulations holding the developer to particular requirements, such as building a sports field. "Spot zoning" and "zoning variance" would allow developers to selectively skirt broader zoning regulations, while "innovative zoning" was interpreted negatively by developers as "more zoning."[58]

Beltway Banditry[59]

A new kind of contracting firm emerged out of the aerospace firms of the 1950s such as Melpar, specializing in Systems Engineering and Technical Assistance (SETA), high-tech producer services developed specifically for the defense industry and US military. The Washington, DC, metropolitan area, an important command, control, and communication center of the US military and home to the core institutions concerned with the military-industrial complex, would become a national agglomeration of SETA companies.[60] As if to geographically signify this separate arm of the state, such organizations, firms, and institutions were absent from the textbook model of US democracy presented on the National Mall downtown, but instead clustered in the emerging suburbs of Northern Virginia.[61] One of those firms was TRW; another was BDM International.

In 1958, in the Department of Physics at Fordham University, Joseph Braddock completed his PhD dissertation titled "An Experimental Determination of the Spins and Moments of Nickel-58,-60,-61." The following year his colleagues, Bernard Dunn and Daniel McDonald, completed their degrees and together they founded a systems analysis company, taking the first initials of their last names as its name, BDM. They moved to El Paso, Texas, in order to receive their first US government contract to conduct analyses of several new US missile systems at White Sands, New Mexico. "In those days, there was considerable opportunity for small companies with a strong scientific staff to provide a lot of direct help to the military in weapons-system analyses. The McNamara era was just beginning and there was great opportunity for people like us," explained McDonald, the M of BDM.[62]

With a desire to influence and stay abreast of US defense expenditures and procurement, the company moved to McLean, Virginia, in 1973. The company's revenues steadily climbed and the three founders recruited an aggressive new president, Earle Williams, so they could use more time for their research projects. Williams led the company as it tried to expand, but BDM ended the decade of the 1970s $8.3 million in debt to a major US bank.[63]

Another young systems house similar to BDM was called Planning Research Corporation (PRC). They relocated their national headquarters from Los Angeles to an office on K Street, NW, in Washington, DC, in September 1977. Like BDM, the company and its subsidiaries provided a host of planning, management, and information services to US government agencies and to private clients. In an official statement, the company explained, "Washington is a more logical headquarters location. Over 60 percent of the company's domestic revenues are derived from the nine PRC subsidiaries that are based in McLean, Virginia."[64]

While Williams had been granted authority at BDM, in an aggressive and unexpected move at PRC, John M. Toupes took over as president within two months after former president and chairman William K. Hodson had retired. By February 1978, Toupes had consolidated his power and added the titles of chairman and chief executive to his office door.[65] The late 1970s and early 1980s was an exciting moment for the aggressive and outspoken company leaders who hoped for further growth, as the post-Vietnam contraction in US defense expenditure seemed to be abating. BDM desperately sought an investment firm willing to back an initial public offering of its stock to help raise money for expansion and coverage of its debt. While PRC's stock was publicly traded on the New York Stock Exchange and they had secured lucrative government and private contracts, the company suffered a $1.4 million loss.

Conclusion

In the late 1970s, there was a striking disparity in understandings of El Salvador and the United States and their relations. In El Salvador, increased violence eventually gave way to full-scale civil war and a significant increase in migration to the United States. Yet a narrative of emigration as a consequence of the violence was absent in dominant Salvadoran accounts of the period, while a sense of the qualities of the violence was absent in popular accounts of increased Salvadoran migration to US cities.

By tracing developments across both places, especially the ways that downtown gentrification and suburban expansion formed an internally related whole in the DC region and that the restructuring of the cotton economy in El Salvador contributed to Sigfredo's experiences, the chapter has sought to show how "the economic," "the political," and "the cultural" are abstracted and generalized qualities of a larger totality. In the next chapter, we will see how the cotton system and Northern Virginia land speculation morphed into the circuit of service-work and remittances that currently join El Salvador and the United States, Intipucá and DC.

CHAPTER FOUR

The Intrusion of Uncomfortable Wars, *Illegals*, and Remittances

Everybody, when they come to the suburbs, they want the trees and bunnies and birds, okay? And that's why we put two swans out there and feed the damn ducks so all the frigging geese and ducks come around and people say "Gee, I work out in a place where they have paths and running tracks, ponds, birds. Do you have a running track where you work?" . . . Power to the persons who are making the decisions so that their overall life—real and perceived—is best. — Milton Peterson, 1989

Actualism is the reduction of the necessary and possible, equally constitutative of the domain of the real, to the actual. — Roy Bhaskar, 1994

This chapter is about the fitful emergence of the three categories mentioned in the title, "uncomfortable wars," "illegals," and "remittances," and how they surreptitiously contained a more complex and broader history that helped to bring them into being and determined the manner of their existence. More concretely, the chapter is about the decade of the 1980s when the cotton and coffee export system in El Salvador collapsed amidst more than a decade of civil war and a fundamentally new relationship emerged as direct US government aid and the millions of dollars sent home by Salvadorans living and working in the United States became the dominant source of national wealth.

Rhetorically throughout the twentieth century, the "Golden Grain" of coffee signaled a national future of splendor and wealth in El Salvador. Cotton, like "fields of snow" that promised "to go on forever," similarly appeared to auger a weighty quality of progress. In the 1980s, such phrases tied to primary agricultural crops gave way to new concepts in El Salvador: Terrorists and communists threatened the nation; a popular front and socialist revolution promised to lead the nation into a new future. The US military leadership described the Salvadoran conflict as an "uncomfortable war"—a new kind of conflict that would threaten the US nation into the future—and such a definition justified direct US intervention and expenditure. *Illegal*, a term already in wide use in the United States, was adopted tactically by the Salvadoran government to refer to its citizens who migrated and worked clandestinely without official documents in the United States. "Remittances" became the technical policy term used in both countries to refer to the money sent through a variety of channels from Salvadorans in the United States to friends and family in El Salvador.

At the end of the 1980s, Milton Peterson, the developer whom we encountered in chapter 3, described the design of his Fair Lakes residential and office park in Fairfax County, Virginia, just west of Washington, DC. He at once glorifies and mocks formal appearance—the actual—and those who are mindful of it, ending a long interview with *Washington Post* journalist Joel Garreau by using a curious sentence that suggests two different categories, the real and the perceived, although the precise quality of their relationship is not completely clear.

Roy Bhaskar's short definition, in spite of its apparent complexity, helps to clarify Peterson's remark by highlighting that the two categories are not as interchangeable as Peterson's use seems to imply. According to Bhaskar's definition, "actualism" involves pulling a specific social form out of and divorcing it from its many determining conditions, the domain of the real. This notion of the real includes "conditions of necessity," such as a law-like physical or material tendency. For example, if a material object of a particular mass and density is propelled at sufficient speed so as to collide with another object of lesser mass and density, it will penetrate and break down this object. A high-caliber metal bullet fired at close range will at least chip, if not break through, a cinder-block and mortar wall. At sea-level on earth, all other things being constant, the fracturing of the concrete is a "necessity." Bhaskar's domain of the real also contains "conditions of possibility," a short-hand manner of saying everything else that did, does, or could play a direct or contingent role.

To the extent that the actual may be humanly sensed, it is close to Peterson's category of "the perceived." As long as connections between "the actual" or (more narrowly) "the perceived" and their conditions of possibility are mystified and invisible, then ongoing dynamic processes and the mechanisms that animate them risk becoming reduced to static things.

A concrete wall will bear the actual scars of gunfire long after the events that yielded them have given way to other conditions. In a similar squeezing manner, Peterson took part in, but cannot be reduced to being the sole agent of, transforming land into a form of capital with his "frigging geese" and "damn ducks." These animals helped to turn space and time into a place with its own quality of tense, literally an "event-full" thing to be rented and sold.[1]

The chapter begins by returning to Marvin, his hurried exodus to DC, and his understanding of the growing civil war and US involvement in El Salvador. The focus is on his attraction to a person or thing that has the capacity to appear as a forceful agent and leader of change in particular contexts. The chapter explores how the US state under President Reagan was able to appear as such a powerful historical actor in El Salvador and in the United States. The goal here is to interrogate this capacity and examine some of the less visible conditions that helped to yield it, especially changes in the meaning of the US dollar that extended throughout the hemisphere and beyond. The chapter suggests that as in the time of coffee and cotton, complex transnational interactions deeply conditioned life for Salvadorans like Marvin and other people living in Intipucá. In spite of the circuitous web of people, money, and products that has enveloped the hemisphere, intertwining El Salvador and the United States, Intipucá and DC, as part of a structured twentieth-century whole, this "circuit" or social field remained a differentiated and uneven realm, shot through with crisis. However, by the 1990s, "uncomfortable war" gave way to "electoral democracy," "illegals" gained amnesty and forms of citizenship, and "remittances" morphed into "family remittances." Coupled with this new and increasingly dominant narrative and rhetorical understanding, the "Intipucá-DC Connection Story" emerges in a particularly abstracted way, the subject of chapters 4–5.

Marvin's Identification with Aspects of the United States

During the late fall of 1980, Sigfredo's son Marvin arrived in Washington, DC, just as Ronald Reagan, also a relative newcomer to the city, was about to assume office as the new US President. On a snowy night Marvin moved into a small apartment with his mother in Mount Pleasant, less than 5 miles north of the White House. Over the ensuing months, like many teenagers in the neighborhood, he attended Woodrow Wilson High

School, traveling on one of DC's public Metro buses each day. At this time he lived only a block away from Hobart Street, where his father later bought a small house and lived part of each year when he was not minding the family farm in Intipucá.

In 1996, four years after the Salvadoran war had ended, Marvin was again living in Intipucá. From this vantage point, he recalled the eight years of the Reagan presidency and his early years in DC:

> I arrived in Washington just as Reagan became President. He was a great president for your country and for my country. I liked him because he didn't let people bother the United States. I remember the attack on the guy in Libya. That was good. In those days [when I was in DC] it was hard for me. I was short and Hispanic. The police called us "illegals." The blacks called us "spicks" and "wetbacks." Every day I was stopped by groups of kids and they took the money I had for the bus and for lunch. Gradually all the Hispanics got together in the school and we would walk together to protect each other. . . . Also, I became a US citizen—just like you! Did you know that?

Marvin used the dominant US term from that time, "*Hispanics*," to characterize himself and retrospectively identified with the force and authority of the Reagan administration. By joining the two statements almost seamlessly he seemed to link challenging aspects of his early life in DC life and their resolution with Reagan's embodiment of the US state's capacity to assert its power and dominate world affairs in the context of the Cold War. By using the term Hispanic, he effaced the highly varied backgrounds of his fellow Spanish-speaking students. With respect to the term *illegal*, he denied its applicability to his life, since he was a US citizen.

At Wilson, Marvin was recognized as a competent student by his teachers. He avidly watched US television programs and steadily increased his reading and speaking ability in English. He especially liked the US magazine *Newsweek* and later the popular cable TV channel called the Nature Channel. During high school and over subsequent years, he closely followed the news as growing violence and US involvement in El Salvador came to dominate the public media in both countries.

In January 1981, the newly formed FMLN launched what it called its "final offensive," a coordinated assault meant in part to help generate a massive social uprising across the country. This was similar to the strategy of the successful Sandinista revolution in Nicaragua. However, in El Salvador the takeover failed to occur. El Salvador splashed across the headlines of US newspapers and magazines. Within two months, Reagan's ambassador to the United Nations, Jeanne Kirkpatrick, spoke to journalists at Marvin's favorite weekly magazine and made the resonant claim that "Central America is the most important place in the world for the US today." According to the four Newsweek writers who jointly authored the essay, "Kirkpatrick insisted that the violence in El Salvador was not caused by social injustice—'a situation that has existed for decades'—but by 'the introduction of arms from the outside.' "[2]

Less than a week before Kirkpatrick had placed El Salvador near the center of the world (a perspective that she may have shared somewhat paradoxically with nationalistic Salvadorans like Marvin—despite his US citizenship), US Secretary of Defense Casper Weinberger had testified before the US Senate Armed Services Committee and attempted to justify the largest peacetime defense budget increase in the history of the Pentagon. *Newsweek* journalists called his proposal "a $222 billion cornucopia of exotic hardware, acronymic readiness programs and fat pay increases, all designed to rescue the nation's defense establishment from inflation and reverse the atrophy of American power abroad."[3]

At this time "Cap" Weinberger's testimony merely outlined a hypothetical wish list, though with several distinct features. Most of the spending would be earmarked for a massive buildup of US conventional forces that Weinberger claimed was needed to counter "Soviet and Soviet-inspired" conflicts around the world, including the growing conflict in El Salvador. Among his many proposals was a system of multiyear contracting that would bolster defense suppliers against the generally boom-or-bust business cycles driven by fluctuating patterns of federal spending. Speaking directly to that sector of the US economy, he urged renewed confidence: "This is a very long-range kind of program," he stressed.[4] When finally approved by the US Congress, the Federal Budget of that year included an increase of $32 billion for defense for 1981 and 1982. This was on top of the $20 billion for defense already added to the budget during the end of the Carter administration.

This expansion in spending and specifically the Reagan administration's interpretation of the growing conflict in El Salvador as a Soviet-inspired uprising that had to be immediately thwarted was inspiring to Marvin and he vigorously supported it. Critics of Reagan's policy argued that the United States risked being dragged into another Vietnam, and Reagan infamously diagnosed those opposed to his interventionist policy as suffering from the "Vietnam Syndrome."[5] This was a kind of timidity and fear of action—the condition of being trapped or constrained—that Marvin had been socialized all his life to detest as the opposite of a virtuous and well-lived life. As Marvin never tired of stressing, "He was a great president for your country and for my country."

The Emergent Allure of the United States

The capacity to marshal great wealth and channel it into the US defense industry and military did not rely primarily on Reagan's greatness or the apparent agentive capacity of Cap Weinberg. They were mere actors, reading from a script as it rolled off a larger historical press—a confluence of events that was orchestrated, nevertheless, in the vicinity of Salvadorans living in DC and to some extent because of their quotidian efforts to work out life in the District.

Several months before Marvin arrived in Mount Pleasant, Paul Volker, the chairman of the US Federal Reserve, who lived less than 20 miles from where Marvin would live, announced that his quasi-state entity no longer would "target" interest rates, but instead would seek to manage the US economy by controlling the circulation of dollars to US banks via an instrument known as the "discount window." This shift meant that "the Fed," as it was known, would control the growth of the money supply by regulating bank reserves and by extension their freedom to make loans, rather than by directly managing interest rates. The effect of this decision was to gradually allow interest rates to climb to unprecedented levels in the early 1980s. Although this rise was devastating for small borrowers, the shift in policy directly favored big lenders and others whose capacity to accumulate wealth was influenced by the combined effects of inflation and interest payments.

In a sense, the US Federal Reserve led a moralizing project that significantly altered future-oriented expectations, beliefs, and practices that involved the US dollar. This quasi-governmental body effectively raised the relative worth of US dollars when they were exchanged for other national currencies or commodities anywhere in the world. Given that, since the early 1970s, US dollars had no other external referent from which they derived their meaning except these transactions as a composite whole, this was a bold attempt to initiate a practical change in the meaning of US money on a global scale.

Two numbers came to stand for the complex interactions of US dollar buyers, sellers, and borrowers around the world: the "nominal" interest rate and the "real" interest rate, which was the posted interest rate minus the rate of inflation. Within this calculus that drew upon a relationship similar to Peterson's distinction between "the perceived and the real," as long as inflation was higher than the nominal interest rate, all holders of interest-bearing capital were in effect losing accumulated wealth over time. Thus, keeping the worth of the US dollar steady, predictable, and relatively high in relation to commodities and other currencies benefited this sector directly.

William Greider, once a journalist for *Rolling Stone* magazine and also an expert on the inner workings of the Fed, explained that

> the fundamental reversal [in how the Fed managed the US economy] was in the advantage between lenders and borrowers of every kind. The debtors, from families buying a home to businesses borrowing for new machinery, had benefited powerfully from rising prices—paying back their old loans in cheapened dollars. Now it was the creditors' turn. Old debts, contracted when inflation was running high and expected to continue, would now be paid back in "hard" dollars—money that not only retained its value but actually increased in purchasing power as prices continued to fall.[6]

This method of reducing inflation, combined with the tax cuts also initiated by the Reagan administration and its allies in the US Congress and with the expanded federal deficit spending, especially in the defense sector, projected a compelling story worldwide in the form of real interest rates—the postinflation profits of loaning money—which dramatically rose in the United States. Signaling belief in this story as it seemed to unfold, foreign capital, especially Canadian, Japanese, and German, poured into the United States. Coupled also with legal changes that allowed more diverse kinds of financial institutions to take advantage of these higher real interest rates and to lend more sources of money across larger regions of the country, the United States became awash in newly mobilized and "hardened" money and the many new kinds of social relations and habits, including moral definitions, that this powerful abstraction generated.

The countless counters, managers, and owners of this money competed to enter into relations of credit where the money would be offered at a fee to a borrower in expectation of future wealth-generating activities. One domain where this occurred was commercial real estate, where developers like Peterson borrowed the new money to pay for the land, labor, materials, and equipment to build high-rise apartments, offices, and shopping malls.

As a social group, developers hoped that through strategic design and placement, their properties would yield rents that would well offset the costs of developing the land, including the interest paid on the initial loans. The promise of future high rents was predicated on attracting tenants whose activities were expanding yet also were tied to particular locations and kinds of production that could not be orchestrated elsewhere.

Stimulated in part by the changing relations among those who trafficked in the two kinds of money described above—rents and interest—the Washington, DC, area became an enormous center of real estate development and giddy speculation during the 1980s. Federal spending in the region tied to the high-tech defense industry helped to transform the sleepy suburbs of Maryland and Virginia into "edge cities" of producer and consumer services. In Maryland, along the I-270 Technology Corridor from Bethesda to Frederick arose a concentration of biomedical research centers, and stretching from National Airport (before it was named after Ronald Reagan) toward Dulles International Airport emerged an array of firms devoted to high-tech military research and service provision.

As significant as the Fed Chairman's utterances were (and seem to remain) in popular understanding, Volker's proscriptions were arrived at through consultation with 11 other member banks of the Fed. For example, at the Richmond Federal Reserve Bank in Virginia, one of his main supporters during the early shift to "monetarism" was Robert P. Black, a conservative man from Kentucky who once said that he had favored "for more than 20 years" the approach of trying to control inflation by controlling the money supply, a view that he acknowledged "puts me fairly strongly in the monetarist camp."[7]

Although their deliberations remained secret, in the late 1970s and early 1980s, the Richmond board was directly influenced not only by Robert Black, but also by representatives of local and regional banks across the state. In addition, the Virginia board decisions were shaped by various corporate interests, including the new concentration of defense companies together with land-owners and property developers, such as Peterson, in Northern Virginia. Politicians and other corporate sectors decried the growing dominance of the banks, defense contractors, and developers in Northern Virginia via the Fed and also through their increasing capacity to influence electoral politics. Their ascendance marked a tenuous shift in power relations that had historically favored Virginia's coal, railroad, and tobacco industries centered in Richmond and Roanoke.[8] This battle among capitals featured a "ground campaign" fought in the suburbs of Washington, DC.

Other Consequences of Changes in State Policy

Supportive of the "hardened" US dollars and the promise of state expenditure in the defense sector, in late March 1981 a consortium of developers and their political and financial backers began a systematic campaign to accelerate the building of a new road that would link otherwise isolated regions of Fairfax County in Northern Virginia. The Fairfax Parkway Coalition included Til Hazel and Milton Peterson, together with Hazel's close friends George W. Johnson, the president of George Mason University, and Earle Williams, the head of BDM International, the large defense contractor in the area, along with other executives and chamber of commerce members in the region. They hired the DCM Group, a public relations firm in Arlington, Virginia, that had worked for conservative Virginia politicians such as Governor John Dalton and Senator John Warner, to promote the bypass as satisfying a community need while paying heed to environmental issues and to downplay their commercial interests in the project. In a statement, a coalition board member, Edward M. Risse, who was also Hazel's main urban planner, said that the bypass would yield only " a very small increase" in the worth of the land, because the present network of roads was already significant.[9] The DCM Group produced a colorful video that featured Milton Peterson explaining how the bypass negotiation grew out of a spirit of cooperation among community and environmental groups and developers.[10]

Behind the propaganda campaign of the DCM Group, the consortium went on the attack. On April 6, 1981, Til Hazel sent a blistering letter to the Virginia State Highway Commissioner Harold C. King, whose body had been granted authority to rule on the final alignment of the road, accusing him of incompetence for not shepherding through the road plan in a more timely manner. Several weeks later Governor Dalton asked Hazel, Wrench, and King to attend a private meeting where he ordered King and other highway officials to comply with Hazel's repeated requests that a final route be chosen after more than five years of study and debate. On June 15, the PR campaign seemed to have had its desired effect and the various citizens groups approved construction on the road. In August 1981, King's highway commission met and Wrench, the Northern Virginia representative, recommended and voted for the final alignment of the road.

At the time, Wrench knew that his recommendation would not only place the road next to property that he owned but also place a cloverleaf intersection partially across the land owned by Hazel and Peterson. Shortly before the vote, he had sent a letter to King, acknowledging the potential conflict of interest regarding his own land, but he did not mention how the alignment would affect Hazel.[11]

On September 17, Wrench's letter became public. With the Virginia gubernatorial election just two months away, J. Marshall Coleman, Virginia Attorney General and Republican candidate for governor (for whom Hazel had served as a campaign finance advisor), returned with great fanfare a $2,000 campaign donation made by Wrench. Democratic politicians, including the competing candidate, Charles "Chuck" Robb, urged a broader investigation into the matter. On September 19, Wrench, as Hazel's sacrificial lamb, resigned from the highway commission, retaining Hazel as his legal counsel in the process. Five days later, the state highway commission reaffirmed its August decision on the road alignment. As the November elections approached, Democratic party politicians and supporters held a series of public hearings on the subject of the bypass, keeping Wrench, Hazel, and their ties to both Dalton and Coleman in the public view. Although Coleman lost the election to Chuck Robb, the road alignment remained fixed in favor of Hazel.

Although firms such as Earle's BDM and PRC (see chapter 3) began the decade of the 1980s in debt, the Reagan military built-up was the lucrative salve that provided the opportunity for sustained and predictable growth. Gradually BDM, PRC, and other firms like them obtained more contracts and their worth as companies climbed—so much that they were eventually bought in aggressive corporate mergers in the early 1990s. BDM annual sales shot upward from $7.7 million in 1972 to $191.4 million by 1984.[12]

The defense money that these firms obtained allowed them to finance expansion of their operations in the DC area, but this flow of money was shaped by patterns of personal interaction. Earle Williams, who led BDM's growth, was a well-known figure in DC and Virginia political circles. According to the president of a small defense contractor in the area:

Earle was involved with everything and by exposure made BDM a name in the community. . . . I've been to his house, and I shook hands with Sen. Warner there. Does that mean that Sen. Warner is going to fix his contracts? No. Of course not. But how can it not help to be rubbing elbows with the [ranking Republican member] of the Armed Services Committee?[13]

Earle Williams frequently rubbed elbows. Warner had used the same PR firm that the Fairfax Parkway Coalition had hired, and Williams had been a member of the Coalition. Williams was also a close friend of Til Hazel, and together they had hosted fundraising events for the Wolf Trap National Park for the Performing Arts in Virginia and served on the Fairfax County Chamber of Commerce. BDM General Counsel James C. Hughes had served as a top campaign aide to the Fairfax County Board of Supervisors chair, John F. Herrity, who had flown in the helicopter with Governor Dalton during the early days of the bypass struggle. These friendships and alliances were reflected in business transactions between developers and defense firms where US military spending helped create the incredibly high rents that surpassed the combined costs of labor, materials, and interest on loans paid by the developers.

In 1981, the firm called PRC moved to a new office complex that had just been developed by Hazel, Peterson, and their partner Duane W. Beckhorn, at Lewinsville Road and Dolly Madison Boulevard in Northern Virginia. To recall a segment of chapter 2, this was the old CDC property that Hazel had acquired the previous year and had successfully rezoned! PRC signed an incredible 15-year, $70-million lease on a new 440,000-square foot X-shaped building in Hazel's new Tyson-McLean Park, a contract that was unprecedented for its size and duration. The building had been designed by DI Design and Development of Toronto, Canada, and built by workers—many of them Salvadoran—employed by Omni Construction Company, a large non-union firm based in Bethesda.[14] Just three years later PRC signed another lease with Tyson-McLean Joint Venture to occupy the Tyson-McLean III building, adjacent to PRC's existing headquarters.[15]

Just after PRC had moved into its new building on Hazel's property, Halpin's West Group Associates announced that construction would begin in March on a 220,000-square-foot corporate headquarters in the West Park Office Complex, that Earle's BDM was planning to lease. This building was designed by Hellmuth, Obata, and Kassabaum, the architects who would later design the headquarters of the large defense firm TRW at Hazel and Peterson's Fairlakes Center as well as the Smithsonian Institution's National Air and Space Museum and the Mobil Oil Company's new headquarters, also in the DC area. "Northern Virginia, and particularly this area of Tysons Corner/McLean, has proved to be one of the fastest growing high-technology centers in the nation," proudly claimed Stanley E. Harrison, executive vice president of BDM International Inc., "and BDM International Inc. is growing along with it."[16]

From Coffee and Cotton to a New Kind of Circuit

In 1981, the Reagan administration responded to the FMLN "final offensive" by commissioning what became known as the Woerner Report, which called for the US military to join with their Salvadoran counterparts to organize a massive project of US aid, armament, and training. Between 1980 and 1984 US military support grew from $5.9 million to $196.6 million. Despite the imposition of limiting conditions by Congress, the direct military aid translated into new hardware and expensive training for Salvadoran forces designed to improve their capacity to "take the fight to the guerilla." According to Cynthia Aronson, a political scientist working in DC at the time, almost 60 percent of US military aid during the decade was not approved by congressional appropriations committees and instead came from presidential discretionary funds. Thus, it was literally the Reagan administration's war in Central America.

In January 1982 the US administration began to stress the singular security threat of political instability in the Caribbean and Central America, distinguishing these regions from the rest of Latin America. Direct economic aid and lower tariffs on exports to the United States were offered to governments in exchange for neoliberal reforms and nascent privatization plans. By July 1982 the Salvadoran government had secured an $87 million loan from the IMF in exchange for a series of reforms, the most significant of which was the creation of a parallel "free" currency exchange market outside of the Central Reserve Bank. This parallel market was dominated by private banks, rather than the state, and would be "free" in the sense that it would fluctuate freely, uncoupled from the 2.5 colones/dollar official rate.

Amidst this gradual usurpation of its monetary authority, the BCR released a new 25-colon note that featured the image of the Cuscatlán Bridge and the more recently completed "Sept. 15 Hydro-electric Dam." This was among the last of a host of state-led development projects initiated since 1948, especially throughout central and eastern El Salvador, meant to facilitate expansion of the cotton and also sugar sectors.

That fall, FMLN forces mounted a major assault across the eastern part of the country, destroying state property, blowing up key bridges, attacking military barracks, and shutting down large cotton and sugar plantations in the lowlands. They swept into towns in several departments across eastern El Salvador as part of a plan to weaken the economic foundations of the Salvadoran state. The high-profile attacks on towns and government barracks were meant to appear as signs of a conventional territory-oriented project of warfare. Less apparent at the time was the more significant objective of shutting down the cotton and sugar production system, especially in the departments of Usulután and San Vicente.

In the middle of the night in November 1983, a column of guerilla soldiers made their way across the corn, watermelon, and cattle-grazing fields on the outskirts of Intipucá, approaching from the southwest. Led by a town resident who had joined them, they left high ground to move down upon the pueblo with the Pacific Ocean only a couple of miles to their south. At this end of the town a small group of the guerilla approached a concrete bunker with several government soldiers stationed inside. They hurled grenades at the bunker and the soldiers fired back. Just as the exchange of gunfire and explosions alerted the town to their arrival, a larger concentration of guerilla forces swept down upon the town from several sides, rapidly making their way to the town hall and central plaza where more government troops were stationed. Quickly a team of FMLN machine gunners set up atop the unfinished second story of a house on the north side of the park across from the town hall. From this vantage they could effectively shoot at vehicles and troops entering the pueblo along its main road and also fire upon the small military garrison next to the town hall. The FMLN occupied the town for three days; some families offered food and shelter to the men and women guerilla soldiers while others cursed their arrival. Many of the wealthiest members of the town had fled in the face of extortion and death threats over the previous years.

After three days, Salvadoran military reinforcements poured into the town and routed the guerilla forces. Like the first assault, this attack terrified most residents, but some ran from their houses to take part in the fighting. In one instance, the younger brother of Roberto, the man who had hurt his nose while looking into the bordello, seized the M-16 rifle of a dead Salvadoran army soldier and fired on a group of fleeing guerilla, killing one of them and gaining notoriety in the town. Some people interpreted his actions as heroic while others were amazed at what they called one more example of his stupidity. Among his friends he was known as

FIGURE 9. Bullet-scarred wall in Intipucá, photographed by author.

"The Puerto Rican." Over a decade later I asked him why he was called this and he replied, "Because I'm so stupid, they say!"[17]

The Salvadoran army fired repeatedly at the machine gun nest on the top of the house, eventually killing the guerilla soldiers who operated it. In the course of the exchange, large pieces of the unfinished concrete block wall of the house were knocked off by the bullets, leaving it pock-marked. Bullets also pierced a large metal pole used to hold a basketball net in the center of town. The construction of the unfinished second floor was being paid for with money saved by the owner and sent by relatives working in the DC area. In a strange moment of meeting, the bullets fired by the Salvadoran army troops were also paid for with US dollars, a transfer of wealth partially arranged in Washington, DC. Two forms of value destroyed each other. Although at the time the connection would be almost imperceptible, the bullet holes lingered like a ghost, pointing to this larger geo-history. Thus the materiality of the hole (the absence of material) lingers into the present reminding potential interpreters of the moment when two kinds of money were joined in Intipucá in a destructive confrontation of opposites although, remarkably, they shared the same ground—US defense expenditures.[18]

In response to the violence of late 1983, many Intipucá families made huge sacrifices to get their children out of the country, especially boys over the age of 15 who risked being forcibly conscripted into the military. Miguel, the man who had picked coffee in the 1940s, sold all of his cows so that his youngest son Manuel could travel to DC. Manuel was a distant cousin of Marvin and the person with whom I played billiards in the late 1980s. Other kids who had been friends of Marvin began to arrive, and there was a quality of reunion in the city, despite the difficult conditions faced by most people. "At that time all the Intipuqueños would get together on the weekend and go to the park to watch the soccer games. We would bring beer and cook meat on the grill. Sometimes the police would come and we would have to run away, but it was always fun to see everyone," recalled Marvin.

In contrast to Marvin who had legal work papers, had just graduated from high school, and was working in a prestigious DC restaurant busing tables, Manuel was obligated to take work as a day laborer on a crew that was periodically contracted by the larger non-union construction firms in the region. Most of this work was concentrated in the suburbs of DC, especially in Northern Virginia. Vans would stop at established points near Mount Pleasant to pick up workers each morning.

Among Salvadorans like Miguel arriving in DC from Intipucá and elsewhere, the non-union Miller & Long and Omni Construction companies were known as relatively well-paying sources of employment. Miguel reflected on his time working for Omni Construction in the early 1980s, after his arrival in DC:

> I worked in concrete, setting up the metal [rebar] and pouring [floors and foundations]. It wasn't as hard as that kind of work in El Salvador, because there were machines. Eventually someone [an Intipuqueño] would get a regular job on a crew and he would recruit others and tell the foreman.[19] Then we could all work together on a job.

Contradictions of the Migrant and Remittance Circuit Become Visible

In response to the FMLN attack across eastern El Salvador, US president Reagan delivered a lengthy speech in December 1983 urging Congress to increase appropriations for the war as well as for the covert contra war in Nicaragua. By early 1984, the US advisors had put together a national strategy for El Salvador with military, political, and social fronts and the Reagan administration had wrested control of US policy from the State Department. A significant feature of the plan called for the political support of a "moderate" candidate to lead the country, José Napoleon Duarte.

US officials urged El Salvador to hold national elections and the CIA spent $2 million to help assure Duarte's victory.[20] On May 20, 1984, Duarte traveled to DC after winning the Salvadoran election. Reagan introduced Duarte and gave a short speech on US policy in Central America.[21] He suggested that if Congress did not approve more aid to Duarte's government and to combat the government of Nicaragua, hordes of people would stream northward into the United States:

> We have an important visitor in Washington, José Napoleon Duarte, the president-elect of El Salvador. The president-elect and I yesterday issued a joint statement in which we agreed on three major objectives for Central America: The strengthening of democratic institutions, the improvement of living standards, and increased levels of US security assistance to defend against violence from both the extreme left and the extreme right. The election of José Napoleon Duarte is the latest chapter in a trend toward democracy throughout Latin America. . . . Our balanced policy can succeed if the Congress provides the resources for all elements of that policy as outlined in the bipartisan recommendations of the Kissinger Commission. But if the Congress offers too little support, it will be worse than doing nothing at all. This excessive communism in Central America poses the threat that 100 million people from Panama to the open border on our south could come under the control of pro-Soviet regimes. We could face a massive exodus of refugees to the United States.

Reagan concluded the press conference by answering a host of questions on domestic and foreign policy with abbreviated vague replies. The threat of migrants streaming over the border was a striking and exaggerated invocation since it was already happening.

During Duarte's short trip to DC, he dined at the Four Seasons Restaurant in the prestigious neighborhood of Georgetown. At that time, Marvin had begun to bus tables at the restaurant with other friends from Intipucá. They all knew of Duarte's election and of his triumphant arrival in DC. On the day of his visit to the restaurant they were told to stay home and not report to work. As Marvin later commented, "I didn't like him, but he was the president of my country. Can you believe that? We weren't allowed to come to work that day!"

Over the following year the US government increased aid and training for the Salvadoran armed forces, and FMLN forces were pushed out of the eastern part of the country. The relative calm allowed Marvin to travel back to Intipucá and visit his grandmother and other family members. In one military sweep during October 1985, a US soldier and some Salvadoran troops under his command were pinned down in Intipucá because of a raid on La Unión. The soldier stayed briefly at Marvin's house and, according to Marvin, was shocked by the English language ability of many people in the town and at the availability of videocassette movies and VCRs in every home.

As the Salvadoran kitchen and wait staff remained away from the restaurant, one of the central contradictions of US-Salvadoran relations in 1984 remained invisible to Duarte, but less so to Marvin and his friends. Indeed, Reagan's speech carried only rhetorical force in their absence from the restaurant. Relations between El Salvador and the United States had transformed faster than the dominant conceptualizations of it; Salvadorans had been streaming northward since the early 1980s, and their remittances rivaled the US government resources that Reagan sought to shift toward El Salvador.

Another indication of this transformation is that on January 1, 1984, FMLN forces destroyed the great Cuscatlán bridge that had appeared on the 25-colon note in 1983. Figuratively, the bridge and the currency that contained its representation were both "built" with coffee and cotton money. The bridge was blown up at the same historical moment when the nation was no longer built on this source of wealth.

Uncomfortable Wars

In 1986 General John R. Galvin, the head of the US Southern Command based in Panama, delivered the annual Kermit Roosevelt Lecture in the United Kingdom. Galvin was a prestigious participant and his address circulated widely as an article and a chapter in an edited book.[22] Galvin embodied the US military's desire to exorcise the ghosts of the Vietnam War defeat by demonstrating that US forces could intervene in a sovereign country and with their proxies win a "small war" that pitted a US-backed national government against a popular urban and rural insurgent movement.

At the time of Galvin's presentation, after six years of military conflict and substantial aid and guidance from the US military and State Department, the government and military forces of El Salvador were locked in a struggle with the armed forces of the FMLN. Neither side appeared able to achieve victory according to their own terms. From the perspective of General Galvin and others who believed that Vietnam had been a defeat of the US military, the stalemate in El Salvador loomed large. Any kind of mutual recognition and negotiated settlement between the adversaries would constitute a failure of the US-led campaign and its associated doctrines of counterinsurgency warfare and nation-building.

In the face of potential defeat, Galvin argued for the complete reformulation of US small war doctrine using a simple rhetorical logic. He began with the premise that the US military habitually viewed potential conflicts as "comfortable wars" that could be won through routine bureaucratic and battlefield preparation, with victory measured in terms of terrain controlled and enemy forces eliminated. By asking a series of questions in four sets, he suggested that historically new "intrusions" threatened the notion of the comfortable war:

- Why did the governments of Haiti and the Philippines collapse so quickly? (Substitute Cuba, Vietnam, Iran, or other countries that have recently undergone rapid political change.)
- Why does the frequency of internal conflict, with its political turmoil, civil disorder, guerilla warfare, and indiscriminate violence continue to grow?
- Why have we seen the rise of terrorism over the last decade? Has the overall level of fanaticism somehow increased?
- How involved are international drug traffickers in the conflicts internal to many Third World states?[23]

Galvin summarized the unspoken answers to each of his questions by declaring that "surrogate war, general violence, subversive activity, multiplication of small wars, widespread training of terrorists—each of these has intruded on our vision of war."[24] According to Galvin, such intrusions should be seen not as peripheral developments but as lying at the center of contemporary warfare. The nature of war itself must be redefined as *uncomfortable* and include typically nonmilitary societal dimensions. He derived three new conditions of such a war:

First, the distinction between soldier and noncombatant has blurred to the point of being unrecognizable. Second, ideological mass indoctrination has become an important part of combat power, particularly (but not exclusively) in lesser developed societies where some common belief system is a dominant part of culture. Third, and closely related, the aspirations of the civilian combatants have exerted an increasingly powerful influence on the military outcome.[25]

Galvin argued for a fundamental reevaluation of the nature of contemporary warfare, announcing to his audience that "we are experiencing something new in warfare, something that requires us to restudy our doctrine, tactics, organization and training."[26] Galvin proposed a deeper analysis that would examine the "structure of the struggle itself" or what he introduced as "the triangle" that included the government (with its armed forces), the enemy, and the people.[27] He concluded his talk by presenting the case of El Salvador where

> military forces fighting a counterinsurgency threat must . . . use other yardsticks to measure success than the traditional indicator of enemy killed or terrain captured. In El Salvador, for example, the military has come to attach greater importance to the guerrillas remaining than the number . . . killed. The Salvadorans recognize that reducing the size of the guerrilla can often be pursued as effectively in ways other than just killing the insurgents—that is, pursued through actions that cause the guerrillas to desert their cause, return to their homes, or surrender. Though harder to measure than "body counts," other indicators of success have been adopted, such as the frequency of insurgent defections, the availability of volunteer informers, and the willingness of former insurgents to collaborate publicly with the established government.[28]

As the final example in his speech, El Salvador was touted as a case study where victory according to these "other yardsticks"—the new paradigm for uncomfortable wars—might be possible. At the moment when he uttered these words in his speech, the FMLN in El Salvador had effectively pushed Galvin to redefine the terms of engagement and measures of success, a powerful though unacknowledged hegemonic victory for the rebels.

Galvin's speech marked the beginning of a broad-based reformulation of US military doctrine that occurred in the context of the stalemate in El Salvador.[29] In 1986, the US Army signed a contract with the Management Services division of BDM International for the firm to produce a new analytic model of counterinsurgency warfare. This project was directed by Maxwell G. Manwaring, a member of the US Southern Command's

Small Wars Operations Research Directorate (SWORD) under General Galvin, and Manwaring was employed by BDM at this time. Besides the analytic model, the contract included a large-scale oral history project on the Salvadoran conflict to be undertaken jointly by BDM and the Strategic Studies Institute at the US Army War College in Carlisle Barracks, Pennsylvania.[30]

BDM released its report on counterinsurgency doctrine, "A Model for the Analysis of Insurgencies," on February 4, 1988, the same day that the US Southern Command made public a 33-page strategic assessment of the situation in El Salvador based on the BDM report and the data from the larger oral history research project conducted during 1986–87. That same year some of the oral history materials were published in a collection called *El Salvador at War: An Oral History of Conflict from the 1979 Insurrection to the Present*, edited by Manwaring and Courtney Prisk, a senior analyst working at the international consulting firm Booz Allen Hamilton.[31] The three publications were an effective operationalizing of General Galvin's call for a new paradigm of counterinsurgency since together they implied that the meaning of a term like Galvin's *uncomfortable wars* would be defined correctly through the scientific procedures necessary to measure and determine it.

The BDM report was developed alongside the oral history research during 1986–87, and well before the report was made public it formed part of the Spanish- and English-language briefing sessions conducted by the US Southern Command in Panama.[32] The BDM report reiterated Galvin's argument about the new kind of systemic threats that constituted uncomfortable wars, and highlighted the social and psychological dimensions of establishing governmental legitimacy. The report suggested that the new threat required "a strong coherent conceptual framework or a set of principles from which doctrine, strategy, and tactics might flow."[33] The report yielded this framework through a six-step method, and from this it suggested seven leading principles for the conduct of counterinsurgency wars.

The study began by deriving analytical commonalities from previous counterinsurgency campaigns, drawing upon published literature and consultations with military and civilian officials who had experience in combating popular struggles in Indonesia (1945–49), Malaya (1948–60), Algeria (1954–62), Mozambique (1964–74), and 39 other conflicts in Africa, Asia, the Middle East, and Latin America. From these interviews Manwaring suggested 72 variables that influenced the outcome of the conflicts. The researchers then circulated a questionnaire using a 4-point scale to a wider selection of civilian and military officials and scholars who knew of or had experienced the conflicts. Besides ranking the variables for each conflict, members of the sample were asked to rate each insurgency as a "win" or a "loss." For example, *General de Division* J. Salavan of the French Army considered Algeria to be a "loss."

The BDM researchers chose six models of counterinsurgency warfare to test using their new data, including two US Southern Command approaches, an approach developed by the US Army War College Strategic Studies Institute, a CIA model, an approach credited to Sir Robert Thompson, and a model developed by SWORD. The researchers identified a specific series of activities, dimensions, and conditions associated with each theoretical model and then associated them with the empirical variables taken from the questionnaire. Using factor analysis, the researchers abstracted from each set of variables the set's first "component of a principle" in order to obtain a single composite variable for each theoretical dimension in each model. Using these factor score coefficients, the researchers undertook a multivariate probit analysis. Probit analysis is meant to yield maximum likelihood estimates of the coefficients associated with the predictor variables—the probit coefficient.

The technical language hides a simple transformation in the authority of positivist social science: the researchers derived a numerical (cardinal) value for an abstract quality, transforming the immeasurable into the measurable. The probit coefficients associated with each abstract dimension or activity then allowed judgments regarding the relative importance of each dimension in predicting the outcome of a given case. In a footnote, the researchers acknowledge the limits of such analysis by likening it to the difficulty of measuring the *probability* of life or death among experimental animals when actually all that can be measured is whether they actually live or die.

The researchers tested each of the six models using the probit coefficient to establish goodness of fit, the percentage of cases that the model classified correctly as win or loss. According to their results, the SWORD model faired best by predicting 88.3 percent of the cases correctly, misjudging five conflicts (in Eritrea, Cyprus, Oman, Togoland, and Aden). From the relative predictive accuracy of the SWORD model, the report suggested seven leading principles for approaching future uncomfortable wars: (1) military force should not be applied *ad hoc*, (2) support for incumbent government should be consistent, (3) the primary struggle is over governmental legitimacy, (4) insurgents should be separated from their sanctuaries, (5) intelligence and psychological operations should be effectively used, (6) incumbent government should support qualified military, and (7) there must be a unity of command.

The principles suggest that "multiple wars" are to be fought and that for each of the seven "fronts," the primary threats must be evaluated in terms of the fundamental nature of the conflict. The wide scope of these multiple fronts suggests not only that all actions contain significant meaning, but also that counterinsurgency war is both the constant preparation for such a material-symbolic war and the conduct of all-out war at the same time.

Simultaneously the US Army released its "SWORD Paper" on El Salvador that directly referred to the BDM model and substantiated its seven dimensions with evidence from the oral history project.[34] The El Salvador report described a combination of strategic and operational threats and suggested that given the current strategy and tactics of both sides, the war would continue in the form of a stalemate as the FMLN slowly attempted to build its moral right to govern and the Salvadoran military held tactical superiority within the country. The report suggested five dimensions of the conflict to be fought simultaneously: the military dimension, legitimacy, unity of effort, external support for government, and limiting external support for insurgents and counter-subversion. Using a simple chart, the paper offered the evaluation that as of early 1988 the US military had achieved success in the first, second, and fourth dimension only.

The report concluded with a series of general recommendations to improve all dimensions or fronts. The overall goal substantiated by the report was for the US military and the Salvadoran government to completely defeat the insurgency and eliminate all possibility that the FMLN and its allied social organizations could establish any grounds for governing or influencing the governance of the country. To this end, the project called for a sustained increase in US spending in the region, including a proposal for a "Mini-Marshall Plan" to build legitimacy for the Salvadoran government.[35]

Illegals and Remittances

In the spring of 1987 while Manwaring and his collaborators were conducting their research on the conflict in El Salvador and US counterinsurgency doctrine, President Duarte sent a confidential letter to Ronald Reagan. The US president received it on April 10, but the letter was leaked to news reporters and on Sunday, April 26, Robert Pear of the *New York Times* published excerpts of the letter in a front page article.[36]

Duarte's letter directly appealed to President Reagan not to deport several thousand Salvadorans who were living and working in the United States without legal permits, visas, or US citizenship. The Immigration Reform and Control Act of 1986 (IRCA) prohibited employers from hiring undocumented workers and made such people liable to deportation, although the law also offered legal status to migrants who could prove that they entered the United States before January 1, 1982, and had lived in the country since then. All Salvadorans who had entered clandestinely after that date were, in the parlance of the INS, *illegals.*

IRCA rewrote circa-1965 US immigration policies that had facilitated large-scale immigration from Asia, Latin America, and the Caribbean. Like military policy that offered a chance to arrive at a future liberated from the memory of Vietnam defeat, the immigration policy change symbolically presented the US state as the entity that would deliver the US nation into a future free from the past immigration of non-European people. The future that IRCA promised was one where a population would be properly regulated and defined as citizens, workers, and employers; sovereignty would be maintained; and territorial boundaries would be protected. In practice, however, IRCA did little to curb human migration and instead forced migrants to enter through more dangerous border regions, to join in a booming economy of forged documents in the United States and sending countries, and to form more clandestine and exploitative productive arrangements with their employers.

Duarte wrote that "some 400,000 to 600,000 Salvadorans have entered the United State illegally since January 1982." In 1986, this was close to 10 percent of the total Salvadoran population. The *Times* writer, Robert Pear, rephrased the letter and selectively quoted Duarte, explaining that El Salvador was experiencing "a severe economic crisis" because of seven years of civil war and an earthquake that left 300,000 Salvadorans without shelter the previous October. Return of Salvadorans "would reduce drastically the amount of money received by poor Salvadoran people in remittances from relatives now working in the United States."

In his letter, Duarte stressed the central role of remittances in the Salvadoran economy. "My government estimates that the total value of remittances is some place between $350 million and $600 million annually, and is thus larger than the United States Government's assistance to El Salvador." At that time the Reagan Administration was providing about $420 million in annual economic and military aid. With this comparison, Duarte suggested that to heed his request would be compatible with the US administration's current support for his government and military. He continued:

> The enormous cost of the war, the destruction the guerillas have caused, the reduction of our sugar export, the loss of the cotton market, and the plummeting of coffee prices all bode ill for the Salvadoran economy in the coming year. To eliminate remittances from the United States would be yet another blow that seems counterproductive to our joint aims of denying Central America to Marxist-Leninist regimes.

Duarte urged Reagan to let Salvadorans stay in the United States under a provision in US law called "Extended Voluntary Departure" (EVD) "until the economic situation has improved." Duarte and his government had privately lobbied the Reagan administration on IRCA, its deportation provision, and Salvadoran remittances. The secret letter was a continuation of these efforts and attempted to skirt the difficult contradiction that many Salvadorans were claiming asylum as political refugees from persecution by a US-supported government.[37] Duarte did not want to risk inflaming the issue even as his government was under pressure from members of the US Congress to reduce levels of government-supported violence against the civilian population. "The improved human rights situation does not justify the granting of political asylum by the United States to Salvadoran illegals," wrote Duarte.[38]

By adopting the term for undocumented migrants, *illegals*, Duarte did not contest directly the US laws that criminalized people for residing and working in the country without legal permission, but instead tried to cast the issue as one about the vital economic health of El Salvador on the basis of the dollars sent back to the country. Throughout the 1980s, the US Congress had debated the plight of Salvadorans in the United States, soliciting expert testimony on the relative levels of political violence in El Salvador and arguing whether to cast them as "economic migrants" or "political refugees."[39] Duarte directly contributed to this debate, but by raising the issue of money alongside people he attempted to sidestep and possibly diffuse the issue of causality that lay at the center of policy debates.

The Duarte letter stimulated long-standing divisions among factions of the US State Department, the Justice Department, and the White House who disagreed on US–El Salvador policy regarding migration and the war. The State Department generally supported Duarte's argument about the centrality of remittances for Salvadoran political and economic stability, while hard-line factions in the Justice Department that were allied with President Reagan wanted no compromise on the provisions of IRCA and also sought complete victory in the Salvadoran war. This division permeated US political culture, pitting an aggressive nationalist faction intent upon erasing the memory of Vietnam, the Iranian hostage crisis, and the image of non-European people coming to the United States to live and work against a more pragmatic developmentalist faction that sought neoliberal reforms and embodied a more internationalist perspective.

Duarte's letter became public at the same time that Salvadoran sociologist and Jesuit priest Segundo Montes published several essays and one book based on research on migration and remittances conducted in El Salvador and the United States.[40] The work yielded estimates higher than Duarte's, but substantiated the new and powerful point that remittances were as important for the Salvadoran economy as dollars from US aid and earned through agricultural exports. In 1988, the US State Department's Bureau for Refugee Programs funded the publication of Montes' research in English through a grant to Georgetown University's Center for Immigration Policy. The small book circulated widely in DC policy circles, and the issue of remittances became prominent in the context of debates about US policy and aid to the Salvadoran government and military. Discursively, the abstraction of remittances became powerful and began to dwarf the concrete experiences of people.[41]

Based on three surveys of representative samples in the United States and El Salvador, Montes' report yielded two quantitative measures and attempted to determine the significance of several other relations. Montes and his collaborator, Juan José García Vasquez, reported that about 1 million Salvadorans resided in the United States and sent home over $1 billion annually. "We find an association between US-bound emigration and the Salvadoran political crisis. Emigration has been greater in the periods and Departments in which violence has been most acute," reported the authors.[42] Montes and his research team attempted to show through their measures that migration was caused by a combination of political and economic variables and that people migrating from rural areas had better education and training than those who remained in the country, suggesting that it was a "middle class" migration and that this was a loss of valuable labor power to El Salvador.

The report concluded with conjectures based on two case studies conducted in the small towns of Intipucá and Casítas. In these studies, a group of university students supervised by Montes visited each town and, with permission from the mayor and National Guard forces stationed in the towns, interviewed residents using a short questionnaire. On the basis of the results and of cursory observations made in the town, Montes hypothesized that the rise of remittances in El Salvador fostered a new relationship of dependency: instead of working, rural populations were waiting idly for their dollars from the United States.

Scientific Explanation

At one level, US policy debates about the war in El Salvador and Salvadoran migration to the United States were contradictory, because one denied the sovereignty of a nation and called for active US politicomilitary intervention, whereas the other sought to reinforce the notion of separate polities and populations. Duarte's secret letter and the divisions in US policy that it exposed suggest the stakes of keeping the contradictory domains separate. At another level, however, there is continuity, since the laws and doctrines in both realms were predicated on an active and powerful US state acting within a neo-imperial system.

More narrowly, both Galvin's speech and Duarte's letter complemented and gained evidence and authority from particular scientific studies conducted at the same time. Galvin's speech was part of a US military project to reorganize US counterinsurgency doctrine and practice, a part of which required the creation and propagation of a new analytic model of such conflicts. Duarte and members of his government knew Segundo Montes and were familiar with his research, as were the US government agencies concerned with El Salvador at the time.

In both instances, the studies adhered to the dominant twentieth-century form of science, empiricism, and its embrace by positivism, or "logical positivism" in its most formal sense and "instrumental (or methodological) positivism" as it has developed in the United States. Within the realm of positivism, the studies implicitly followed three principles of deductive reasoning. In both cases, the research attempted to establish invariant principles or laws based upon observing empirical regularities within closed "experimental" situations. Second, the authority of the BDM report and Montes' study was built upon the assumption that law-like claims could be confirmed or falsified simply by their instances. Finally, the studies followed a specific theory of meaning whereby to explain or make sense of something means to deduce it from a set of initial conditions and universal laws. This suggests that if one possesses the knowledge to explain something before it occurs then one can predict it. By extension, a failed prediction falsifies the explanation.

By following the principles of deductivism, the two scientific studies directly contributed to materializing and separating the abstractions so that they became discursively powerful. The specific history of the Salvadoran conflict and US relations to it became an *uncomfortable war*. The lives and experiences of Salvadorans who migrated to the United States and worked under specific conditions were *illegals*. All that facilitated their time used for working in the United States yielded their wages and the portions sent home were *remittances*. As powerfully as these terms echo in their respective discursive realms, they are built upon an unstable and contradictory system of meaning because the universal cannot also be the particular and the empirical, or at least always risks being overthrown by it. Nevertheless, the terms partially and in a highly obscured fashion represent a broad and extremely violent transformation in meaningful relations among specific places, people, and money across El Salvador and the United States.

Conclusion

The low-level services that Salvadorans provided in DC went to the high-level service workers of the region who in turn made up the public and private institutions that produced "services" for clients like BDM and the US military. It might be possible to see that as they worked in DC, Salvadorans were producing services that connected to the services that were being exported to El Salvador as part of the US effort to support the Salvadoran army and government in its civil war. Thus the abstract categories "remittances" and the United States' "uncomfortable war" were connected in concrete ways by money, people, and products.

US federal spending contributed to conditions in Northern Virginia that resulted in rising buildings and ground rents and also yielded specific commodities that could be wielded to affect people's capacity to get their way against the wishes and interests of others. These products comprised a panoply of advanced services and manufactured goods that could project deadly force in particular ways. The ability to alter social conditions through the direct influx of US dollars was also part of the state's capacity to exert force and bolster, weaken, or alter structures of domination and exploitation in particular ways. For the US state in the 1980s, all of these means were dressed in the garb of "national security." In their deployment in Central America and especially El Salvador, what occurred within the unifying logic of national security was a more complicated and contradictory drama where no single actor or agent held a monopoly on the use of violent force nor ever completely got its way against the wishes of others.

Although after 1983 the United States increased aid to the Salvadoran military, which then made notable gains, by 1986 a deep stalemate had formed between opposing forces and had become apparent to many people involved with the conflict. In the face of this, the United States and Salvadoran hardliners called for all-out victory against communism. They took part in producing the uncomfortable wars doctrine as a redefinition of the Vietnam-era counterinsurgency doctrine. But the approach was chasing after a reality that was vanishing. Duarte wrote his letter in desperation to Reagan, drawing upon the Montes research, and BDM took part in revamping US counterinsurgency strategy with a similar urgency. But while US counterinsurgency strategy came into crisis, the understanding of remittances became more deeply established.

PART II

CHAPTER FIVE

The Wealth of Pueblos

This chapter continues the inquiry into the way that Intipucá and Washington, DC, gradually began to stand in certain ways for El Salvador and its changing relations with the United States. While chapters 2–4 explored how this capacity rested on determinants that had emerged in the decades of coffee and cotton production leading to the 1980s war, large-scale migration, and remittance transfers, chapters 5–6 focus more narrowly on events in the late 1980s and early 1990s connected with migration and remittance circulation that specifically propelled Intipucá and DC into the public spotlight. Yet even as Intipucá and DC became better known in both countries during this time, the larger process of remittance circulation, upon which the pueblo's appearance rested, became obscured by the growing discursive glow of the town. The present chapter explores this process, beginning with an account of the town that emerged in 1989 and the way that, like a photograph, it presented a highly partial and limited truth.

Returning to Picture and Article

After the public debate around Duarte's letter to Reagan and widespread circulation of the Montes research, Intipucá became increasingly well known to journalists in the DC area and also throughout El Salvador. As I have examined briefly, on July 18, 1989, the *New York Times* published a short account of Intipucá written by Lindsey Gruson under the heading "Intipucá Journal" and with the title "Emigrants Feather Their Old Nests with Dollars." Immediately below the title was the picture of Marvin astride his motorcycle, taken by Robin Lubbock. The vocabulary and rhetorical logic deployed by Gruson in the short article (about 1,200 words) showed a particular conceptualization of Intipucá, its people, and their relation to DC and the pueblo. In contrast to the *Washington Post* articles that had appeared a decade earlier, the short essay interpreted changes in Intipucá as directly related to the Salvadoran war. Gruson's narrative draws upon dominant understandings of several important categories and concepts, including violence, emigration, work, money, and wealth, and establishes a series of causal relations among them that unfold according to a particular logic: (1) although the first Intipuqueños moved to DC in the late 1960s, wartime violence caused hundreds of people to leave the pueblo and find work in DC where they were able to save money and send it home to those who did not leave, but lived in a more or less unified way in the pueblo; (2) these US dollars have allowed people to purchase a host of consumer items never before available in the pueblo, nor elsewhere in this generally poor agricultural region of El Salvador; (3) as a result, the town appears to be wealthy and heavily influenced by "US culture" as it is borne by the dollars and the commercial items that people purchase; and (4) in turn, this has bred unease among some town residents who fear that the money and products as well as the allure of migrating to DC are changing patterns of Salvadoran life in negative and potentially irreversible ways.

In the title and throughout the essay, the author chooses the word "emigrate" and "emigrant" to suggest the one-way movement away from a particular locale. He also refers to Intipucá metaphorically as the "old nest" that people now "feather" with their US dollars. This choice of words corresponds with the dominant US understanding of migration as a one-way movement from one situation or country (usually understood as undesirable and unworkable, e.g., "the Old Country") to a new one that might promise a kind of upward social and economic mobility or "American Dream." It also suggests another dominant account of migration as a process containing "birds of passage" or people who temporarily live and work abroad, only to return home later with accumulated wealth. As Roger Rouse has noted in his study of Mexican migration to the United States during the 1980s, these two conceptualizations of human movement, the emigrant and the "bird of passage" suggest a "bipolar" understanding of the migration process, where people in their life course are assumed to wholly orient themselves around a single unified place either in the sending or the receiving zone.[1] Such logic is reflected in this article and conforms to the foundational myth of the United States as a sovereign and territorially delimited "nation of immigrants."

According to Gruson, as emigrants find work in "the restaurants of Washington and on its construction sites," they are able to earn a wage and also save money and send a portion of it home on a regular basis, which has in turn altered the conditions of life for many people in the pueblo. According to the article, Maximiliano Arias, a resident of the town and "director of a committee that decides how to spend money raised for the town, estimates that Intipuqueños working in Washington send their families here [in Intipucá] $100,000 a month." The visible record of this transfer of wealth is the appearance of Intipucá as "probably the country's richest town." This definition of wealth, like that formulated by nineteenth-century classical political economists and interrogated by their critics, is the "immense collection of commodities" that fills Intipucá: TVs and sky-high antennas, VCRs, a town radio station, freshly painted concrete houses and church, gardens, and paved roads with 4-inch high curbstones. Intipucá is contrasted with its surrounding region and the apparent absence of these items beyond the pueblo. In a meaningful opening sentence, Gruson claims that Intipucá is "a pastel oasis of plenty with more in common with an exclusive United States suburb than a destitute and devastated land."

If we explore the history of social relations that brought those commodities not only into being, but also into Intipucá so as to yield the appearance of town wealth, we find a story vastly more complex than that suggested by the logic of one-way exchange in the article by Gruson. Indeed, Gruson's opening sentence is doubly meaningful because Intipucá is directly connected to the DC suburbs of Maryland and Virginia in ways that can be seen better by following with considerably more detail the story of Marvin Chávez and his motorcycle.

The Significance of the Motorcycle

At the time of the photograph, Marvin had traveled to Intipucá and shipped his motorcycle via ground transport. When it arrived, he picked it up at the customs office in Cutuco, the same place where the coffee picked by Miguel forty years before had been shipped out to the United States. In the late 1980s in eastern El Salvador Marvin was probably the only person with a high-powered Japanese-built *grand prix* style motorcycle, and he relished the messages about his wealth and status that it sent to all onlookers. In the weeks before Robin arrived in the pueblo and snapped the photograph, Marvin had ridden the bike through the hills to the beach called Cuco, where he was friends with the son and daughter of the main landowner in the area.

Marvin especially enjoyed gunning the motorcycle up and down the beach, forcing chickens, cows, dogs, and the many people who lived along the shore and made their living by fishing and caring for the beach houses of wealthy San Miguel families, to scatter in amazement as he barreled through. After racing up and down the beach he returned to the more concentrated urban part of Cuco comprised of several buildings. "I went out onto the street and did those things that you call 'donuts' in the US. You know, the thing that everyone with a car did in high school. I had always wanted to do that, so I tried it there in Cuco on my motorcycle."

After a while a group of government soldiers surrounded him and ordered him to stop his bike. They had their rifles pointed at him and he obeyed. They took the motorcycle and led him to the National Guard office in the town (a three-story building constructed before the war) where they interrogated him for a while. " 'Where did you get that motorcycle?' they asked me," said Marvin later. " 'Where did you get the money? You have too much money! You come down here and show off your motorcycle—next time you do that we're going to lock you up and take that motorcycle!' " After several hours, the Guard released Marvin and returned his motorcycle to him—after several of the Guardia had taken a turn riding it up and down the beach.

In Intipucá, Marvin was a celebrity. During his visits to the pueblo in the later 1980s, like most people who returned for periods, he brought with him a variety of new consumer items. For Marvin these included expensive clothing, new televisions and VCRs, and several pure-bred dogs. Several times he delivered sports equipment for the local school. And always he had cash that he was willing to spend. One year, with great notoriety, he shipped a 17-foot motorboat with a large outboard engine to Cutuco. On its maiden journey in the Pacific Ocean swells, it took on water that swamped the engine. The craft rapidly sank under Marvin and his friends, who were rescued by nearby fishermen. "Too bad that happened. We were going too fast, I think," Marvin reflected.

In 1982, Marvin graduated from high school and was offered the chance to enlist in the US Army. "On that paper in front of me I had two boxes. One said yes and the other said no. I checked no. Maybe that was a mistake," he said, again looking back on his experiences with some regret.

After graduating high school I began to work in different restaurants. Intipuqueños were everywhere and it was easy to get a job. My cousins owned a restaurant in Adams Morgan, and all our parents and friends who had come up from Intipucá worked in restaurants. One guy would get a job and then help the rest of us to work there. The money was okay and it was fun. The only problem was going home at night. We were always afraid that we would get robbed by a black in the neighborhood.

When I spoke with Marvin in 1996 about the motorcycle, the boat, and other items and activities, he frequently recalled aspects of his life during the 1980s with a sense of having made significant errors in judgment that began at a particular moment. "It all happened when I met Billy," Marvin once sighed.

"Billy" was the child of wealthy parents and lived in the area called Potomac in the state of Maryland. It was a popular and affluent neighborhood constructed after World War II and known for its substantial tax base and excellent public schools. The Salvadoran government owned a house in Potomac to provide a home for the ambassador and his family during their residency in DC.

Billy's father ran a successful business in the area, and his mother was part owner of a large high-rise office building on Connecticut Avenue in the District. Underneath the building was a commercial parking garage operated by a private family-owned company that maintained garages and lots throughout the DC area. In the years after high school, Marvin had begun to work for the company, eventually becoming a manager. Among his responsibilities was to close the garage late at night on the weekends. One Friday night he noticed on his closed-circuit video security camera that there was a BMW brand car that remained parked in the lot, but that he had no record of the driver purchasing a parking ticket. "I could zoom the camera to three different levels of magnification and see people inside," Marvin later explained.

After noting the car and its occupants several weekends in a row, Marvin cautiously walked down to the level where it was parked while his friend the security guard watched on the camera. As he approached the car, he saw two young women in the car together with a young man. Marvin knocked on the rolled up window and the young people looked at him with great surprise. The young man in the driver's seat quickly jumped out and ran around the car to confront Marvin. "Who are you?!" demanded Marvin as the young man approached him. Speaking very rapidly and with fear, the man explained that he was just parked there to talk and listen to music with two of his friends and that he had access to the building because his mother was part-owner of the building. He seemed especially concerned that Marvin, as an employee of the parking garage, might in some way be able to reach his mother and tell of her son's trespassing. "Please don't tell my mom you saw me here," he pleaded.

"That is not a problem," replied Marvin, who thought that the fellow must be about his age and seemed nice enough, although greatly nervous. Over the following weekends, the BMW would pull in late at night, often filled with people who would remain in the car listening to loud music. They would carry on late into the night drinking beer and wine, as Marvin watched on the camera. After more than a month of this, Marvin ventured down again to visit the car. "These were rich, beautiful white people. I didn't know people like this! I was curious about their life," Marvin said, "so I walked down again and they invited me to stay."

The weekend car crowd began to regularly include Marvin, and one day Billy asked Marvin if he would like to snort some cocaine with them. "I had never done this, ever in my life. I didn't even drink when I was in high school." Billy shared several lines of cocaine with Marvin. "After I tried it I said to myself, this is GOOD! I LIKE this!" Marvin recalled.

After several more cocaine parties in Billy's car at the parking garage, Billy asked Marvin whether he could obtain cocaine for him. "Can you get this stuff? You live with all the Hispanics. You must be able to get it," Marvin remembered him asking. Marvin explained this important exchange to me: "SHIT! I lived in Mount Pleasant, I could get anything! I talked to the people I knew and then I began to sell to Billy. He bought a lot and kept asking for more. I could buy a kilo for $16,000 and I would sell it to Billy for $17,500."

After several months Billy began to invite Marvin to join him at parties in Potomac and gatherings at popular bars like Third Edition and Spy Club. According to Marvin, Billy lived much of the time in what appeared to be his own house in Potomac and frequently threw parties there. The events were extraordinary affairs for Marvin. "Once I met Miss Canada at a party. Her nose was so beautiful when she snorted coke," Marvin reported. Gradually Marvin was accepted into this group and became well known to many of Billy's friends:

> Every time that I would go to the bathroom two guys would follow me and ask me if I would sell them coke. They said that Billy was selling them one kilo for $24,000 dollars. I couldn't believe that. He was making over $6,000 in profit! I confronted Billy and he told me that he was sorry, but that was just how he did business. Gradually I got many of Billy's customers and began to make over $40,000 dollars a week. Can you believe that?!

Marvin and Billy remained friends, and Billy continued to buy quantities of cocaine from Marvin to sell to his acquaintances in the suburbs. He and Marvin fancied themselves as outlaws of sorts. Periodically they would spend the weekend at Billy's house, apparently given to him by his parents. One day they piled Billy's bed full of money, kilos of cocaine, and all of their small arms that they had acquired. They reclined across all these items and placed a camera on an opposite shelf. Years later Marvin showed me the picture, "We were gangsters back then! Just like in the movies."

According to Marvin, however, Billy was becoming increasingly unstable. He would smoke cocaine and then become convinced that his house was being assaulted by troops or attacked by bands of robbers. Billy would climb under his bed and remain there for hours, waiting for the attack, unable to move. Gradually Marvin began to spend less time with Billy, and within several months they were completely estranged. Marvin's share of the distribution business continued to expand. He later heard that Billy had "gone crazy." Apparently after smoking cocaine and hiding under his bed, he emerged with all his firearms and began to shoot wildly in the house. "He destroyed that house from the inside out, just shooting and shooting all afternoon," Marvin explained to me later with amazement. Eventually police arrived. Marvin did not know what happened to Billy after this episode, but he heard from several of Billy's friends that he eventually spent time in a private detoxification center, paid for by his parents, to help him overcome his heavy use of cocaine. "We never really spoke again; he became crazy," said Marvin.

Leisure Services for the Wealthy

Gradually Marvin began to sell ever larger amounts of cocaine directly to several of Billy's wealthiest friends, who in turn passed on his name to others involved in DC's fast-lane suburban coke scene. During the heyday of his lucrative middleman business, transferring cocaine from a Dominican supplier to wealthy Anglo-European children in the suburbs who had large amounts of discretionary income, Marvin was able to live out some of his fantasies as much as they were presented to him as desirable by the example of suburban wealth that he was exposed to at parties and elsewhere. In one instance, a young man introduced his father to Marvin:

> I think that he was a US senator or someone important in the government. He wanted to have some cocaine for a big party so I sold him a kilo. He paid me all

in cash with very small bills. It was just like in those movies where the guy brings a briefcase with the money. We met in his parking lot downtown and he opened the case, just like in those movies.

Nevertheless, Marvin limited his consumption habits. "I always wanted a red sports car. But what do you think the police do when they see a short Hispanic driving an expensive sports car? Forget it. That's why I had to settle for the motorcycle."

Cocaine served as a powerful social lubricant during the 1980s in Washington, DC, as well as in other US cities, and fit well with the pumped-up aggression of corporate take-overs and the rapid dismantling and reselling of companies for profit. Wealthy white suburban residents were a significant part of the DC regional drug trade; 42 percent of people arrested on possession charges between 1985 and 1987 were from outside the District, and a third of these people were white. Among sellers who were arrested, over 20 percent came from outside the District and at least 10 percent of these people were white.[2]

As Marvin's network of buyers grew, he found that he could not keep up with business. He recruited one of his closest friends from Intipucá who also had moved to the area to avoid fighting in the war after 1983. One was the son of one of Marvin's father's closest boyhood friends. He and Marvin had known each other well in Intipucá and they remained close friends in Washington, DC. "He was like a brother," Marvin later recalled.

A central problem for Marvin was that he had growing amounts of cash that he needed to keep safe and available for other transactions. At first he laid out the money flat, under a rug in his small apartment bedroom. Then he asked his friend from Intipucá to look after several boxes of money. Marvin was happy that his friend would do this for him and in time they had built a deep level of trust between them. Marvin also drew upon other friendships and acquaintances from Intipucá to help in the distribution business. One man became a trusted carrier who would transport large quantities to the growing network of suburban buyers. Another fellow, the eldest son of a man who became the mayor of the pueblo in the early 1990s, also became involved as a periodic buyer from Marvin. Marvin assumed that this colleague was using it for his own consumption and possibly selling some on the side as well. Marvin and his closest friend from Intipucá remained at the center of the business and had direct contact with a young man whom I shall call Richard. Richard was originally from the Dominican Republic and was the main supplier to Marvin. According to Marvin, he obtained his cocaine from an unknown source who in turn received it from a member of the so-called cartel of Columbian producers and illicit transshipment organizations that brought the drugs to the United States.

Billy's friends who bought cocaine from Marvin were people whose parents and relatives occupied during the 1980s some of the most powerful positions in the DC regional economy that was growing in part because of the expansion of federal spending in high-tech military technologies, most notably the Strategic Defense Initiative introduced by President Reagan in 1983. During the 1980s most Intipuqueños found work in the expanding service sector tied to these expenditures. Marvin worked as a commercial middleman, selling a popular and illicit good that was used, in this case, together with other leisure and recreational activities of wealthy young adults. It was a risky job since it involved transferring large amounts of money on a regular basis to relative strangers in exchange for an expensive commodity. All of these transactions were conducted under hurried and insecure conditions since there was no central authority that wielded the power to enforce the terms of the exchange, especially the property rights that undergirded them.

Inside the Motorcycle

Cocaine is a fiercely addictive drug. Like alcohol and nicotine and many other chemicals, if it is absorbed rapidly in highly concentrated amounts it can produce potentially deadly physiological changes in the human body. Yet, it is derived from a complex process of agricultural production, processing, and export much like coffee beans and cotton fiber. The cocaine that Marvin was selling to people (such as the winner of the Miss Canada Beauty Pageant) came to him from a single supplier who obtained the cocaine from regional distributors who were connected to the consortia of processors, shippers, and merchants concentrated in Colombia, dominated during the 1980s by a cartel founded in the city of Médellin and run by its infamous "godfather," Pablo Escobar. During the 1980s, between 500 and 700 tons of prepared cocaine were shipped out of Columbia annually.[3]

The merchants of Columbia bought the raw materials in the form of coca paste from processors and shippers in the Santa Cruz and Bení regions of Bolivia, who traded with the proprietors of the many small and medium-sized farms concentrated in the central lowland area of Chaparé. Like remittances for El Salvador, during the second half of the 1980s, the sale of coca paste became for Bolivia the single largest source of foreign exchange, easily outstripping its traditional exports, tin and natural gas. The other source of raw paste for the Colombian processors was Peru, especially growers concentrated in the 150-square-mile Upper Huallaga Valley on the eastern slopes of the Andes Mountains. As in Bolivia, raw coca became Peru's most important export during the 1980s, generating about $1 billion annually or about one-third of the foreign exchange earned from all other exports.[4] In these poppy-growing areas, people supported themselves through a mixture of commercial and subsistence farming, much like people in Intipucá before the migration to DC. Also similar to El Salvador in the later 1980s, the US dollars generated from the new export flooded the financial and commercial sectors and cushioned the effects of IMF-dictated restructuring plans.

Although one could trace such a chain of commodities through its production and consumption backward through time and across space, following out how money and products traveled and transmogrified relationally at each moment, such boundless representation that almost mirrors the reality it proposes to stand for is unnecessary for the purposes of this chapter. Nevertheless, the exercise suggests a structured world that combines different people and experiences, objects and places, in an uneven way. In the small segment considered so far, Billy and his friends dealt and snorted relatively free from police inquiry, and Marvin was their trustworthy middleman who maintained more dangerous commercial relations that were invisible from the parlors of Potomac mansions.

The wealth in the form of money used to buy the cocaine had been accumulated through the highly abstracted buying, selling, and renting of rights to land, money, and shares of future production of other goods and services that the parents of Billy and the parents of his friends were involved with in the DC area. In the form of trust funds, where money appeared to make money, or of generous allowances that yielded the power to buy and sell from a position of power, this wealth was based on past and future accumulation and the basic human capacity to imagine, invent, make, and do things. Much of this harnessed capacity was (and will be, hope the speculators) the low-wage work performed by Salvadorans living alongside Marvin in Mount Pleasant who built the buildings and provided many of the services (such as restaurant dining) that were bought and sold in the booming region. In an indirect and highly abstracted way, Gruson's narrative of remittances from hard work in the United States flowing back to El Salvador as US dollars is correct. But the conditions out of which particular forms of wealth circulate are highly uneven and partially invisible.

Policing One Moment in the Circuit

On April 11, 1989, President George Bush's newly appointed "Drug Czar," William Bennett, spoke at a national press conference and announced that Washington, DC, was to become an exemplary case of the new US "war on drugs." He announced that $80 million would be spent primarily on enforcement activities in the District, featuring the hiring of federal prosecutors, drug agents, and military analysts. Bennett blamed the DC city government for its failure to stop the drug trade in the US capital city; representatives of the city government had not been invited to attend the press conference.

The increased enforcement strategy in the District was led by the US Drug Enforcement Agency. They placed undercover agents throughout the city try to infiltrate the distribution businesses. They went after small-time dealers on the street corners, many of whom were juveniles who sold small amounts to local consumers. In Mount Pleasant this took place on Park Road, where buyers would drive along a one-way section and make quick curbside deals. The DEA also attempted to work their way up the chain of supply by threatening or playing apprehended dealers off of one another in an attempt to get them to "snitch."

In 1990, one of Marvin's colleagues in the growing business called to say that he knew of a trusted friend who would be interested in buying a large amount of cocaine. To Marvin this appeared to be a good opportunity, and he sold the fellow a kilo via his colleague. After several deals like this Marvin's colleague called to say that the client wanted to purchase an especially large amount and would like the chance to meet with Marvin's supplier. Marvin consulted with Richard and they agreed to meet Marvin's colleague and the prospective client at the Ramada Inn on Connecticut Avenue in Bethesda. The hotel was located adjacent to the sprawling grounds of the National Institutes of Health's Library of Medicine and across the street from a popular seafood restaurant called O'Donnell's.

Marvin was delayed in traffic and arrived at the hotel fifteen minutes late for the planned meeting. As he headed north on Connecticut Avenue and turned left across traffic into the parking lot, he saw people being escorted out of the building in handcuffs surrounded by DEA agents. Marvin kept driving and quickly returned to Mount Pleasant. "I was freaking out," he explained later. Over the following week, Marvin went to visit his friend Richard in jail and when he arrived he encountered members of his colleague's family from Intipucá who had flown up to visit him and stay with him through the ensuing trial. "They looked at me with such anger like they blamed me for everything," said Marvin. "But that guy [his colleague] was the coke-head and had been stupid, but of course they didn't believe that because he was their son!"

Within a short time Richard was released because the police had insufficient evidence to charge him with a crime. Several months later, Marvin was driving in the area, heading to a party, and was pulled over by an unmarked police vehicle. DEA agents jumped out, questioned him, and searched his car. They found a moderate supply of cocaine, and he was arrested for narcotics possession with intent to distribute. "In jail that night they put a gun to my head and said that they would kill me if I didn't tell who my suppliers were. They also tried to be nice and promise me things if I became a witness for them." The next day Marvin consulted with a lawyer who was able to get him out on bail before his upcoming court hearing. The lawyer spoke with the prosecuting attorney and agents and informed Marvin that the least severe punishment that he could expect would be five years in prison with the possibility of up to forty years. Marvin described the moment when he learned of these terms:

> I said no way, so on the seventh day I woke up, put on a wig and walked out the back door of my apartment. The agents were sitting in a garbage truck watching the building but they didn't recognize me. My friend picked me up and we drove to Wheaton, picked up some things and just drove straight back here to Intipucá!

With Marvin's clandestine return to Intipucá in 1992, his friend was left at the center of the business. This person continued to meet with Richard and attempted to sell cocaine through various channels, but it was an operation in decline. Marvin's partner began to plan his exit from the business and how he would transfer what assets he could back to El Salvador.

From the vantage point of the pueblo in 1996, Marvin recalled his experiences of the "go-go 80s" in Washington, DC. "Cocaine is powerful because it made me high and it gave me money like I had never seen in my life! I never could control [the effects of] that. When I had the chance to join the US Army after high school, I should have taken it. I never would have met Billy." Marvin's life in DC during the 1980s was extremely complex, and he worked it out to the best of his abilities. In his capacity as a cocaine middleman he extracted a fee that allowed him access to people, goods, and services that were otherwise unavailable and that were deemed highly desirable according to his upbringing in Intipucá and Washington, DC. But as much as he tried to make a life for himself, certain things took part in making him, especially the conditions into which he was virtually thrown, beginning at least with the growing violence in El Salvador that obligated him to move to the United States in 1983. He grew up in DC in the midst of a period of expansion. Through chance and his own volition, he came to occupy a unique position as a Salvadoran who had regular contact with wealthy cocaine buyers and users and also with someone who offered a reliable and relatively inexpensive supply for him to purchase. In many ways cocaine made him, as in the US saying, "money makes the man," and Marvin's recollection suggests an inversion of typical assumptions about the relative agency of subjects and objects.

From Cocaine to Coca-Cola

On one of his trips to Intipucá before his final return, Marvin had met a jovial fellow, whom I shall call Jorge, at a small restaurant and bar located at the beach called Icacal at the southernmost edge of Intipucá. Throughout the early 1980s Jorge had worked at the Coca-Cola bottling factory that was located at the western edge of San Salvador. During the war, the factory was attacked several times by FMLN forces, and it became increasingly difficult for large trucks laden with Coca-Cola products to safely travel beyond the capital, lest they be robbed or destroyed by guerilla forces. The executives of the plant effectively subcontracted the transportation of products to conflicted zones by offering especially low wholesale costs to anyone who would deliver products using their own vehicles, assuming all the risks. At that time Jorge was able to obtain a small truck and he cautiously plied the roads between San Salvador and the eastern part of the country, distributing in the region of Intipucá and its nearby beaches.

Jorge was attracted to the daughter of the owners of the beach restaurant, and he liked to visit on his rounds. There, he first met Marvin, and over drinks they made a deal together. Years later Marvin explained the evolution of the arrangement:

> A few months later, after I got back to Washington, I bought an old UPS delivery truck in Rockville [Maryland] for about $10,000. Then I drove it with a friend down through Mexico to Intipucá and sold it to Jorge. In San Miguel they have a place where they strip it down and build racks on the back for cases of soda and beer. Those brown [UPS] ones are good trucks—strong motors, brakes, and suspension—what we need here in El Salvador.

Jorge's business dramatically expanded with the new truck, and he eventually moved to Intipucá, storing crates of drinks in the back yard of his modest house and redistributing them throughout the region with his first truck, which was considerably smaller. Marvin periodically returned to Intipucá to visit, and several times he helped Jorge drive the large load of drinks lashed to the converted UPS truck between San Salvador and Intipucá. Marvin explained the challenges and also one surprise encounter on the trip:

> The war was still going. Because we were Coca-Cola, we always thought that we would be targets for the guerilla. Once when I was driving they stopped us. They were young guys, but an older guy, their commander, had a lot of money and bought our soda from us! Usually when the [Salvadoran] military stopped us they made us give out the soda to the soldiers for free!

Marvin also explained some of the dynamics of Jorge's drink distribution business and his participation in during the 1990s:

> When I moved back here [Intipucá] to care for my grandmother [and avoid serving time in jail for selling cocaine to wealthy suburban users], I became the main driver. It was a good business then and I made a trip almost every day. Now [1996] business is down. We have competition from people like Daniel who are growing watermelons. You take your family to the beach and the kids are thirsty. What will you do, buy them each a soda and yourself a beer or one big watermelon for ten colones? It's not a problem; when the season is over we will go up again.

In the late 1990s Marvin was an accomplished truck driver with the distinguished record of never having been involved in an accident with the soda delivery truck. He was proud of this personal achievement and also of his knowledge of how to drive the large diesel vehicle. "I took some truck driving courses in the United States," he explained, as he deftly slowed the truck by downshifting.

A typical delivery run began in Intipucá at around 4:45 a.m., when Marvin would pick up the truck from Jorge's back yard. Marvin had a helper, whom I shall call Guillermo, who accompanied him on many of the trips. Guillermo's job was to act as an extra set of eyes and ears on the road, as well as to load and unload the cases of bottles. Guillermo came from a small village on the western outskirts of San Salvador, known as an indigenous settlement. Compared to Marvin, he had straighter hair, darker skin, and narrower eyes. Marvin frequently teased him, calling him indio and asking him to speak in "his dialect." Guillermo never showed any concern for the ribbing and on occasion he and I would offer a counter to Marvin, remarking about his shorter height, compared to both Guillermo and myself. Marvin's nickname in the pueblo was "caveman" and Guillermo always used this appellation. Each morning, Jorge would give Marvin some money to cover breakfast and lunch for himself and Guillermo as well as fuel for the truck. Marvin would depart Intipucá around five o'clock in the morning carrying a full-load of empty bottles for return to the plant in San Salvador. By six o'clock he usually passed the intersection called El Delirio, turning onto the Littoral highway where remnants of the old maguey workers' settlement still stood. Now there were many new concrete houses, paid for with money earned in the United States, according to the residents. Families that did not have a connection to the United States tended to live in the older stick huts with galvanized corrugated steel roofing, occasionally supplemented with cardboard and plastic trash bags.

Just past El Delirio and adjacent to the highway was a small house with a gravel field that served as an informal parking lot. Marvin frequently stopped there to eat breakfast. An elderly woman offered scrambled eggs, plátanos, cheese, and tortillas along with fruit drinks and coffee, which she served from her house. We sat at tables next to the gravel lot and discussed the landscape and the upcoming drive. "From here to San Salvador was really dangerous during the war, especially as we get closer to Usulután. One day I saw the guerilla everywhere, attacking the military checkpoints along the highway with mortars and grenades. Then the next day, the military was back in control. We never knew what was going to happen each day," Marvin recalled.

Leaving the breakfast stop and passing through Usulután, the next landmark was the famous Puente de Oro Bridge. It had been destroyed by guerilla forces at the beginning of the conflict and existed as no more than a tangle of metal and concrete in the late 1990s. During the war, the US Army had supplied a temporary bridge that still served as the only way to cross the river at this juncture. Frequently there were bottlenecks as traffic slowed across the bridge, and heavy trucks had to cross one at a time in order to decrease the load on the structure. In 1996, preliminary work began on a new bridge, financed mostly by the Japanese government. Japanese government funds also paid for the reconstruction of the Littoral after the war. From the front seat of Marvin's truck, one could see that the new bridge was progressing slowly. In San Salvador I had heard rumors of corruption and disagreements over the design.[5] Moving on from the bridge, Marvin continued driving across the low-lying plains of south central El Salvador, which once had been dominated by cotton production.

By 8:30 in the morning Marvin arrived at the outskirts of El Salvador, passing one of several congested "Export Processing Zones" before entering the city. These production centers had been established by the Salvadoran government towards the end of the war, through tax breaks, liberalized foreign exchange rules, and tacit guarantees of non-unionized labor. This was directly encouraged by the US State Department in conjunction with US policy changes (the Caribbean Basin Initiative) that gave such factories in the isthmus region duty-free access to the US market. One of these centers, the "San Bartolo" Export Processing Zone, surfaced in a story that Marvin liked to tell in the pueblo.

Shortly after he returned to Intipucá, Marvin had received a birthday gift from his mother, who lived in Maryland and worked in a major hotel downtown, cleaning and preparing rooms for guests. She cared deeply for her son, missed his friendly company, and was sad that he had decided to return to Intipucá. She frequently sent him money when she was able and invited him to visit her whenever possible. Marvin opened the gift and saw that it was a package of underwear. He was especially happy to see that they bore the brand label of "Playboy" and carried the familiar bunny-rabbit motif associated with the infamous magazine and more generally a lifestyle and manner of comportment promoted through the large company's many "entertainment" ventures. "Nobody has underwear like this here in Intipucá," he told me jokingly. "And they are good for me because I'm a playboy," he continued in a jesting way.

As he took out the underwear he saw that they carried not only the Playboy label, but also a tag with the Spanish language phrase *Hecho en El Salvador* (Made in El Salvador). "I couldn't believe it," Marvin laughed, recounting the event. "They came all the way from the United States, but they were made here in El Salvador—by a girl in San Bartolo I bet!" He laughed again loudly. Marvin often recounted the underwear story for different audiences, often generating a slew of jokes that made fun of him and his indirect relationship with the anonymous seamstress in San Bartolo. Occasionally the joking would lead to more serious discussion about recent changes in El Salvador and the decline of commercial agriculture in the region around Intipucá.

After dropping off cases of empty bottles and replacing them with full cases of both Coca-Cola products and the "national" soda and beer brands produced at the facility, Marvin would begin the return trip to Intipucá. By the late afternoon he would park the truck in the yard behind Jorge's house. Guillermo and several other employees unloaded the cases of soda and beer and stacked them on a smaller truck that would make the rounds to Cuco and the other beaches as well as to other nearby pueblos, such as Chirilagua.

Pulling Out Particular Kinds of Entrepreneurs

In January 1995 the neoliberal Salvadoran policy research organization FUSADES published a research paper by noted Salvadoran economist Gabriel Siri and two of his colleagues, Pedro Abelardo Delgado and Vilma Calderon.[6] The report, *Uso Productivo de las Remesas Familiares en El Salvador* (Productive Use of Family Remittances in El Salvador) briefly surveyed the phenomenon of remittance transfers worldwide and compared evidence of the Salvadoran experience with that of countries in southern Europe, especially Portugal.[7] The authors' concern was that Salvadoran remittance flows should be regularized and formalized as a kind of capital transfer, according to the neoclassical definition of the term. In that regard, the authors offered eleven policy recommendations designed to more effectively draw remittances into the Salvadoran financial system, potentially at their source in the United States as savings, which could be held as US dollars rather than converted to colónes in a Salvadoran bank. The development of more widespread use of private banks across Salvadoran society and the setting up of affiliated transfer agencies in the United States coincided with broader policies of financial liberalization supported in El Salvador by the World Bank since the early 1980s. More subtly, the report took part in a slight alteration in the language of money transfers. Throughout the 1980s, remittances were referred to popularly as "help" in El Salvador and in Intipucá as "Washington money." The FUSADES report adopted a new kind of technical term: "family remittances." The deft addition of family to the category employed by economists identified the money, its source, and its purpose in a particular way.

Though FUSADES was a well-funded and powerful policy research organization in El Salvador at the time, supported in part by the US Agency for International Development, other development organizations also formed in the aftermath of the conflict to offer policy options and development strategies for the country. They recruited scholars and activists from El Salvador and abroad, including the United States, obtaining their financial support from a host of European social democratic public and private institutions. Like FUSADES, another private organization, founded in 1991 and known by its acronym FUNDE (Fundación Nacional para el Desarrollo), sponsored several research projects designed to assess the use of remittances in Salvadoran society and to identify more precisely their influence and impact on Salvadoran social life.[8] FUNDE also sought new ways to concentrate and channel these funds. However, they were oriented more toward developing smaller-scale, "grass-roots" projects of cooperative savings and community reinvestment in certain kinds of productive activity than toward encouraging the immediate recirculation of the dollars through the dominant banks in El Salvador. To substantiate this line of argumentation, FUNDE drew upon a variety of research materials, including interviews conducted throughout the eastern part of the country, that were designed to identify successful models and cases of small-scale remittance-led investment and development.[9]

Among the people interviewed in this research was a young man originally from Intipucá who had lived and worked in DC during the 1980s and had returned in 1994 to start several businesses with his saved earnings. He purchased two large buses, named each of them *Caballo de Troya* (Trojan Horse), written in large green letters on the side, and paid drivers to operate them on the established line between San Miguel and La Union, collecting the total fares at the end of each day and paying the drivers and the fare collectors who worked with them. He also purchased portable well-digging equipment and began a lucrative business building wells for new homes under construction throughout the region.

The FUNDE-affiliated researchers interviewed the man and included his story as part of their data set on successful and productive investment of money earned in the United States. The research report argued for policies that would facilitate and encourage such "productive use of remittances." Like the FUSADES report, FUNDE also cautioned against the tendency for remittances to go into "nonproductive" end-use consumption of imported domestic goods, such as refrigerators, TVs, and VCRs.

In 1996, I spoke with this businessman who invited me to share lunch with him and his cousin, who still lived in Intipucá. He repeatedly asked why I was living in the pueblo and seemed unsatisfied with my description of myself as a student and anthropologist interested in writing the history of the town. Eventually he stopped questioning me directly and we began to speak more informally about his own life.

"It is not hard to live like a king here with a little money. Most people here are not experienced with how to run a good business. I have been very successful. You should just get some money and come back here and start a business. You will do very well." By the standards of both the neo-liberal and the alternative development agencies, the fellow appeared as a living example of one who had acquired wealth and investment savvy in the United States and brought both back to El Salvador, contributing to desirable change in the country. Indeed, people from Intipucá had played this role since Sigfredo returned with his picture of the red Ford Mustang convertible.

Also in 1996, someone in Intipucá told me the following story: After Marvin had returned to Intipucá, his "business partner" had made a large final deal in DC and returned to San Miguel to start several business ventures. Among them was the purchase of the two buses. In Intipucá one day in late 1996 as the bus pulled up to take on and let off passengers, a well-known woman in the park muttered out loud with a twinkle in her eye for those who cared to listen, "Ha! Nobody knows what's in a Trojan horse!"

The Problem of Perception

The newspaper article through its picture and text showed not how the conditions of the cocaine trade in DC made Marvin, but how he as the owner of the motorcycle took part in making Intipucá—"feathering the nest," as Gruson called it. In the text, the author vaguely described the restaurants and construction sites of Washington, DC, and urged the reader to infer that such work in DC is yielding the modern goods like a motorcycle that make the town appear wealthy in contrast to other pueblos in the region. The newspaper is a narrative of that which is immediately present to the reader (and the journalist), and it compresses all the conditions that brought Marvin and his motorcycle to Intipucá into an abstract and highly partial account. Into this form, the complex geohistory of Marvin and his motorcycle are squeezed and the model of Intipucá as a wealthy pueblo is constructed. The power of the discursive model of the flow of remittances built upon the Intipucá-DC connection is that it simultaneously draws upon and obscures the concrete experiences of not only Marvin, but also Billy, his friends, their parents, and the DEA agents who arrested Marvin, among many other people.

CHAPTER SIX

Immigrant Entrepreneurship

In the early 1980s, four Intipucá residents, Fernando Leonzo, Eberth Torres, Ursulo Márquez, and Lionel Salinas, founded an informal Banquito (Little Bank)—as its many clients then called it with a quality of affection. They maintained an office in Intipucá and in the nearby city of San Miguel. Two thousand miles northeast of Intipucá, the Banquito operated its busiest office out of a storefront at 1704 R Street, NW, in Washington, DC. Using a fax machine in conjunction with informal modes of bookkeeping and transporting cash, the Banquito owners charged a small fee to send US dollars back to family members remaining in the pueblo or elsewhere in southeast El Salvador. At its offices in El Salvador, the Banquito converted those dollars to Salvadoran colónes at a rate slightly higher than what formal banks and exchange houses charged. At the DC office, the Banquito provided savings accounts and other financial services for Salvadorans in the DC area who did not have legal residency documents and thus could not open an account with an official US bank.

During the autumn of 1990, the Banquito faced a severe cash shortfall as clients in the DC area and in Intipucá withdrew portions of their savings in anticipation of the holidays and, for many, to offset the effects of a growing US recession that had led to a decline in jobs and wages. During most of its short history, the Banquito had existed clandestinely, remaining free of governmental regulation in both countries, especially US reserve requirements necessary for depositors' insurance. The owners had used their clients' deposits to make loans to friends and family members, start several small businesses, and purchase land, houses, buildings, and securities in El Salvador and the DC area. At the same time that many legal DC area banks were going into crisis, failing, or being taken over by larger US banks and holding companies during the regional recession, many of the

Banquito's investments ceased to yield sufficient revenue flows to meet the cash demands of its clients and the debts of the owners. The drop in deposits further threatened the four founders' highly leveraged situation. Pinched between personal losses and a possible run on their bank, and without any depositor insurance or ability to obtain short-term emergency loans, the Banquito founders simply closed their doors, absconding with about $7 million of deposits.

The crash of the Banquito echoed across Intipucá and Washington, DC, lingering in the memory of people in a way that affected the later operations of other banks in the pueblo. Since 1990, little of the stolen money has been recovered; the four founders have avoided serious penalties; and few depositors have received compensation. For almost thirty years, Intipuqueños have referred to the DC area as *la mina de oro* (the gold mine). In El Salvador, Intipucá currently is known as "gringo city" and the "city of dollars." Since the Banquito's collapse, many residents of the pueblo and throughout the DC area caustically refer to Intipucá as *el pueblo de los ladrones* (the town of thieves).

These competing conceptualizations of the town grew out of the contradictions of the remittance and migrant circuit that itself had formed out of the coffee and cotton systems. This chapter traces out aspects of this history and the way that it threw Intipucá into crisis by the early 1990s, threatening its capacity to offer a compelling model of the future for El Salvador. This history also threatened the capacity of Washington, DC, to offer a compelling model of successful Salvadoran migrant life in the United States. In order to understand the emergence of this dual crisis, it is necessary to situate it within the broader rise of the phenomenon of Salvadoran migrant remittances.

Entering the Remittance Circuit

Throughout the 1980s, the Washington, DC, area appeared especially lucrative for lenders of US dollars, and major US banks sought access to the regional money market that was tied to particular kinds of land and labor use in the area. Banks like New York's Citicorp informally lobbied members of the DC government to assist them in finding favorable conditions within the District. In this context, Charlene Drew Jarvis, the Democratic member of the DC City Council representing Ward 4 and chair of the council's Committee on Housing and Economic Development, organized the drafting and passage of a bill to establish the District of Columbia Banking Office. As its sponsor, Jarvis argued that the new office would help establish Washington, DC, as an international financial center. According to the law, the DC Banking Superintendent would have the main responsibility to "promote a climate in which financial institutions will organize to do business in the District and contribute to the economic development of the District through the increased availability of capital and credit." At the center of the bill was the provision that allowed banks from outside the District to acquire local institutions. For the first time in the history of the District (but like all 50 US states), the bill gave the executive branch of the District government jurisdiction over banking in the city. Supporters touted the new bill as a way to bring money into the city's poorer neighborhoods through its requirement that banks make substantial investments in these areas.

Bank regulators from outside of the District criticized the bill for its lack of enforcement provisions and suggested that Jarvis had maintained control of local banking issues before the creation of the office and continued to do so with its inception. This dispute reflected a struggle over the authority to attract and control forms of wealth in the nation's capital. As in El Salvador, a country with limited exports relying on reserves of foreign currency to purchase the goods that circulate domestically, political leaders in DC courted sources of investment to stimulate property development to push up rents while yielding greater tax revenue (the major landowner, the US federal government, as well as numerous nonprofit agencies, paid no taxes to the District government). The central role that Jarvis played reflected the social geography of the city. Ward 4, which she represented, contained significant poorer regions but was also home to many of the wealthiest African American business owners in the city. Historically, DC banks tended to be run by and for the city's white establishment. Under the leadership of Jarvis, the newly arriving banks would be steered toward the African American elite of Ward 4 who, in turn, would gain new access to credit for their commercial endeavors.

Just as big US banks sought access to the DC end of the value circuit under favorable terms, the largest Salvadoran banks began to explore how to move up the trail of remittances to obtain the US dollars earlier in an effort to better control the market of floating exchange rates in El Salvador. One strategy of the large banks was to open transfer offices in the US cities where most Salvadorans lived, so that the bank could obtain dollars in the United States but pay out colónes at their offices in El Salvador, charging a small fee for the transfer. By convincing other institutions that they had a stable long-term stream of remittance dollars, the banks in turn could buy and sell other financial instruments backed by this income.

In 1988, after opening such a transfer office in the New York metropolitan area, executives of Banco Cuscatlán, also among the largest Salvadoran banks, contacted the DC government about setting up a similar transfer office in the city. In a short time, they received a letter granting them permission to begin activities from an office at 18th Street and Columbia Road, NW, in the heart of the Adams Morgan neighborhood of the District, just south of Mount Pleasant where most Salvadorans in the District lived. In a supportive yet ambiguous letter, the DC Banking Office replied to Cuscatlán: "You should know, however, that this office expects to exercise jurisdiction over the types of activities described, once our statutory authority in this area has been clarified. Until that time, [you] need not obtain approval from our office before engaging in business." Thus Banco Cuscatlán opened in Washington, DC, named after the Pipil word for a large indigenous population settlement that became the capital city of El Salvador, San Salvador, after three centuries of colonialism.

Banking on the Banquito

Like Citicorp, Fernando Leonzo, who had moved from Intipucá to the District in 1969, sought to connect in a particular way to the emergent value circuit that the DC and US federal governments had helped to shape. Like the directors at Cuscatlán, he was aware of the growing number of Salvadorans living in the DC area and the thousands of dollars they were sending to southeastern El Salvador each month during the 1980s. With his childhood friends Eberth Torres, Leonel Salinas, and Ursulo Márquez and his sister Elsy, who lived in Intipucá, he organized an informal money transfer and exchange service. Using a fax, they would transfer information about people's "accounts" much like a wire service. In DC, they sold "money orders" that could be sent from the DC office to San Miguel and Intipucá, where a local town "radio" (public address system) would announce the arrival of people's money orders. The order would be converted to Salvadoran colónes at a rate determined by the bank operators that was slightly higher than official bank rates. In practice, they kept a supply of cash at both offices, and the physical transfer of the orders was unnecessary as long as occasionally someone made a trip to transport quantities of dollars from the DC office back to El Salvador.

In 1983, the group incorporated themselves as Latin Investment Corporation (LIC) in Washington, DC, and began to offer saving accounts for their customers in DC, paying them about 3 percent interest on their deposits. After two years as a corporation, they had built up accounts totaling over $400,000, two of which they maintained at Perpetual Savings and Loan and one that they kept as an official business account at Riggs National Bank, both prominent DC lenders. Flush with funds, Leonzo and his associates began to cash US checks at the DC office so that people could buy Banquito money orders. The "bank tellers" also began to pay bills for depositors directly out of their accounts. Depositors could withdraw up to $1,000 in cash at the bank office and, if they requested more money, they were issued a check against the business account at Riggs. Depositors were also given small red books where their daily transactions and accrued interest were recorded.

These interactions among people and objects helped establish a series of meaningful relations of trust out of which relations of credit could be built and extended. Leonzo, as a representative of the group of owners, publicly worked to foster a special connection between Salvadorans in the DC area and himself as an icon of the bank. He frequently referred to himself and the many Salvadorans in DC as all sharing a similar condition in that they came from modest agricultural origins in Oriente, the eastern part of El Salvador, and were obligated to work hard and make sacrifices in DC to support their extended families in both countries. He frequently mentioned to journalists for Spanish- and English-language publications reporting on the growing Salvadoran presence in the city that he had been a farm worker in El Salvador and, after his arrival in DC in the 1970s, he had begun working as a janitor and cook. Although he had obtained legal documents to live and work in the DC area, he identified himself as Salvadoran and stressed this kind of orientation over the less visible relationship that he had with the US state as a naturalized citizen. His situation contrasted with that of other Salvadorans who did not have legal papers and risked apprehension and deportation by the US Immigration and Naturalization Service.

Leonzo and his associates were able to build the image of a uniquely Salvadoran bank out of the notion of a shared Salvadoraness that was defined by ties to an agricultural lifestyle in El Salvador, the migration experience, and low-wage service work in DC. While the Banquito performed useful activities for undocumented Salvadorans, the owners also took advantage of the fact that many Salvadorans could not open a conventional US bank account nor cash their paychecks at the end of the week. With little time or resources to learn English, to have the bank pay their bills and negotiate with city offices seemed like a service.

In return for peoples' trust, dependency, and deposits, the bank made a more incredible offer in the form of paying depositors 3 percent interest on their accounts. From the perspective of the bank, this was the cost of holding and using other peoples' money. To the depositors, their money appeared to make more money as it "sat" in their account. By recording transactions, especially interest earned, in the small books issued to depositors, the bank offered the image of transparency and the opportunity for people to participate in and visually chronicle a sophisticated form of financial capitalism. For many Salvadorans who had never earned interest and were accustomed to working week by week without the possibility of saving in El Salvador or in the United States, the bank seemed to represent a new way of life but with the familiar trappings of Salvadoran nationalism, regionalism, and paternalism.

When the Banquito incorporated itself as LIC, the owners entered into different relations with the DC and US federal governments. This formal title allowed them to open accounts with two major DC banks and thickened the foundation of trust among Salvadorans by suggesting that deposits ultimately lay within a bank that had US government insurance against default. Again, the Banquito owners were attempting to substantiate their relations of belief and credit with depositors by linking themselves with the prestige and authority of the US government. This "safety net" allowed the Banquito to assure depositors of the security of their money while the Banquito earned interest for them as well.

During the late 1980s, the Banquito transferred millions of dollars, and the partners invested their money throughout the San Miguel, Intipucá, and DC area. They founded Tuco y Tico, a propane gas distributorship in the San Miguel area, and purchased property in downtown San Miguel where Ursulo Marquez opened a popular restaurant, El Gran Tejano, and a Burger King franchise. In Washington, DC, Leonzo and his associates purchased commercial real estate and made substantial loans to other business, including a small company called L&L Construction. Leonzo was part owner of the company together with Manuel Leiva, another Intipucá native. Leiva, in turn, made loans to the Intipucá local government where Ursulo's other brother served as a political official. In DC, Leonzo used depositors' money to purchase a 30 percent stake in *El Latino*, the largest Spanish-language publication in DC, making him the majority stockholder. His shares represented ownership of future wealth that could be obtained in relation to this newspaper's circulation in the DC area. All of these investments were transactions oriented toward future production and pursuit of different kinds of capital (diversification). They tied the bank into a system of credit, rent, and wage relations that extended throughout DC and El Salvador. This was facilitated by associating directly with the power and prestige of US banks and the US state, a relationship that also carried with it the possibility of state regulation.

The ties between the Banquito and Riggs National Bank showed up in the form of a great amount of activity in the account—too much for a small corporation—arousing the suspicion of the US Securities and Exchange Commission (SEC), which decided that the Latin Investment Corporation must be offering banking services in the District without being legally chartered. In spite of the enforcement capacity that the SEC and other institutions could potentially bring to bear in the realm of money circulation, the federal and municipal authorities were uncoordinated in their inquiries and actions. Following a brief investigation, the SEC alerted Jarvis's District of Columbia Banking Office.

In August 1987, a member of the DC Office of Comptroller of Currency also notified the DC Banking Office that the Latin Investment Corporation appeared to be an unincorporated bank in the District. In January 1988, the DC Banking Office contacted Leonzo at LIC and requested that he file documents to become legally chartered as a bank operating in the District or face enforcement action, although this was presented in vague terms, much like the letter that had been sent to Cuscatlán. Indeed, at this time the Banking Office struggled to clarify its enforcement role and contacted the DC Corporation Council in this regard. They received a short memorandum stating that neither the Banking Office nor the Council had any jurisdiction over the case.

Even as they began to encounter minimal inquiry by federal agencies and the DC Banking Office, the Banquito owners had become celebrities in Intipucá and Washington, DC. In May 1989, Charles Lane, the Central American correspondent for the weekly magazine *Newsweek*, published a short essay in the popular (and now defunct) DC monthly *Regardie's Magazine*. He described the apparent wealth and prosperity of Intipucá and linked it with the success of the Banquito and especially the entrepreneurial spirit of Leonzo, Torres, Márquez, and the other bank principals. According to the article, the bank had $6 million in capital and the partners grossed about $1.15 million from their combined investments in DC and El Salvador.

Exactly like Gruson's later piece in the *New York Times*, the short article provided a powerful dual representation of the Intipucá-DC circuit that contributed to dominant accounts in both countries. In the DC area, the bank owners seemed like successful entrepreneurs who were realizing a contemporary version of the American dream. In El Salvador they appeared as important agents in a new development model for El Salvador. Their ties to the visible wealth of Intipucá provided a positive image of El Salvador–US relations defined by migration and remittances. Paradoxically, the Banquito's success was predicated on the transgression of national borders through the relatively unregulated movement of people and money, yet it also buttressed tenets of US and Salvadoran nationalist discourse based on the integrity of these very same borders.

"The Banquito Is in Trouble"

On Thursday, November 29, 1990, an important public evaluation of the relations into which the bank was woven circulated among Salvadorans living in Mount Pleasant and Columbia Heights neighborhoods of the District: "The Banquito is in trouble." On the door that day hung a sign explaining that the bank was closed for auditing. By the following week, several hundred Salvadorans in DC gathered outside the office in hope of withdrawing their savings, and the president of Latin Investment, Fernando Leonzo, spoke on WMDO (Radio Mundo), a Spanish-language station in the District. "The current economic situation is critical, but we want to face our obligations," he said. On the program, Leonzo apologized to the depositors and assured them that their money was "safely invested in real estate."[1]

For depositors' money to be invested in real estate meant that it had been exchanged for land and buildings (or shares in them) in the belief that these places would become sites of new productive activity and yield substantial rents for the owners. During the fall of 1989, the great real estate and construction boom in the DC area, in which the Banquito and many other banks and investment groups had participated during the previous decade, came to a crashing halt. Commercial buildings and shopping centers stood empty across Maryland and Virginia. As physical shells with thousands of feet of unrented space, they were the visible representation of a bubble that was in the process of bursting. At this time, the Washington, DC, area became one of the most concentrated regions of bank and

S&L failures in the United States. Among the institutions that collapsed was Perpetual Savings Bank, where the Banquito kept two accounts. Riggs also experienced a rash of "nonperforming loans," which provoked initial fear of a collapse. For Perpetual, federal insurance for depositors with up to $100,000 dollars would shift the losses into the future and spread them across an abstract national space and population. Investors with more substantial sums were usually given preferential treatment and warned well in advance of an actual collapse so that they might shift their accounts to more solvent institutions.

The Banquito had no emergency government insurance if its loans and investments ceased to yield income beyond the costs of their operations, including the cash necessary to service their depositors. With depositors' balance plus interest due, but with rapidly declining income, the owners of the bank risked losing all that had made them the living examples of successful immigrant capitalists and exemplary models of national development in El Salvador. They simply closed the bank and kept what they could.

The shutdown of the Banquito provoked concern among Salvadoran depositors, who almost immediately sought to mobilize the same kind of high-level political authority that the Banquito had used to build its legitimacy. Jorge Guerrero, president of the newly formed Depositors Committee of Latin Investment Corporation, visited the Salvadoran Embassy in Washington, DC, to ask that the Salvadoran government intervene in the matter on behalf of its citizens who resided in DC. According to the ambassador at the time, the Salvadoran Consulate in Washington could gain jurisdiction over the problem only if the US government formally recognized the problem and officially denounced it to the Salvadoran government.

The relative disinterest in the Banquito situation reflected conflict among US and Salvadoran governmental factions and the emergence of Intipucá as an important discursive locus in these conflicts. In 1987, two years before members of the Salvadoran armed forces murdered him, the Salvadoran sociologist and Jesuit priest Segundo Montes had published the pioneering study of Salvadorans living in the United States and sending money home. Among the case studies in the book was one based on research conducted with university students in Intipucá. The Ford Foundation supported some of Montes's research in the United States, and as discussed in chapter 4, a version of the book was published in English supported with funds from the US State Department. In the context of the

Salvadoran war and US involvement at this time, Intipucá and the success story of the bank owners served as an important positive symbol of US relations with El Salvador; it suggested a workable model of future capitalist development in El Salvador that also echoed the American dream of immigrant entrepreneurship in the United States. In spite of the strong criticism of the growing remittance economy as a new form of dependency in the Montes report, the bank and its visible forms of wealth helped contribute to these two powerful narratives.

When high-level government officials neglected to intervene, the pursuit of the depositors' money shifted to the hands of local organizations and law firms that sought to recover a percentage of the money for themselves. Shortly after the collapse, about 1,500 people gathered at La Peña, a community center in the basement of a Catholic church in the Mount Pleasant neighborhood. There, a group of lawyers headed by Brian Leitch of the large DC law firm Arnold & Porter urged people to seek direct negotiations with Leonzo as soon as possible. Outside the building, Richard Deering, another lawyer in competition with Leitch, handed out flyers as the depositors entered and left the building, saying that he would represent them for $75 to $100 plus 15 percent of any recovered money. There was great urgency among all parties to determine the amount of money that was to be recovered. Elaine Grant and the staff of the Wilson Community Center in Northwest DC began to collect the names of all depositors and examine their savings and checking account documents. She estimated that altogether about 2,000 people had lost close to $13 million.

As the number $13 million circulated in discussions, competition over recovering a portion of the money pitted the two lawyers against each other. Enough people had picked up Deering's flyer so that he shortly filed a restraining order on behalf of 300 people in the DC Superior Court, prohibiting Leonzo or anyone on his behalf from gaining access to their accounts at Riggs. Jorge Guerrero (president of the Depositors Committee of LIC) began to regularly consult with the lawyers led by Leitch, and they suggested how he might file charges on behalf of the depositors against Leonzo, forcing him into involuntary bankruptcy and guaranteeing that all depositors would have equal access to any recovered funds.

On Friday, December 14, 1990, the SEC opened a formal investigation and subpoenaed the financial records of LIC and two related businesses. One name frequently appeared in the record books: Manuel Leiva, Leonzo's partner in L&L Construction. Leonzo had made substantial loans to L&L with no record of repayment. A week later more connections became public as the *Washington Post* ran a front-page story on Intipucá, the hometown of Leonzo, his associates, and many of the depositors. On Saturday, December 22, 1990, on the front page of the *Post*, the SEC announced their findings that the owners of LIC had, in fact, used depositors' funds in a host of personal investments without their knowledge. Although the case had not been acknowledged publicly by either the US or Salvadoran governments, in early January 1991 SEC investigators visited El Salvador with the goal of seeking out and freezing company assets. They received assistance from staff at the US embassy under the direction of the US ambassador, William Walker.

On Thursday, March 21, 1991, Leonzo spoke in public for the first time and admitted that he and his associates had "diverted" depositors' funds. On April 6, Leonzo testified in detail at his own bankruptcy hearing, and over the ensuing week more details of the money use become public. The federal judge denied LIC's attempts to reorganize, setting the stage for the sale of all properties owned by the Banquito in the United States. Based on its investigation into the material assets of LIC that could be turned back into liquid form, the SEC estimated that in the best of circumstances, investors would recover only 25 cents for each dollar deposited.

Since fall 1990, depositors had been concerned about the bank closure, yet the sense of doubt and disbelief that accompanied the SEC report was stunning. The most obvious culprits were the bank founders and owners whose relationship of trust had been constructed upon the shared experience of being a Salvadoran migrant in DC with ties to Intipucá and Oriente. "Our own countrymen!" was the incredulous refrain delivered by many Salvadoran depositors. "It was a bank where everyone spoke Spanish," said a man who lost $28,000 with the collapse. "It was my bank and the bank of other people. We felt good," said another. At another level, the abstraction of "the United States" had failed the depositors. "This could have happened in El Salvador, but not here," said a woman whose family had lost close to $7,000. "In this country we believed the law was respected and everything was okay. If you park your car in the wrong place, there is someone to give you a ticket right away. But this time . . . everyone knew about this bank, and they did not take the care," explained a man. The failure also prompted a crisis in the DC Banking Office, angry public exchanges between Jarvis and her critics, and an emergency rewriting of the DC banking laws. In the absence of DC municipal or US state authority, the Salvadoran government was similarly held to blame, but there was little expectation of redress among Salvadorans in either country. Finally, the many places where the depositors' money had been paid out in expectation of future returns was to blame, for these projects did not generate the income needed to cover the withdrawals. Salvadorans had lost the materialization in money of their life and activity in DC. Much of that money was now gone, as was the future that the bankbooks and their multiplying numbers promised to deliver.

The Incredible

This was an extremely difficult time for Salvadorans in DC and El Salvador. The collapse of the Banquito and numerous other DC banks and a slowdown in new construction work directly affected many families. Pending changes in US immigration law also threatened deportation for those without legal papers. Finally, only several months before, the FMLN had conducted its infamous "Final Offensive," which had been followed by massive government bombing of the Salvadoran capital and the murder of the Jesuit priests and professors at the University of Central America (UCA). Against this bleak picture, Mount Pleasant, the main neighborhood where many of the Salvadorans lived, was in many ways a place of recovery and escape from both the war and poverty of El Salvador and the rhythms of wage work in the DC area, at least for most men who gathered with friends during off-hours and on weekends. For women, it was the place of all kinds of unpaid labor that facilitated the work of both the men and women elsewhere in the city and suburbs.

During the 1980s, the neighborhood had become increasingly popular with young professional families who sought to buy up and restore the many historic homes in the region, boosting land values as they participated in what they felt was a vibrant "mixed" and "multicultural" urban neighborhood. The longest-term residents, however, were African Americans who had lived in the neighborhood since the 1940s and felt the encroachment of both new populations. There were frequent disagreements among members of all groups, and the wealthier residents put increasing pressure on the DC government to police the public areas of the neighborhood. One objective of this work was to keep large groups of men from gathering and drinking, especially on weekends and holidays.

Many days later Daniel Gómez remembered the moment when he believed that he would live. The young man from El Salvador did not expect to be shot at 7:30 p.m. on May 5, 1991, during a Cinco de Mayo celebration, near the corner of 17th and Lamont streets in Northwest Washington, DC, as he faced Angela Jewell, a young DC police officer from the 4th District. She fired her service revolver once and the bullet tore through his shirt and flesh and lodged deep in his upper right side, under his armpit. He felt a throbbing burning sensation and lapsed in and out of consciousness. During subsequent moments, his feelings gave way to the thought that he was about to die. Four days later at Washington Hospital Center, located several miles east of the neighborhood, nurses removed tubes from his throat. "I figured if I could talk, I would live," he remembered thinking to himself.[2]

Shortly before he was shot, Daniel had walked into Don Juan's, a popular restaurant on Mount Pleasant Street in the neighborhood of the same name. While holding a beer can in his hand, he asked Juan Llerena, the Cuban owner of the restaurant, if he and his two friends might enter the restaurant and finish their drinks. Juan told Daniel no and suggested that he leave the restaurant. "The truth is the man who came in had been drinking. He was under the influence," explained Juan a couple of days after the shooting.[3]

Daniel stepped back out on to the street corner in front of the restaurant and together with his friends encountered Angela Jewell and another officer on foot patrol, Girsel Del Valle. The two officers commanded the group of men to empty their beers and to stop drinking in public. The men protested and the officers called for assistance on their radios. Officers Irwin Harris and Tymia Prince shortly arrived as Jewell and Del Valle began to arrest and handcuff the men, citing them for disorderly conduct. In the course of the arrest, the officers and the group of Salvadoran friends began to struggle. Officer Jewel stepped back, leveled her gun at Gómez 12 inches away, and fired into his torso.

Juan Llerna and his restaurant staff heard the gun report inside the restaurant. Juan quickly finished with his customers and three to four minutes after the shot, he gingerly stepped outside of his restaurant. He saw Gómez lying on the ground, obviously in terrible pain, writhing and cursing the police officers in Spanish. Next to Gómez lay a six-inch knife and the shiny steel of a police handcuff visibly encircled at least one of his wrists. From across the street, Jorge Urizar, a 36-year-old man from Guatemala, stood in front of Corados Restaurant and watched these events unfold. Jorge noticed that one of Daniel's friends seemed to struggle with an officer during the arrest and the other officers began to beat him. At that moment, according to Jorge, Daniel jumped in and attacked the officers. Three officers were now wrestling with and punching Daniel, his friends, and two additional men who had been standing on the street and had joined the melee on the side of the Salvadoran friends. In Jorge's account, Officer Jewell took several steps back and yelled, "Freeze!" before firing her gun. Jorge later argued with police and maintained that both of Gomez's hands were handcuffed when she shot him and that he had never seen any knife at the scene.

As Gomez lay bleeding at the edge of Lamont Street in front of Don Juan's, a crowd of residents gathered in a nearby small park abutting the neighborhood's central bus stop on Lamont Street. Within about 30 minutes of the shooting, an ambulance arrived to transport Daniel to the hospital. Several more officers reached the scene and the police clustered on the corner. People from throughout the neighborhood ran up to the park and began to yell and hurl bottles and rocks at the police. By 9:00 p.m., the 4th District police began to send more officers to the neighborhood, including some who could speak Spanish. Police sedans and wagons streamed north up 16th Street from the District headquarters. As vehicles and police converged two blocks away at 16th and Lamont, the police on the corner moved into the crowd to arrest the rock throwers. Fights broke out and the crowd in the park surged forward surrounding the remaining group of police standing around the blood-soaked asphalt where Daniel had been lying. According to one person who was present, "The police started to beat them. . . . All hell broke loose."[4]

People chanted loudly and threw more bottles and bricks. The police were severely outnumbered and began to run east on Lamont Street toward the corner at 16th Street to escape the growing crowd. Several hundred people surged toward 16th and Lamont. Simultaneously, more police vehicles arrived at the corner. In one instance, an officer drove his car up 16th and was showered with rocks and bottles. He opened the door, jumped out and drew his pistol, but did not shoot. As debris smashed into him and his car, he desperately ran from the crowd. People attacked the car, smashed the windows, and flipped it over before lighting it on fire. The officers at 16th and Lamont scattered, running north to Park Road and south to Columbia Road. A police helicopter swooped overhead as the crowd massed on 16th Street. Between Lamont and Park Road youths set upon two abandoned police cars and one wagon, setting them afire with road flares carried in the car trunks which they thrust into the gas tanks. Officers on motorcycles swerved to avoid attacks, and more people filled the streets and watched from the roadside. As the vehicles exploded and burned, heavy smoke choked the area.

Strategically Localized Difference

As events unfolded that night, police and media competed to define and shape the meaning of the events. DC police spokesman Lt. Reginald Smith tried to explain and justify the shooting. "You need to underscore the fact that the man was armed with a knife." DC council member Frank Smith Jr. of Ward 1, where the violence was concentrated, stated to reporters the same evening, referring to the violence: "This takes me by surprise; its magnitude concerns me very much. This is an intimation of the flashpoints in the community."[5] The newly elected mayor, Sharon Pratt Dixon, did not officially comment on the events that night, but she was notified at 10:00 p.m. and followed the situation through the night from her home.

Early in the morning of May 6, only hours after the violence had subsided, Reginald Smith publicly explained that the confrontation and violence was the result of "misinformation communicated to the community." The same morning of Smith's statement, the *Washington Post* ran an article on the front page suggesting that the violence was the outcome of "simmering tension" and a "language gap" between police and "Hispanics" in the neighborhood. Featuring interviews with neighborhood residents during the evening of and the morning after the outbreak of violence, the article powerfully narrowed the parameters of emerging interpretations and explanation of the events: The violence was related to the "Hispanic" habit of public drinking, poor police work and the lack of Spanish-speaking officers in the neighborhood, the large number of local liquor stores, and conflicts with wealthy home-owners who were concerned about their property values and had put pressure on the police to "clean up the neighborhood."[6]

Later in the day, DC police released their first detailed report of the arrest and shooting on Sunday night. The report identified four officers involved and suggested that four men on the street had taken part in the altercation that led to the shooting. According to the report, as officer Jewell began to arrest two men for drunk and disorderly conduct, a third person became disorderly. As the officers struggled to subdue him, a fourth person assaulted one of the officers. The third man was not fully handcuffed and he pulled out a knife and pointed it toward the officers. Jewell drew her revolver ordered the man to drop the knife. When he lunged at her, she fired, said the report. The man was later identified as Daniel Enrique Gomez.

Several hours after her breakfast, Dixon visited Mount Pleasant for the first time since the outbreak of violence. Crowds turned out to watch and follow her down the street. Several people booed and jeered her, while others yelled, "Give us justice!" and "We need jobs!" For the day, she requested that police make only a limited appearance in the neighborhood and avoid any kind of confrontation with residents.

In the afternoon of May 6, Dixon met with religious and Latin American business leaders from the neighborhood. They criticized her for leading an administration that was out of touch with their concerns. "I hear you loud and clear," she conceded. "Clearly we have to improve the dialogue. Not the least of which is for me to be out in the community." She explained to the group that she had not ventured to the neighborhood on Sunday night because her advisors suggested that it would be too dangerous and also that the evening was understood as an outburst of "criminal activity," not any kind of response to historic conditions and relations in the neighborhood. "When it became clear that we had something much more than that, we began to treat this much differently," she explained.[7]

That evening crowds returned to the street, and by 6:00 p.m. Dixon ordered police to disperse the crowds but not to make arrests. At least 1,000 police officers were deployed in the neighborhood. "I'll do whatever it takes to put an end to it, but we will put an end to it. It's part of deep frustration . . . and it won't be solved overnight."[8] More fires and looting marked the night as people from all over the District joined the melee. By 10:00 p.m. the Mayor called the situation a "state of emergency" and ordered police to begin making arrests as she imposed a curfew from midnight until 5:00 a.m.

Washington Post staff reporters continued to collect words on the street and used this information in another article on May 7 to suggest that that public understandings of the events differed markedly from police accounts. Journalists interviewed Jorge Urizar, who had been standing across the street. He maintained that Gomez had been fully handcuffed and that there was no knife in sight. The *Post* article stated that:

> Along Mount Pleasant Street yesterday, almost everyone accepted Urizar's account and said the shooting of a defenseless man was what led to the violence. But in interviews with dozens of people, almost all of them did not have first-hand knowledge, there were widely divergent accounts. Some said Gómez was armed only with a nail clipper. Others said a police sergeant unfastened his handcuffs moments after he was shot. Still others said police planted a knife. A waitress at Don Juan's supports Urizar's account and said Gómez was handcuffed.

In the discursive struggle between the *Washington Post* and the DC police, the crisis was immediately localized in the Mount Pleasant area and a limited set of questions related to improper violent actions framed inquiry into the causes of the disturbance.

On the night of the May 7, there were only sporadic small groups that formed and then dissolved as police set upon them. As the acts of property theft and destruction subsided, conditions relaxed in the neighborhood and conflict shifted to a different realm. The localized interpretive frame remained, but one group struggled to expand definition of the issues. Over the subsequent weeks an organization of Salvadoran community leaders and activists formed the Latino Civil Rights Task Force and attempted to frame the violence as part of an emerging new civil rights struggle for Latinos in the United States, with particular emphasis on the lack of citizenship and political representation for Salvadorans in the United States.

The political project included alliances with national Latino political organizations, and as the debate sharpened, the Salvadoran and African American populations in the District became increasingly polarized. These growing divisions allowed the events in early May to be subsumed within debates about "multiculturalism" in the United States and changes in the racial and ethnic politics in the United States. Over the following year, in the context of uprisings in Los Angeles and other US cities, the violence in Mount Pleasant became part of a larger national discourse on conditions in urban centers of the United States. The 20-year history of changing relations between El Salvador and the United States receded into the background, especially with the end of the Salvadoran conflict in 1992. A logical hierarchy was established that encased US neighborhood within city, and city within nation. There was one significant connection that escaped this logic.

The North Americanization of Intipucá

Within three weeks of the uprising in DC, the US Ambassador to El Salvador, William Walker, visited Intipucá and met with the newly elected mayor and other town officials. He delivered a short speech in the town and donated about $10,000 directly to the town, via the mayor. This cash award was part of a USAID program of direct payment to town mayors called Municipios en Accion (Municipalities in Action), begun near the end of 1986 as part of a shift in the overall US military effort in the country.

The MEA program was designed to foster local democratic process, and sow legitimacy for the Salvadoran government and military.

Before this program was implemented, USAID would usually design, fund, and hire contractors to build a project (school, road, or public utilities). Frequently the projects were not completed; there was little collective sense of proprietorship and responsibility and no legal recourse to sue a delinquent or negligent contractor who had no ties to the region. In principal, under MEA, local townships would meet and vote on a project, establishing a sense of local participation and ownership. As part of the overall project, USAID officials instructed mayors how to conduct town meetings, occasionally inviting them to the United States for conferences. In some cases, actors were hired in El Salvador to enact a theatrical representation of effective local politics. USAID characterized its project as a "quiet revolution," although critics in the US government argued that "since the program is conceived and financed by the United States, and since its orientation is specifically local, it establishes little loyalty toward the government and the armed forces of El Salvador."[9]

When the ambassador visited and spoke publicly, he stressed that although the $10,000 was a gift to the town, it was not from the US government, but from hard-working people in the United States who paid their taxes, including the many Salvadorans who lived and worked in the DC area with legal documents. By suggesting that it was money earned partially by Salvadorans, he attempted to unify Salvadoran national sentiment across the town and DC. The ambassador never spoke publicly of the Banquito and its direct ties to Intipucá, nor did he mention the unrest in Washington, DC, that had occurred earlier in the month.

In 1997, when Walker was serving as Vice President of the US Naval War College in DC, he recalled to me how he had heard of Intipucá, why he had made the trip to the town, and what he had done during his visit.

By 1988, of course, there were lots of people from Intipucá already in the Washington area, so I heard of this town. I'm not sure if I can remember when I sort of zeroed in on the fact that it was a very unique place and it had this back-and-forth traffic to the Washington area specifically. I expressed a desire to go to Intipucá just to see what it was because my curiosity was there. I wasn't sure what to expect, but I can assure you I sort of underestimated, I guess, what I would call the Americanization of Intipucá.

Although Intipuqueños had spoken of his visit to me in detail and stressed the story of the money and its origins, I asked the ambassador what he spoke about that day. "I'm sure I was conveying the special relationship between this town, and by extension I thought of El Salvador itself, with the United States, and that we're growing closer together and that they were sort of a symbol of this," he replied.

The most visible legacy of his visit is that a main street in Intipucá was paved with the $10,000 and named after him, Calle Central William Walker. I asked him how this came about.

> Well, [US] AID had lots of funds for infrastructure and infrastructure improvement and when I was asking around to see what could be done, what I could bring in the way of a token gesture our support for Intipucá, our AID people said that they could probably put together some money to—I can't remember what it was—help pave it or do something with the street. So when I was there, I announced that AID would be doing this. We left and I swear it was three months later, five months later, six months later, a delegation came to San Salvador from Intipucá to tell me that they were naming the street after me.

In Defense of the "K-Mart Look"

The business owners and landowners of Intipucá and DC were relatively powerful within the pueblo and also among circles of Salvadorans in DC, despite the crisis provoked by the Banquito collapse. However, from the perspective of US Ambassador Walker, the elite of the pueblo were of a different moral order. Near the end of our conversation in 1996, the Ambassador told me of an encounter he had in Washington, DC, after his 1991 visit to Intipucá.

> As the American Ambassador, I was very much involved in getting TACA [the Salvadoran airline] landing rights here in Washington, DC. I don't know if you're familiar with civil aviation, but it's very tough if you're not one of the big European carriers to get landing rights at Dulles [International Airport in Virginia], and TACA wanted to have direct Washington-San Salvador access. After months and months of struggle we finally got it. So when they had the inaugural flight from Salvador to Washington, they invited me to go on board along with the Supreme Court of El Salvador and all sorts of other dignitaries. We got up here and there was a very nice reception given at the Hayes-Adams Hotel, which is one of the fancier hotels across from the White House. I was there and it was a pretty flashy operation—at least, TACA spent a lot of money on it—and the audience, the participants, were of several varieties: There were US

government types, you know, Congress folks and stuff that TACA had invited, and I guess I was in that group. Then there was sort of the Taca Airlines and other airlines and people who obviously had good jobs, good money, dressed well. And then there was a sprinkling through the crowd of fairly humble-looking people, and the humble-looking people, I mean I'm sure you've seen them in Salvador where the women are perhaps over-made-up and their hair is a bit fu fu and their dresses are not quite as stylish, but flashy. And there was a sprinkling of these folks and enough people knew me from my picture or from Washington that people were coming up and shaking hands and introducing themselves, etc.

And finally this woman came up who was dressed this way and was obviously of the poorer class from El Salvador—mestizo-looking, etc.—and she introduced herself and asked me if I'd have my picture taken with her kids who were there. And there were 4 or 5 of her kids—different ages. And I said sure, so she brought over her husband and her kids and the kids were similarly dressed, overdressed, and, you know, [with a] sort of K-Mart look to them and the husband was kind of scruffy and pot-bellied and, you know, looked like a campesino type who had put on a suit. So we're standing getting our pictures taken and I'm talking to them and I'm saying to myself don't ask them, you know, if they are here legally, just don't, don't get, I mean this is going to embarrass them! For some reason they'd been invited to this, maybe they're the, maybe this is the gardener or something of the head of TACA or something, you know. Who knows?

But I was getting my picture taken with each of the kids, and then with the family and we were sort of talking and they asked me if I knew Intipucá and I said yes, I'd been there as a matter of—Oh! So they're from Intipucá! We talked about that a bit, and the conversation got interesting enough that I finally said, how do you like Washington? Have you been here a while? And the father said well, we've been here, I think it was four years or something like that. "And I've brought my wife up, two years later, and then each kid has come up and we're all here now." And I said well, you know, how are you doing? How's life here—giving him the chance if he wants to say well, I'm here illegally so I can't find work or something like that. And he said, well, "I'm doing pretty well." And I said, Oh good. What are you doing? Are you in a restaurant or something like that, which is what many of them are. He said, "No, no, I've started a little construction business." And I said, Oh, terrific. Are you doing well? He said, "Yes, Mr. Ambassador, I'm doing fairly well." I said, well, that's great. He said, "As a matter of fact, just yesterday," I think it was he said, "I signed a contract to do one of the Metro [subway] stations for seven and a half million dollars."

I said hoooooly shit! Talk about a success story. I mean he could have knocked me over with a feather. I really assumed from the way he looked, the way he was dressed—I'd seen many people like that in Salvador, sort of lower middle class trying to get one step up on the ladder—and here this guy who'd been here four or five years [and] was doing very well indeed. Very well indeed. So, you know, I'm always impressed by the work ethic of Salvadorans in general, but the folks from Intipucá seem to have it in spades.

The man to whom the ambassador referred was Manuel Leiva of L & L Construction who had received the large "loan" from the Banquito.

Conclusion

The ambassador's telling phrase in reference to his visit continues to reso-nate well beyond the pueblo: "I was conveying the special relationship between this town, and by extension I thought of El Salvador itself, with the United States, and that we're growing closer together and that they were sort of a symbol of this." The paved street with his name helped make Intipucá such a symbol. Yet contained in the paved street named after William Walker is the larger history of the financial and speculative real estate market collapse in the DC area, triggered in part by the end of the Cold War and the possibility that US defense spending would contract. The Banquito founders had profited in this system and lost many of their investments when it came into crisis. However, what is most remembered is that they escaped accountability for these losses and protected them-selves by keeping people's deposits.

In spite of the geographical and historical emergence of the new trans-national value circuit linking El Salvador and DC, divisions within it were an extension of social relations that had pitted different kinds of capital-ists, landholders, and workers against each other throughout the century. The money relations were new, yet the new bosses were quite similar to the old ones. In the period of crisis after the Banquito failure, the town ap-peared divided from the perspective of the ruling elite, a member of whom once expressed the short and desperate question: "What happened? We were once a beautiful and united pueblo!"

PART III

CHAPTER SEVEN

Welcome to Intipucá City

This chapter marks a shift in the mode of analysis from considering the geographically and historically larger conditions from which the Intipucá-DC model emerged in the 1980s and early 1990s to an examination of contemporary social relations in the pueblo that are not accurately captured or represented by the model. Overall, the temporal and spatial scale of analysis has been progressively narrowed and tightened over the course of the book. This chapter focuses on the way that the President of El Salvador, Armando Calderón Sol, attempted to link a national project of governance with the particularities of the pueblo and its ties to Washington, DC. The chapter first considers a visit he made to Intipucá in 1995 and a short speech that he delivered, focusing on its main rhetorical features. The chapter then moves to an analysis of relations in the pueblo. Through consideration of three sets of events, the chapter explores why Calderón Sol was not able to successfully link this national project with the specificity of Intipucá. The chapter concludes with reflection on the paradoxical situation confronted by Calderón Sol and an additional illustration of the sort of crisis faced by the Salvadoran state in the contemporary period.

Mr. Calderón Sol Goes to Intipucá City

In the morning of July 5, 1995, Calderón Sol flew by helicopter from his presidential home in San Salvador and alighted on a soccer field not far from Daniel's watermelon patch at the southwestern edge of Intipucá. The President was accompanied by his wife, adolescent son, and several government officials. As word spread that the aircraft had touched down, the Intipucá school marching band nervously assembled and began to play, leading the arriving group to the town square. Dr. Calderón Sol and his wife smiled broadly and waved to townspeople who looked out of their doors and stood on the edge of the road. Their son was less visibly extroverted, appearing slightly bored as he walked holding his mother's hand.[1]

The recently elected Intipucá mayor from the Democratic Christian Party (PDC), whom I shall refer to as Oscar, greeted the President without smiling and followed him up onto the concrete stage in the center of town. Calderón Sol and his family were flanked by several officials who had traveled from San Salvador, including an especially dark-skinned man who acted as the local liaison with Intipucá government officials. Also on the stage were several members of the organization called *Unidos-por-Intipucá* (United for Intipucá), a consortium of business owners and landowners living in the Washington, DC, area and in the pueblo who had organized a series of private investment projects in the town, financed with money donated by Intipuqueños who were living and working in the United States. Members of this "hometown association," as some social scientists might typologize it, generally had controlled the local government until the election of Oscar, and all were loyal *Areneros* (ARENA party members) who vigorously supported the Calderón Sol presidency.

Before he was elected President in 1994, succeeding Alfredo Cristiani, Calderón Sol had served two terms as the mayor of San Salvador, winning elections in 1988 and 1991. He was known to be an ally of the less moderate factions of the party, but also considered as someone who would follow in the spirit of Cristiani and continue the neoliberal restructuring of Salvadoran society. One of his well-known campaign slogans was "This Must Continue." In his inauguration speech, Calderón Sol had promised to continue Cristiani's economic policies and especially stressed the need for the privatization and decentralization of public services. Famously, he announced the goal of turning El Salvador into "one big free trade zone."

The portly Salvadoran President stepped up to the small public address system and began to speak slowly, inflecting his delivery with evident emotion and sincerity. After several gestures of gratitude toward town officials, he began his presentation, announcing that recently he had traveled to the United States and met with President Clinton. He intoned that he had "seen with . . . [his] own eyes" many Intipuqueños living and working in Washington, DC. "They—you—are all sacrificing to help your families, to provide more opportunity for your children, to build a better pueblo. You are all sacrificing for the *Patria* (fatherland), for El Salvador!" With each word, he built a gradual crescendo, ending emphatically *"para El Salvador!"* Despite this manner of speaking, the crowd stood in solemn attention, for the most part not applauding or showing any actual excitement that might correspond with the tenor of the president's delivery.

After concluding with the rousing "for El Salvador," Calderón Sol momentarily relaxed and then began to speak in glowing terms about Unidos-por-Intipucá, describing how this organization coordinated fundraising for reinvestment in the town. He acknowledged that many members were active supporters of his ARENA party. He nodded towards the Unidos representatives who had accompanied him on stage and who were much larger in physical stature and with fairer skin color than the diminutive and unsmiling Mayor, Oscar. Calderón Sol mentioned in particular the Unidos' efforts to build a large soccer stadium on the outskirts of town that had been suspended the previous year for lack of funds. He implored the audience—and by extension their family members and friends in the United States—to help support the efforts of the group, especially with the stadium project. "These people who are members of the ARENA party are developing the pueblo!" he stressed. At this moment in his delivery he paused again and asked rhetorically, "How could such a great pueblo as Intipucá NOT have a mayor from the ARENA party?" The President then brought the short talk to a conclusion, waved to the politely applauding townspeople and walked down off the stage. He shook hands with admirers as he slowly moved through the town center toward the home of the director of Unidos-por-Intipucá, where members had organized a special reception and dinner for the President.

Through the speech and visit, Calderón Sol sought to draw together and consolidate a host of disparate entities, activities, and events to create a singular paradigmatic chain. From his first gesture of affiliation with the town derived from a visit to Washington, DC, and a meeting with US President Clinton, he sought to link his government's official efforts to persuade the Clinton administration against large-scale deportation of nearly 200,000 undocumented Salvadoran migrants working in the United States with the specific concerns of residents, both in the town and in the DC area. Because of its history of ties to DC, Intipucá provided a unique venue for this project. By promoting the interests of local members of his ARENA party whose candidate had lost in the previous year's municipal elections and advocating on behalf of the organization Unidos-por-Intipucá, he lent his prestige to the reputation of this faction, after it had been tarnished because of members' ties to the Banquito. By stressing the continuity through party membership, Calderón Sol strung together a normative story of formal equivalences: the President and his party help all Salvadorans, of which Intipuqueños are highly representative, to work hard in the United States and send money back to El Salvador; Intipuqueños, via the organization Unidos-por-Intipucá and hopefully soon with an ARENA mayor—both of which are extensions of the President and his government—take part in the development of themselves, their families, their pueblo, and their nation. It was a masterful form of rhetorical suture and synthesis. Judging by the lukewarm response, it may not have been completely effective. From the Salvadoran government's perspective, the visit was part of an overall effort to promote remittance flows back to El Salvador and describe this as a viable source of "national" development. But why was Calderón Sol not able to successfully link this project with the specificity of Intipucá, despite the town's status as one of the most successful remittance-led towns in El Salvador? This chapter pursues three interrelated events, using them as clues through which to develop an answer to the question.

Clue No. 1: Signs of Welcome

At the time of the Banquito failure, Intipucá landowning elite controlled the local government and shared an interest in erasing the social memory of the Banquito debacle through promoting the town in particular ways through forms of public boosterism. The visit by US Ambassador Walker contributed to this campaign; the town leadership, via the mayor's office, took advantage of this opportunity to record photographs, which they reproduced later in a significant way. Also at this time the son of one of the Banquito founders, who had been living in the DC area, returned to the pueblo and worked hard to organize several projects in the town in conjunction with the "Woman's Voluntary Committee for the Improvement of Intipucá," a group headed by a woman whose brother-in-law was also a Banquito founder. Among these projects was a campaign to plant trees along several of the main streets.

One of the most visible improvement projects was the construction of a large sign that advertised Intipucá at the intersection of the San Miguel–La Union leg of the Littoral and the winding uphill road that led to the pueblo, a junction popularly known as *el desvio* (the intersection). It was located at the southern end of the Chávez family's land, and at its edge

FIGURE 10. "Welcome to Intipucá City" sign, photographed by author.

lived the family that had been ostracized from Caulotio by Marvin's grand-mother for cutting wood. After the sign's installation, it stood out in a dramatic way, immediately noticeable to any passerby. It remains in place and is referred to in popular accounts of the town in El Salvador and the United States.

The most striking feature of the sign, especially at the time of its place-ment, is the phrase "Welcome to Intipucá City," written in English. Above the English lines is the slightly different Spanish, "Bienvenido a Intipucá," and below are several numbers that provide measures of the population and altitude. The sign lists the names of three beaches within 6 kilometers of the town. At the bottom, the sign comments on its own origins in Span-ish, translatable as "Courtesy of Gavilan Express, Washington, DC, ABY General Store, and the Mayor's Office."

In its most general capacity, the sign represents Intipucá to some would-be interpreter so as to create other equivalent or more developed messages. However, the way that it presents its object for interpretation is curious since in English, Intipucá is coupled with City, and in Spanish, Intipucá stands alone. In addition, at the bottom there is evidence that the sign has had an exchangeable quality in the sense that some people likely paid to have others create and install it. This story of the sign's value in the form of its price leads to a small metal workshop in the pueblo and the labors of the young kids who built and painted it in exchange for a wage that came from the owners of a store in the Mount Pleasant neighborhood of northwest Washington, DC, a store in Intipucá, and the Mayor's office. By naming themselves on the sign, the suppliers of the money appeared as primary agents in the realization of the sign.

Like many representations of Intipucá, the sign tends to reflect the perspective of the elite of the town. Gavilan Express, a small store in the DC area, is owned by members of a large landowning family in Intipucá whose patriarch traveled to DC shortly after Sigfredo Chávez and also was among the first in the pueblo to receive a private high school education outside of the town. The store has achieved consistently high rates of profit by being among the most popular markets among the thousands of Salvadorans living in the DC area. Comercio ABY is a small general store in Intipucá owned by members of a wealthy family not originally from Intipucá but from the nearby city of La Unión. The brother of one ABY co-owner is the owner of a successful restaurant in DC that occupies the building once used by Sigfredo Chávez when he ran his pool hall in the early 1970s. ABY has been a successful business in Intipucá, supplying food and an array of inexpensive consumer goods, the majority of which are imported from China. It also served as a money-transfer and money-changing center in the town (until 2001 when US dollars could circulate).

Overall, the sign tells several stories. At its most general, it marks Intipucá as a town distinguished by the naturalization of the English language and in this way contributes to a host of claims about the consequences of the pueblo's strong ties with the Washington, DC, area. From another perspective, the sign represents specific town agents, whose capacities to present themselves this way rests on the efforts and activities of many other people within the pueblo and beyond. There is a third story that is less visible, but it is the one that dominates within the pueblo. According to most residents, it is "Hugo's sign."

Clue No. 2: More Pictures

Hugo is the talented and hard-working son of one of the Banquito founders who led many of the most successful improvement projects in the pueblo. Besides the sign, which he had envisioned, designed, and helped to realize through promotion and fundraising efforts, among his most important contributions to Intipucá was a self-published colorful 48-page magazine about the town. It was released in conjunction with the yearly festival in honor of Intipucá's patron saint, St. Nicholas Tolentino, that was held during the first week of March. The 1992 magazine was unique in that it contained a comprehensive and well-researched history of the town written by Hugo.[2] One significant part of this narrative was an extensive discussion of the visit of the US Ambassador, William Walker, in 1989, shortly after the Banquito collapse, although this connection was never acknowledged in the magazine. Along with text that listed other important guests in the town, like the *New York Times* journalist Lindsey Gruson, the historical account reproduced several pictures of Walker's visit.

The beautifully assembled brochure circulated widely, and many Intipuqueños in DC and in the pueblo kept well-worn copies in their homes. The festival in March was a popular time for Intipuqueños in DC to return to the pueblo, and the brochure was addressed as much to them as to visitors from elsewhere in El Salvador. As a formal descriptor of Intipucá, it joins the words of Sigfredo Chávez and others whose representations of the town were picked up by journalists and researchers and recast as popular accounts of the pueblo for a Salvadoran and US audience. However, in contrast to the popular journalistic accounts, Hugo's brochure presents particular people who have been important actors in shaping the dominant images of the town, but who have assiduously avoided journalists, most photographers, and public speaking. These behind-the-scenes players were (and remain) among the most powerful actors in the town. They continue to shape the public form that the town has taken and the way it is known well beyond its environs or among Intipuqueños in DC.

Inside Hugo's brochure, page eight and nine open to face each other and together offer a powerful depiction of Intipucá and its ties to DC and the United States. On the top of page eight is a large map of El Salvador, showing Intipucá and stating its longitude and latitude. Beneath it is an advertisement for Tuco y Tico, the propane distributorship founded with Banquito funds. All of page nine is devoted to an eight-paragraph glowing profile of the recently elected mayor, Juan de Dios Blanco (ARENA), and the various local institutions and ministries under his control. At the top of the article is a well-focused photograph of Juan flanked on his right by US Ambassador William Walker and on his left by the brother of one of the Banquito founders. He is partially cut out of this picture. However, in this next section I would like to place him and some of his family and friends more at the center of how one understands contemporary social relations in Intipucá.

Among the largest landowners in Intipucá, and of the same generation as Marvin's grandmother, was a man known as Ursulo. He owned most of the territory that Intipucá currently occupies, and he deeded large portions to the municipal government while also selling off lots to individuals. His three sons each inherited part of the vast hacienda. One son left the pueblo, attended medical school, and moved to San Miguel, allowing a number of tenant farmers to continue to work his land. He was one of the Banquito founders and a part owner of Tuco y Tico. He also opened El Gran Tejano, the popular steak restaurant in San Miguel. The second son, who was a close friend of Sigfredo, sold all of his inheritance and continues to live from the interest that his money earns in a Salvadoran bank. The youngest son, the man in the picture, was the only one who continued to farm the land; I shall call him Raúl. He used this operation to capitalize several other businesses and investment ventures, including a modest general store that he and his family operated out of the front of their house to sell basic foodstuffs as well as more expensive consumer items, which they purchased in San Miguel and resold in the pueblo. They also changed dollars and colónes according to their own established rate of exchange.

Despite the visible signs of wealth in the form of the hacienda and the store, in the late 1990s Raúl was greatly concerned about the viability of his way of life in the town. His temper flared often at this time, especially when events did not unfold according to his choice. In particular, the farm owner was angry at his eldest son because this young man seemed to have little interest in or aptitude for taking on any of the varied family businesses. He also was angry at his wife, blaming her for spoiling this son and contributing to his aversion to taking over the family business. Increasingly he viewed all of his four children as a significant drain on the family assets. "It's tremendous!" he sighed in a slightly humorous, but mostly exasperated, way to me once.

Raúl's eldest son was in his middle 20s at this time and, besides helping out in the store, his main responsibility was to collect milk from the workers early each morning after they had milked the cows. These workers lived in small houses adjacent to the fields and received a small wage each Saturday, in the late afternoon, paid out at the store. After collecting the milk in large plastic containers, the son would sell it to several older women who operated a small cheese-making business in the center of town.

Most days and evenings the son was relatively free to live as he pleased, and his mother gave him a substantial allowance as he needed or requested it. He had access to the family car, a blue Toyota sedan with tinted windows that was decidedly more exciting than the diesel pickup used for transporting milk or commercial goods from San Miguel. On the weekends he usually traveled to San Miguel, which he and other friends called "Saint Michael City," affecting an English translation of the name.

A typical evening for this son and his male friends would involve first a trip to a small bar on the south side of San Miguel where it was possible to sit outside and eat small portions of food "cocktails" that accompanied each round of beer. After an hour or so of drinking, eating, and joking, the young men would climb back into the blue Toyota, roll up the tinted windows, and turn up music that they referred to as "techno." They would drive across to the northern side of town to a large intersection where the Pan-American Highway entered San Miguel. The 3rd Brigade, the Army force responsible for the infamous El Mozote massacre, was stationed at this juncture. The section of the Pan-American Highway that continued out of town and headed north was known informally as the *Ruta Militar* (Military Route) since convoys of troops would depart on the road to head north into the most conflicted and mountainous fighting areas north of San Miguel, where the FMLN had established its rear guard since the 1970s. The intersection was popularly known as *El Triangulo* (The Triangle) and featured an array of discotheques, nightclubs, and bordellos. In 1996 a large discotheque called Hollywood opened, and this was often the ultimate destination of the young men.

On occasion, however, a member of the entourage would propose that they first visit a bordello called Tony's and more colloquially "Carnitas Tony's," which was, in fact, the largest bordello in San Miguel. The men would park the Toyota, enter the building after being searched for weapons, and sit down in the darkly lit space. The large room was surrounded with mirrored walls and featured a dance space in the center. As women walked around in tight-fitting outfits, they would watch the mirrors to see if any of the men were staring at any of them. If a man's gaze had been caught and identified with a particular woman, she would receive a message from her colleagues and venture over to talk with the man. Typically she would ask him to buy her a nonalcoholic drink and a beer for himself. Often with little more conversation the man would propose that the two of them have sex in one of the back rooms. The woman would collect several hundred colónes from the man and obtain a key to one of the rooms from the manager. The couple would depart and the man would return sometime later to his seat. Gradually all of the entourage who chose to purchase sexual relations with the women in this way completed their exchanges, and the group walked next door to the discotheque for more drinking and dancing. These encounters with sex workers were not completely anonymous. The son and other people from Intipucá were well known to the manager and also to some of the employees. The son often spoke of his "favorites" at Tony's, and they greeted each other as acquaintances when he would visit.

Sex work in San Miguel, like elsewhere in El Salvador, is a structural feature of a highly patriarchal society. Most of the women were from very modest backgrounds and in many ways driven to this line of work. Almost none of the women employees was from San Miguel; they had come from other cities or small villages in El Salvador and wished to remain anonymous at their jobs. Women also arrived from Honduras and Nicaragua to work at Tony's, and frequently these women had young children whom they were raising without a spouse or other assistance. One way to understand the business is to trace the way in which one woman came to it in the course of her life, part of which included time spent in Intipucá.

Subplot of Clue No. 2

When Raúl's son was a teenager, he employed a young woman from the outskirts of the pueblo to cook and clean their home and work in the store. She and the son became close friends and periodically they stole off to a back room by the garden for romantic interludes, much against the wishes of Raúl and his wife. Eventually the young domestic servant became pregnant. Raúl and his wife were quite concerned and offered to raise the child in their family. Although the exact conditions of the agreement are not completely clear, the woman left the household and Raúl's wife raised the child as her own. The child grew up referring to Raúl's son as Papi and Raúl's wife as Mami. The birth mother of the child returned to her settlement south of Intipucá and rarely visited the home again.

When Duarte visited the Four Seasons Restaurant in Washington, DC, and Marvin and his fellow workers were forbidden to come to work, among those who stayed away was a fellow known as Tommy to his friends in Intipucá. Like Marvin and others in DC, he periodically returned to Intipucá to visit and then traveled back to DC, bringing dry cheese and also leather belts, which he sold in Mount Pleasant. "With one load of cheese I can buy a refrigerator for my house here in Intipucá," he told me in 1993. That year he had a child with the sister of the young domestic servant who had left Raúl's household after giving birth. Tommy and the woman were living together in the pueblo, and she was not happy that he was planning to return to Washington, DC, to work for at least six months until his next visit. She also was concerned that he would not send adequate money for her to live and take care of their house and infant child in Intipucá.

Tommy was a heavy drinker in the pueblo, and in DC he also consumed cocaine on a regular basis. These practices affected his ability to work and save money. His ability to set limits on drinking and taking other drugs apparently decreased, and he eventually lost his job in DC. He spent a period in a city detoxification center, paid for by his mother who was working as a hotel maid in DC. His wife in Intipucá was destitute; she could not adequately feed herself and the child as well as pay the electricity and water bills for the new house in the pueblo. In this context she left her child with a relative nearby and moved to San Miguel with the goal of working for a period at Tony's in order to save up money for herself and the child. Word spread back to the pueblo that "Tommy's wife was working at Tony's," and many of the young men in Intipucá found this especially appealing. They frequently traveled to the bordello to purchase her capacity to have sex with them.

One evening Raúl's son met her at Tony's and proposed that she provide sexual services to him in exchange for the usual fee. She angrily refused, saying that he was her brother-in-law. He replied in a yet more angry way that he was her client, a client of the business, and that as long as he had money he could buy her product. She went to the manager and complained that the man was her brother-in-law and that she refused to have sexual relations with him for any amount of money. The manager told her to accept "the client's" money or prepare to leave work. With great regret she had sex with the man, which he viewed as a kind of consumer-rights triumph. The next day when his hangover had cleared and he had returned to the pueblo, he told several people that he regretted what he had done. His main reason, however, was that he feared that Tommy would get out of treatment for drug abuse and come back to the pueblo to confront him. Tommy's wife was not a concern of his since "she had chosen to work there."

Neither Raúl nor the rest of the family learned of these events, but the father did begin to notice that a great deal of cash was being paid out of the store account. He accused his wife of not carefully regulating the weekly allowance for the children. At that moment, he suddenly became furious, yelling loudly at his wife over all the money that was being wasted on his son who never worked and showed no interest in taking over any of the farm responsibilities. His wife was distraught over this outburst and cried to herself most of the evening.

The next day she asked me if I ever fought with my wife and if fighting among married people was common in the United States. She also told me that she had heard that many married people in the United States sought and obtained legally sanctioned divorces. She wondered how women lived when they were alone, without a husband. "But people separate here, too," I proffered. "Well, yes. We always separate for a little bit of time each month," she said, slightly laughing and bringing this line of discussion to an end. "I think that you are a less jealous society," she stated, referring to the United States as a whole. "Here we are really jealous. That's why we can't separate."

This section began with the half-hidden picture of Raúl and ends with his wife's use of the term jealousy as a general explanation for why many Salvadoran women remained in unhappy relationships with men. The significance of these events and their connecting strand in the form of the son and his activities is that, at numerous conflicted junctures, important features of intimate human relations were measured in terms of their price, even as they also were evaluated in terms of love, fear, jealousy, anger, and impropriety. Raúl feared that his son could not adequately run the family business and seemed to use accumulated wealth only for "leisure" activities. He was angry at his wife for facilitating these practices and for their cost to the family business. Raúl's wife likely feared the implications of her husband's anger. Tommy's wife feared that he would not help her with money to live with their newborn child, whom she dearly loved. She also later feared Raúl's son and his authority as a "client" of Tony's. The son in turn feared the return of Tommy as a consequence of his "purchase." All of these sentiments emerged out of relations that were in part shaped by the money-form.

Although I have traced a short series of interrelated events, I believe that they reflect broader patterns of relations in the pueblo and beyond. When the Salvadoran President made the simple association between individuals, families, and the nation of El Salvador, the unity of one category, "family," was assumed along with the others, as was the assumption that remittances flowed neatly and uniformly, although not without "sacrifice" across all three entities, appearing to create wealth. However, across DC, the pueblo, and San Miguel, this circulation of money was more complex and uneven, as was the constitution of "individuals" and "families."

Clue No. 3: The Absence of an ARENA Mayor

Also posing next to the US Ambassador in one of the photographs reprinted in Hugo's brochure was the Mayor of Intipucá at the time, Oscar. He was a member of the ARENA party and had participated in a
USAID-sponsored program that brought Salvadoran municipal leaders
to the United States during the war as part of a campaign to shape political leadership in rural areas. These same programs, as a kind of secular
counter-liberation theology, are what sponsored the US Ambassador's
visit and his donation of money to the town.

At the end of the conflict in 1992, despite the recent Banquito failure
and several half-constructed houses in Intipucá that signaled the moment
of the Banquito collapse and the theft of their owners' money, Intipuqueños living in the DC area deepened their orientation to the pueblo. They
tended to visit more frequently in the years immediately after the war and
also to invest what money they could marshal in their Salvadoran properties, whose potential sale prices seemed to be rapidly rising. Indeed, after
the war there was a widespread speculative housing boom across all of El
Salvador driven to some extent by shared anticipation of return migration
from the United States.

Juan took advantage of this climate and levied a tax on all Intipucá residents. Since many of the people in the pueblo were heavily reliant upon
remittances from family members working in the DC area, it effectively
was a tax on wage earners in DC as well. Ostensibly the tax was to help
expedite paving of all the town's roads, a project that had been stimulated
with Ambassador Walker's $10,000. However, the tax was perceived as ar-
bitrary and excessive by many residents, and they directed their resentment
at Juan and his connections to ARENA and also Unidos-por-Intipucá,
of which he was a member. Many pueblo residents assumed that he was
enriching himself with the tax, and there was a recurring rumor that he
owned a large house on the other side of the country in the city of Sonsonate. Among the excessive luxuries that it contained was an electric garage door opener, the rumors suggested. Other people claimed that he had
used the mayor's office to alter personal documents of people so that they
might obtain legal US residency papers under laws that encouraged the
reunification of immediate family members.

As a result of the tax and suspicions of personal enrichment, as well as
the revelations about the Banquito that continued to surface into the early
1990s, well after Walker's palliative visit, Juan's popularity in the pueblo

dropped precipitously. Several years later, I asked several residents about this time and how Juan's political demise affected Unidos-por-Intipucá and its project of building a large soccer stadium in Intipucá. They summed up the situation by saying that Juan had a "character defect" and that this had tainted many things in the pueblo, including the reputation of his political party in the town, ARENA, and the prospects that it could offer a competitive candidate in the next election. As the 1994 elections approached, Juan was gently pushed aside by Raul, and other power brokers in the pueblo selected a new ARENA candidate, whom I shall call Max. Despite Hugo's brochure and other concerted efforts to overcome the stigma of the Banquito collapse, the contours of corruption were apparent to the majority of voters and a man of much humbler origins won the Intipucá mayoral elections. Considered the archenemy of ARENA, he was a member of the PCD, the party of José Napoleon Duarte.

Oscar was a soft-spoken man who worked extremely hard as mayor, constantly explaining that his job was just to help people with their basic needs. He surrounded himself with a group of advisors, all drawn from the poorer classes of the pueblo who had been employed by the landowning elite over several generations. They set modest goals of completing a number of projects that had been started under Juan. In these endeavors, his administration was not able to draw upon Unidos-por-Intipucá funds, like Juan, nor to link local government activities as directly with Intipuqueño business owners in the town or the DC area. In this way his constituency represented the members of the pueblo who had more tenuous ties to the DC region and, in some cases, none at all. Many of these people were more recent arrivals in the town who had come to work on cotton farms in the 1960s or who had fled fighting elsewhere in the country during the 1980s.

When the Salvadoran president asked rhetorically why Intipucá did not have a mayor from ARENA, the answer rested in people's lived experiences of the Banquito, members of the local ARENA party, and the mayorship of Juan. The election of the new mayor and his presence (marked by visible discomfort) on the stage with Calderón Sol in 1995 was a reflection of this sentiment. The rise of Oscar to political office in the pueblo also played out a complicated history of personal relations between him and Raul.

Clue No. 4: The Personal and the Political

When Raul was a young boy, his father, Ursulo, deemed Oscar among his most trusted workers on the hacienda called *Los Morenos*. Oscar was able to save the money that he earned from Ursulo and start his carpentry business. As a carpenter he earned significantly more money than as a hacienda worker and could more easily control his work routine each day. After several years he approached Ursulo and asked him if he would be able to purchase some land from him in order to build a small house. Ursulo offered to sell him a lot for 3,000 colónes, carved from Los Morenos. Many years later the neighborhood in which Oscar lives is still called Los Morenos, though the hacienda by this name no longer exists.

Oscar built his house and also a workshop and continued to expand his business, even as Ursulo refused to give him the title to the land. On the basis of their long relationship, Oscar trusted that Ursulo would do so eventually. However, once Oscar had developed the property, Ursulo approached him and told him that he had changed his mind and that he preferred not to sell the property. He proposed that he would return Oscar's money to him gradually over a period. "What do you want me to do, lift up my house and move it?" Oscar reportedly said to Ursulo.

Oscar went to the town judge and requested that there be a hearing where he and Ursulo could present their sides of the case. The judge refused, saying that since no document had ever been signed by anyone, there could be no legal case brought to the court. Oscar was furious and refused to speak with Ursulo or any member of his family. Oscar contacted a distant cousin who worked in the presidential palace in San Salvador and asked if the fellow might write a letter to the judge, requesting that he allow Oscar to open his case against Ursulo. Despite receiving the letter, the judge refused.

At this time Ursulo's son, Raúl, was in his teens and owned a small .22 caliber rifle. The wooden stock had cracked and broken off and he asked Oscar if he would repair the gun. Oscar was brusque with Raúl and told him that he had no time, but would consider doing the job sometime in the future. Raúl, prone to temper tantrums, screamed at Oscar and ran to his father and insisted that he make Oscar repair his gun. Oscar refused to meet with either of them.

At the entrance to his property, there was an old farm gate that occasionally hindered Oscar when he tried to move large logs and boards into his workshop. He had given up on Ursulo ever moving it and wrote to his cousin in San Salvador. His cousin in turn contacted an official in the Ministry of Public Works in San Miguel. In short order the office dispatched several members of the Hacienda Police, a rural military unit similar to the National Guard. The police tore down the gate and left. Apparently Ursulo was surprised at the social connections that Oscar had been able to marshal. Within a short time he presented Oscar with title to the land. After defeating Juan in the 1994 mayoral elections, Oscar privately took great pleasure that he could continue to refuse to respond to the wishes and interests of Raúl with impunity.

Oscar has a son who served in the Salvadoran army during the war as a communication specialist and then went to live in Washington, DC, keeping in touch with his father and other friends in town. He saved a good amount of money and purchased a host of consumer items that he brought back to the pueblo when he returned with his wife and baby girl in 1996. As someone of modest background who had received education through the military and then moved to DC, where he had earned a high wage as the manager of a retail store, he brought a unique critical perspective to the changes in the pueblo that had helped to propel his father into office. "See all these farms. They are all going down," he said to me as we walked across a farm near the pueblo.

> They are owned by the old guard that doesn't want anything to change. They don't want to see my father as mayor. They don't want any of the poor people to change their position in life. Look at me. They don't like it that I have an education and a car that I brought back from DC. In the past you could get rich in this country without going to school, just by exploiting people. Raul's wife thought that she never needed to learn how to read. She's illiterate. Did you know that? These kids of the old families, they are stupid. They don't know how to work and they don't want to work. If their fathers stopped working all the businesses would collapse. Things are changing. They are selling their land. If you are selling, you're going down. The people buying are doing better. These old guard are selling.

This young man's observations were astute and captured important aspects of aggregate change. Production based on highly exploited agricultural labor in El Salvador was giving way to the dominance of service work in the United States and the host of transnational commercial and financial activities stimulated by the remittances. Some landowners like Sigfredo had taken part in this transition relatively early. The Mayor's son was remarking on people like Raúl who had remained in El Salvador throughout the war and continued to base their activities around farming. This transformation in the pueblo mirrored shifts at a larger scale as Salvadoran coffee growers who were not part of the Cristiani-led neoliberal faction of diversified capitalists chaffed at the restructuring of El Salvador toward international finance, which was stimulated especially by the remittance process. However, there was another cross-cutting contradiction in Intipucá that suggests the complexity of the contemporary moment.

After Calderón Sol's speech, local ARENA members and the town elite hosted a private reception for the President and his family in the home of a man whom I will call Jacinto, a member of the Washington arm of Unidos-por-Intipucá who resided most of the year in the DC area. In their efforts to welcome the President, the hosts of the party had purchased imported Heineken beer and served it along with the Salvadoran brand, Pilsner. The president made a great point to drink only Pilsner, "the national beer," brewed by the Constancia brewery that was partially owned by Calderón Sol's cousin. The hosts remarked about this later and found it curious that he would drink what they considered to be an inferior beer. The second lingering memory of the visit, according to town residents who attended the speech, was that Calderón Sol announced that in his talks with Clinton, the US president had mentioned Intipucá and asked Calderón Sol if he had ever visited the pueblo. He had not, and for this reason he chose to deliver a speech there. Some Intipucá residents suggested that Calderón Sol had been ordered by Clinton to travel to the pueblo and make the speech.

Although the visit was well choreographed and carried out by all of the lead participants, especially the president, the beer story and the notion that the Salvadoran president was both ignorant of Intipucá and acting at the behest of US President Clinton suggested some of the lurking contradictions behind Calderón Sol's visit that he was unable to completely efface or mend. Imported commodities whose brand names were associated with metropolitan centers, such as the Heineken beer and its origins in the Netherlands, told a complex story of both progress and lack of progress in El Salvador. The beer signified the relative inferiority of the national product and at the same time it lent prestige to those who drank it, for it suggested that they had access to superior goods and their associated practices. In the case of Intipucá, much of the wealth that allowed the hosts to spend extra money on imported beer came from business ventures being conducted in DC that were also connected with the pueblo. Calderón Sol had affirmed this in his speech, but had wanted to emphasize how the wealth from the United States yielded Salvadoran national progress. By drinking Pilsner he tried to signal a kind of popular nationalism in the face of the transnational origins of "national" wealth. Similarly, when residents repeated the story that Calderón Sol had been effectively ordered to Intipucá by Clinton and that he was ignorant of the pueblo, they were supporting a hierarchy of authority and affiliation that collided with the national orientation stressed by the Salvadoran president during his visit to the pueblo.

These contradictions that lingered behind Calderón Sol's visit shed light on broader historical patterns that extend beyond Intipucá and are occluded in the popular representations of the town and its ties to DC. A subset of the landed elite of the town has made a transition to becoming transnational entrepreneurs of sorts. They are a strange sort of vanguard since their emergence conflicts with the national idioms and orientation of the Salvadoran state. Yet they also represent a form of continuity, since they continue to take part in the exploitation of landless wage-laborers, not only as employers, but also as merchants and commercial capitalists. The dominant account of Intipucá and DC makes the whole town appear as such a conglomeration of business owners, who were once peasant farmers. The reality is that long-term social divisions based on property ownership are being reproduced even as they are being modified transnationally.

These trends are difficult to perceive from the perspective of the Salvadoran state and from the vantage offered by most accounts and representations of Intipucá. Indeed, the current scholarly and popular fascination with identifying "immigrant entrepreneurs" obscures the history of inequality upon which their appearance as successful capitalists rests. In order to show this more clearly, the next chapter tightens the overall focus yet again, looking more deeply into quotidian occurrences in the pueblo. By seeking forms of evidence at this small-scale level of analysis, it becomes possible at the end of the book to consider Intipucá and DC from the much larger perspective of twentieth-century El Salvador–US relations and to project some of the century-long continuities, not just the empirical newness of migration and remittances, into the near future. This final move is meant to shed light on some of the hidden possibilities and futures that lie nascent in this present but are suppressed by dominant accounts.

CHAPTER EIGHT

The World in a Park

The young man who videotaped the visit in 1995 of the Salvadoran president to the pueblo focused for several seconds on the Catholic priest in the region, John King, a missionary from Cleveland, Ohio. This diocese had been active in the region since the 1960s in the context of the US Alliance for Progress and the first US Peace Corps workers who were sent to the region. John had arrived the previous year as the youngest member of the group, and he was working hard to expand his influence and stature in the pueblo.

John was from Akron, Ohio, but had lived much of his life in the city of Cleveland. He had been born in the late 1960s at the crest of Akron's post–World War II expansion. As he grew up with his family, he witnessed the major corporation in the area, Firestone Tires, close factories and relocate aspects of production to other regions of the United States, leaving behind large numbers of people without jobs and a widespread sense of social disequilibria in the city. It was at this time that John moved to Cleveland and eventually began to study at a Catholic seminary in the central downtown area. During that time he wrote a short history of this church in Cleveland, focusing on its missionary activities in El Salvador, and prepared to join the mission after being ordained. Also at that time, a woman working for one of the missions in the seaside town of La Libertad, Jean Donovan, was murdered along with three other church workers by Salvadoran members of the *Guardia Nacional*.

In 1995, after he completed his studies, John began to work for a five-year period in the eastern part of El Salvador, traveling and preaching in the region near the border of the Departments of San Miguel and La Unión while based at the mission headquarters in Chirilagua. Several miles to the southeast of Chirilagua was Intipucá, and one of Padre Juan's first experiences as a missionary was to watch the president of El Salvador, Armando Calderón Sol, arrive by helicopter and deliver his short speech. Over the following year, Padre Juan (Father John) became increasingly well known in Intipucá and frequently delivered sermons in the town's refurbished church.

Although he was no longer likely to receive death threats or be murdered by the Guardia or right-wing paramilitaries, this period in the country was challenging for the tall trim man with short light hair. He found himself into the ongoing competition between the Catholic Church and the rising number of Protestant evangelical sects that proliferated, especially among poorer sectors of Salvadoran society. During a sermon on September 22, 1996, Padre Juan recalled his childhood in Akron and described the experience of riding his bicycle to a store where he would buy candy. He explained that along the route he would pass a towering billboard with huge letters just before arriving at the store. At a distance, the sign was a vaguely visible object and signaled to him the general location of the store. As he peddled toward the sign, he could make out the faint outline of letters that rapidly came into focus as he approached. For a brief period he could clearly read the sign and take part in the advertising message that it was designed to impart. Yet within moments he would be right upon the sign and, glancing up, then could only see bright swatches of color, too huge to read. The next moment he had passed by the sign and his feelings shifted toward anticipation since he would soon arrive at his destination.

The Padre continued to speak, weaving a tale of how this experience of riding a bike and attempting to interpret a large sign suggested to him the problem of understanding one's place in the world. Though he did not specify it, the story highlighted the difficulty of fixing forms and meaning when (and where) both subject and object seem to be in rapid motion relative to each other. From his story he extrapolated to suggest that churchgoers were similarly living in a world where the decipherability of "the big perspective" was at best only a fleeting experience. Through his oratory delivered with apparent sincerity, he gradually merged his story with a typical biblical interpretation of the Catholic faith, replete with an omnipresent god who "saw the big perspective" and a telos of life, death, and eventual salvation. He concluded the sermon by emphasizing that through active following of church tenets, both the lived world of Intipucá and one's sense of self might seem more stable and understandable, and by allusion, the youthful joy that one might experience by arriving at a candy store could be shared by the devout.

As I looked around the church, it was difficult to tell how the sermon constructed around John's childhood experience resonated with the audience. If one followed the tale that John delivered comfortably, using many idioms of rural Salvadoran speech, and found it meaningful, then the sermon might provide a kind of narrative template or framework into which each listener could situate themselves and their experiences and link them to being a member of the Catholic church. To the extent that this occurred and the congregation grew and more actively practiced their Catholic faith, the Padre was a successful missionary priest. Unfortunately for the Padre, the congregation was gradually becoming smaller.

The story was alienating for some people in the audience because it relied on a set of experiences that were not as universally familiar to people in the town as John had assumed. The naturalization and externalization of certain objects and activities through John's story-as-parable actually promoted the feelings of social disequilibria, especially among older residents, that the Padre sought to quell. Many of the people listening to the Padre's sermon that day supplemented their household income or relied completely upon the money remitted by friends and relatives in DC, Maryland, and Virginia and had spent significant periods of their lives working in the DC area. As a result of work abroad that yielded the remittances, many of the objects and practices mentioned in Padre Juan's story—children owning and riding bicycles, paved roads, billboard-like signs, and a store where a youngster could purchase candy, not to mention the availability of money as discretionary income—were relatively new features of life for the majority in the pueblo. During the time that I was living in Intipucá, residents frequently spoke of the time "before" and the time of "now," marking the shift with an almost endless array of observations that centered on particular people and their activities in relation to new commercial goods and services.

The Problem of Scale and Perspective

I begin with the story of the Padre and his sermon that day because it helps to illustrate a central problematic of the book as it has so far unfolded. Padre Juan remarked that Catholicism provides the "big picture" for the congregation, and he illustrated this concept with an example from his youth and how his capacity to make sense of a large sign rested on, among many things, his position relative to the sign. He attempted to make a connection between his own experience and the experiences of those in

church that day, stressing that they also should be aware that one's "position" determined the capacity to grasp the "big picture." Most impor-
tantly, the proper vantage point was that of being an active member of the
Church and a follower of Church doctrine.

Recalling chapter 1, the Padre essentially was offering a perfect map
of the world, "the big picture" into which all the details and dilemmas
of everyday life would fit in neatly resolved fashion. More precisely, he
was saying that such a map could be found through the active practice
of Church doctrine. In a more secular fashion, such a perfect map is also
being constructed out of the complexities of everyday life for people in
Intipucá and DC and being presented to the "congregation" of people
in El Salvador and the United States. There is no single padre or church
in this process, but rather it is emerging out of specific historical processes,
which are the outcome of the complex interaction of a host of people,
institutions, and doctrines.

One place where this can be seen at a more granular level of analysis
is the central park of Intipucá, a place dominated by a row of "chalets,"
welded metal kiosks where merchants sell drinks and prepared food to the
many residents who congregate in the area during the day and evenings.
Visitors from other pueblos and residents alike consistently remark that
they know of no other small town in the region with such a busy and commercial park area. At the same time, however, many people in Intipucá
have mixed feelings about the park, judging it to be too loud and rowdy,
not a "recommendable" place to visit or be seen. Many residents believe
that it is especially inappropriate for the park to be filled on Sunday when
the Catholic church across the street holds its sessions. The chalet operators in return assert their right and also the necessity to operate, and
there is no shortage of customers, particularly on the weekends. In the late
1990s, the town mayor tended to side with the merchants, despite several
requests by Padre Juan to curtail park activities on Sunday.

As I have alluded to, this chapter focuses yet more closely on everyday
life in the pueblo. From the vantage of the park as a central place for exchanging money, drinks, food, and varied forms of communication, this
chapter traces out some of the social relations that intersect at the park
and also lie behind its capacity to appear as such a controversial center of
life in Intipucá. The chapter begins by examining several occurrences and
events that played out in the park during the late 1990s and then traces out
some of the less visible participants and social relations reflected, but also
hidden, in the events.

Perceptions of Inequality in Intipucá

About six months after the visit of the Salvadoran president to Intipucá, members of Unidos-por-Intipucá held a public meeting in the central park area of the pueblo to stress the need for more funds to complete the large soccer stadium that they had begun to build on the outskirts of town. They appealed to residents to make donations to the committee and to ask their relatives in the DC area to contribute as well. Among those listening to the short speeches were several women who sold drinks at their chalets. "They are all thieves," muttered one of the older and most respected drink-stand proprietors. Although none of the presenters that day were directly associated with the Banquito, this utterance reflected the feeling among many residents they were part of a unified group of allied families, the wealthiest in the pueblo. "The bankers, the ex-mayor, Unidos por Intipucá, the *Areneros* [members of the conservative ARENA political party], all of them—*ladrones* [thieves]!" she spat out in a sharp whisper.

Just six months after this episode, on August 26, 1996, Banco Agrícola Comercial, the largest bank in El Salvador, opened a branch office in Intipucá, adjacent to the corner of 2a Calle Poniente and 1a Avenida Norte, just off the central park area. Many residents and the Agrícola officials, of course, were proud of the bank's arrival, for it suggested that within the pueblo both the subjective values of financial capitalism and its dominant form of value, money, circulated in ample fashion. Referring to this, the owner of a store across the street from the bank cautiously appraised this moment and smiled: "With Agrícola we are no longer a pueblo. We are a *ciudad* [city]. No, we are a *villa* [large town]—something in between."

After the well-publicized opening of the Agrícola office, which included a complimentary lobster dinner for the town's elite and visiting bank officials, a rumor began to circulate that brought the bank's promise of progress radically into question. A compelling counter-narrative of corruption described a secret door and a short tunnel at the back of the new office through which depositors' money could be secretly moved into the adjacent residence of a man who had been a guest at the celebratory feast and from whom Agrícola rented its new office. This narrative, with its hinting at the presence of a regressive morality of embezzlement and theft, disrupted the forward-looking aura cast by the bank's presence with its bright, marquee-like sign (*rótolo*). Supporters of the new bank, like the storeowner across the street, harshly criticized purveyors of this fantastic story for their *estrechez de miras* (narrow-mindedness). However, *estrechez de miras* may also be translated, less literally, as "tunnel vision," suggesting how the tale and its tellers comprise an accurate "counter-model" to the bank and its significance for the pueblo.

Over the following 16 months, few residents opened savings and checking accounts or used the bank office to exchange US dollars sent to them by relatives and friends living and working in the United States, especially in the Washington, DC, metropolitan area, for they strongly believed that their money would be passed surreptitiously to the man who lived next door. "They're all thieves," muttered the same well-known drink-seller in the town square, referring to the bank's neighbor and his brother, the storeowner who lived across the street.

In December 1997, a member of the Agrícola bank office provided me with an explanation that neither addressed the possibility of a mysterious opening in the wall nor directly explained the significance of the man next door. This person's account hinted at a history that had altered people's habits, shaping the social environment within which the new bank operated:

> We have not done well in this town. We know how much money is sent back here [from the United States] and we see very little of it. People from farther away, from Cuco, Chirilagua, and so on use the bank, but here in Intipucá we are not very popular because of the events that happened in the past. If we had known about this history, we might have opened in a different pueblo.

Residents had crafted the story of the porous connection between the Agrícola office and the adjacent dwelling on the basis of past perceptions and experiences. A large number of them had lost all of their savings in the collapse of the informal Banquito in 1990. One of the Banquito founders was the brother of Banco Agrícola's neighbor and the store-owner across the street. The story of the secret passageway was a figurative extension of a longer history of bank failure, doubt, and mistrust that was linked with these three brothers and their associates.

Shortly after the opening of the new bank, the drink-stand operator who had rendered the judgment "They're all thieves!" burst into tears one evening near her chalet. "Why are you crying?" some of her customers yelled, with a mix of sympathy and jest. "Because I'm poor!" she sobbed, clutching her dirty apron with tears on her face. Quickly, Marvin jumped up and hugged the woman, comforting her by saying, "We're all poor. We're all poor. Don't worry. It will be alright." She hugged him, relaxed, and then went to sit back down at her drink stand.

Several nights later the woman, Marvin, and others in the park ban-
tered in a friendly way over the price of beer that she charged. "You've
got so much money in your apron!" Marvin called out. As she walked
over to talk with him, he stood up and, winking to the small crowd, dramatically reached into her apron pocket, pretending to take her money.
She slapped his arm and he pulled back in a theatrical manner. At that
moment she had the attention of most of the people gathered around her
stand as Marvin briefly turned. "*Laaaadrrrooone* (thief)!" she whispered
in an exaggerated drawn-out fashion to her impromptu audience, gesturing to the man. "He's one of the thieves!" With his lips turned up, the man
shook his head and waved a finger at the audience, signaling "no, she is not
to be believed" in a similarly dramatic and playful way.

The people gathered began to laugh and yell comments about each of
the "performers." Some people complimented the woman for what a fine
person she was, a hard-working business owner who always settled her
debts. "Better than your old job!" yelled one person in a lewd reference.
"Besides that, did you know she was also a witch?" someone added. "Here
we are with a witch and a caveman. What kind of a town is this?" someone
asked rhetorically. "Intipucá, El Salvador!" replied another fellow, pitch-
ing forward, visibly drunk. The "performance" gave way to a long period
of exchanging stories about Marvin, the drink-stand proprietor, and others who knew both them as everyone chimed in with details and accounts
of past events.

Amidst the anger, sorrow, humor, playfulness, and sense of shared experience expressed not only in the exchange above, but also in the events
that occurred in the park over the previous months, lay the reality of social relations within and across Intipucá and the Washington, DC, area.
A relatively small group of elite land-owning families had dominated aspects of life in the pueblo for much of the twentieth century. These were
the families that become wealthy through a productive system based on
sharecropping. Their members ran the generator business in the 1950s,
were members of the cotton cooperative in the 1960s, had capitalized new
ventures by working in the DC area during the 1970s, and profited greatly
during the 1980s as Salvadoran migration to the United States increased.
Members of this group had founded the Banquito, had controlled the local
government more or less consistently, and were responsible for naming the
street after the US Ambassador. They had founded Unidos-por-Intipucá,
started the booster campaigns, and welcomed the Salvadoran president to
the pueblo. These were also the people who had negotiated with Agrícola
about its office in the town.

When Marvin hugged the woman and claimed to share a similar social position with her ("We're all poor"), he was invoking a claim that had been used for many years among the town elite as part of their project of rule and exploitation. It was the same kind of claim that Fernando Leonzo had frequently tried to make to build trust in his bank in Washington, DC. Relative to real estate developers like Til Hazel in Northern Virginia or the Calderón Sol family in El Salvador, Intipuqueños all shared a subaltern class position. However, internally, the population across DC and the pueblo was deeply divided. The park events reenacted this tense history as people were simultaneously unified and divided in an uneven manner. The play-like performance of pick-pocketing and being caught mirrored the experience of many people with regard to the town elite. The woman stood for those whose lives were limited, and the man embodied the elite who had control over people's lives. Remarkably, the highly playful spirit suggested these two groups did share some common experiences in the pueblo and in particular contexts could be moderately reconciled, especially in moments of exchange.

At the Margins

Moving from exchange to some of its conditions of possibility, the well-known and greatly liked drink-vendor purchased an important aspect of her operation — small blocks of ice — on a daily basis from another woman who lived nearby. This woman, whom I shall call Sonya, had fled wartime fighting in the town of Sesori located north of San Miguel and had found work on a large farm owned by one of the wealthiest families in El Salvador, the Regelado dynasty. The Regelado family member who owned this large parcel rented the land to a consortium of Jamaican investors who operated a rudimentary juice packaging plant there. Sonya worked for a period on the farm and in the packing plant. She eventually heard of Intipucá, located only about 8 miles away, as a place where one could find work taking care of houses owned by residents living in the DC area. She eventually traveled to the town and found exactly this kind of work.

Sonya was immediately accepted into the household where she worked as a maid and became very close with a senior member of the family who resided in the house. When he died of a stroke in the early 1990s, Sonya was invited to remain in the house and care for it because most members of the family had moved to San Salvador or to the Washington, DC, area. The surviving heir to the house lived in the Mount Pleasant neighborhood of Washington, DC, and worked as a maid at the Hilton Hotel on Connecticut Avenue, several miles south of her apartment residence. This woman would send money each month to Sonya to pay the electrical and water bills, but Sonya received no money for additional food or supplies. Resourcefully, Sonya used the refrigerator in the house to make small blocks of ice, which she sold to the kiosk operator in the park. With the money that she earned from the ice sale, she was able to buy tortillas each day to supplement her meals.

Sonya's son, whom I shall call Manlio, had been conscripted into the Salvadoran Army near the end of the 1980s. He had fought in the region near Intipucá with his platoon and received training from US advisors, Puerto Ricans who spoke Spanish, he told me. After his discharge, Manlio received about 2,400 colónes and was able to build a small house out of thatch and pieces of wood with a galvanized steel roof along a small path that linked Intipucá with the Pacific Ocean. There were several other huts adjacent to his, and not far away was a more substantial settlement of people who worked on farms owned by Intipucá families, known as Santa Juliana. Manlio was able to farm a small plot of land that he rented by returning a portion of his corn harvest to the owner, a prominent landowner in the pueblo. When not minding his small plot of corn, he obtained his food and a small amount of cash income by fishing in the Pacific Ocean or in Lake Olomega. This was the lake that Sigfredo's mother had traversed with the corn that her family brought to market in San Miguel during the early part of the twentieth century. Depending on the size of his catch, Manlio usually would sell a portion, keep some for himself and his wife, and give some to his mother. Other than purchasing tortillas with her ice-money, she was almost wholly dependent on the food that Manlio obtained for her.

Obtaining Food and Money

On a typical fishing trip to Olomega, Manlio would walk up the hill from his hut to the house where his mother lived in Intipucá, arriving in a remarkably cheery mood at about 4:45 am. Manlio does not own a watch, but was almost perfectly on time whenever we made the fishing trip together. I once asked him how he could tell the time and always arrive so that he could catch the 5:00 a.m. bus to Tierra Blanca. "From the stars," he replied. "My father taught me how to read the stars through the walls of my house. I can lie in the hammock and look up to see the stars and know if it is morning." Manlio's reply was remarkably similar to the opening sequence of Argueta's famous novel, *One Day in the Life*:

> I have a trick to be punctual: the cracks between the sticks that make up the wall . . . I peek at the night through the cracks in the wall . . . I can see the morning star through a little hole. I know it because it is so big. It flickers, on and off. At first I can't see it; then it arrives at the little hole as the stars and the moon and the sun walk across the sky. When the big star gets to the little hole (I know exactly where it is), it's four in the morning, and by then I'm awake.

In spite of the prompt arrival of Manlio at 4:45 one day, he and I still missed the 5:00 bus since it left unexpectedly early. We returned to Sonya's house to drink another cup of coffee and then caught a bus going to San Miguel. Not far into the trip, we jumped off at the intersection of the road to Tierra Blanca. Manlio had told me that he suspected that a friend from San Miguel who sold cheese in the area might be driving by on his delivery route at about this time. Sure enough. At 6:30 sharp his friend drove by and we flagged him down and got a ride for about five miles to Tierra Blanca, passing Chichipate where Marvin's cousin "Manuel" now lived. We jumped out of the back of the truck at Tierra Blanca and walked down the steep hill to the area known as Puerto Viejo at the southwest end of Laguna Olomega. Before the Littoral highway was built, this was the disembarkment point for small boats that carried people and supplies across the lake where they would catch the train to continue on to San Miguel. Above Puerto Viejo all along the dusty steep hills, people who had come to the area during the 1980s to flee the fighting to the north had carved out flat surfaces and built adobe and stick huts.

We arrived at the dwelling of Manlio's sister, Daisy, where she lived with her husband and young son and daughter. The door to the hut was made of a vertical array of sticks nailed together and suspended by wire from the walls of the adobe house. A plastic table cloth divided the large room, creating a sleeping area in the back and open eating and cooking space in the front. Over the beds hung several well-worn brown mosquito nets. Daisy explained that during the winter rainy season the mosquitoes were unbearable.

Manlio and Daisy recalled that their mother, Sonya, had come to the area to work during the second half of the 1980s. Manlio then boasted that he was the first from the family to come to the area, arriving as an army soldier with his patrol when he was sixteen years old. "They got

me at Esteron when I was fifteen and I stayed in for two years," he said
of his conscription. "People always ask me why I didn't join the guerilla,"
Manlio continued. "When I was twelve-and-a-half years I went to their
training camp for fifteen days. We learned how to disassemble and shoot
a rifle. I hated it. We were near El Triunfo in the mountains. How was a
little kid like me going to be able to carry that old gun—let alone shoot a
well-armed government soldier with it?!! I left the camp. 'This is not for
me,' I said to myself."

After more chatting, we hurried off to the house of a fellow whom Manlio addressed as Napito (short for Napoleon) and who I later learned was a
cousin of Manlio. Napito's father, also named Napoleon, owned a small outboard motor that could be attached to a launch. He had lived in the Washington, DC, area during the 1980s and worked a variety of low-wage jobs,
returning to build his house, fish, and work a small piece of land nearby.
Napito agreed to lend us the motor and also come along to help catch fish.

After securing use of the motor for the day, we walked to another
house to arrange to borrow a small boat. A very young boy wearing rub-
ber boots, dirty trousers, and a faded Washington Redskins football team
t-shirt was minding the house. He told me that he had four older brothers
who were living in the Washington, DC, area and that they all worked and
regularly sent home a portion of their income. The yard was larger than
most in the area, and there were two small houses made of concrete block
with tile roofs. One was strung with Christmas lights. This more substantial design was typical of new homes often paid for with US remittances.
In Intipucá they were called "Washington homes." The yard contained
several cows and chickens as well as a covered wash area. A radio was
playing loudly in the background, broadcasting evangelical preaching. The
young boy was visibly proud to be looking after everything. He shrugged
his shoulders and told us that his father was out drinking and had not been
home for a week.

We attached the motor to the launch and with barely an ounce of gaso-
line in the tank, we motored along the shore down to another house where
the residents sold gas out of large plastic containers stacked in their living
room. The whole house smelled of gas and oil fumes. We bought all they
had for sale, mixing in the proper amount of oil with the gas as we filled
up the red plastic tank with the fuel, and then ran the boat back to Daisy's
house in order to get ready to fish. We changed into shorts and T-shirts,
ate some tortillas and avocados with salt, and headed out at about 2:00 in
the afternoon, just as the hot midday sun seemed to be cooling slightly.

At medium speed, we motored out around a point and then the lake seemed to expand almost to the horizon, speckled with clusters of floating nymphs. As we headed around the point and out to the open lake we saw several people fishing from a boat along the western shore and we headed toward them. They appeared to be successfully bringing in full nets of fish, one after the other. Yelling back and forth, we all acknowledged that this was the best shore from which to cast nets.

Manlio had stored the net rolled up at his sister's house. It was a long rectangle of nylon mesh with small lead weights attached along one of the long edges. The weights served to hold this edge down along the bottom of the lake. With a long stick we anchored one end of the net into the mud near shore, and then in a slow paddling motion dropped the net gradually into the water, creating a large arc or circle extending out into the lake as we returned back to where the stick was anchored. Once the net was "thrown" in this manner, we began the difficult process of drawing it in and trapping the fish. Napito stood in the chest-high water and held one end of the net secure, keeping it tight against the bottom of the lake with his foot. Manlio also stood in the lake and pulled the net toward him using his toes and hands. With his left foot he hooked his toe into the net and dragged it along the bottom, up his other leg and then grabbed it with his hand, pulling it up and across his chest and then bundling it together. Gradually, be brought in the net.

At a certain point in the process, the weight and tug of the fish could be felt by both Manlio and Napito. They both nodded silently to each other and smiled. As Manlio pulled in the final yards of the net, the fish that were trapped began to jump out of the water into the air, sometimes escaping over the net and swimming back out into the lake. Manlio would pull in the net and the fish were trapped by their gills in the mesh. He would free the fish, hold it in his hand and kiss the fish, sucking water out of the fish's mouth and then spitting it out himself. Then he would smile and throw the fish in the boat.

Once the net was fully drawn up, Manlio re-set it by casting it over his head. It was a complex motion that involved swinging the whole net above his head and then releasing it so the weighted edge fell in an arching circle. He performed this deftly each time, slowly pulling it in again, each time with fish hung up in the mesh. By the late afternoon a small breeze was picking up and Napito started to shiver in the water. "Get some balls!" yelled Manlio with a grin at his younger cousin.

With the last cast pulled in, we sorted the fish in the bottom of the boat, distinguishing them by size. As the sun was setting, Manlio pulled on the starter rope, bringing the engine to life. We sped across the lake, yelling to a woman on the far side, whom Manlio knew as a regular purchaser of fish. After some haggling, Manlio agreed to sell her thirty of the larger fish for fifty colones.

When we arrived back at Puerto Viejo, we dragged the boat up on the shore near the large house with the young child from whom we had borrowed it. His sister was with him, but the father still had not returned. Napito dragged the heavy motor back to his father. Daisy came down to the edge of the lake with several buckets, and we carried the fish up to the hut while Manlio bore the net over his shoulder.

Sitting outside as it got dark, Manlio and Daisy worked quickly to scale the fish. Daisy cut several of the big ones in half and dropped them in a pot of boiling water already filled with cabbage, tomatoes, potatoes, and an ample amount of salt. As we were eating the soup with a stack of re-heated tortillas, I asked Manlio and Daisy whether they thought of fishing as work. Without answering the question negatively or affirmatively, Manlio quickly began to explain that if I wanted to become a fisherman I would have to begin learning as if I were a young child. "You have to start with the small net, like we used at Esteron," he said, recalling another fishing trip we had made to the river delta south of Intipucá. Only after I was competent with the small net would he allow me to try fishing with the big net. He explained in careful detail that the big net required a significant amount of specialized skill because one had to use one's feet together with the hands in order to properly draw it in, keeping the fish from escaping.

I believe that Manlio had interpreted my question as if I were asking whether the activity of fishing was such a general form of work that I could simply copy him, since I was capable of work just like anyone else. His answer in the form of a long explanation suggested that he did not agree with this basic premise. He specified in great detail the skills involved and pointed out that they were learned over time, in the course of one's development from youth into adulthood. Proper fishing was not abstract work that anyone could accomplish. It was a practice developed over time and in this way was tied with one's personal experiences and capacities. He was visibly proud of his learned abilities and attributed this, like other aspects of his life, to his strong sense of self-discipline, such as when he teased his cousin about shivering in the water. I agreed that it probably would take a long time and a great amount of effort for me to learn to become a fisherman using the net.

The next morning, we awoke at around 5:00 and Daisy immediately started a cooking fire with wood. The smoke filled the hut before it slowly dissipated up through cracks in the corrugated steel roof. She then began to soak corn kernels in lye to soften them in order to make tortillas. For breakfast, we ate packaged cakes that Daisy purchased at a small tienda down the hill; they had been made by a Mexican company and brought to the area by distributors based in San Miguel. We drank what everyone called "café indio"—a small bag of pungent ground coffee boiled in water with large amounts of sugar added. After washing up, Manlio packed up our fish and walked up to catch the bus back to Intipucá.

Manlio's Sense of Self-Discipline

Over the course of the two-day visit, Manlio had registered a series of criticisms about Daisy and her children. Several times he coaxed the daughter to come close to him and then he would swat her with his hand. She would interpret it as a game until it hurt and then she would cry and run inside the house. Manlio immediately yelled across the yard to his sister telling her that this crying was a bad habit and should be stopped. She should not bring up her children in such a way, he admonished her. Once when Daisy's son ran into the house and pulled the door behind him, snapping it on its hinges, Manlio yelled at him and lectured him on taking care of the house. "If you want to be a man, you have to take care of the house, understand me?" Earlier in the week, several kids had killed one of Daisy's hens with a slingshot. Manlio chastised his sister for not reporting this to the police. "I'll talk with the kids," Daisy tried to reassure him.

Manlio's strong opinions about discipline and conduct may have been shaped in part by his two years in the army. Coupled with his explanation about the particular difficulties of learning to fish, his attitudes suggest that he placed great importance on one's ability to live as a properly self-disciplined person, willing to work hard to learn special skills and techniques. Giving in to hardship, whether by shivering in the cold, crying from being struck, or not seeking proper redress for a poached chicken, was something that he abhorred. Masculinity and maturity together were defined as responsible comportment and care for property. This apparent rigidness, despite the possible discomfort of those he imposed it upon, helped sustain Manlio in a life that was organized around meeting basic subsistence needs on an almost daily basis. It was less a psychological tendency than the outcome of life as a young man without even the guarantee that he and his family would have enough to eat each day. It was this quality of selfhood that, in part, allowed Sonya to be relatively sure that she would never be short of food. "He's a good man, my son," she frequently remarked.

Steak and Cheese

Sonya and her children in the area lived on the margins of a circuit of relations that extended to Washington, DC, yielding the boat and motor for fishing and the ice that Sonya sold in the park. In turn, the availability of handmade drinks chilled with Sonya's ice helped to distinguish the one kiosk from others whose operators sold different kinds of drinks, using other methods for cooling them. One "competitor" kiosk sold a much different line of food and beverages, and it was owned by the fellow whom I introduced in chapter 2 as Roberto.

Roberto grew up in the settlement of La Leona and moved to the outskirts of the pueblo when he was a boy. In the early 1970s, his mother traveled with a group of people from the pueblo overland via Mexico to Washington, DC. Like many Salvadoran women during the 1970s in DC, she found work as a maid cleaning rooms in various city hotels. As a young man, Roberto was an exceptionally talented soccer player. During the late 1970s and early 1980s, when Sigfredo was organizing the soccer team in DC with sponsorship from the popular restaurant Adam's Rib, he knew of Roberto and his abilities and arranged to help Roberto make the trip to DC so that he might find work and be able to play on the Intipucá team in DC. Roberto joined his mother in the city and worked odd jobs in construction, house painting, and a variety of restaurants. He led the team to several championships against the various informal teams organized by Latino, European, and African enthusiasts of the game who were living in the DC region.

Roberto gradually was welcomed into the circle of more established Intipucá residents in DC and eventually found steady and relatively well-paying work as a cook at a well-known Chinese restaurant in the District. Among Intipuqueños this was considered more favorable employment than construction, since it provided the opportunity for free food and it was less demanding physically than outside labor. He and his mother carefully saved their money, and eventually they were able to help his younger stepbrother leave the pueblo in the later 1980s to avoid military service. They were also able to purchase a small brick and concrete house on the outer edge of the pueblo where other, more distant family members from La Leona were able to move and live. During this time the younger brother, known as "the Puerto Rican," had a difficult time in DC, and Roberto and his mother frequently were concerned for his welfare. They were upset that he was not attending school regularly and frequently coming home drunk and stoned. He was not working at a regular job, and he was becoming a financial burden for Roberto and his mother.

At this time Roberto was working in the Chinese restaurant, and he began to quarrel with another cook, a Chinese man. The cook accused Roberto of stealing food from the kitchen and called him a "fucking lazy Hispanic." Roberto denied taking food beyond what he was allowed to eat as an employee. The Chinese man grabbed Roberto and pulled a large knife out, threatening Roberto with it. He pushed Roberto out the back door and said for him not to come back to work or he would kill him with the knife. Roberto walked away. Later that night Roberto returned and waited for the chef to leave through the same back door As the man walked out, Roberto attacked him with a metal bar, beating him severely around the face, head, and torso. Several other cooks ran out and restrained Roberto. Police officers soon arrived and Roberto was arrested and brought to the DC jail.

Roberto was convicted of assault and ordered serve a brief term in prison. Upon his release he was immediately deported to El Salvador, and he returned to Intipucá. Those people who remembered him agreed that he was right to respond to the cook's threat with a counter-assault, although Roberto later admitted that it was excessive and that the man barely survived his attack. In Intipucá, residents spoke poorly of Chinese and Korean migrants in DC who served as their coworkers and bosses in area restaurants. "They are mean and they are cheap," was a general refrain.

With the help of some money sent by his mother who remained in DC, Roberto quickly made plans to take care of himself in the pueblo, moving back into the small house and arranging to obtain a metal "chalet" to put in the park from which he might be able to sell drinks and food. Like the son of the mayor, Roberto occupied a unique social position as a person with considerable experience in DC, but with ties to Intipucá that were much different than those of the circle of landowners like Sigfredo, who continued to move back and forth developing business ventures in DC and Intipucá. As a soccer player who had gone to DC and earned a relatively good living in restaurant work, he was a model for poorer residents who had neither the money nor the contacts to leave the pueblo and travel to DC.

Roberto soon opened his chalet and was able to obtain a free refrigerator from Jorge, the soda and beer distributor with whom Marvin worked, since he agreed to sell exclusively Coca-Cola products. This was a strategy that the company pursued throughout El Salvador to help build its network of small retailers. Roberto connected his chalet to the town power line that ran overhead in order to run the refrigerator and also to hang a low-wattage bulb so he could remain open into the night. During and after the war, electric power was limited and sporadic in the region. Frequently drinks remained less than completely chilled, and Roberto would work by candlelight and lantern. Nevertheless, Roberto's chalet was popular, and he began to offer a specialty item that he called "steak and cheese," using the English words. It was a small sandwich with cooked and seasoned meat, locally produced cheese, and a sweet cole slaw–like topping all served on a small roll, freshly baked in the pueblo. They immediately became popular with residents who had the three colónes to pay for one of them.

In 1992 when Marvin returned permanently to the pueblo, he missed many aspects of life in DC. He began to work for Jorge as the regular truck driver and at the end of each trip he would stop at Roberto's chalet to eat several "steak and cheese" sandwiches. "It's not Burger King, but it's good," he often said to me. He and Roberto, though of much different class backgrounds, became close friends. What they shared in common was over a decade of living and working in the DC area and the experience of having encountered the police and having been obligated to return to the pueblo. They knew of each other while in DC, but had not been part of the same social circles. From Roberto's perspective, he liked Marvin's regular purchases, and through negotiations with Jorge he was able to receive advances on soda and beer to correspond with increased sales during holidays. Despite their differences, Marvin and Roberto were very loyal friends and much enjoyed wagering on pool matches and card games whenever possible.

Market Competition and the Intipucá Service Sector

In 1996, a man whom I shall call Omar, the friend recruited by Marvin to help him distribute cocaine in the 1980s, completed his ten-year prison sentence and was deported back to El Salvador. He returned to the pueblo much as Roberto did in the late 1980s and Marvin did in 1992, but in contrast to Roberto, Omar came from a family that owned a large house in the center of the pueblo and also several large plots of land nearby. Omar was encouraged by his mother, also successfully working in a DC hotel for almost two decades, to try to restart the farm. Omar had limited resources

and complained that he was not able to find competent workers or a foreman to run the farm. As a child he had not been raised to run the farm and
did not know how to begin, although his mother promised that she could
send him up to $7,000 of her savings to help him. Instead, Omar decided
to convert part of the large family home into a restaurant that would specialize in selling US-style food, especially for people who returned to the
pueblo for holidays.

He, Marvin, and Roberto worked hard to clean and repaint the house
in time for the festival to honor the patron saint of the town during the
first week of March. "We worked fast," Omar recalled, using the popular English terms for the different types of painting mixed with Spanish.
"Steak-and-Cheese and I 'cut' and Marvin 'rolled'; we painted the whole
house in a day." With facilitation by Marvin, Omar ordered beer and soda
from Jorge along with a large refrigerator. He passed the word around that
he was looking for a woman to hire as a waitress so that his new restaurant
could open for business in time for the festival.

Around the time that Sonya had fled Sesori, a teen-aged woman whom
I shall call María left her mother and younger sisters and brothers in that
town to travel to the capital city of San Salvador. She sought work as a
servant in a private home, where she would clean and cook in return for
board and a small wage that she could share with her family who remained
in Sesori. She eventually came to work for a prominent attorney whose
family owned a moderate amount of agricultural land outside of Intipucá.
This lawyer and his siblings and cousins had attended prominent universi-
ties in El Salvador because their family had significant resources accumulated from growing cotton on their land, renting land to other cotton
growers, and working for extended periods in Washington, DC, since the
1970s like other residents of Intipucá.

María and the lawyer became close friends and periodically she traveled with him to Intipucá. Slowly María established ties to the town, and
eventually she stopped working for the family in San Salvador and moved
to Intipucá to work as a servant in private homes, much like Sonya. Her
mother, sisters, and brothers eventually moved to Intipucá as well and
found small rooms to rent. The mother also took a job cleaning homes,
while the oldest son occasionally sold ice cream and found day jobs clear-
ing other people's fields.

During her early time in Intipucá, she encountered a young woman
whom I shall call Mélida. Mélida and her brother inherited from their
father a large piece of property where he had grazed cattle and grown cot-

ton. Mélida's brother was the fellow introduced in chapter 3 who had left for Los Angeles in the late 1970s and started a construction company, employing Mexicans and Salvadorans. Mélida had remained in El Salvador to look after the family property. Mélida agreed to take María to San Salvador to help her find work in another home as a servant, as she had once worked for the lawyer and his family. When Mélida picked up María with her truck, instead of driving to San Salvador they arrived at a popular seaside town and beach where Mélida lived and owned several buildings—the same place where Marvin had ridden his motorcycle on the beach. Mélida forced María, who was broke, to live and work in a small bordello, and told her that she could leave once she had earned enough to pay for the food and shelter that she received. María remained at the beach for less than a week until she was able to arrange an escape with the help of a friend.

When she returned to Intipucá, she learned that Omar wished to hire a woman to cook and serve at his restaurant, and she went to speak with him. He agreed to hire her, anticipating a lucrative business with the return of hundreds of Intipuqueños for the festival. While working for Omar, María took part in the celebration of the town's patron saint and had a liaison with a young man in the town, a son of a prominent political leader. During the resulting pregnancy, María became increasingly concerned about the role of the young man in relation to her and the child. Initially he denied that he could be the father, a habitual claim among men in rural El Salvador. Later he admitted that he was the father, but made little effort to contact María or play an active role in her life or later in the life of the child.

One evening after a heated argument, María stormed out of the restaurant. "She's dirty. She doesn't take care of herself. She doesn't comb her hair," Omar explained, acting as if he had fired her. Roberto, echoing his own encounter with the Chinese cook, offered the interpretation that she had been stealing food for her family. Marvin suggested that she had rebuffed his demands that she sleep with him. Later in the evening she explained her reason for quitting to me: "He got drunk today. I'm not working for a drunk!"

Without María, Omar was somewhat ashamed that he had to stand over the stove while his friends were drinking and eating. He often insisted that he needed another female assistant. A young woman from La Leona whom I will call Sandra joined him to work in the restaurant and eventually began to stay there each night as she became romantically involved with Omar. Sandra was tough and smart, and she helped Omar run a better business. Mostly she discouraged him from giving out free drinks to his friends and also tried to keep him from getting too drunk as he was trying to run the restaurant.

The romance and steady hand of Sandra suited Roberto and allowed him to appear more like a successful proprietor and popular man rather than an overworked cook, waiter, and ex-con living off the largesse of his mother. His main competition, however, was his apparent friend, Roberto Steak-and-Cheese, who worked less hard to court visitors from the DC area with parties and expensive food, but instead was extremely frugal and careful—in a sense a better business operator than Omar.

The competition between the two purveyors of US-style food, each focusing on the market of Intipuqueños accustomed to living in the United States, came to a head near the end of the 1990s. A rumor began to circulate that Roberto had had a romantic relationship with Sandra while she was living and working at Omar's restaurant. Omar did not confront Roberto, and Roberto tended to avoid going near the restaurant. Most people assumed that it was a one-time event and would slowly fade away in everyone's memory, not disrupting the more established relationships. Indeed, this seemed to be happening until one evening when Omar and Roberto were playing checkers together at the Desvio.

Omar was losing small amounts of money in the betting that accompanied each game and was growing increasingly frustrated—and drunk. As Roberto bested him once again, Omar jumped up and stabbed a metal fork into Roberto's abdomen. Roberto fell over, clutching his stomach as blood flowed from the wound. Omar ran up the hill into the pueblo, leaving Roberto on the ground. Roberto eventually made it back to the pueblo, but had lost a considerable amount of blood. He went to his house, cleaned the wound, and rested carefully over the next several days. Rather than begin to heal, the wound became badly infected, and Roberto had to be taken to a hospital in San Miguel. Over two weeks later he returned to the pueblo, after having received several pints of plasma and large doses of antibiotics. "I almost died," he told us when he returned. In the meantime, Omar had fled the pueblo, taking the last of the money that he had left from his mother and moving to live with an old girlfriend in San Salvador.

The Future Viewed from the Margins of the Intipucá–Washington, DC, Circuit

Meanwhile, María, Omar's first employee, continued to live in the pueblo, being provided for by her mother and siblings as her pregnancy progressed.

During these months, María occasionally visited the home of a friend who had just given birth to a child. The child's father and mother, both in their late teens, had grown up in the Mount Pleasant neighborhood in DC. The father had been an accomplished soccer player, but had become involved in selling small amounts of drugs on a popular corner of Park Road in the neighborhood as a youth. He had been apprehended by the police and sent to live in a juvenile detention center for a period; now he was back in Intipucá along with his wife. The couple explained to María that in Washington, DC, "the government gives you money, food, and clothing to have children. They pay you to have a baby!" María was incredulous.

Also during the pregnancy María made periodic trips to the town clinic to be checked on by a nurse. She frequently borrowed money to pay for these visits. About a month before the birth, María experienced severe pain in the region of her womb and went to visit a woman who lived on the outskirts of the town and was popularly known as a witch or *bruja*. The woman massaged María's stomach and said that this would help align the heads of what she guessed were twins and prepare them for birth.

In late November María went into labor and was in great pain. According to several people present, the infant was not emerging safely. The town ambulance was called, and she was driven to the public hospital in San Miguel. Later in the night, a doctor performed a caesarian delivery, and by the next day María was recovering in a room shared by about twenty other women.

The next day, her mother and I and several family friends visited and talked briefly with María. During our conversation she was especially concerned about having enough money to pay for the unexpected operation and also that she needed a man to sign the birth certificate as the legal father or guardian of the child. In the absence of money and a father's signature, the child potentially could be placed in an orphanage.

Later in the day I had a more extended conversation with María's mother who was extremely frustrated over the situation and burst out forcefully in an uncharacteristic manner. "She needs the father to sign for the baby with two witnesses and to pay 600 colónes for the operation! And [the father] has not come by and I will not go get him! It was not like this before!" A friend asks, "Why didn't she have the child here?" motioning around the room with his arm.

"There were problems and they had to cut her open. Two days of intensive care," replied Maria's mother with patience and deference to the older man that she could maintain only for a brief moment. Then she raised her voice:

A woman could have a child and leave with the child! I raised my children because their father was killed in the war, not because they did not have a father!
I am humble (*humilde*), but I am not going to go asking for money so Maria can
have her child! This makes me angry! I am angry about this!

María eventually obtained the money and a passable signature and was
able to leave the hospital with her child to rejoin her mother and sisters
and brothers in Intipucá. Over the following year María raised the child
and tried to find work in Intipucá. Without any support from the child's
father, the family was in a situation similar to before the childbirth.

In 1997, María secretly borrowed $3,000 from a series of friends in the
area and made arrangements to travel overland to Mexico and then cross
into the United States. Her objective was to make it to Northern Virginia
near Washington, DC, where she had several friends. It was an extremely
difficult trip. She was robbed near the US–Mexican border and lived in a
trailer for six days without food, water, or access to a toilet. Once across
the Rio Grande and staying in a temporary house in the desert, she had
to pay an additional $2,000 to be driven to Atlanta, Georgia, where she
worked for a period.

Almost three months after leaving Intipucá, she arrived in Virginia and
soon found work at a Pancake House Restaurant in the city of Alexandria,
living in an apartment complex populated by many other Salvadorans.
Over time she came to know a young man from El Salvador, and they
began to share an apartment with other family members. Within the year
she became pregnant again, and together they planned for the arrival of
their child. She was able to earn a steady wage at Pancake House and send
home between $20 and $50 periodically to her mother and the rest of the
family in Intipucá, who now rented a more substantial home from one of
the wealthier landowning families in the town. She was especially happy
that her baby in Intipucá would be able to eat and live better than when
she lived there and was cautiously optimistic about her future in Northern
Virginia.

Shortly after the birth of her second child at Alexandria Hospital she
encountered a city social worker. "I asked her if I could take my child
with me to El Salvador and she said no. 'That baby is an American baby
and must remain here,' she said. I need to get [her] a passport and a social
security card."

María told me that the social workers seemed especially kind and concerned about the health of the child. She told me that she received some

clothing and blankets for the child and a small amount of money for food and medicine. She said that she did not understand everything that the social worker said to her regarding the child and how it was a US child. She was particularly concerned that if she were deported to El Salvador, the baby would not be able to accompany her.

Conclusion: To Service and Subsist

This chapter began with the bustling appearance of the park in the center of town and then traced out several people's lives and the different ways that they were linked through park activities. Their lives were radically different, and each was enveloped in particular conflicts shaped by competing interests, outlooks, and objectives. Overall, Sonya, Manlio, Sandra, Roberto, Omar, and María were living at various social positions within the Intipucá-DC circuit. To live, each person took part in a simple service economy organized around preparing and selling food and drinks in the town and driven to a large extent by customers with particular ties to and experiences in the DC area.

Of everyone considered, María was the only person who later traveled to DC. Several of her brothers have successfully joined her in Virginia and have found work there as well. All of them prefer not to visit restaurants or markets owned by the well-known Intipucá families in the region, and they have changed their name so that they cannot be linked with the pueblo. As María's young child grows up as a US citizen with Salvadoran parents, she will be confronted with many understandings of El Salvador–US relations during the decades of the twentieth century, including the dominant Intipucá-DC account. Of the many challenges that she faces, one will be to recognize her role in the making of this history.

FINALE

CHAPTER NINE

Options and Models for the Future

This final chapter builds on the materials covered so far in the book and performs two kinds of inquiries. First, it describes a dominant US model of counterinsurgency warfare that has guided the US policies in Iraq since the invasion. This account shows the public appearance of El Salvador as the source of an exemplary model of warfare and also uncovers some of the historical content of this warfare doctrine, including an explicit connection to Intipucá. The second part of the chapter moves in a similar way, tracing out a dominant US development and foreign aid strategy that, remarkably, also contains within it the attenuated presence of Intipucá and DC. These two US foreign policy projects—counterinsurgency warfare and grass-roots entrepreneur-based development—are complementary, defining the stick and carrot of a revitalized US interventionist agenda at the edge of the twenty-first century. One idealized figure at the center of this project is a kind of compassionate multicultural soldier-turned-entrepreneur, perhaps similar to the figure of Greg Mortenson as he has portrayed himself in the popular book *Three Cups of Tea: One Man's Journey to Change the World . . . One Child at a Time.*[1]

This chapter goes inside the contemporary counterinsurgency option and the new model of development, showing that part of their content is exactly the geohistorical terrain covered in the previous chapters of the book. Figuratively, the previous eight chapters are like the story of the three women in the introduction—necessary for, but hidden within, what now appears as a crisis-ridden twenty-first-century US imperial project.

The El Salvador Option

In English, an "option" usually is understood to be a choice or a course of action that may be taken but without compulsion. For example, in US financial markets, to trade in "options" means buying and selling the rights, but again not the obligation, to make a future transaction, usually around some other security or contract.[2] The general definition of an option and the technical financial term have something in common. At any particular moment, something already known or completed may be set for repetition. The effect is to render an open-ended future into a set of possible choices—bringing it somewhere between the completely unknown and the utterly predictable. To have an "option" is to carve out a quality of tendency, of reasonableness, and of meaning. Exactly such a social process historically unfolded in the context of the US invasion and war in Iraq.

On March 20, 2003, the US military led a sustained air-, land-, and sea-based assault on the country of Iraq, seizing control of the capital city, Baghdad, after just less than three weeks of fighting. From the perspective of the US war-planners and commanders as well as the numerous media reporters who had been invited to cover the attack, it seemed like a masterful military success, echoing the swift US-led invasion of Afghanistan carried out the previous year. On May 1, US President Bush hailed the incursion as an unqualified US military "victory," famously landing as a passenger in a 1970s-era Lockheed S-3 antisubmarine reconnaissance airplane on the aircraft carrier USS *Abraham Lincoln* and delivering a short address under a fluttering banner that read "Mission Accomplished."[3]

In remarkably short order, however, small-scale guerilla-style attacks on US forces and their newly recruited, trained Iraqi Security Forces as well as on sites of vital infrastructure in the country began to climb dramatically, especially in the provinces of Baghdad and Al Anbar. This growing and increasingly multiplex insurgency initially was dominated by former Saddam and Baath Party supporters and later included an array of religious and nationalist militias from within and outside of Iraq—hardly unified, but all deeply opposed to the US invasion and occupation. Civilian and combatant casualties climbed into the thousands as a result of both the insurgency and US-led "counterinsurgency" operations, notably in Fallujah and Mosul at the end of 2004 and continuing into 2008. Several US officials acknowledged that they were fighting a difficult guerilla war that included a significant level of popular support and that there was little possibility of a quick resolution to the conflict.

From the perspective of the US military especially, a central challenge was how to diminish the appearance that US forces were illegitimate invaders and occupiers of Iraq. A key part of this endeavor entailed promoting popular elections in the country and the formation of a national Iraqi civilian government by January 2005. In the face of widespread criticism that popular elections amidst the violent fighting would be little more than a propaganda charade, US General John Abizaid, Commander of the United States Central Command—which oversees all US military activity across northeast Africa, the Arabian Peninsula, and southern and central Asia—appeared on the popular US television show "Meet the Press" (that aired on September 26, 2004). Host Tim Russert peppered the General with questions about the viability and legitimacy of such an election in Iraq, pointing out that regions of the country were so stricken with conflict that fair balloting would be impossible.

"My belief is that elections will occur in the vast majority of the country. I can't predict 100 percent that all areas will be available for complete, free, fair, and peaceful elections. . . . That having been said, if we look at our previous experiences in El Salvador, we know that people who want to vote will vote," said Abizaid. At that moment, for a US TV news–watching public, 1980s El Salvador had been rhetorically transformed into as successful "model" to be applied in Iraq. The next day *New York Times* columnist David Brooks echoed and expanded on Abizaid's Iraq–El Salvador comparison with a short op-ed titled "The Insurgency Buster." Recounting the violence surrounding El Salvador elections in the early 1980s, Brooks argued that the elections, among many things, "proved how resilient democracy is," "undermined the insurgency," and "produced a President, José Napoleón Duarte." Gesturing toward the possible future in Iraq (and also with respect to impending elections in Afghanistan), Brooks referred in a particular way to a period in Salvadoran history. "A democratically elected leader . . . can do what Duarte did. He can negotiate with rebels, invite them into the political process, and co-opt any legitimate grievances. He can rally people on all sides of the political spectrum, who are united by their attachment to the democratic idea."

Slightly more than a week after this call to "do what Duarte did," US Vice President Cheney made the same comparison in the context of a public debate with Democratic vice presidential challenger John Edwards.

"Twenty years ago we had a similar situation in El Salvador," Cheney said. "We had a guerilla insurgency controlled roughly a third of the country, 75,000 people dead. And we held free elections. I was there as an observer on behalf of the Congress. . . . And as the terrorists would come in and shoot up polling places, as soon as they left, the voters would come back and get in line and would not be denied their right to vote. And today El Salvador is a whale of a lot better because we held free elections. . . . And [that concept] will apply in Afghanistan. And it will apply as well in Iraq."

The following month, on November 11, 2004, Donald Rumsfeld offered a version of the El Salvador comparison when he visited El Salvador and gave an address at the US Embassy, thanking El Salvador for sending troops to Iraq. He also touted El Salvador as an exemplary model of how a country can move from civil war to become a stable democracy and close US ally.[4]

Two months later, on January 8, 2005, *Newsweek* carried an article by Michael Hirsh and John Barry suggesting that US military leaders privately were discussing the Salvador Option as a way to combat the insurgency in Iraq.[5] As in the other references to El Salvador, features of the country's recent history were culled to provide a model for future US conduct in Iraq. However, the *Newsweek* article marked a significant alteration. In this case, the "El Salvador Option" referred not to elections, but to the possibility of training special Iraqi attack groups by US advisors. The article quoted anonymous sources within the US defense establishment who said that officials were directly discussing the tactic, but that no official decision had been reached about deploying it. The article also described private debate about whether the CIA or US Pentagon would have control over the project. Most glaringly, however, the article performed a rhetorical move in its second full paragraph, linking such training with the formation of paramilitary "death squads" as, the article suggested, the United States had done in El Salvador during the 1980s. This triggered a veritable tidal wave of public discussion and echoes of the claim worldwide. "El Salvador–Style Death Squads to Be Deployed by US against Iraq Militants," announced the *London Times* on January 10, 2005, citing the *Newsweek* story.

At a news conference on January 11, Rumsfeld called the idea of an El Salvador option "nonsense." Yet within two weeks, Seymour Hersh published an essay in the *New Yorker*, effectively substantiating the claim that the US Pentagon was discussing the Salvador Option for Iraq. Quoting an anonymous source in the intelligence community, Hersh also linked the "Option" with a specific kind of clandestine fighting. According to Hersh,

> the President has signed a series of findings and executive orders authorizing secret commando groups and other Special Forces units to conduct covert operations against suspected terrorist targets in as many as ten nations in the Middle East. . . . The new rules will enable the Special Forces community to set up what it calls "action teams" in the target countries overseas which can be used to find and eliminate terrorist organizations. "Do you remember the right-wing execution squads in El Salvador?" the former high-level intelligence official asked me, referring to the military-led gangs that committed atrocities in the early nineteen-eighties. "We founded them and we financed them," he said. "The objective now is to recruit locals in any area we want. And we aren't going to tell Congress about it." A former military officer, who has knowledge of the Pentagon's commando capabilities, said, "We're going to be riding with the bad boys."[6]

Within days of the appearance of the article, US Department of Defense spokesman Lawrence DiRita issued an impassioned statement that attempted to identify several errors in Hersh's article, though without addressing its central argument about expanded Pentagon authority for covert actions and tactics abroad.

Throughout 2004 and 2005, the "El Salvador Option," as it publicly circulated, moved from promotion of wartime elections to also include specially trained "action teams" for covert activities, including assassinations. Its appearance as a kind of ideological formation was tied to official and unofficial statements publicly circulating in the media. Its authorship was collective and diffuse and included the media together with state officials, but as a discursive entity it referred to Salvadoran history in particularly sharp ways for its audience. In its first variant it was an example of democratic consolidation under US leadership; in the second, it was US-orchestrated small-scale warfare with targeted killings and abductions of specific people.

Two-sided, the Salvador Option, nevertheless, appeared as a viable model for dealing with the multiplex Iraq insurgency. It seemed a rational response to an unexpected situation, though critics decried it as an especially brutal manner of reacting. The sense that the US state was a rational entity, acting in the form of decision making, properly (or not) selecting from a quiver of options, was the dominant image.[7]

A False Choice

As a chief architect of the US military invasion of Iraq in 2003, Paul Wolfowitz helped translate what has been known as "neoconservative" political doctrine into concrete policy under the presidential administration of George W. Bush. Among the features of the loose body of principles that make up the "neocon" perspective is an unabashed celebration of the US nation-state as the preeminent political, military, and moral leader of the world. Accordingly, this entails unquestioned global military superiority coupled with the capacity and commitment to act with "moral clarity" and to pursue issues unhindered by forms of tolerance and accommodation. One feature of the doctrine called for reorganizing the US military into a more rapid strike force, so that it could be used more widely and with greater frequency. Neocon doctrine, the desire for quick action, and the expectation of swift results informed the invasion of Iraq and the goal of transforming the country into a US-modeled "free-market democracy in short order."[8]

Shortly before President Bush made the infamous carrier landing, Paul Wolfowitz contacted an "old friend" named Jim Steele and suggested that he join the newly appointed Jay Garner as an advisor on restoring and developing electrical power in Iraq.[9] At the time, Mr. Steele was president and CEO of a large electrical utility company, TM Power Ventures, based in Houston, Texas. Steele also had served as a vice president and managing director at Enron Corporation, participating in a controversial project in Guatemala that included illegal hiding of Enron's taxable US income.[10] According to Steele, Wolfowitz suggested that this professional background in electrical power and energy development would be useful in Iraq and that he might serve as senior US advisor to the Iraqi Electricity Commission.

Upon arrival in May 2003, however, Steele switched his orientation and took command of a US advisory team that organized, trained, and then regularly operated with a special team of police known as the National Iraqi Police Service Emergency Response Unit. Steele publicly claimed that in March 2004, he "participated in the raid that resulted in the capture of Saddam's former Minister of Interior, General Mohammed Zimam Abdul Al-Razzaq, the four of spades with a bounty of one million dollars on his head."[11] Consistent with the desire to diminish the appearance that the United States was an occupying or invading force, the White House issued a press release in February that placed a slightly different emphasis

on the agents of this capture as well as marking the date as the weekend of
Saturday, February 14, 2004:

> Iraqi police are helping to make their country more secure by investigating,
> identifying, and arresting former officials of Saddam's regime. This weekend,
> the National Iraqi Police Service Emergency Response Unit arrested Muham-
> mad Zimam abd al-Razzaq al-Sadun, who is a former Ba'ath Party Regional
> Command Chairman. His arrest shows that the new Iraqi police force is taking
> responsibility for Iraq's security.[12]

Behind this manner of representation, by May 2004 Steele's Emergency
Response Unit (ERU) had become the seed from which the US military
began to develop a "third force" to work along with the reconstituted Iraqi
police and army. A private contracting agency, US Investigations Service
(USIS), owned at the time by the DC-based investment consortium Carlyle Group (that also had once owned BDM International), took over and
expanded the training program as part of a $64.5 million no-bid contract it
had secured. Initially rejected by Iraqi authorities, the ERUs functioned
largely as a counterinsurgency force, working as a direct extension of US
Special Forces in Iraq.[13]

Through the rest of the summer Steele also advised and worked with
an additional counterinsurgency group known as the Iraqi Special Police
Commandos. Unlike the ERUs, this group explicitly drew on Baathist vet-
erans of Hussein's special forces and Republican Guard, a strategy that
Steele's friend Wolfowitz had argued for originally as part of US war strategy. The Special Commandos as a counterinsurgency force and Steele's
supervision of them became more publicly recognized through the publication of Peter Maas's essay, "The Salvadorization of Iraq?" in the *New
York Times Magazine* in May 2005. This was the second public identification of Steele as a former US Special Forces soldier who had been
stationed in El Salvador during the war and the first one that linked his
presence in Iraq with the repetition of a model of "successful" counterinsurgency warfare derived from El Salvador

With these various news reports, a simple chronology was being put
into place that made it appear as if the US state were a rational actor:
The anti–United States insurgency in Iraq was unexpected (pure chance)
but there existed a viable response that now (2005) could be chosen. This
option was in fact a model of counterinsurgency derived from the success
story of US involvement in El Salvador during the 1980s. The so-called
success, as US officials liked to note, had yielded the defeat of a popular

(and in part anti–United States) insurgency and the establishment of a US-allied government in El Salvador, completely open to neoliberal restructuring (see Introduction).

Behind this appearance of rational decision-making, the training of special teams by US forces—one side of the El Salvador Option—was a path already actively pursued since the beginning of the war by Wolfowitz and Steele. To call on the option in the face of the insurgency was to falsely gesture toward an action as if it were an untried choice—something known but new. What was new, as has become clear, was simply that Wolfowitz and Steele's project became augmented and expanded. Public figures and the media had jointly coauthored a story of rational choice, of choosing an option in the face of the unexpected.

Rather than being a complete facade to be discarded, however, this appearance of "the option" had real effects. At the least, it helped set the ground for public and US congressional approval of the subsequent "surge," as if the US military had new kinds of more effective and yet untried tools at its disposal. In reality it seems that counterinsurgency was a consistent part of the strategy from the beginning of the war, though largely hidden from view as it was enacted. James Steele's presence in both El Salvador and Iraq signaled one simple connection.[14] But behind his name was another less visible story of continuity. The guiding model for US counterinsurgency warfare had been abstracted from the 1980s Salvadoran war and it similarly purported to be a success story. Yet like the public image of the El Salvador Option as a rational choice for the US state, this counterinsurgency model hid its formative historical conditions that actually were largely the opposite of the model's promises.

"Made in El Salvador"

James Steele, a veteran of the Vietnam War, had gone to El Salvador in 1984 as part of a major increase in the US role in the Salvadoran war. This was not long after Manuel, introduced in chapter 1, had traveled to DC. Colonel Steele's mandate as commander of the US Military Group (USMILGP) was to build up the Salvadoran armed forces capacity to defeat the FMLN. One part of this project involved establishing strategically located training centers within the country. Under the rubric of advising, US Special Forces and their Salvadoran counterparts could train and undertake military missions in specific parts of the country deemed important in the conflict. The training centers were meant to help organize small-scale forces that could effectively "decapitate" the FMLN insurgency, weakening its leadership and civilian support structure while also gaining valuable intelligence information.

The first of these strategic training centers was established near the port city of La Unión, slightly more than 25 kilometers from Intipucá. Known as CEMFA (*Centro de Entrenamiento Militar de la Fuerza Armada*), the facility was constructed under US supervision and could hold up to 2,000 soldiers and as many as 100 trainers, with the potential to graduate 7,500 soldiers annually.[15] When the Honduran government ordered that the United States stop training Salvadoran soldiers at the US Regional Military Training Center (CREMS) built in 1983 at Puerto Castillo, Honduras, CEMFA became the main US training base in El Salvador, especially for "counterinsurgency" warfare, known by its US military acronym, COIN.

Greg Walker, a US Special Forces soldier who served in El Salvador, recounted an early episode in the creation of CEMFA, offering his perspective of wartime southeastern El Salvador not far from Intipucá:

> A fifteen-man advisor element in La Union discovered itself tasked to establish a regional training camp (CEMFA) for the Salvadoran military. Deep in Indian country, the trainers were dismayed at the lack of perimeter defenses and a competent security force for the badly needed project. Within one week they were on alert, a sizable force of guerrillas reported to be preparing to storm the ragged *cuartel.*

Though it is not clear that all participants shared Walker's "frontier symbolism," the US advisory team did establish a 25-kilometer defensive zone around the site of the base as a "training area."[16] On this dual purpose of the zone, Walker quotes one member of the fifteen-man US team: "Our primary concern was to be able to fight from inside the *cuartel* if attacked. But we had our people out in the bush conducting training both day and night. We went on patrols, during one of which a suspected guerilla was captured spying on the base from a tree."[17]

FMLN forces in the region took great interest in the new training center and were specifically concerned with the techniques of counterinsurgency warfare that US trainers would be imparting to new Salvadoran recruits. According to one former guerilla (an intelligence expert) with whom I spoke in 1993, "We learned the most about the US forces and how they would advise the Salvadoran military by talking with the [North] Vietnamese. Those old generals knew how the US fought and they told us what to expect."[18]

On October 10, 1985, the FMLN launched a coordinated assault with at least 300 soldiers on the newly constructed center. This was among the largest operations undertaken by the FMLN in this period of the war. Their explicit goal was to capture or kill the US advisors at the base and curtail the training operations. Five US Green Beret soldiers were stationed at the base and according to Walker, "fought back against the advancing guerillas, rallying ESAF (El Salvador Armed Forces) security forces deep within the confines of the base and leading a valiant counterattack."[19] The US embassy officially denied that US forces had actively participated in repelling the attack. The US soldiers survived, but 40 Salvadoran soldiers were killed and more than 60 were wounded in the fighting. The FMLN also reported a high number of casualties.

During its existence, CEMFA was well known in Intipucá since the pueblo was located east of the base just outside the 25-kilometer perimeter zone. One of the larger land-owning families in the pueblo used personal ties to military officials there to gain permission to move to the base after receiving direct threats from FMLN soldiers operating on the outskirts of the pueblo. Intipucá residents also occasionally encountered US Special Forces soldiers in the pueblo. There are at least two well-known stories of such meetings. The first, already mentioned in chapter 4, is the tale of an African American soldier who walked into the town, looking desperately for food and water. He said that he had gotten separated from his small group in the context of a mission and needed to rest briefly before making his way back to the base. He was offered avocado, boiled eggs, and tortillas by members of Marvin's family and remained with them in their house for several hours. According to people who sat with him, he was extremely pleasant ("nicer than blacks in DC," said one person) and consistently remarked that he was amazed to learn that Salvadorans from Intipucá had been living and working in DC for nearly two generations. In particular, he was shocked when he saw so many homes with TVs and VCRs as well as when several residents began to speak with him in English. According to residents, he left in the evening, and they never saw him again.

The second story is slightly more cryptic, but seems also to correspond with the development of the training center close to the pueblo. According to residents, one morning after an evening of intense fighting near the cantón of La Leona, just to the east of Intipucá (and within CEMFA's security perimeter), townspeople found a US soldier dead, shot, lying on the ground. Most people skirted the body all day as it lay in the sun attracting flies to the bloodied wounds. Yet by the evening, his boots were conspicuously gone. "Everybody wanted those boots," someone told me year later. According to residents, by sunrise the next day the soldier had vanished. "They took him away. We don't know if it was the guerilla or the US."

According to most accounts of the war, the US training strategy was effective and the FMLN guerilla forces appeared to change their tactics in response, reducing the scale of their active operations and standing troop levels. Nevertheless, they maintained the capacity to rapidly move in and out of regions, destroying infrastructure and military resources, while keeping a high level of popular support throughout the country. US officials, not unlike their counterparts in Iraq two decades later, acknowledged that they were bogged down in a difficult and unconventional insurgency. Some went so far as to call it a stalemate by 1986–87.

Manwaring's Modeling

As chapter 4 already has explored, during this time of stalemate in El Salvador the US Army signed a contract with a private company called BDM International for the firm to produce a new analytic model of counterinsurgency warfare. Among the main conclusions reached by the director of the project, Maxwell Manwaring, and his collaborators is that establishing, building, and defending forms of "legitimacy" while subverting others lies at the heart of the doctrine.[20] In this regard, counterinsurgency is fundamentally oriented around the culturally and historically specific task of putting into place a particular kind of systemically meaningful world for people.

Over the next year, the stalemate continued. The Salvadoran war was resolved eventually through joint talks brokered by the United Nations. Among the results were that the Salvadoran military was drastically reduced and placed under civilian control. The main protagonists in the "insurgency," the FMLN (also called "terrorists" at the time), became a legitimate political party in El Salvador. Indeed, years later in 2009, their candidate Mauricio Funes became the popularly elected president of El Salvador.

The El Salvador Option as a success story to be duplicated in Iraq was a kind of social conjuring act. The Manwaring Paradigm that partially undergirded the option is a set of principles greatly abstracted from real events. It is not an actual account of a particular victory or a history of actual events, but a future-oriented proscriptive model, derived through quantitative inference. In its invocation for Iraq, it hides its own lack of success in El Salvador, as well as the 1986–87 stalemate that immediately led to its production. The hidden death of the US soldier is also part of the model's formative history, as is the chance that a resident of La Leona would happen upon and make good use of his functional boots.

Optioning the Option

During the same decade that the United States supported the Salvadoran military with money, arms, and training at places like CEMFA, including the sophisticated model-building associated with the BDM report, the US government also dramatically expanded its efforts at anti-narcotics policing and law enforcement worldwide. By the end of the Salvadoran war, the total US budget oriented toward enforcing drug laws was $8.2 billion, divided among about 40 different federal agencies and programs. The majority of these were administered by officials in the departments of Justice, Treasury, and Defense, although what some scholars have dubbed the "Narco-Enforcement Complex" also included the departments of the Interior, Transportation, Agriculture, and Forest Service as well as the federal, state, and local court systems.[21] In the late 1980s, the George H. W. Bush administration created several military Joint Task Forces to coordinate military-civilian cooperation in the "War on Drugs."[22] Among the best-known has been Joint Task Force Six (JTF-6) of Fort Bliss, Texas, founded in November 1989. Much like the US advisory teams in El Salvador, JTF6 has been responsible for providing operational, training, and intelligence support for any requesting law enforcement agency within the continental United States, including the US-Mexico border regions in California, Arizona, New Mexico, and Texas.

According to an innovative survey conducted by Peter Kraska and Victor Kappeler, more than 40 percent of 690 police officers interviewed mentioned direct experience with US Special Forces and counterinsurgency training. One of these respondents reflected on police force members and their counterinsurgency background, likely in El Salvador—perhaps even working at CEMFA, though La Unión is a port city, not a dense tropical forest or swamp:

> We've had [US] Special Forces folks who have come right out of the jungles of Central and South America. These guys get into real shit. All branches of military service are involved in providing training to law enforcement. US Mar-

shalls act as liaisons between police and military to set up the training—our go-between. They have an arrangement with the military through JTF-6 [Joint Task Force 6]. . . . I just received a piece of paper from a four-star general who tells us he's concerned about the type of training we're getting. We've had teams of Navy SEALs and Army Rangers come here and teach us everything. We just have to use our judgment and exclude information like: "at this point we bring in the mortars and blow the place up."

In 2004, US Major General Alfred Valenzuela coauthored (with Col. Victor Rosello) an essay in the well-known journal *Military Review*.[23] He explicitly mentioned the "El Salvador Model" and argued: "If the United States is serious about countering terrorism and drug trafficking in Columbia, it might be worthwhile to dust off the El Salvador archives and examine the model used there to create the necessary organization and structure with which to respond." Though Valenzuela did not mention the Manwaring Paradigm, he did cite the exemplary US training provided under the overall leadership of Colonel Jim Steele after 1984, mentioning CEMFA as evidence of the model's success. Manwaring also has published important extensions of the model, arguing explicitly that it is applicable to the "small wars" of anti-narcotics policing worldwide and also arguing for the reinvigoration of US state sovereignty against the threats of "gangs and other illicit transnational criminal organizations."[24] In this way, despite its initial 1980s wartime formulation, it continues to undergird US political-military relations with El Salvador as anti-gang and anti-narcotic policing have become the central area of cooperation in the aftermath of the war.

Chance, Determinacy, and the Problem of Induction

In November 2003, as the anti–United States insurgency in Iraq was expanding, an organization called the Highlands Forum, funded by the US Defense Department, convened a private conference titled "Risk in a Networked Environment." They held the meeting at the famous Bellagio Hotel and Casino in Las Vegas, Nevada. Among the invitees were several skilled gamblers who were banned from casinos worldwide for their card-counting acumen. According to Richard P. O'Neil, the founder and president of the Forum, his organization had to obtain special permission and escorts from the Bellagio to allow these "black-listed" gamblers into the casino. Another guest was Jeff Jonas, currently an engineer and scientist at IBM, best known for inventing a computerized facial recognition system used by casinos to protect themselves from aggressive card-counters working in teams. He also has been recognized for his ongoing contributions to US national security and counterterrorism systems, especially in the tracking and aggregating of complex networks.

According to O'Neil, one the most popular presentations at the meeting was one by Naseem Taleb, at the time well-known for his popular book, *Fooled by Randomness*. Taleb's talk that night in Las Vegas was titled "Gambling with the Wrong Dice" and, according to a public account of the meeting, he offered a succinct point, "When we don't know how much we don't know, no mathematics will ever yield a meaningful answer." Again, according to records of the meeting, "his message for investors and for DoD [US Department of Defense] alike is to 'Look for ways to foster serendipitous developments while preparing broadly for disaster.'"

This paraphrasing of Taleb's argument may be taken in at least two ways with respect to the issue of chance. One is simply to say that the risk or, more neutrally, the chance of "disaster" justifies preparing for anything and everything. Second, risk cast more broadly as "chance" yields an escape hatch of sorts. In April 2008, Paul Wolfowitz invoked this chance defense when he publicly said that the US government was "pretty much clueless on counterinsurgency" in the first years of the war, not having factored the potential for popular anti–United States uprisings into its models of warfare.[25] This claim was disingenuous given James Steele's operations since the onset of the invasion at the direct behest of Wolfowitz, as well as published studies conducted by US State Department officials that stressed the great probability of an insurgency as a result of the invasion.

Naseem Taleb has translated his reverence and respect for chance, particularly disaster, into a successful company, Empirica Capital, that focuses on "options" trading; two popular books: *Fooled by Randomness: The Hidden Role of Chance in Life and in the Markets* (2008), and *The Black Swan: The Impact of the Highly Improbable* (2007); and a third, more technical book, *Dynamic Hedging: Managing Vanilla and Exotic Options* (1997). On one wall of his office hangs a modest ink drawing of Karl Popper, the philosopher of science known among many things for his reworking of David Hume's classic identification of "the problem of induction."[26]

In *Enquiry Concerning Human Understanding*, Hume clarifies the basic problem of how experience of past events warrants or provides a foundation for beliefs about similar future events. In a famous proposition he states,

> When I see, for instance, a billiard ball moving in a straight line towards an-
> other; even suppose motion in the second ball should by accident be suggested
> to me, as a result of their contact or impulse; may I not conceive, that a hundred
> different events might as well follow from that cause? May not both these balls
> remain at absolute rest? May not the first ball return in a straight line, or leap
> off from the second in any line or direction? All these suppositions are consis-
> tent and conceivable. Why then should we give preference to one, which is no
> more consistent or conceivable than the rest? (part 4, para. 10)

Hume's answer is to the effect that only through previous observation can it be predicted what actually will happen to the balls. He then carefully points out that this presupposes, as a foundation, that the future will re-semble the past. And yet, according to his own reasoning and logic, he acknowledges, this is impossible to maintain. Nevertheless, the Humean observation about observation undergirds positivist accounts of knowl-edge where a fact can be established on the basis of the observations of constant conjunctures within closed systems. In basic terms, this is the proposition that "whenever x, then y" (discussed in the introduction). Hume in fuller form, however, brings up the dilemma of induction that has invited continuous discussion and debate.

Taleb's hero, Karl Popper, took up the induction problem in the domain of scientific inquiry and method, claiming that it was impossible to confirm a universal scientific theory with any kind of probability. Instead, the best that could be achieved is its falsification. In other words, no number of identical observations will conclusively establish the positive truth of a universal claim. However, one observation of its opposite would defeat it.

Popper joins a broader number of scholars who have questioned the foundationalism associated with positivist forms of scientific inquiry and, more generally, instances where followers of a theory refuse to relinquish it in the face of contrary evidence or its apparent inability to offer an em-pirical prediction. In this regard, any inference, any model, any option for the future derived from the past is provisional and purposeful, not a permanent truth with a capital T. Hence it is judged according to the inter-ests at stake. In Naseem's case, they are very narrow interests of making a profit on the basis of a bet. And it is no wonder that Popper guides him in this. As many critics have pointed out, the limitation of Popper's paradigm is that it tends to assume that the grounds of falsification are universally understood and shared. Cast in Taleb's popular terms, the observation of one black swan may falsify the claim that all swans are white. But there is little room to admit that the falsification is predicated on and involves open and collective debate and judgment about what constitutes blackness and whiteness. Who gets to decide the grounds of falsification? Who is this decider?

Nevertheless, induction as the measurable probability that a member of an experiential class will have a certain character guides the Manwaring Paradigm that, in turn, formed part of the appearance of the "El Salvador Model" for Iraq. In its highly partial appearance as an option, the Salvador model contributed to the appearance of the US state as the rational follower of a kind of crude induction, much as a person might judge the future on the basis of past experience.

Across the varied contexts with their different types of induction, there was a great deal of forgetting that occurred. Most broadly, within the current US counterinsurgency approach to the Iraq war lies the real history of Manuel, his fleeing forced induction into the US-backed Salvadoran military, his migration to DC, and also the dead US soldier not far from his parents' home in Intipucá. The lesson of the account is that to really accept chance means to embrace "the infinite long run" with integrity. It entails an opening up of history to a fuller kind of realism that includes would-be's and could-be's along with actual events in their "here and now" as well as real tendencies or causal forces that may be at work beyond any single empirical instantiation. Such an inclusion of chance would mean a fuller account of any historical process.

Faithful Service

In January 2007, US President George W. Bush delivered his State of the Union Address in an embattled state. The US-led invasion and reorganization of Iraq had stalled amidst a multifaceted insurgency. Bush's Republican party had been rousted from Congress in midterm elections, largely because of opposition to the war. Bush had fired his Secretary of Defense, Donald Rumsfeld, after earlier reassigning Rumsfeld's deputy assistant, Paul Wolfowitz, to run the World Bank. In national polls, the US president's national approval ratings had dropped into the low 30-percent range.[27]

The 2007 address contrasted with the more grave and "no compromise" style that had dominated his speeches, especially in the aftermath of the attacks on the two towers of the World Trade Center and the wing of the Pentagon on September 11, 2001. The speech was remarkably upbeat, delivered with the panache of a campaign address. Notably, it featured a rhetorical strategy of give-and-take, with constant movement between muscular assertions of strength and fortitude always gently offset with conciliatory gestures and deferential asides. The speech was peppered with couplets like "courage and compassion," "strength and generosity," and "heroic kindness." The speech moved sequentially through what were assumed to be discrete themes, separating domestic policies regarding "the economy" from foreign policies organized around "security." In the concluding section, the speech then deftly shifted from political and military intervention to the realm of foreign aid and "development," offering a resounding claim of US benevolence and generosity worldwide: "American foreign policy is more than a matter of war and diplomacy. Our work in the world is also based on a timeless truth: to whom much is given, much is required."

Some listeners might have recognized this reference to "a timeless truth" as a phrase taken directly from one of the biblical parables of Jesus, specifically that of "the faithful servant" recorded in the Gospel of Luke (12:35–48). In this tale, often interpreted as an allegory of devotion to the resurrection of Jesus, the story describes slaves in a household being instructed to be vigilant and protective of their master's estate in his absence. The slave most entrusted with running the household and keeping authority over the other slaves bears the greatest responsibility, but potentially receives the greatest reward. Yet to knowingly fail in this task of stewardship is worse than to be simply ignorant of what it requires. "From everyone to whom much has been given, much will be required; and from one to whom much has been entrusted, even more will be demanded," concludes the passage.

Bush followed the allusion to the parable with a brief explanation of US foreign aid efforts in Africa and an oblique reference to administration efforts to reorganize the World Bank (under Wolfowitz) as a tool of US bilateralism. There was little noticeable applause from the audience. Michael Gerson, the principal author of Bush's address (and noted evangelical Christian), commented later that he was especially disappointed that this portion of the speech on foreign aid seemed to cause little positive reaction. "We had two paragraphs on foreign aid, about the compassion of America, which is unusual for a presidential speech, and there was no applause," said Gerson. "I don't know—it might be a bad line, or it could be a sign that aid abroad doesn't sell."

Yet just after this moment in the speech, the audience came to life in response to a slightly modified tack. The US president continued: "When

FIGURE 11. Dikembe Mutombo standing in the audience while being introduced by President Bush. Used with permission from G. W. Bush Library.

America serves others in this way, we show the strength and generosity of our country. These deeds reflect the character of our people. The greatest strength we have is the heroic kindness and courage and self-sacrifice of the American people. You see this spirit often if you know where to look." With this turn of a phrase, Bush gestured to the audience, "And tonight we need only look above to the gallery. Dikembe Mutombo grew up in Africa, amid great poverty and disease. He came to Georgetown University on a scholarship to study medicine, but Coach John Thompson took a look at Dikembe and had a different idea."[28]

The television cameras swung to focus on Mr. Mutombo, who stood up to face the president, smiling. Over seven feet tall, the former NBA basketball player who was known for his record of blocking offensive shots dwarfed First Lady Laura Bush, seated next to him on the left. Business entrepreneur Julie Aigner-Clark (whose husband William E. Clark had donated thousands of dollars to Republican political candidates in the United States) smiled at eye level standing a row behind Mutombo on his left. The audience erupted in laughter at President Bush's well-choreographed comment on John Thompson's opportunistic basketball coach "look" at Mutombo.

Bush continued: "Dikembe became a star in the NBA and a citizen of the United States, but he never forgot the land of his birth or the duty to share his blessings with others. He built a brand-new hospital in his hometown. A friend has said of this good-hearted man, 'Mutombo believes that God has given him this opportunity to do great things.' And we are proud to call this son of the Congo a citizen of the United States of America." The audience applauded resoundingly. The President then went on to call on several other men and women in the gallery whom he presented as figures exemplifying "courage and compassion," the speech's overall theme, before concluding the Address with his typical "God bless."[29]

To shift the speech from national security (strength) to international development (generosity), Bush emphasized specific dimensions of Dikembe Mutombo besides his height. As a non–Anglo-European immigrant, Mutombo had left behind a supposedly unworkable past in Africa and taken up a new life in the United States. He was educated in a private (Catholic) US university, became a US citizen and successful professional (athlete), and, echoing features of Lindsey Gruson's article about Marvin's Intipucá nearly two decades earlier (chapter 1), transferred money and resources back to the place of his birth to aid in its "development." While Marvin and Intipucá came into the view of a newspaper-reading audience in 1989 through the mildly exotic "Journal" series of the *New York Times*, Dikembe's appearance in 2007 next to First Lady Laura Bush signaled a significant domestication of this figure, the non–Anglo-European US immigrant entrepreneur as source of hometown development.

Doctrinal Consolidation

At the time of Gruson's article about Marvin and Intipucá, Dikembe was still a young college student in DC, spending his summer as an intern at the headquarters of the World Bank. By the time Dikembe appeared in the audience at Bush's speech, the World Bank had made migration and especially the role of people like Dikembe, who sent money back to their home country, a central part of its financial analysis and development policy. The main difference, however, was that the Bank well understood that most migrants earned much less than an NBA salary and remitted on average no more than a few hundred dollars monthly. Collectively, however, such migrant remittances could be marshaled for modest development projects and, by nature, carried specific positive effects.

In 2003, the Bank's *Global Development Finance* contained a chapter devoted to the phenomenon of remittances titled, "Workers' Remittances: An Important and Stable Source of External Development Finance," written by senior Bank economist Dilip Ratha. That same year, the Bank had convened the "International Conference on Migrant Remittances: Development Impact, Opportunities for the Financial Sector, and Future Prospects" in London, England, subsequently publishing a book based on the proceedings, edited by Samuel Munzele Maimbo and Ratha. A revised version of Ratha's 2003 paper formed the first chapter. Late that same year, the World Bank released its influential 2006 "Global Economic Prospects" report, subtitled *Economic Implications of Remittances and Migration*, with Ratha as a lead author.

Ratha's research and writing on remittances formed the core of the Bank's perspective on the topic by the early twenty-first century and may be summarized as a series of "findings" or claims. Perhaps most significantly, Ratha has consistently argued that "remittances reduce poverty" in the receiving countries, allowing households to spend greater shares of their income on health and education. The argument is substantiated through research at the scale of the household and builds on dominant "human capital" analyses, arguing that such expenditure on health and education enhances such "capital." More generally, Ratha suggests that increased migration of people from poor to wealthy countries, their participation in wealthy-country labor markets, and the transfer of a portion of their income back to the sending countries offers more benefits to poorer countries than direct financial aid or expanded commercial trade. Finally, Ratha's research and the work of the Bank more generally have substantiated the empirical claim that migrant remittances over the past two decades have become the largest source of external financing in poorer, especially smaller, countries worldwide.[30]

Ratha's research and the World Bank publications joined other work at the time, especially publications produced by the United Nations Global Commission on International Migration (GCIM), formed by UN Secretary-General Kofi Annan in December 2003. Their first major report, "Migration in an Interconnected World: New Directions for Action," appeared in 2005 and directly complemented and reinforced the Bank perspective, offering a series of arguments about how governments should craft policies that properly facilitate both migration and remittance transfer. Indeed, the World Bank's 2006 "Global Economic Prospects" report explicitly directs the reader to the work of GCIM.

Across the international organizations, their research and publications, and the collective discussions and debates associated with them, a relatively durable model of "development" combining immigration and remittance transfer had become consolidated. As practices, migration and money transfer obviously had existed in various contexts well before their documenting and codification in this emergent model. In addition, each of the two phenomena had been the object of substantial inquiry, popular reporting, professional academic scholarship, and political rhetoric over many years. Nevertheless, in the first decade of the twenty-first century, the World Bank and United Nations together played a central role in deriving a positive model of "poverty reduction" and development based on migration and remittance transfer. This perspective is in contrast to the World Bank report on El Salvador released in 1996 (and discussed in chapter 1). That report acknowledged the growing importance of remittances, but placed no emphasis on their role in poverty reduction. Instead, the report invoked the "Dutch disease" model for understanding remittances as a windfall of foreign currency that must be properly channeled through macroeconomic policy-oriented liberalization of the financial sector.

Institutional Ordering

Bush's introduction of the figure of Mutombo as a virtuous immigrant who succeeded in the United States and assembled money for his hometown, as well as the consolidation of a model of migration and remittances as poverty reduction by the World Bank and UN, can be understood as part of a broader effort in the face of a crisis in the legitimacy not just of the Bush presidency in 2007, but also more generally in the US-directed project of "structural adjustment," begun under US President Reagan in 1980 and foisted especially on specific countries in Africa, Latin America, and Asia. In essence, adjustment meant for national governments to institute a series of policy changes designed to "liberalize" and "privatize" national economies. One, if not the central, institution behind this project was the World Bank, beginning exactly at the time when Mutombo was working there as an intern. And the immediate context for this project was sub-Saharan Africa, including Congo.

In 1981, the World Bank under the leadership of Robert McNamara invited a University of Michigan economist named Elliott Berg to conduct a far-ranging study of the economic development of sub-Saharan Africa. Popularly known as the "Berg Report," it suggested that World Bank loans designed to alleviate poverty should be tied to recipient governments' willingness to systematically adjust their macroeconomic architecture to promote expanded private-sector activity and export-oriented growth. In essence, "structural adjustment"—and later the variant focused on Latin America known as "the Washington Consensus" (first coined by John Williamson of the Washington, DC–based Institute for International Economics) and led by US-dominated multilateral lending organizations—was born in Africa by way of the UM Economics Department in Ann Arbor, Michigan. It received substantial codification in the Bank's World Development Report of 1987, and by the end of that decade provided the dominant contours of what constituted "neoliberal globalization" throughout the 1990s.

In this context, US President Clinton appointed James Wolfensohn in 1995 to head the Bank, in part to consolidate the neoliberal project, but also especially to address growing criticism of structural adjustment and "austerity" policies emanating from popular sectors worldwide. Wolfensohn initiated a series of efforts to reach out to popular organizations, inviting them to share at least figuratively in the formulation of Bank policies. One of the first of these public sector meetings occurred in Washington, DC, and included "migrant entrepreneurs" from Intipucá who operated small businesses in the DC area and in El Salvador.

The main designer and spokesperson of this "reorientation" at the Bank was Vice President of External Affairs Mark Malloch-Brown. Malloch-Brown had spent his early life in the British colony of Southern Rhodesia as the child of a South African diplomat. He attended Cambridge University and then began graduate study in the department of political science at the University of Michigan, leaving with a master's degree in 1976. Years later Malloch-Brown recalled the influence of Michigan: "Politics and development have been the two driving issues in my career. I learned just enough quantitative skills at the University of Michigan . . . to be able to run an opinion research company when I was a political consultant."[31] Malloch-Brown told me that he never encountered Elliott Berg while he was at Michigan.[32]

Before becoming a political consultant, however, Malloch-Brown worked as a journalist at the *Economist*, helping to found its regular "Economist Development Report." He then went on to serve as a member of the UN High Commission for Refugees where he came to know Kofi Anan. (Malloch-Brown had worked as an intern at the UN while a student at Michigan.) In 1986 he joined the Sawyer-Miller group, an international political consulting firm. Drawing on his "quantitative skills" learned in Ann Arbor, Michigan, he advised presidential election candidates in Bolivia, Chile, Peru, and Colombia at the end of the 1980s, helping

their campaigns and also working to enhance US public perceptions of
these countries. After a stint with Refugees International, collaboration
with George Soros in the context of the Bosnian war, and cofounding the
International Crisis Group, Malloch-Brown joined the World Bank, leading Wolfensohn's effort to bring poverty reduction and "accountability"
back to the bank's public image. Malloch-Brown served as vice president
of external affairs in 1996–99, and worked as well coordinating relations
between the Bank and the United Nations.

In 1999, he left the Bank to work again directly with his friend and colleague Kofi Anan at the UN, who appointed him to serve as administrator
of the UN Development Programme. In that capacity he oversaw significant strengthening and expansion of UNDP's 135 country program offices, doubling the overall budget to $4 billion. One recipient of these new
resources was the UNDP office in El Salvador, that undertook a famously
comprehensive research project to study and document El Salvador's reorganization around migration to the United States.

The project was coordinated by Salvadoran economist William Pleitez
and involved several teams of researchers and writers. In 2005, UNDP–
El Salvador released *Informe Sobre el Desarrollo Humano 2005: Una
Mirada al Nuevo "Nosotros," el Impacto de las Migraciones* (Human Development Report for El Salvador 2005: A Look at the New "Us," the Impact of Migration). The comprehensive report contained ten chapters and
was immediately noteworthy for its tremendous assemblage and review of
recent empirical evidence related to Salvadoran migration and remittance
circulation.

In public presentations in El Salvador and in the United States, Pleitez
has discussed and summarized the research project and the report. He has
acknowledged that exodus to the United States and proper "human development" in El Salvador may be at cross-purposes, given the "brain drain"
caused by migration. But, echoing the tenor of Lindsey Gruson in the *New
York Times* almost two decades earlier, as well as Bush's introduction of
Dikembe Mutombo and the arguments of World Bank economist Dilip
Ratha:

> Migration can also be seen as a resource of the underprivileged, who have de-
> cided to run these risks to find a more direct way to achieve their human de-
> velopment. . . . Through hard work and sacrifice many migrants have become
> sufficiently prosperous and send aid to their families, as well as to others who
> remain in precarious circumstances, contributing to reduced poverty rates and
> improved human development indexes.

In this regard, migration has facilitated self-generated solutions to problems of poverty and insufficient human development. Not willing to wait for official programs, migrants have managed to advance their own development and that of their families by investing in social and human capital: their own inventiveness, sacrifice and hard work, with the support of social networks. . . .

Why should human development wait for official programs if, on their own initiative, people have made progress in this regard? How can one deny that migration—which provides more opportunities for and a better use of a country's primary resource—also facilitates the human development of those who leave as well as those who remain?[33]

On the cover of the UNDP El Salvador report is a collage of images meant to represent some aspects of the country's transformation through migration. The UNDP cover contains several photographic images from the Salvadoran newspaper *La Prensa Grafica*, which are overlaid on a reproduction of the middle part of a complex serigraphy (silk-screen) triptych, made by Salvadoran artist Romeo Galdámez. One of the images created by Galdámez and reproduced on the UNDP report is a one-way road sign with the name "Intipucá City."[34] Although the term has a particular concrete history, it has become highly ubiquitous in El Salvador well beyond the pueblo proper. The phrase remains widely used in the town in popular discourse and appears on the sign that has stood at the intersection of the San Miguel–La Unión leg of the Littoral Highway and the winding paved uphill road that leads into Intipucá.

Model Formation

The second part of this chapter has charted the emergence of the immigrant entrepreneur figure with regard to presidential accounts of US foreign aid and also in the development framework of the World Bank and the United Nations. This later appearance rested in part on the institutional coordination between the two agencies, led especially by Mark Malloch-Brown. Under Brown's leadership, the UN helped produce an exhaustive study of El Salvador's deep and rapid restructuring around US migration and remittance circulation. One meaningful referent in the account that helps grant it its representational quality is the phrase Intipucá City, reproduced artistically on the cover. Taken as a whole, this configuration of people, events, and outcomes suggests the consolidation of a particular kind of development model, produced in part by a quasi-

FIGURE 12. Cover of the UNDP El Salvador report with road sign pointing to Intipucá.

transnational state apparatus whose institutional form is a composite of such entities as the World Bank and the UN, in some sort of relation with the US government.

There is a now well-known story of a clandestine meeting held in early 2004 at the New York apartment of Richard Holbrooke, the US ambassador to the UN, appointed by then-President Clinton. The meeting included Kofi Anan, the UN Secretary General at the time, as well as the

US National Security Council member Robert Orr, Harvard University professor John Ruggie, and Nader Musavizadeh, an associate editor of the US magazine the *New Republic*. In this context, Malloch-Brown was "assigned" to join Anan directly as Deputy Secretary General. Ruggie and Musavizadeh also received UN appointments in the ensuing months. Instead of a conspiracy, the meeting suggests the further consolidation of a loose coalition of "neoliberal" capitalist representatives, stretching across the US state and various international organizations, meeting to plan the rescue of the legitimacy of the UN and its leader in the face of the US-led invasion of Iraq and Anan's corrupt involvement with the Iraq "Oil for Food" Program.[35]

As much as President Bush and people in his administration like Paul Wolfowitz followed a more aggressive US unilateralism, informed by the tenets of "neoconservatism," they benefited—if only for a while—from this intervention. In 2007 Bush again drew on the face of neoliberal internationalism when he introduced the figure of Mutombo, focusing on his efforts to develop his hometown in Congo. At the edge of the twenty-first century, the "transnational immigrant entrepreneur" has become a powerful ideological formation. Its invocation by the Bush administration probably was a sign of his administration's weakness and decline. Yet like the "El Salvador Option," more directly associated with Bush's neoconservative agenda, it similarly was socially pulled out or abstracted from the past three decades of El Salvador–US relations. Amidst this complex history, the town of Intipucá and its ties to Washington, DC, have made their appearance, providing important source material and leaving significant traces.

Conclusion

This book began with two general orienting questions: Across El Salvador and the United States, how and why have certain dominant but highly partial accounts of life formed and circulated, hiding the fuller history from which they emerged, including other stories, which are completely at odds with theirs? How and why does the continued circulation of dominant stories hide the way that they contribute to perpetuating conditions that actually contradict their accounts? Over nine chapters, this book has pursued these questions, organized principally around consideration of what I have called the Intipucá-DC connection story, though the actual ground covered by the book goes well beyond this entity.

Among the greatest challenges of this project has been to show that all the entities considered—the stories, value forms, discursive categories, doctrines, everyday practices, and patterns of social relations—and the process of occlusion that the orienting questions point to, are cumulative social and historical products or outcomes of the whole under consideration: El Salvador and the United States over roughly the past fifty years. Now at the end of the book, it should be clear that although each chapter covered different people, events, periods, and places, all the chapters were at the same time considering aspects and features of what was presupposed as a more or less coherent moment or whole within a larger and decidedly open totality of relations.[1] Since this goes against the logic of assuming that separate and discrete parts are contained within a closed set, like marbles in a bag, I introduced this book with the metaphor of waves and water, adapted from Calvino's opening chapter to his book *Mr. Palomar*. In this spirit, what follows is a brief recapitulation of waves, water, and a particular current within them.

The Waves

The surface contours of the Intipucá-DC connection story now fall into relief. El Salvador and the United States appear to have been relatively separate and autonomous nations until the migration of people and the circulation of remittances. Rural regions of El Salvador, such as Intipucá, have become modern only as a result of the migration and remittances. In Intipucá, this process has been the outcome of the combined efforts and abilities of modest farm workers, even peasants, who ventured to the Washington, DC, area and through hard work and sacrifice obtained the trappings of wealth for themselves and their pueblo, Intipucá. Initially, they migrated because of economic conditions; later migration was stimulated by political conditions connected with the civil war (1980–92.) The war was a particular kind of "low intensity" conflict that forced people to move clandestinely and live in the United States as "illegal" migrants. After the war, the different categories of people—"economic," "political," and "illegal" migrants—presented a dilemma as it became clear that Salvadoran migration to the United States was integral to the expansion of the service sector in US cities like Washington, DC, and migrant remittances provided the most important single quotient of Salvadoran national wealth. Both the Salvadoran and US governments, led by their respective presidents, have cooperated in resolving this problem of categories and their legal ramifications in both countries. In particular, the Salvadoran government has sought to work on behalf of families so that they might contribute to developing their pueblos and, by extension, the nation of El Salvador. One of the most promising kinds of participants in this collective project are "hometown associations" comprising "transnational migrant entrepreneurs." Intipucá and its history of ties to Washington, DC, provides a compelling and successful example of this. The future development of rural El Salvador rests on the expansion of these kinds of activities.

The Water

Beneath the surface ripples lies a conflict-ridden systemic transition from coffee to cotton to labor-power as El Salvador's dominant twentieth-century exports and sources of national wealth; also beneath the surface is a related shift in the United States as major cities have gone from being centers of manufacturing to agglomerations of service production. This transition was shaped by the actions and interactions of particular class fractions that struggled and coalesced to control the Salvadoran and US states. In El Salvador, the state facilitated cotton production through its development of transportation and communication infrastructure as well as an expanded police apparatus. These changes rested in part on the accumulated wealth from decades of coffee production and export, which in turn was predicated in part on the reproduction of coffee-laborers' capacity to work. This labor-power was fueled with staple foods grown and sold in the non–coffee-producing regions of El Salvador, including the area around Intipucá. A nascent professional class formed out of the farming regions devoted to corn and dairy goods through three interrelated conditions. First, it became profitable to rent land to cotton growers. Second, expanded money income from these rents combined with new electrical power, transportation, and communication infrastructure made it possible to obtain advanced education and professional skills in urban areas, such as San Miguel, as the city itself expanded as a result of cotton production. Finally, professional jobs in cities as well as the growth of state bureaucracies in rural areas helped to consolidate a more mobile outward-oriented class of potential US-bound migrants, such as Sigfredo and his friends from Intipucá.

Over the same period, expanded US state spending in defense-oriented aerospace technologies stimulated patterns of change in specific US cities, creating pockets of low-rent housing in relatively close proximity to regions of highly speculative real estate development. Members of the new Salvadoran professional class with ties to agricultural life as major land-owners in their hometown of Intipucá moved to Washington, DC, throughout the late 1960s and 1970s. They astutely took advantage of business opportunities in the Washington, DC, area and were well positioned to provide employment and services to the growing Salvadoran migrant population in the area during the 1980s as well as to the expanding population of wealthy investors and professionals. When the DC real estate and financial sector collapsed in the wake of the end of the Cold War, these elite protected themselves from personal costs by passing their losses on to their many clients and employees. In this moment of crisis, a history of exploitation tied to coffee and cotton production in El Salvador now included the more abstracted processes of financial and land speculation and forms of commerce in the DC area and in El Salvador. In this context, state actors in both countries have struggled to efface these contradictions and the sense of continuity that it has generated, because dominant social groups in El Salvador wish to encourage the nationalist allegiances (that now extend to Salvadorans in the United States) that facilitate remittance circulation. Nevertheless, many people's real experiences in Intipucá go against the forms of tutelage offered by both state institutions and the growing number of government and privately funded "development" organizations.

The Intipucá-DC connection story emerged out of this more complex history as a particular kind of abstraction from a fixed perspective. The dominant model plays a role in the perpetuation of this history, hiding its origins as it takes part in the production of doctrines and practices that shape the dispositions of people and influence the possibility of producing certain kinds of products. As a relatively influential truth that transfigures social life, it cannot be divorced from the social history from which it emerged. This book has sought to critique it by showing its partiality, highlighting the way that it has percolated out of a complex process with no single or dominant author. This critique is meant to help clarify the conditions of contemporary life and illuminate some latent possibilities. In this way the model and its occluded origins together comprise a more dynamic and interactive kind of critical explanatory "model" of social life across both countries.

The Current: Value and Transvaluation

The category value has lurked throughout. It is a nebulous concept, fraught with disagreement and misunderstanding among its users. In this book, however, its enigmatic qualities were central for the analysis. As I sought to explain in the introduction, it is not an actual thing that can be found as a discrete entity. Rather, it is a systemic tendency of representation. By systemic, I mean that it cannot be explained in terms of any single instance or empirical instantiation. Nevertheless, it is real, like a structure or causal mechanism. (Marx called it the law of value.) It is tempting to say that it is "out there," too, but that would be to formally separate it from the quotidian processes of its substantiation. The logic here is one of chicken and egg together. A great deal of capitalist life in El Salvador and the United States has been defined by its money price, in the process effectively pulling out and presenting only the most abstract qualities of human work capacity that went into whatever bears the price—even work capacity itself—but one does not cause the other. It is a real tendency of representation.

That said, as the book has sought to show, it is a directional geohistorical tendency, not a fixed immutable thing. In this respect, there are countless moments, both possibilities and actualities, that are within the generality of the tendency. The many stories uncovered behind the dominant stories brought this to light. Marvin and his motorcycle in Lubbock's picture composed just one moment in the whole history of each and their coming into relation. Some of this was uncovered, though hardly the infinite whole. Nevertheless, the effect of this inquiry was to transvalue the motorcycle, the rider, and the photographic image, ever so slightly.

As I began this book, the three women on the street that morning were effectively doing the same thing, transvaluing the story of Intipucá substantiated by Lubbock's photo and Gruson's narrative. Their comment to me that day is a reminder that the most excluded and marginal social position in El Salvador currently is to be without access to any source of remittances or the chance to migrate and find work. Like those without land and livelihoods in previous periods, this marks the most unstable social fault line in El Salvador today.

This book concludes by recounting a recent event in El Salvador that gestures to the future that is coming to pass. Remarkably, it suggests the possibility of a significant transvaluation along the lines of what this book has covered and what the three woman in the introduction requested. In June 2010 in San Salvador, El Salvador, a group of people were having an informal discussion on the general topic that much of what one often hears to be popularly true in the country, turns out to be quite false. Each speaker took turns offering examples of this phenomenon, both in their experience and also more hypothetically. One person, who had never visited the pueblo, provided the following example: "Yes. It is just like when you hear that in Intipucá everyone is rich from all the remittances and then you go there and find out that isn't true."[2]

Acknowledgments

It is challenging to appreciate that a full account of what something *is* would include all that gave rise to it, all that continues to shape its existence, and also all the absences that it potentially could make go away. Short of this impossible task, at least with respect to books, we have the Acknowledgments section. One important moment in the process of this book's emergence is the period 1988–1992 when I worked at the Institute for Policy Studies (IPS) in Washington, DC, researching and writing about US foreign policy and recent immigration from parts of Asia, the Caribbean, and Central America. Saul Landau taught me how these processes could be studied together in DC literally by walking around, listening to, watching, and talking with people, whether mediated by a camera and notepad or not. Saul also provided the first book I read about US immigration, race, and ethnicity, the popular two-volume *To Serve the Devil* that he had written in 1973 together with Paul Jacobs and Eve Pell. The second book I read on the subject, Saskia Sassen's *The Mobility of Labor and Capital: A Study in International Investment and Labor Flow*, was given to me by another IPS friend and colleague, Sasha Natapoff, whose mother, Flora, had painted the picture that appeared on the cover of the book. I am grateful for Saskia's example of studying large-scale connections and transformations and for her interest in this project over the years. The third piece that I read on migration during this early period came to me by way of a student working at IPS who passed on a copy of a soon-to-be published essay by Roger Rouse, titled "Mexican Migration and the Social Space of Postmodernism." I contacted Roger, which eventually led to the opportunity to begin graduate studies in the Department of Anthropology at the University of Michigan, guided by him and his example of multi-sited ethnographic inquiry into transnational migrant life. I am grateful to

Roger for opening this door for me and also for his tremendous political acuity, intelligence, and friendship over the years.

While at the University of Michigan, my various research trips to El Salvador and Washington, DC, were supported by grants from the National Science Foundation, the Mellon Foundation, the US Fulbright Scholars Program, the Rackham Graduate School, the Department of Anthropology, and the Latin American and Caribbean Studies Center. I also was fortunate to spend one year as junior member of the Michigan Society of Fellows and one as a postdoctoral scholar in the Department of History at Michigan.

During my first trip to El Salvador in spring 1993, I stayed in San Miguel with Helen Hopps who was working for the United Nations at the time. She generously introduced me to many people there, helping to launch my inquiries by driving me in her car for my first visit to Intipucá. I thank Professors Manuel Artiga and Fabio Melgar at the San Miguel campus of the National University whto generously included me in many events, projects, and discussions. During the time I lived in Intipucá, I interacted closely with several extended families and circles of friends that I will acknowledge somewhat cryptically by way of just a few first names. I especially thank Miguel, Gilberto, Marvin, Carlos, Felix, the other Carlos, Chele, Melida, Santos, Adan, Melvin, and Henry for all that they shared and taught me. There are many other people in Intipucá and DC who should recognize their presence in this book, though, with my apologies, they remain unnamed for now. I am grateful to the staff of the Archivo General de la Nación (AGN) and especially to US-based historian of El Salvador Aldo Lauria-Santiago, who introduced me to much of AGN's content. I thank Kay Eekhoff for her friendship and advice and Knut Walter for a helpful discussion of contemporary El Salvador that influenced this book. I thank members of the Batres, Fontg, and Franco families, especially Guillermo, for their great friendship and generosity during my visits.

In between periods of research in El Salvador and among Salvadorans in Washington, DC, I regularly met with Fernando Coronil, my teacher at Michigan who also became a dear friend. He constantly provoked me with variations of his extension of William Blake, urging me to seek after both the world in a grain of sand and that grain within its unfolding world. As a result of these discussions and the example of his own work that he shared, I expanded the depth and breadth of my inquiries and switched my degree to the Doctoral Program in Anthropology and History at Michigan.

Fernando died in August 2011, much too early for all of us, leaving behind a scholarly and personal echo that we will be listening to forever, I hope. His influence on this book should be obvious to all who are familiar with him and his work. For this, and his living example that "the struggle for life is the matter," I am thankful without end.

Also at Michigan during this time, Val Daniel was a great influence. Our frequent discussions always began as a kind of two-some, usually a comparison of cash crops, agricultural life, war, violence, migration, refugees, money circulation, or popular fiction in south Asia and Central America. Invariably our talks moved toward the inclusion of a third, C. S. Peirce. I learned much from his example of going deeply into philosophical problems and ethnographic evidence together and thank him for suggesting that the category of value, variously defined, might be valuable for making sense of my research.

Julie Skurski carefully read and discussed chapters and papers then and since, helping me both to start and finish various drafts at crucial times. Sueann Caulfield, David W. Cohen, and Jeff Paige provided helpful input after they had read significant portions of this book in early form. Fred Cooper, Jane Burbank, and Ann Stoler also provided critical feedback at various stages. I thank also a special group of friends who generously read and commented on portions of the book, including Marty Baker, Chandra Bhimul, Sharad Chari, Laurent Dubois, Mani Limbert, Setrag Manoukian, Aims McGuiness, Penelope Papaillias, Steven Pierce, Josh Reno, and Genese Sodikoff. I send out a special thanks to my comrade Paul Eiss for his unceasing friendship, fine sense of humor, and tremendous intellectual influence, the value of which, I like to say, is beyond measure.

Since fall 2005, I have been fortunate to be a member of the anthropology department at UCSD, surrounded by a generous and talented group of colleagues and students. I could not have completed this book outside of this academic home and I thank everyone there. Joel Robbins' intellectual engagement, careful reading, and sage advice have been helpful from day one. Joe Hankins offered detailed comments on several chapters and has joined me in numerous conversations about labor, capitalist value, and Peirce's semeiotic. Nancy Postero read a draft of the book and offered helpful comments infused with her perspective on contemporary Latin America. I also thank Rupert Stasch for carefully reading the whole manuscript at a key moment in its production. Many thanks also to Michael Berman, John Bialecki, Marisa Peeters, David Keyes, Raquel Pacheco, Paloma Rodrigo, Ana Pimental-Walker, Kit Wollard, Keith McNeil, Esra

Ozyrek, Jonathan Friedman, Guillermo Algaze, and John Haviland for their feedback on various papers and presentations that eventually became part of this book. During winter and spring 2007, I was a Visiting Fellow at the Center for Comparative Immigration Studies at UCSD. This provided the opportunity to research and write what has now become chapter 9. I thank Wayne Cornelius, David Fitzgerald, Everard Meade, and Ane Minivielli for their generosity during this stay.

In the process of bringing this book manuscript to "the market," I received close readings of chapters and important feedback from Julia Adams, Geoff Eley, Webb Keane, George Steinmetz, Lydia Lieu, and Mugge Gocek. I thank George and Julia for their unflinching belief in the project amidst the US recession and crisis in the academic publishing industry. Andreas Glaeser encouraged me to share the manuscript with his co-editors of the book series, Chicago Studies in Practices of Meaning. I thank him, Bill Sewell, and Lisa Wedeen for providing helpful suggestions on several chapters, especially the introduction. I am deeply grateful to Bill Sewell, Keith Hart, Terry Turner, Bill Maurer, and Susan Coutin for their critical and encouraging comments on the whole manuscript. I also thank Julia Elachyar, Paul Kockelman, and Beatriz Cortez for their engagement with aspects of this project in recent years.

At the University of Chicago Press, I thank Mary Corrado for her careful edits and also Priya Nelson and Ryo Yamaguchi for their assistance and advice during the production process. I am especially grateful to David Brent, who took a keen interest in this book from the beginning and moved it along with remarkable speed.

This book in all its dimensions has been most shaped by my long companionship with Julianne O'Brien Pedersen. I thank her for joining me and contributing to every aspect of this project, from DC to Michigan to El Salvador, to San Diego and back—several times! I am honored also to thank our daughter, Clara, for her encouragement as she has lived amidst this project. Finally, without Frank, Esther, Sarah, and Jim, these sentences simply would not exist. Thank you.

Notes

Introduction

1. Descartes is one main source for the assumption that proper inquiry should proceed from such a set or foundational perspective. "Archimedes, to move the earth from its orbit and place it in a new position, demanded nothing more than fixed and immovable fulcrum; in a similar manner I shall have the right to entertain high hopes if I am fortunate enough to find a single truth which is certain and indubitable." René Descartes, *Meditations on First Philosophy*, trans. Laurence Lafleur (Indianapolis: Bobbs-Merrill Company, 1960), 23.

2. Three months before Huntington's book appeared, one of its chapters was published in the journal *Foreign Policy*, titled "The Hispanic Challenge" and provoking an upswell of public commentary and debate. *Foreign Policy* published several long responses, a reply by Huntington, and a series of letters signed by academic scholars and political figures, of whom some vehemently denounced the essay and others strongly endorsed it. Samuel P. Huntington, "The Hispanic Challenge," *Foreign Policy* (March/April 2004). As a note, the image of an inexorable tide or wave of migrants swamping the United States is not in the same spirit as my use of the wave-water metaphor here.

3. Susanne Jonas, "Reflections on the Great Immigration Battle of 2006 and the Future of the Americas," *Social Justice* 33, no. 1 (2006): 6–20.

4. See Leo Chávez, *The Latino Threat: Constructing Immigrants, Citizens, and the Nation* (Palo Alto: Stanford University Press, 2009).

5. See George Steinmetz, "The State of Emergency and the Revival of American Imperialism: Toward an Authoritarian Post-Fordism," *Public Culture* 15, no. 2 (spring 2003): 323–45.

6. Giovanni Arrighi, *Adam Smith in Beijing: Lineages of the 21st Century* (London: Verso Books, 2009).

7. On transnational migration, see the field-defining essays by Roger Rouse, "Mexican Migration and the Social Space of Postmodernity," *Diaspora* 1, no. 1

(1991); "Thinking Through Transnationalism: Notes on the Cultural Politics of Class Relations in the Contemporary United States," *Public Culture* 7, no. 2 (1995): 353–402; and "Making Sense of Settlement: Class Transformation, Cultural Struggle, and Transnationalism among Mexican Migrants in the United States," part of the important book-length development of transnationalism as concept and approach in *Nations Unbound,* edited by N. Glick Schiller, L. Basch, and C. Blanc-Szanton. See also the comprehensive review by Michael Kearney, "Border and Boundaries of the State and Self at the End of Empire," *Journal of Historical Sociology* 4, no. 1 (1991): 52–74. More recently the "transnationalism" framework has been taken up by sociologists of migration who have debated whether and to what extent migrants empirically move back and forth across multiple nation-states. See Roger Waldinger and David Fitzgerald, "Transnationalism in Question," *American Journal of Sociology* 109, no. 5 (March 2004): 1177–95.

8. Huntington, *Who Are We? The Challenges to America's National Identity*, New York, Simon & Schuster, 2004, p.206.

9. Other works that cite and make use of Schoultz's mention of Intipucá's 20 percent include Darrell Y. Hamamoto, Rodolfo D. Torres, eds., *New American Destinies: A Reader in Contemporary Asian and Latino Immigration* (New York: Routledge, 1997), 30; Rubén G. Rumbaut, "Origins and Destinies: Immigration to the United States since World War II," in "Multiculturalism and Diversity," special issue, *Sociological Forum* 9, no. 4 (December 1994), 583–621; Birgit Leyendecker and Michael E. Lamb, "Latino Families," in *Parenting and Child Development in Nontraditional Families*, ed. Michael E. Lamb (Mahwah, NJ: Lawrence Erlbaum Associates, 1999), 251.

10. Accepting both Huntington's and Schultz's arguments, one could infer that US foreign policy in Latin America was a threat to US national culture.

11. Schoultz, "Central America and the Politicization of US Immigration Policy," in *Western Hemisphere Immigration Policy and United States Foreign Policy*, ed. Christopher Mitchell (University Park: Pennsylvania State University Press, 1992), 189.

12. As a private affiliate of the National Endowment for the Humanities, this organization has provided public grants for humanities-related events pertaining to the city Washington, DC, emphasizing especially its nonfederal dimensions, since 1980. In 1981 they awarded a grant to the Adult Education Center of the Psychiatric Institute Foundation in Washington, DC, to convene two roundtable discussions among humanities scholars and representatives of the Salvadoran community in DC, which yielded the 41-page booklet that the Humanities Council published. One copy of this booklet currently is held by the American University library in Washington, DC.

13. Schoultz actually had cited a 1981 report titled "Survey of Central American Population in the United States," by Patricia Ruggles, Michael Fix, and Kathleen M. Thomas, published by the Urban Institute, a Washington, DC–based policy re-

search center. Unable to find a reference to Intipucá in this report, I contacted Schoultz and he told me that the correct citation was the Humanities Council report.

14. I was born in Mount Pleasant, adjacent to Adams Morgan, though my family later moved north to the state of Maryland where my father found new employment. In 1988 I returned to live in Mount Pleasant, staying until fall 1992.

15. Altogether, I have lived in or near the town for 30 months, supported with several research grants, including a fellowship from the Fulbright US Student Program.

16. David Pedersen, "American Value: Money, Migrants, and Modernity in El Salvador and the USA" (PhD diss., University of Michigan, Ann Arbor, 2004).

17. In this sense, following a perspective developed by scholars affiliated with the journal *Public Culture*, Intipucá and DC may be understood as part of the circulation of varied cultural forms within an international mass media–dominated public sphere, itself worthy of critical study.

18. See for example, José Luis Benítez, "Transnational Dimensions of the Digital Divide among Salvadoran Immigrants in the Washington, DC, Metropolitan Area," *Global Networks* 6, no. 2 (2006): 181–99; José Itzigsohn and Daniela Villacrés, "Migrant Political Transnationalism and the Practice of Democracy: Dominican External Voting Rights and Salvadoran Home Town Associations," *Ethnic and Racial Studies* 31, no. 4 (May 2008): 664–86; and Manuel Orozco, "Central American Diasporas and Hometown Associations," in *Diasporas and Development*, ed. Barbara J. Merz, Lincoln C. Chen, and Peter Geithner (Cambridge, MA: Harvard University Press, 2007).

19. One of the most prominent codification of this perspective that I will take up in chapter 9 is the 2005 UNDP report, *Informe sobre Desarrollo Humano de El Salvador 2005: Una Mirada al Nuevo Nosotros. El Impacto de las Migraciones*. An image of Intipucá appears on the front cover of this report.

20. Though hardly a systematic measure, I invite any airplane traveler to El Salvador taking a taxi from the airport to the capital city, San Salvador, to strike up a conversation with the driver by mentioning the town of Intipucá.

21. "Immigrant entrepreneurship" is a large topic in the sociology of US immigration as scholars have sought to identify it and the conditions of its emergence in order to produce more general models of the phenomenon. See especially Roger Waldinger, Howard Aldrich, and Robin Ward, *Ethnic Entrepreneurs: Immigrant Business in Industrial Societies* (Newbury Park, CA: Sage, 1990). Also, Alejandro Portes, Luis Eduardo Guarnizo, and William Haller, "Transnational Entrepreneurs: An Alternative From of Immigrant Economic Adaptation," *American Sociological Review* 67, no. 2 (April 2002): 278–98. The topic also has been taken up in a European context by Robert Kloosterman and Jan Rath. See their edited collection, *Immigrant Entrepreneurs: Venturing Abroad in the Age of Globalization* (Oxford: Berg Publishers, 2003). The most substantial examination of Salvadorans

in the United States in relationship to these US debates is by the anthropologist Sarah Mahler, in *American Dreaming: Immigrant Life on the Margins* (Princeton: Princeton University Press, 1995).

22. Evidence for this claim about the nesting of the Intipucá-DC connection story in broader national models of development in both countries is considered in the subsequent chapters of the book.

23. Mentioned subsequently in this paragraph, these future-oriented metamodels are examined in chapter 9.

24. This is the topic of chapter 9. See Alfred A. Valenzuela, Victor M. Rosello, "Expanding Roles and Missions in the War on Drugs and Terrorism: El Salvador and Colombia," *Military Review* (March-April 2004); Maxwell G. Manwaring, *A Contemporary Challenge to State Sovereignty: Gangs and Other Illicit Transnational Criminal Organizations in Central America, El Salvador, Mexico, Jamaica, and Brazil* (Carlisle Barracks, PA: US Army Strategic Studies Institute, December 2007).

25. As I will explain, this recognition goes against the assumption that one must separate and choose between inquiring into on-the-ground reality and examining the effects of its circulating discursive representations.

26. For an argument about how concrete historical processes and events become selectively compressed into more limited written accounts, see Michel-Rolph Trouillot, *Silencing the Past: Power and the Production of History* (Boston: Beacon Press, 1995).

27. This is not to say that everyone directly worked on coffee farms, but rather that the coffee sector was the social and productive center of gravity in El Salvador. Most other activities were conditioned at least in part by their relationship to coffee production and export. See Héctor Lindo-Fuentes, *Weak Foundations: The Economy of El Salvador in the Nineteenth Century, 1821–1898* (Berkeley: University of California Press, 1990); Aldo A. Lauria-Santiago, *An Agrarian Republic: Commercial Agriculture and the Politics of Peasant Communities in El Salvador, 1823–1914* (Pittsburgh, PA: University of Pittsburgh Press, 1999); and Victor Bulmer-Thomas, *The Economic History of Latin America since Independence* (Cambridge: Cambridge University Press, 1994).

28. Michael F. Jiménez, " 'From Plantation to Cup': Coffee and Capitalism in the United States, 1830–1930," in *Coffee, Society, and Power in Latin America*, ed. William Roseberry, Lowell Gudmundson, and Mario Samper Kutschbach (Baltimore: Johns Hopkins University Press, 1995).

29. David Browning, *El Salvador: Landscape and Society* (Oxford: Clarendon Press, 1971).

30. David Pedersen, "The Storm We Call Dollars: Determining Value and Belief in El Salvador and the United States," *Cultural Anthropology* 17, no. 3 (August 2002).

31. In his lucid introduction to Peirce in the opening chapter of *Fluid Signs: Being a Person the Tamil Way* (Berkeley: University of California Press, 1987),

E. Valentine Daniel paraphrases Milton Singer's endorsement of Peirce's framework: "By adopting the semeiotic perspective of the sign, we are, thankfully, precluded from executing a cultural analysis that neglects the empirical subject as well as the empirical object" (p. 15). Fortunately, the growing scholarly literature on Peirce has helped to bring his insights to practical use in new kinds of social and humanistic inquiry.

32. I have discussed this in relation to William Sewell's notion of history as "fateful" in an exchange published in *Social Science History* 32, no. 4 (Winter 2008).

33. Other adaptations of Peirce have done much to isolate discrete signs and unpack them according to Peirce's typologies. Iconic, indexical, and symbolic are the three best-known ones. I place more emphasis on semeiotic as process and especially the tension between the immediate object of a sign and the real or dynamical object from which it is abstracted.

34. I thank Kit Wollard for pointing out that my distinction between stories and storytelling is similar to the perspective developed by contributors to the volume *Natural History of Discourse*, ed. Michael Silverstein and Greg Urban (Chicago: University of Chicago Press, 1996), who argue against mistaking "texts" for the process of "entextualization."

35. Karl Marx, *Capital: A Critique of Political Economy*, trans. Ben Fowkes (New York: Vintage, 1977), 1:127.

36. For more on this perspective, see David Pedersen, "Brief Event: The Value of Getting to Value in the Era of 'Globalization,'" *Anthropological Theory* 8, (2008): 57-77.

37. See Diane Elson, "Value Theory of Labor, " in *Value: The Representation of Labour in Capitalism*, ed. Elson (London: CSE Books, 1979), for a careful explication of Marx's parsing of the internally related qualities of human work capacity along the lines of personal, social, abstract, and concrete. Her relational perspective on capitalist value formation as the objectification of the most abstract dimensions of labor-power is different from the characterization made by Lowe and Lloyd in 1997 that "Marx theorized that it is the tendency of capital to use 'abstract labor.'" This analytical reading of Marx lends weight to their critical observation that "in most capitalist situations capital lays hold of labor that is precisely not abstract but differentiated by race, gender, and nationality." See Lisa Lowe and David Lloyd, eds., *The Politics of Culture in the Shadow of Capital* (Durham, NC: Duke University Press, 1997), 31.

38. See discussion of the wealth/value distinction in Moishe Postone, *Time, Labor, and Social Domination: A Reinterpretation of Marx's Critical Theory* (Cambridge: Cambridge University Press, 1996).

39. Marx, *Capital*, 1:80.

40. In an essay that he later developed into a chapter in *Provincializing Europe: Postcolonial Thought and Historical Difference* (Princeton: Princeton University Press, 2000), Dipesh Chakrabarty describes his gradual recognition of how Marx's value analysis rested on being able to abstract or pull out what are otherwise

internally related qualities of open-ended human work capacity. Chakrabarty later found Heidegger helpful for emphasizing what was radically exterior or at the limit of capitalist subsumption. See Vinay Gidwani's critical discussion of Chakrabarty's approach in *Capital Interrupted: Agrarian Development and the Politics of Work in India* (Minneapolis: University of Minnesota Press, 2008).

41. On this circulatory perspective toward value formation, see Paul K. Eiss and Pedersen, eds., "Value in Circulation," special issue, *Cultural Anthropology* 17, no. 3 (August 2002).

42. Fernando Coronil has emphasized this holistic and relational perspective on value in *The Magical State: Nature, Money, and Modernity in Venezuela* (Chicago: University of Chicago Press, 1997).

43. This historical perspective on value is developed in Pedersen, "Brief Event," and also in Paul K. Eiss, "Beyond the Object: Of Rabbits, Rutabagas, and History" *Anthropological Theory* 8, no. 1 (March 2008): 79-97.

44. Terrance Turner, Nancy Munn, and the summary of their work by David Graeber emphasize this more synchronic approach to value. See the discussion by Paul Eiss in "Beyond the Object."

45. Building on a broader trend of positing small-scale accounts in opposition to larger, more encompassing ones (the modern/the metanarrative), recent historical work on Central America specifically distinguishes itself as focusing on "the local" in distinction to other scales, primarily the national. See Lauria-Santiago, *An Agrarian Republic*; Greg Grandin, *The Blood of Guatemala* (Durham, NC: Duke University Press, 2000); David McCreery, *Rural Guatemala, 1760–1940* (Palo Alto, CA: Stanford University Press, 1994); Jim Handy, *Revolution in the Countryside* (Chapel Hill: University of North Carolina Press, 1994); Jeffrey Gould, *To Lead as Equals* (Chapel Hill: University of North Carolina Press, 1990); Elisabeth Jean Wood, *Insurgent Collective Action and Civil War in El Salvador* (Cambridge: Cambridge University Press, 2003); Deborah Levenson-Estrada, *Trade Unionists against Terror: Guatemala City, 1954–1985* (Chapel Hill: University of North Carolina Press, 1994); and Lynn Horton, *Peasants in Arms* (Athens: Ohio University Press, 1998).

46. Though not focused primarily on Central America, two collections on the relative power of the United States in relation to other countries in the hemisphere and beyond address this split perspective, though by tending to choose the micro over the macro. See Gilbert M. Joseph, Catherine C. Legrand, and Ricardo D. Salvatore, eds., *Close Encounters of Empire: Writing the Cultural History of US-Latin American Relations*, (Durham, NC: Duke University Press, 1998); and Amy Kaplan and Donald E. Pease, eds., *Cultures of United States Imperialism* (Durham, NC: Duke University Press, 1993).

47. Most book-length studies of Salvadoran migration to the United States have not focused on its "transnational" dimensions, but rather on migrant incorporation in the context of US deindustrialization. See Mahler, *American Dreaming*; Menjívar, *Fragmented Ties*; Nora Hamilton and Norma Stoltz Chinchilla, *Seeking*

Community: Guatemalans and Salvadorans in Los Angeles (Philadelphia: Temple University Press, 2001); Repak, *Waiting on Washington*; Beth Baker-Cristales, *Salvadoran Migration to Southern California: Redefining El Hermano Lejano* (Gainesville: University Press of Florida, 2004). Several scholars have begun to explicitly adopt a "transnational" perspective for understanding aspects of El Salvador-US relations, especially migration and related themes. See Susan Coutin, *Nations of Emigrants: Shifting Boundaries of Citizenship in El Salvador and the United States* (Ithaca, NY: Cornell University Press, 2007); and Elana Zilberg, *Transnational Geographies of Violence: An Inter-American Encounter from the Cold War to the War on Terror* (Durham, NC: Duke University Press, forthcoming).

48. This threesome or its dyadic variant is present in nearly all the work on Central America and relations with the United States.

49. William Robinson invokes these distinctions, reproducing the ideological appearance of a separate and discrete market, state, and civil society upon which the threesome and their disciplinary correlates exist. As he says in the introduction to his book, *Transnational Conflicts*, "The conceptualization I advance here posits material over an ideational determinacy and assigns structural determinacy to the global economy."

50. I have developed this concept in "Step into Anthrohistory," a chapter in *Anthrohistory: Unsettling Knowledge, Questioning Discipline*, ed. Edward Murphy, David William Cohen, Chandra D. Bhimull, Fernando Coronil, Monica Eileen Patterson, and Julie Skurski (Ann Arbor: University of Michigan Press, 2011).

51. For example, Borges' 1941 story "Library of Babel" contains exactly the sort of infinite set worked out by Cantor. Borges concludes the story, explaining, *"The Library is unlimited and cyclical.* If an eternal traveler were to cross it in any direction, after centuries he would see that the same volumes were repeated in the same disorder (which, thus repeated, would be an order . . .)"; the story is in Borges, *The Garden of Forking Paths* (Buenos Aires: Sur, 1941). Alain Badiou similarly acknowledges Cantor and calls for the complete "secularization of infinitude." See Badiou, *Conditions* (London: Continuum, 2009). Some readers of Marx have found a notion of "open totality," notably US political scientist Bertell Ollman, whose work on the matter frequently has been cited and paraphrased by the British geographer David Harvey. See also Jay, *Marxism and Totality*, especially pages 276–99 on Lefebvre.

Chapter One

1. "Tanto va el cántaro al agua, que por fin se quiebra" is the way that I have heard the expression.

2. From Hegel, Marx, and Engels to modern physicists, biologists, and theorists of "complexity," the phenomenon of quantity-to-quality transformation is well recognized, if not often used in contemporary social and historical analysis.

See Robert L. Carniero, "The Transition from Quantity to Quality: A Neglected Causal Mechanism in Accounting for Social Evolution," *Proceedings of the National Academy of Sciences* 97, no. 23 (2000): 12926–31.

3. In *The Science of Logic*, Hegel defined "Measure" as exactly such a whole, "where quality and quantity are in one." *Hegel's Logic*, trans. William Wallace (Oxford: Oxford University Press, 1975): 157.

4. Personal communication, October 29, 2003. Lubbock currently is Director of New Media at the Boston radio station WBUR.

5. Quayle delivered a list of three officers who the US embassy believed were responsible for the attack. See Philip J. Williams and Knut Walter, *Militarization and Demilitarization in El Salvador's Transition to Democracy* (Pittsburgh: University of Pittsburgh Press, 1997): 145–46.

6. Around this time in 1989, US sociologist Jeff Paige began to speak regularly with members of the Cristiani faction and other elite groups in El Salvador. This interview research identified their business-related interest in ending the war more quickly through negotiations. See Paige, *Coffee and Power: Revolution and the Rise of Democracy in Central America* (Cambridge, MA: Harvard University Press, 1997).

7. See Elisabeth Wood, *Forging Democracy from Below: Insurgent Transitions in South Africa and El Salvador* (Cambridge: Cambridge University Press, 2000), 52–77.

8. See Rosa, *AID y las Transformaciones Globales en El Salvador*; and Cuenca, *El Poder Intangible*.

9. See LeoGrande, *Our Own Backyard*.

10. Lindsey Gruson, "Intipucá Journal: Emigrants Feather Their Old Nest with Dollars," *New York Times*, July 18, 1989, 4.

11. According to Lubbock, he had been asked by the *Times* to travel to Intipucá to take photographs for the Gruson article. "I think that they told me to look up this Chávez fellow," Robin explained.

12. Almost ten years later I first came across Charles Lane's *Regardie's* story that Gruson's article directly echoed, obtained via microfiche at the University of Michigan. The magazine appeared between 1980 and 1992 and is no longer in print. In 2011, Lane sent me an original copy of the magazine issue with his story.

13. See "El Asesinato de los Jesuita," *Proceso* no. 409, Nov. 29, 1989, San Salvador: UCA/Centro Universitario de Documentación e Información; Teresa Whitfield, *Paying the Price: Ignacio Ellacuría and the Murdered Jesuits of El Salvador* (Philadelphia: Temple University Press, 1995); Martha Dogget, *Death Foretold: The Jesuit Murders in El Salvador* (Washington, DC: Lawyers Committee for Human Rights and Georgetown University Press, 1993); John Hasset and Hugh Lacey, eds., *Towards a Society that Serves Its People: The Intellectual Contribution of El Salvador's Murdered Jesuits* (Washington, DC: Georgetown University Press, 1991).

14. Confidential interview in Northern Virginia, spring 1997.

15. As of this writing, one version of the ad may be found on the popular website, YouTube. I thank Andrew Harris for this reference. www.youtube.com/watch?v=n7PEMGuA6tw.

16. Public Radio International, January 28, 2003. According to the report, "The El Salvadoran economy depends on cash and credit that relatives in the United States send back home. Last year, those remittances totaled almost $2 billion. That's nine times the total amount El Salvador earned from exporting coffee and sugar. Salvadoran families use the money to purchase basic necessities and consumer goods. But one town in El Salvador [Intipucá] is putting the cash into local development."

17. I am grateful to Rupert Stasch for his example of analyzing the rhetorical logic of news reports. See his "Textual Iconicity and the Primitivist Cosmos: Chronotopes of Desire in Travel Writing about Korowai of West Papua," *Journal of Linguistic Anthropology* 21, no. 1 (2011): 1–21.

18. Segundo Montes, *El Salvador 1987: Salvadoreños Refugiados en los Estados Unidos* (San Salvador: UCA, Instituto de Investigaciones, 1987); Pedro Ticas, *Cambios Culturales, Economia, y Migracion en Intipucá, La Union* (El Salvador: Universidad Tecnológica de El Salvador, 1998).

19. Patricia Landolt, "Salvadoran Economic Transnationalism: Embedded Strategies for Household Maintenance, Immigrant Incorporation, and Entrepreneurial Expansion," in "New Research and Theory on Immigrant Transnationalism," special issue, *Global Networks: A Journal of Transnational Affairs* 1, no. 3 (2001): 217–42 . Daniela Villacrés, "Remitting Trans-local Governance: Diaspora Associations as Vehicles for Deepening Democracy" (PhD diss., Brown University, 2011).

20. José Roberto López and Mitchell Seligson, "Small Business Development in El Salvador: The Impact of Remittances," in *Migration, Remittances, and Small Business Development: Mexico and the Caribbean Basin Countries*, ed. Sergio Díaz-Briquets and Sidney Weintraub (Boulder: Westview, 1991), 175–206.

21. At its embassy built on the outskirts of San Salvador—so far from the official city limits that the Salvadoran government was obligated to revise the city boundaries so that the compound legally lay within the national capital proper—US commercial attaché Matthew Rooney acknowledged that "the principal factor that makes dollarization feasible is remittances."

22. Rafael Rodriguez Loucel, "La Sorpresa Económica," *Opiniones*, 2000.

23. In a related manner of generalizing the particular, an accomplished writer and surgeon who was born in the pueblo calls his hometown of Intipucá part of the "puertoricanization" of El Salvador.

24. Wood has written two excellent books on the war in El Salvador, informed by remarkable ethnographic field research conducted in Usulután during the last five years of the war.

25. These charts are part of Wood's effort to build explicitly on Paige and implicitly on Lungo and their arguments that these shifts were especially visible to a particular class fraction in El Salvador, shaping their outlooks and future-oriented capitalist projects.

26. See for example, Susan Coutin's discussion of remittance accounting in El Salvador in the fifth chapter of her book *Nations of Emigrants: Shifting Boundaries of Citizenship in El Salvador and the United States* (Ithaca: Cornell University Press, 2007), 122–48.

27. Wood, *Forging Democracy from Below*, 55.

28. Natural resources and the unpaid labor in the home are the two classic examples. See Op-Ed by Eric Zencey, "G.D.P.R.I.P.," *New York Times*, August 10, 2009.

29. Grandolini, Gloria M.1996. *El Salvador: Meeting the Challenge of Globalization* (Washington, DC: World Bank), xix-xxiii.

30. Ibid., 14.

31. For a critical analysis of national economic accounting, see Anwar M. Shaikh and E. Ahmet Tonak, *Measuring the Wealth of Nations: The Political Economy of National Accounts* (Cambridge: Cambridge University Press, 1994).

32. Fernando Coronil, *The Magical State: Nature, Money, and Modernity in Venezuela* (Chicago: University of Chicago Press, 1997).

33. Grandolini 1996, 16.

34. "La Emigracion de Salvadoreños y Su Impacto Economico y Social." *Boletín Economico y Social* 98 (1994). San Salvador: FUSADES.

35. CEPAL, "El Salvador: Remesas Internacionales y Economia Familiar" (Mexico City: CEPAL, 1991).

36. Segundo Montes Mozo and Juan José García Vásquez. *Salvadoran Migration to the United States: An Exploratory Study* (Washington, DC: Center for Immigration Policy and Refugee Assistance, Georgetown University, 1988).

Part I Introduction

1. Besides the rhyme, research on human brains has shown them to be remarkably historical ("plastic" is the technical term), constantly changing their neurological configuration in relation to environmental conditions encountered over their lifespan.

Chapter Two

1. Gabriel Escobar, "Rural Hardship Acquires a Gilt Edge," *Washington Post*, June 21, 1993, A1. Currently Escobar is the city editor at the *Post* after serving as the paper's bureau chief in South America.

2. Interview on December 14, 1997, with Armando Duke at his home in San Salvador. Considered to be part of the Salvadoran oligarchy, Duke's ancestors owned large indigo plantations near San Miguel during the colonial era but shifted their wealth into coffee farming and commercial enterprises by the late 19th century. See Manuel Sevilla, "El Salvador: La Concentration Económica y los Grupos de Poder," in *Cuaderno de Trabajo* no. 3 (Mexico: Centro de Investigación y Acción Social, 1984), 37.

3. Gavidia may have been born in 1865, according to some sources. See Luis Gallegos Valdés, *Panorama de la Literatura Salvadoreña* (San Salvador: UCA Editores, 1981), 83–98.

4. On early nineteenth-century indigo production and trade in the vicinity of San Miguel, see David Browning, *El Salvador: Landscape and Society* (Oxford: Clarendon Press, 1971), 155–57; Héctor Lindo-Fuentes, *Weak Foundations: The Economy of El Salvador in the Nineteenth Century, 1821–1898* (Berkeley: University of California Press, 1990), 111–16. A recent analysis of the colonial indigo system throughout Central America is Jose Antonio Fernandez Molina, "Colouring the World in Blue: The Indigo Boom and the Central American Market, 1750–1810" (PhD diss., University of Texas at Austin, 1992).

5. ECLA (CEPAL) report (E/CN.12/435), April 20, 1957, presented at seventh session, May 15–29, 1957, in La Paz, Bolivia. Reprinted as *Coffee in Latin America* (New York: UNFAO, 1958), 130.

6. The street is named *4 Calle Poniente* on the maps of the *Direccion General de Estadistica y Censos,* drawn up after completion of the 1992 national census.

7. Interview conducted in Intipucá, Wednesday morning, November 21, 1996, translated from Spanish by author.

8. In absolute terms, in DC Sigfredo was earning over six times his San Miguel wage.

9. "Pedro" is a pseudonym for a man who was Sigfredo's closest friend from childhood.

10. In 1996 Sigfredo could not recall if he used this term specifically to describe himself to Escobar three years earlier, but he thought that it was sufficiently accurate for the US readership.

11. In 1896, Serapio Chávez (who would become Rosa's father-in-law) and Manuel Leonzo, both of Intipucá, queried the government to see if lands near the Rivas farm were titled. Archivo General de la Nación (AGN), San Salvador, Col. Ministerios, Tierras, Dep. La Union, 1889–1925, document 13.

12. See the local history and promotional magazine *Intipucá,* written and published by Hugo Salinas. According to Salinas, this short history draws from common memories in the pueblo and sources that he consulted at the *Museo Nacional David J. Guzman* in San Salvador.

13. Younger members of the pueblo corroborated this story. Historian David Browning cites documents housed at the Archivo General del Gobierno in Guatemala City (A1.24, exp. 10226, leg. 1582, fol. 223) that mention the reestablishment

of Intipucá by 1770 "after its former site, now described as Pueblo Viejo, had been absorbed into an hacienda." See Browning, *El Salvador: Landscape and Society* (Oxford: Clarendon Press, 1971), 97n28. I believe that this was the hacienda that Juan Rivas acquired.

14. Many people pointed out that the pueblo had three additional previous locations that were marked by stones carved with indigenous iconography. Archeologists have suggested that the region near Intipucá was on the periphery of dominant Mesoamerican indigenous groups and contained pockets of Lenca settlements. See the literature review by Karen Olsen Bruhns, "El Salvador and the Southeastern Frontier of Mesoamerica," in *Paths to Central American Prehistory*, ed. Frederick W. Lang (Denver: University Press of Colorado, 1996), 285–96. Intipucá residents often jokingly referred to the migration to DC as a continuation of this long history of indigenous mobility.

15. An important work that draws upon limited evidence of rural land-owner perspectives to show how the two terms overlapped is Héctor Pérez Brignoli's "Indians, Communists, and Peasants: The 1932 Rebellion in El Salvador," in the collection of essays, *Coffee, Society, and Power*, ed. William Roseberry, Lowell Gudmundson, and Mario Samper Kutschbach (Baltimore: Johns Hopkins University Press, 1995), 232–61.

16. See AGN, Sec. Jurídica C, 1920, no. 20.

17. In September 1996 I conducted a two-hour tape-recorded interview with Rosa in her current home in Intipucá, which was less than a block from Sigfredo's.

18. See Nora Hamilton and Norma Stoltz Chinchilla, "Central American Migration: A Framework for Analysis," *Latin American Research Review* 26, no.1 (1991): 75–110.

19. According to one Intipucá resident born in the early 1960s, "We were always fighting them [Chirilagua] with machetes—it was just like the gangs they talk about in the newspapers today. After a soccer match there was always blood."

20. Thomas P. Anderson, *Matanza: El Salvador's Communist Revolt of 1932* (Lincoln: University of Nebraska Press, 1971), 193.

21. The American Bank Note Company formed officially in 1858 after the US government took over printing of US domestic currency, but the firm traces its origins to a Philadelphia printing shop that began printing US dollars during the 1790s after the US Constitution was ratified and US states chartered note-issuing banks. As of 2001, the company was a publicly owned corporation traded on the New York Stock Exchange that continued to specialize in the production of documents, currency, and holographic emblems designed to resist forgery and counterfeiting.

22. According to Miguel and his friend, the town has a proud history of defending its water supply from the aggressions of La Union dwellers who periodically sought to divert it to the city below.

23. In our discussions Miguel provided few details of his life at that time and his friend frequently corrected his sense of time, reminding him that they had worked

together on the harvests over fifty years before, although Miguel tended to say "at least thirty years ago."

24. E/CN.12/490, "Coffee in Latin America: Productivity Problems and Future Prospects, I: Colombia and El Salvador," report prepared under the Joint Programme of the Economic Commission for Latin America and the Food and Agriculture Organization of the United Nations, 1958, 103–44.

25. In July 1994 I lived for a week with a family in the settlement called El Delirio and interviewed residents about the history of sisal production in the region. According to Leon Hirsch who visited the region in the early 1960s, the town name referred to the effects of chronic malaria that racked the region until the widespread use of pesticides that was associated with expanded cotton production during the 1960s. Leon V. Hirsch, "The Littoral Highway in El Salvador," in *The Impact of Highway Investment on Development*, ed. Barbara R. Bergmann, Leon V. Hirsch, Martin S. Klein, and George W. Wilson (Washington, DC: Brookings Institution, 1966), 87–126.

26. Ostensibly to keep employment levels high, but also to subvert resurgent campesino–urban worker alliances, Martínez had effectively prohibited the importation of powered machinery for the sisal industry as well as for shoe manufacturing; he also limited cotton processing in the area by levying a huge tax. David Luna, "Analisis de una Dictadura Fascista Latinoamerica, Maximiliano Hernández Martínez 1931–44," *La Universidad* 94, no. 5 (September-October 1969): 62.

27. See Patricia Parkman, *Nonviolent Insurrection in El Salvador: The Fall of Maximiliano Hernández Martínez* (Tucson: University of Arizona Press, 1988), 21.

28. E/CN.12/490, "Coffee in Latin America: Productivity Problems and Future Prospects, I: Colombia and El Salvador." Report prepared under Joint Programme of the Economic Commission for Latin America and the Food and Agriculture Organization of the United Nations, 1958, 103–44.

29. "Statement of Andres Uribe, Acting Chairman of the Pan-American Coffee Bureau, New York, N.Y.," in *Utilization of Farm Crops*, Hearings, Subcommittee of the Committee on Agriculture and Forestry, United States Senate, 81st Congress, Part 3, 1214.

30. In 1948 the top US importers of coffee worldwide were A&P, J. Aron & Co., General Foods, Otis McAllister, and J. A. Folger & Co., according to the US Department of Commerce and presented at the Senate Hearings above, 1267.

31. Interview (September 12, 2001) with Bob Hatch, former president and owner of Wilkins Coffee before it was sold to Royal Cup Coffee in 1989. Wilkins was founded by John Wilkins in 1899 and opened its first roasting shop on Rhode Island Avenue in the District. In 1947 the company opened a large roasting facility in Capital Heights, Maryland. A decade later, Jim Henson, then a student at the University of Maryland, had his first commercial success with two puppets, "Wilkins" and "Wonkins," which appeared in a popular TV ad for the coffee.

Henson later developed a host of puppet characters known as the Muppets with his earnings from the ad.

32. On US coffee capitalists see the excellent chapter by the late Michael F. Jiménez, " 'From Plantation to Cup': Coffee and Capitalism in the United States," in *Coffee, Society, and Power in Latin America*, ed. William Roseberry, Lowell Gudmundson, and Mario Samper Kutschbach (Baltimore: Johns Hopkins University Press, 1995), 38–64.

33. See Fred L. Block, *The Origins of International Economic Disorder: A Study of United States International Monetary Policy from WWII to the Present* (Berkeley: University of California Press, 1977).

34. See Thomas J. McCormick, *America's Half Century: United States Foreign Policy in the Cold War* (Baltimore: Johns Hopkins University Press, 1989), chaps. 1–2.

35. *Utilization of Farm Crops*, Hearings, Subcommittee of the Committee on Agriculture and Forestry, United States Senate, Eighty-First Congress, part 3, 788–97.

36. See Lynn Eden, "Capitalist Conflict and the State: The Making of the United States Military Policy in 1948," in *Statemaking and Social Movements: Essays in History and Theory*, ed. Charles Bright and Susan Harding (Ann Arbor: University of Michigan Press, 1984), 233–61.

37. See Gregory Hooks, *Forging the Military-Industrial Complex: World War II's Battle of the Potomac* (Urbana: University of Illinois Press, 1991).

38. See especially Ann Markusen, Peter Hall, Scott Campbell, and Sabina Deitrick, *Rise of the Gunbelt: The Military Remapping of America* (Oxford: Oxford University Press, 1991).

39. "Thomas Meloy, Melpar Chief, Dies; Founder of Electronics Research Firm," *Washington Post*, January 6, 1979.

40. Peterson quoted in Joel Garreau, *Edge City: Life on the New Frontier* (New York: Doubleday, 1991), 375.

41. Ibid.

42. See Kenesaw M. Landis, *Segregation in Washington, DC: A Report of the National Committee on Segregation in the Nation's Capital* (Chicago: National Committee on Segregation in the Nation's Capital, 1948); Karl E. Taeuber and Alma F. Taeuber, *Negroes in Cities: Residential Segregation and Neighborhood Change* (Chicago: Aldine Publishing Company, 1965); Kenneth T. Jackson, "Federal Subsidy and the Suburban Dream: The First Quarter-Century of Government Intervention in the Housing Market," in *Records of the Columbia Historical Society* (Charlottesville: University Press of Virginia, 1980), 50:421–51.

43. Isabelle Shelton, "Foggy Bottom Area Gets Face-Lifting," *Evening Star*, February 12, 1950; William R. Barnes, "A Battle for Washington: Ideology, Racism, and Self-Interest in the Controversy over Public Housing, 1943–46," *Records of the Columbia Historical Society* (Charlottesville: University Press of Virginia, 1980), 50:452–83.

44. See Philip J. Williams and Knut Walter, *Militarization and Demilitariza-tion in El Salvador's Transition to Democracy* (Pittsburgh, University of Pittsburgh Press, 1997), 37–62.

45. An almost complete collection of the *Boletín* is kept at the AGN in San Salvador.

46. See the government document "Inauguración de los Trabajos de Colada de Concreto por el Pdte. de la República" stored in the "government magazine" sec-tion of the AGN in San Salvador.

47. Hirsch, "Littoral Highway in El Salvador," 87–126.

Chapter Three

1. "La guerra es la continuación de la política por otros medios y la política es solamente la economía quintaesenciada," in Roque Dalton, *Las Historias Prohibi-das del Pulgarcito* (San Salvador: UCA Editores, [1977] 1988), 197.

2. Eladio is the wartime name of a member of the *Resistencia Nacional* (Na-tional Resistance), a splinter group that formed out of the People's Revolution-ary Army (ERP) after members of this militant faction had murdered Salvadoran poet Roque Dalton. Eladio's adaptation of Dalton's famous phrase was part of a long statement delivered at a clandestine meeting of RN members in eastern El Salvador in June 1993.

3. John Beverley and Marc Zimmerman, *Literature and Politics in the Central American Revolutions* (Austin: University of Texas Press, 1990).

4. Argueta, 141–44.

5. Argueta, 144.

6. Conversation with Daniel, Friday afternoon, August 2, 1996. I have tried to reproduce the colloquial expression above, which is short for the exclamatory form of *hijo de la puta* ("son of a bitch"). I thank Manuel Artiga, a professor of philoso-phy at the National University of El Salvador (Oriente campus), for helping me to listen for this expression.

7. See David Mena, "Estado y Grupos Dominantes en El Salvador," paper pre-sented at III Congreso Centroamericano de Sociología, Tegucigalpa, April 24–29, 1978.

8. Conversation with Daniel, August 2, 1996. Daniel told me of these wages, as did others in the pueblo.

9. Dirección General de Estadística y Censos d El Salvador, *Censo Agropecu-ario*, 1950–51, 1970–71.

10. Cooperativa Algodonera Salvadoreña, *Informe de la Cosecha de Algodón, 1961–62* (San Salvador: Cooperativa Algodonera Salvadoreña, 1962).

11. See Ridgeway Satterthwaite, "Campesino Agriculture and Hacienda Mod-ernization in Coastal El Salvador, 1949–1969" (PhD diss., University of Wisconsin, 1971), 96.

12. John Coatsworth, *The Clients and the Colossus* (New York: Twayne Publishers, 1994), 106–7.

13. Interview while visiting Daniel's land, Wednesday afternoon, July 10, 1996.

14. William Stanley, *The Protection Racket State: Elite Politics, Military Extortion, and Civil War in El Salvador* (Philadelphia: Temple University Press, 1996), 107.

15. Stanley, 110.

16. Ibid., 112.

17. Interview, September 22, 1996.

18. Ibid.

19. Ibid.

20. Stanley, 117.

21. Cited in Stanley, 118.

22. Roberto López, "La Nacionalización del Comercio Exterior en El Salvador: Mitos y Realidades en Torno al Café," Latin American and Caribbean Center Occasional Papers, no. 16 (Miami: Latin American and Caribbean Center at Florida International University, 1986), 31, cited in Paige, *Coffee and Power*, 196.

23. Jeffrey Paige, a US sociologist who interviewed members of the coffee elite in El Salvador, has suggested, "Because most coffee holdings were not affected by the first phase of the agrarian reform and the majority of the coffee growers were not bankers (although almost all banks were controlled by coffee capital), export nationalization had a greater immediate economic effect on coffee growers than the other two reforms." *Coffee and Power*, 195.

24. Sigfredo's racial hierarchy is similar to that contained in an elaborately bound glossy book that profiles El Salvador in English and Spanish, printed in 1904.

25. "Police Battle Angry Mob of Rock Throwers," *Evening Star*, August 6, 1965.

26. "DC Officials Close Carnival after Rock-Throwing Melee," *Washington Post*, August 7, 1965.

27. Paul Valentine, "An Alley Game That Became a Near-Riot," *Washington Post*, September 25, 1965. According to the *Post* report, police-community relations were not good in the 10th Precinct. The city assigned 159 officers there, but only 121 in Precinct No. 14 in the far Northeast, which had a larger population and twice the area of No. 10.

28. The account always referred to the rank of the police officers, although Michael Norman was a member of the US Air Force.

29. Valentine, "Alley Game."

30. Paul Valentine, "Ex-airman Goes to Trial in Alley Football Incident," *Washington Post*, March 25, 1966, B8.

31. Cited in "2 Policemen Criticized in Boys' Arrest," *Washington Post*, September 10, 1965.

32. Valentine, "Alley Game."

33. "Mr. Sullivan Speaks," *Washington, DC, Afro-American*, October 16, 1965.

34. This account is based on 12 newspaper articles published between 1977 and 1999.

35. At Westgate, Halpin served as president with Seeley as executive vice president and board chair. They joined with Charles B. Ewing Jr., an engineer who served as vice president of Westgate, and Thomas F. Nicholson, a real estate agent who was vice president and treasurer of Westgate.

36. This lasted until 1970 when they demolished the structure.

37. Michael D. Shear, "Group Honors Tysons Builder," *Washington Post*, April 15, 1999, V01.

38. Leith was a DC native who graduated from Western High School in 1933 and attended American University in the District before obtaining a law degree from the University of Pennsylvania. He joined Peoples after serving with the US Army in the Mediterranean and China-Burma-India theaters during WWII and became president of the company in 1959. See "William T. Leith Dies at 77," *Washington Post*, January 25, 1995, D5.

39. Peoples, founded in 1903, was one of the oldest firms in Washington, DC, and occupied a five-story building at 601 New Hampshire Ave, NW.

40. In 1977 they paid contractors to construct an assemblage of 36 buildings with nearly 3 million square feet of office-related space and formed their own management company to lease space at $3 a square foot. By the end of the 1970s they rented space for $10 a square foot. By 1988, the land that Halpin had bought for 8 cents a square foot in 1962 sold for $54 a square foot.

41. This discussion of Hazel's activities is based on a review of 149 newspaper articles published in 1977–90.

42. Peterson had graduated from Middlebury College in Vermont, where he gained a reputation as a shrewd businessman for almost driving the college bookstore out of business with his own used-book venue.

43. Thomas Grubisich, "Master of All He Surveys," *Washington Post*, July 14, 1979, A15.

44. John F. Harris, "Peterson: Hard-Driving Partner Who Deals without the Spotlight," *Washington Post*, October 2, 1988, A16.

45. In April 1978 they pleaded guilty and were fined $1.381 million by the US government for paying an unnamed foreign government at least $380,000 between 1967 and 1976 in order to ensure receiving a contract. Three months later in July, the company's top seven officers faced a lawsuit brought on behalf of all stockholders calling for reimbursement of $1.761 million to the company for the combined kickback and government fines.

46. This account is based on the Hazel articles and 155 additional articles published from 1977–99.

47. John F. Harris, "Hazel: Horns and Halo; Developer Defines Region's Personality," Washington Post, October 2, 1988, A1.

48. Ibid.

49. Athelia Knight, "Dalton Predicts Building of Bypass in 1980," *Washington Post*, August 3, 1978, Virginia Section, 1.

50. Frances Suave, *Washington Post*, August 10, 1978, Virginia Section, 6.

51. Liza Bercovici, "Developer Offers Fairfax County Land Package for New Headquarters," *Washington Post*, December 9, 1978, A12.

52. Bercovici, "Developer Offers."

53. Thomas Grubisich, "Major Fairfax Route May Be Jeopardized by Money Problems," *Washington Post*, May 5, 1979, C1.

54. Ibid.

55. Ibid.

56. Ibid.

57. "Fairfax Board Votes to Let State Make Decision on Springfield Route Proposal," *Washington Post*, June 19, 1979, C3.

58. Amy DePaul, "Buildspeak," Washington *Post*, January 11, 1987, C5.

59. From Frank Zappa's Reagan-era composition, "The Beltway Bandits," *The Jazz from Hell*, produced by Frank Zappa, 1986.

60. This foundation on federal expenditure led to the emergence of the DC area as a primary national center for high-tech information-based private companies in the late 1990s. See *New York Times*, October 12, 1999, A1.

61. See Pedersen, "States of Memory and Desire: Transnational Migrants in Washington, DC, and El Salvador."

62. Caroline E. Mayer, "Successful BDM Floats Restructuring to Foil Potential Takeovers," Washington Business, *Washington Post*, September 26, 1983, 1.

63. The bank was Manufacturers Hanover Trust Company, at that time among the 16 largest banks in the United States and the third largest in New York City, where it was colloquially known as Manny Hanny.

64. Area Roundup, Business & Finance, *Washington Post*, August 13, 1977, C9.

65. Toupes was later implicated in the failure of a prestigious DC bank.

Chapter Four

1. Among many processes that contributed to this transformation was the effective displacement of the native beaver population.

2. Bob Levin, Beth Nissen, John Walcott, and Jane Whitmore, "Storm over El Salvador," *Newsweek*, March 16, 1981, 34.

3. Levin et al., *Newsweek*.

4. Levin et al., *Newsweek*.

5. As one of many examples, in September 1984 I heard historian Barbara Tuchman speak at Connecticut College in New London. She compared the pace of US buildup in Central America with the early years of the Vietnam War and predicted a massive deployment of US ground troops in El Salvador by that winter.

6. William Greider, *Secrets of the Temple: How the Federal Reserve Runs the Country* (New York: Simon & Schuster, 1987), 551.

7. John M. Berry, "Va. Fed Chief 'in Monetarist Camp,'" *Washington Post,* Washington Business, November 3, 1980, 21.

8. Confidential interview with shareholders of the Norfolk and Southern Railway.

9. Thomas Grubisich, "Powerful Coalition Puts Springfield Bypass on the Road Again," *Washington Post,* June 16, 1981, C1.

10. VHS copy of this video, narrated by Milton Peterson, is available at the UM media union.

11. Fred Haitt, Sandra G. Boodman, and Glenn Frankel, "Coleman to Return Contribution," *Washington Post,* September 17, 1981, B1.

12. "Fairfax Chamber of Commerce Chooses 1985–86 Officers," *Washington Post,* June 3, 1985, Washington Business, 19.

13. Sandra Sugawara, "Secret Success for BDM May Be President's Style," *Washington Post,* July 4, 1988, F1.

14. Omni Construction Company is part of Clark Enterprises that also is the holding company for George Hyman Construction Company, a Bethesda-based national general contracting and construction company. Clark was founded in 1906 as the George Hyman Company and continues to be privately owned. In 1980, A. James Clark was president and Benjamin Rome was chairman.

15. The signing completed informal agreements reached between PRC and Tyson-McLean, a joint venture of Hazel/Peterson and Metropolitan Life Insurance Co. "Planning Research Corp. Leases McLean Building," *Washington Post,* November 19, 1984, Washington Business, Commercial Realty, 54.

16. The West Park Office Complex included more than 2 million square feet of office space in 17 buildings with 170 acres of land zoned for an additional 3.5 million square feet of office development and 1,000 residential units. See M. B. Regan, "Commercial Realty; BDM Plans Headquarters in Tysons Corner," *Washington Post,* January 13, 1986, 42.

17. Twelve years later the same boy killed another boy in the town in a personal struggle at almost the same spot, stabbing him with a knife. In this instance he was sentenced to one year in jail and transformed into the assumed source of most violence and criminality in the town.

18. The haunting quality of an indexical sign is described by Charles S. Peirce in a manner that is apt for our story. "An index is a sign which would, at once, lose the character which makes it a sign if its object were removed, but would not lose that character if there were no interpretant [the interpreter of the sign]. Such, for instance, is a piece of mould with a bullet-hole in it as sign of a shot; for without the shot there would have been no hole; but there is a hole there, whether anybody has the sense to attribute it to a shot or not."

19. During the early 1980s, Omni, Miller & Long, and other firms advertised for bilingual foremen at local high schools, including the one that I attended, Walter

Johnson High School, named after the famous pitcher for the then-defunct Washington Senators baseball team. While playing on the team, Johnson resided in a large house on Old Georgetown Road in Bethesda, Maryland, just two miles from where the school was later built.

20. This story was leaked by Sen. Jesse Helms.

21. Wednesday, May 23, 1984.

22. General John R. Galvin, "Uncomfortable Wars: Towards a New Paradigm," *Parameters: Journal of the US Army War College* 26, no. 4 (December 1986): 2–8, and *Uncomfortable Wars: Towards a New Paradigm of Low-Intensity Conflict*, ed. Maxwell G. Manwaring (Boulder: Westview Press, 1991), 9–18. Galvin graduated from the US Military Academy at West Point and held a master's degree in English from Columbia University. He authored four books and over 50 articles on military strategy, tactics, history, and leadership. He had been a member of the staff of the US European Command and he served as the Supreme Allied Commander in Europe. Galvin served in infantry units in Puerto Rico and as a Ranger instructor in Colombia; he completed two tours in Vietnam with the 1st Cavalry Division, commanding the division's 1st Battalion.

23. Galvin, "Uncomfortable Wars," 11.

24. Ibid., 11–12.

25. Ibid., 13.

26. Ibid., 15.

27. Ibid., 13.

28. Ibid., 16.

29. See Maxwell G. Manwaring and Court Prisk, acknowledgments in *El Salvador at War: An Oral History of Conflict from the 1979 Insurrection to the Present* (Washington, DC: National Defense University Press, 1988), xliii–xliv.

30. The report was prepared under the provision of Amendment 1 to Task Order 723, "Low-Intensity Conflict Cell Support," and followed stipulations of US military contract number DABT60-86-C-1360. I thank William Arkin for his expert advice on how to conduct research on US military contracts via the Internet and through Freedom of Information Act (FOIA) requests.

31. Currently over 2,000 pages in 40 volumes of unpublished interviews remain at the US Army War College in Pennsylvania.

32. When it was published in 1988, the report contained versions in English and Spanish as well as copies of 35-mm slide projections used in the briefing.

33. Maxwell G. Manwaring, *A Model for the Analysis of Insurgencies* (Washington, DC: BDM Management Services, 1988), 2.

34. SWORD Paper, "Strategic Country Assessment: El Salvador," February 4, 1988.

35. Within four years of the report, the Salvadoran war ended through negotiated settlement and the FMLN became a legal political party—a resounding defeat for the Galvin-SWORD-BDM approach to the war.

36. In fall 1998 I spoke with Pear, who told me that he no longer had "any of

those materials," referring to the letter, and that his article had quoted "all the most important things."

37. Salvadoran Foreign Minister Ricardo Acevedo Peralta had met with US officials on March 19 to ask for an exemption from the law for Salvadorans.

38. At the end of April, the *New York Times* published its editorial opinion proposing how to finesse the contradictions, titled "Refugees Are Not Subsidies." The next day on May 1, Duarte sent off a reply, and on May 12 it was published under the headline "Humanitarian Adjustments to Immigration Act."

39. See "Hearing before the Subcommittee on Immigration, Refugees, and International Law of the Committee on the Judiciary," House of Representatives, November 7, 1985, and "Hearings before the Subcommittee on Human Rights and International Organizations and the Subcommittee on Western Hemisphere Affairs of the Committee on Foreign Affairs," House of Representatives, September 23 and 29, 1987 (Washington, DC: US Government Printing Office).

40. Segundo Montes, *El Salvador 1987: Salvadoreños Refugiados en los Estados Unidos* (San Salvador: Instituto de Investigaciones, Universidad de Centroamerica, 1987).

41. According to Patricia Pessar, Research Director of CIP at Georgetown at the time, "We were concerned with the exceptionalism of the case. The remittances going back to ES were part of the drama. IRCA was being debated and Duarte had made that famous speech explaining the centrality of remittances. This was a moment of dramatic transformation in the history of El Salvador" (interview, September 14, 1998).

42. Segundo Montes and Juan Jose Garcia, *Salvadoran Migration to the United States: An Exploratory Study* (Washington, DC: Hemispheric Migration Project, Center for Immigration Policy and Refugee Assistance, Georgetown University, 1988).

Chapter Five

1. Roger Rouse, "Making Sense of Settlement: Class Transformation, Cultural Struggle, and Transnationalism among Mexican Migrants in the United States," in *Towards a Transnational Perspective on Migration: Race, Class, Ethnicity, and Nationalism Reconsidered*, ed. Nina Glick Schiller, Linda Basch, and Christina Blanc-Szanton, Annals of the New York Academy of Sciences (New York: New York Academy of Sciences, 1992), 645:25–52.

2. See Lynn Duke, "Drugs Are Shadowy Force in DC's Area Economy," *Washington Post*, July 19, 1989, A1, and Peter Reuter, Robert MaCoun, and Patrick Murphy, *Summary of Money from Crime: The Economics of Drug Dealing in Washington, DC*, (Washington, DC: Greater Washington Research Center, 1990).

3. Peter R. Andreas and Kenneth E. Sharpe, "Cocaine Politics in the Andes," *Current History* 91, no. 562 (February 1992), 74–79.

4. Andreas and Sharp, "Cocaine Politics in the Andes."

5. In 1997 I spoke with an engineer contracted by the Japanese construction firm, who had resigned from the project, claiming that the bridge was not being built correctly.

6. In March 2001 I spoke with Gabriel Siri, who at that time was residing in Washington, DC, and working for the World Bank.

7. Gabriel Siri and Pedro Abelardo Delgado, with Vilma Calderón, *Uso Productivo de las Remesas Familiares en El Salvador* (FUSADES, January 1995).

8. See for example, the two-volume collection edited by Mario Lungo, *Migracion Internacional y Desarrollo* (San Salvador: FUNDE, 1997).

9. Discussion with Kay Eekhoff, research director of FUNDE in 1996–97.

Chapter Six

1. Carlos Sanchez and Joël Glenn Brenner, "Investors in Limbo after DC Firm Shuts," *Washington Post*, December 6, 1990, C1.

2. Ruben Castaneda, "Four Months Later, Learning from Mount Pleasant's Turmoil: Shooting Victim Gains New Lease on Life," *Washington Post*, September 8, 1991.

3. Gabriel Escobar and Nancy Lewis, "For Every Witness, Yet Another Account of the 'Real' Story," *Washington Post*, May 7, 1991, A28.

4. Nancy Lewis and James Rupert, "DC Neighborhood Erupts after Officer Shoots Suspect," *Washington Post*, May 6, 1991, A1.

5. Ruben Castaneda and Neil Henderson, "Simmering Tension between Police, Hispanics Fed Clash," *Washington Post*, May 6, 1991, A1.

6. Ibid.

7. Rene Sanchez and Christine Spolar, "Dixon's Longest, Darkest Day as Mayor," *Washington Post*, May 7, 1991, A1.

8. Carlos Sanchez and Rene Sanchez, "Skirmishes, Looting Spread under Cloud of Tear Gas," *Washington Post*, May 7, 1991, A1.

9. Benjamin C. Schwarz, *American Counterinsurgency Doctrine and El Salvador: The Frustrations of Reform and the Illusions of Nation Building* (Santa Monica: National Defense Research Institute, 1991), 53, cited in Scott W. Moore, "Gold Not Purple: Lessons from USAID-USMILGP Cooperation in El Salvador, 1980–1992" (MS thesis, Naval Postgraduate School, 1997), 61.

Chapter Seven

1. The visit was recorded by a resident on videotape from which I draw this account.

2. "Hugo got a good private education in Mexico paid for with Banquito money. That's where he gets his talents," said Marvin once with a quality of disdain for his friend.

Chapter Nine

1. Army Gen. Stanley A. McChrystal sought Mortenson's advice on building trust among villagers in Afghanistan. Laura King, "'Three Cups of Tea' Enters Troop Lexicon," *Los Angeles Times*, August 22, 2010. According to Maj. James Spies, the counterinsurgency operations course director at West Point, "Mortenson's involvement in central Asia is critical to a holistic approach to assisting other countries. The military has re-learned the lessons of counterinsurgency that point out the need to build up the whole of a society to assist them in solving the core problems that created an insurgency." See Alexa James, "Mortenson Tells West Point Army Cadets How to Win in Afghanistan," *Times Herald-Record* (Hudson Valley, NY), March 13, 2009.

2. This is different from a "future," which is the actual requirement to buy or sell something on a specified date. In the United States, the first sophisticated market for options and futures formed in the 1860s in Chicago around aggregate wheat prices. William Cronon, *Nature's Metropolis: Chicago and the Great West* (New York: Norton, 1991), 97–147.

3. In 2009 at the end of his presidency, Bush admitted, "Clearly, putting 'Mission Accomplished' on an aircraft carrier was a mistake."

4. Associated Press, San Salvador, November 11, 2004. See also Secretary Rumsfeld's press conference in El Salvador the next day, US Department of Defense, Office of the Assistant Secretary of Defense (Public Affairs), news transcript.

5. Michael Hirsh and John Barry, "The Salvador Option," *Newsweek*, January 8, 2005.

6. Seymour M. Hersh, "The Coming Wars: What the Pentagon Can Now Do in Secret," *New Yorker*, January 24, 2005.

7. In 2006 President Bush famously defended Rumsfeld's prosecution of the war, saying "I'm the decider, and I decide what is best. And what's best is for Don Rumsfeld to remain as the Secretary of Defense."

8. See Mark Ayyash's essay, "The Appearance of War in Discourse: The Neoconservatives on Iraq," *Constellations* 14, no. 4 (2007), 613–34.

9. See John Lee Anderson's interview with Steele, "The Uprising: Shia and Sunnis Put Aside Their Differences," *New Yorker*, May 3, 2004.

10. US congressional hearings, March 2003.

11. Premiere Motivational Speakers Bureau, "Jim Steele Bio," http://premiere speakers.com/jim_steele/bio.

12. White House website, http://www.whitehouse.gov/news/releases/2004/02/20040216–1.html.

13. Pratap Chatterjee, "The Boys from Baghdad: Iraqi Commandos Trained by US Contractor," *CorpWatch,* Sept. 20, 2007.

14. See Greg Grandin, *Empire's Workshop: Latin America and the Roots of US Imperialism* (New York: Metropolitan Books, 2006).

15. Michael Childress, *The Effectiveness of US Training Efforts in Internal Defense and Development: The Cases of El Salvador and Honduras* (Santa Monica: National Defense Research Institute, 1995), 25.

16. See Richard Slotkin, *Gunfighter Nation: The Myth of the Frontier in Twentieth-Century America* (New York: HarperCollins, 1992).

17. Greg Walker, *At the Hurricane's Eye: US Special Operations Forces from Vietnam to Desert Storm* (New York: Ivy Books, 1994), 98–99.

18. Confidential interview, San Miguel, July 1993. See also David E. Spencer, *From Vietnam to El Salvador: The Saga of the FMLN Sappers and Other Guerilla Special Forces in Latin America* (Westport, CT: Praeger, 1996), 1–15.

19. Walker, *At the Hurricane's Eye,* 99.

20. John T. Fishel and Maxwell G. Manwaring, "The SWORD Model of Counterinsurgency: A Summary and Update," *Small Wars Journal* (2006).

21. Eva Bertram, Morris Blachman, Kenneth Sharpe, and Peter Andreas, *Drug War Politics: The Price of Denial* (Berkeley: University of California Press, 1996), 126–27.

22. Peter B. Kraska and Victor E. Kappeler, "Militarizing American Police: The Rise and Normalization of Paramilitary Units," *Social Problems* 44, no. 1 (February 1997), 1–17. Quote is from p. 12.

23. *Military Review* is printed bimonthly in English, Spanish, and Portuguese and is dstributed to readers in more than 100 countries. It is also printed in Arabic on a quarterly basis.

24. Maxwell G. Manwaring, *A Contemporary Challenge to State Sovereignty: Gangs and Other Illicit Transnational Criminal Organizations in Central America, El Salvador, Mexico, Jamaica, and Brazil* (Carlisle Barracks, PA: US Army Strategic Studies Institute, 2007).

25. Hudson Institute Symposium, "War and Decision: Inside the Pentagon at the Dawn of t53. War on Terrorism," with author Douglas Feith and panelists Paul Wolfowitz, Peter Rodman, Dan Senor, April 28, 2008. See also Eli Lake, "Wolfowitz Admits 'Clueless" on Counterinsurgency," *New York Sun,* April 29, 2008. Lake quotes Wolfowitz: "No one anticipated this insurgency; a lot of people were slow to recognize it once it started."

26. Taleb is thoughtfully profiled by Malcolm Gladwell in "Blowing Up: How Nassim Taleb Turned the Inevitability of Disaster into an Investment Strategy," *New Yorker,* April 22, 2002, 162–73.

27. CBS News Poll recorded the lowest level at 28 percent. "The President, the

State of the 7171ion, and the Troop Increase, January 18–21," CBS News Poll, January 22, 2007.

28. *Congressional quarterly*, Transcripts, January 23, 2007.

29. Ibid.

30. Dilip Ratha, "World Bank Programme on Migration and Remittances," Fourth Coordination Meeting on International Migration, Population Division, Department of Economic and Social Affairs, United Nations Secretariat, New York, October 26–27, 2005.

31. "Former Michigan Student Becomes UN Deputy Secretary-General," *University of Michigan Department of Political Science Newsletter* (Fall 2006), 11.

32. On March 6, 2009, Mark Malloch Brown wrote to me via e-mail: "I amazingly never did come across Elliott Berg and only understood his significance—and what I had missed—later!"

33. William Pleitez, "International Migration and Human Development in El Salvador: A Contradictory Relationship," special edition, Canadian Foundation for the Americas *Focal Point* (May-June 2007).

34. I asked Galdámez what motivated him to choose "Intipucá City," and he told me it clearly was an important part of the more general theme of transnational movement in the twenty-first century that his work addressed. For this reason, he was pleased to have the work as a whole taken up to form the cover of the UNDP report.

35. Perry Anderson, "Our Man," *London Review of Books*, May 10, 2007.

Conclusion

1. Even such an unreconstructed Kantian as Marshall Sahlins recently began to explore how distinct cultures necessarily exist in relation to that which they geographically and historically are not.

2. I am grateful to Marisa Peeters, who heard this story during fall 2010 in the context of her research on Pentacostalism and democracy in El Salvador. She relayed it to me and gave me permission to recount it in this way here.

Bibliography

Argueta, Manlio. *Un Día en la Vida*. San Salvador: UCA Editores, 1980.

Barnes, William R. "A Battle for Washington: Ideology, Racism, and Self-Interest in the Controversy over Public Housing, 1943–46." In *Records of the Columbia Historical Society of Washington, DC*, Vol. 50, edited by Francis Coleman Rosenberger, 452–483. Charlottesville: University of Virginia Press, 1980.

Block, Fred L. *The Origins of International Economic Disorder: A Study of United States International Monetary Policy from WWII to the Present*. Berkeley: University of California Press, 1977.

Browning, David. *El Salvador: Landscape and Society*. Oxford: Clarendon Press, 1971.

Bruhns, Karen Olsen. "El Salvador and the Southeastern Frontier of Mesoamerica." In *Paths to Central American Prehistory*, edited by Frederick W. Lang. Denver: University Press of Colorado, 1996.

Comisión Económica para América Latina (CEPAL). *El Salvador: Remesas Internacionales y Economia Familiar*. Mexico City: CEPAL, 1991.

Coatsworth, John. *The Clients and the Colossus*. New York: Twayne Publishers, 1994.

Cuenca, Breny. *El Poder Intangible: La AID y el Estado Salvadoreño en los Años Ochenta*. San Salvador: CRIES/PREIS, 1992.

Dalton, Roque. *Las Historias Prohibidas del Pulgarcito*. San Salvador: UCA Editores, 1988.

Dogget, Martha. *Death Foretold: The Jesuit Murders in El Salvador*. Washington, DC: Lawyers Committee for Human Rights and Georgetown University Press, 1993.

Economic Commission for Latin America and the Caribbean (ECLAC). *Estudio Económico de América Latina y el Caribe*, 1987. El Salvador.

Eden, Lynn. "Capitalist Conflict and the State: The Making of the United States Military Policy in 1948." In *Statemaking and Social Movements: Essays in History and Theory*, edited by Charles Bright and Susan Harding. Ann Arbor: University of Michigan Press, 1984.

Fernandez Molina, Jose Antonio. "Colouring the World in Blue: The Indigo Boom and the Central American Market, 1750–1810." PhD diss., University of Texas at Austin, 1992.

Gallegos Valdés, Luis. *Panorama de la Literatura Salvadoreña.* San Salvador: UCA Editores, 1981.

Galvin, John R. "Uncomfortable Wars: Towards a New Paradigm." In *Uncomfortable Wars: Towards a New Paradigm of Low Intensity Conflict,* edited by Maxwell G. Manwaring. Boulder: Westview Press, 1991.

Garreau, Joel. *Edge City: Life on the New Frontier.* New York: Doubleday, 1991.

García, Juan José. *Remesas Familiares y Relaciones Sociales Locales: El Caso de San Isidro.* Aportes no. 1, Programa El Salvador de la Facultad Latinoamericana de Ciencias Sociales (FLACSO). El Salvador: FLACSO, 1996.

Grandolini, Gloria M. *El Salvador: Meeting the Challenge of Globalization.* Washington, DC: World Bank, 1996.

Grumley, John E. *History and Totality: Radical Historicism from Hegel to Foucault.* London: Routledge, 1989.

Hamilton, Nora, and Norma Stoltz Chinchilla. "Central American Migration: A Framework for Analysis." *Latin American Research Review* 26.1 (1991): 75–110.

Harris, Nigel. *The New Untouchables: Immigration and the New World Worker.* London: I. B. Tauris/Penguin, 1995.

Hasset, John, and Hugh Lacey, eds. *Towards a Society That Serves Its People: The Intellectual Contribution of El Salvador's Murdered Jesuits.* Washington, DC: Georgetown University Press, 1991.

Hirsch, Leon V. "The Littoral Highway in El Salvador." In *The Impact of Highway Investment on Development,* edited by George W. Wilson, Martin S. Klein, Barbara R. Bergmann, Leon V. Hirsch, and Brookings Institution, 87–126. Washington, DC: Brookings Institution, 1966.

Hooks, Gregory. *Forging the Military-Industrial Complex: World War II's Battle of the Potomac.* Urbana: University of Illinois Press, 1991.

Jackson, Kenneth T. "Federal Subsidy and the Suburban Dream: The First Quarter Century of Government Intervention in the Housing Market." In *Records of the Columbia Historical Society,* Vol. 50, 421–51. Charlottesville: University of Virginia Press, 1980.

Jay, Martin. *Marxism & Totality: The Adventures of a Concept from Lukacs to Habermas.* Berkeley: University of California Press, 1984.

Jiménez, Michael F. " 'From Plantation to Cup': Coffee and Capitalism in the United States." In *Coffee, Society and Power in Latin America,* edited by William Roseberry, Lowell Gudmundson, Mario Samper Kutschbach, 38–64. Baltimore: Johns Hopkins University Press, 1995.

Landis, Kenesaw M. *Segregation in Washington, DC: A Report of the National Committee on Segregation in the Nation's Capital.* Chicago: National Committee on Segregation in the Nation's Capital, 1948.

Landolt, Patricia. "Salvadoran Economic Transnationalism: Embedded Strategies for Household Maintenance, Immigrant Incorporation and Entrepreneurial Expansion." In "New Research and Theory on Immigrant Transnationalism," special issue, *Global Networks: A Journal of Transnational Affairs,* 1, no. 3 (2001):217–42.

LeoGrande, William M. *Our Own Backyard: The United States in Central America, 1977–1992.* Chapel Hill: University of North Carolina Press, 1998.

Lindo-Fuentes, Héctor. *Weak Foundations: The Economy of El Salvador in the Nineteenth Century, 1821–1898.* Berkeley: University of California Press, 1990.

Lopez, Jose Roberto, and Mitchell Seligson. "Small Business Development in El Salvador: The Impact of Remittances." In *Migration, Remittances, and Small Business Development: Mexico and the Caribbean Basin Countries,* edited by Sergio Diaz-Briquets and Sidney Weintraub, 175–206. Boulder: Westview Press, 1991.

López, Roberto. *La Nacionalización del Comercio Exterior en El Salvador: Mitos y Realidades en Torno al Café.* Latin American and Caribbean Center (LACC) Occasional Papers, no. 16. Miami: LACC, 1986.

Luna, David. "Analisis de una Dictadura Fascista Latinoamerica, Maximiano Hernández Martínez 1931–44." In "San Salvador," *La Universidad* 94, no. 5 (September–October 1969).

Lungo, Mario. *Migracion Internacional y Desarrollo.* San Salvador: Fundación Nacional para el Desarrollo, El Salvador (FUNDE), 1997.

Lungo, Mario, and Susan Kandel, eds. *Transformando El Salvador: Migracion, Sociedad y Cultura.* San Salvador: FUNDE, 1999.

Mahler, Sarah. *American Dreaming: Immigrant Life on the Margins.* Princeton: Princeton University Press, 1995.

Manwaring, Max G., and Court Prisk. *El Salvador at War: An Oral History of Conflict from the 1979 Insurrection to the Present.* Washington, DC: National Defense University Press, 1988.

Markusen, Ann, Peter Hall, Scott Campbell, and Sabina Deitrick. *Rise of the Gunbelt: The Military Remapping of America.* Oxford: Oxford University Press, 1991.

McCormick, Thomas J. *America's Half Century: United States Foreign Policy in the Cold War.* Baltimore: Johns Hopkins University Press, 1989.

Mena, David. "Estado y Grupos Dominantes en El Salvador." Paper presented at III Congreso Centroamericano de Sociología, Tegucigalpa, April 24–29, 1978.

Menjívar, Cecilia. *Fragmented Ties: Salvadoran Immigrant Networks in America.* Berkeley: University of California Press, 2000.

Montes, Segundo. *El Salvador 1987: Salvadoreños Refugiados en los Estados Unidos.* San Salvador: Universidad de Centroamerica, Instituto de Investigaciones, 1987.

Mozo, Segundo Montes, and Juan José García Vásquez. *Salvadoran Migration to the United States: An Exploratory Study.* Washington, DC: Center for Immigration Policy and Refugee Assistance, Georgetown University, 1988.

Ollman, Bertell, and Tony Smith, eds. "Dialectics: The New Frontier," special issue, *Science & Society* 62, no. 3 (1998).

Paige, Jeffrey. *Coffee and Power in Central America.* Cambridge: Harvard University Press, 1996.

Parkman, Patricia. *Nonviolent Insurrection in El Salvador: The Fall of Maximiliano Hernández Martínez.* Tucson: University of Arizona Press, 1988.

Pérez Brignoli, Héctor. "Indians, Communists, and Peasants: The 1932 Rebellion in El Salvador." In *Coffee, Society, and Power,* edited by William Roseberry, Lowell Gudmundson, and Mario Samper Kutschbach, 232–61. Baltimore: Johns Hopkins University Press, 1995.

Repak, Terry A. *Waiting on Washington: Central American Workers in the Nation's Capital.* Philadelphia: Temple University Press, 1995.

Reuter, Peter, Robert MaCoun, and Patrick Murphy. *Summary of Money from Crime: The Economics of Drug Dealing in Washington, DC.* Washington, DC: Greater Washington Research Center, 1990.

Robinson, William I. *Transnational Conflicts: Central America, Social Change and Globalization.* New York: Verso, 2003.

Rosa, Herman. "AID y las Transformaciones Globales en El Salvador: El Papel de la Política de Asistencia Económica de los Estados Unidos desde 1980." Managua, Nicaragua: Regional Centre for Economic and Social Research (CRIES), 1993.

Rouse, Roger. "Making Sense of Settlement: Class Transformation, Cultural Struggle, and Transnationalism among Mexican Migrants in the United States." In Annals of the New York Academy of Sciences, vol. 645, *Towards a Transnational Perspective on Migration: Race, Class, Ethnicity, and Nationalism Reconsidered*, edited by Nina Glick Schiller, Linda Basch, and Christina Blanc-Szanton, 25–52. New York: New York Academy of Sciences, 1992.

Satterthwaite, Ridgeway. "Campesino Agriculture and Hacienda Modernization in Coastal El Salvador, 1949–1969." PhD diss., University of Wisconsin, 1971.

Siri, Gabrel, and Pedro Abelardo Delgado, with Vilma Calderon. *Uso Productivo de las Remesas Familiares en El Salvador.* La Libertad, El Salvador: Fundación Salvadoreña para El Desarrollo Económico y Social (FUSADES), 1995.

Sevilla, Manuel. *El Salvador: La Concentration Económica y los Grupos de Poder.* Cuaderno de trabajo no. 3. Mexico: Centro de Investigación y Acción Social, 1984.

Shaikh, Anwar M., and E. Ahmet Tonak. *Measuring the Wealth of Nations: The Political Economy of National Accounts.* Cambridge: Cambridge University Press, 1994.

Singer, Audrey, Samantha Friedman, Ivan Cheung, Marie Price. *The World in a Zip Code: Greater Washington, DC, as Region of Immigration.* Washington, DC: Center on Urban and Metropolitan Policy, Brookings Institution, 2001.

Stalker, Peter. *Workers without Frontiers: The Impact of Globalization on International Migration.* Boulder: Lynn Riener, 2003.

Taeuber, Karl E., and Alma F. Taeuber. *Negroes in Cities: Residential Segregation and Neighborhood Change.* Chicago: Aldine Publishing Company, 1965.

Ulloa, Roxanna Elizabeth. "La Remesa Familiar del Exterior: Dependencia o Desarrollo para El Salvador." *Realidad: Revista de Ciencias Sociales y Humanidades* 50 (March–April 1996): 213–40.

Whitfield, Teresa. *Paying the Price: Ignacio Ellacuría and the Murdered Jesuits of El Salvador.* Philadelphia: Temple University Press, 1995.

Williams, Philip J., and Knut Walter. *Militarization and Demilitarization in El Salvador's Transition to Democracy.* Pittsburgh: University of Pittsburgh Press, 1997.

Zappa, Frank. "The Beltway Bandits." *The Jazz from Hell.* Produced by Frank Zappa. 1986.

Index

Page numbers in italics refer to figures and maps.

A&P, 75, 283n30
abduction, 23
Abdul Al-Razzaq, Mohammed Zimam, 240–41
Abizaid, John, 237
ABNC (American Bank Note Company), 67, 282n21
Abraham Lincoln, USS, 236, 240
"actualism," 117–18, 288n1
Adams Morgan, 5–6, 42, 151, 170
aerospace industry, US, 77–78, 82, 113, 263
Afghanistan war, 8, 236–38, 293n1
African Americans, 79, 102–7, 119, 151, 169, 178, 183, 244, 286nn27–28
Agrarian Reform Decrees, 100–101
Agrícola office. *See* Banco Agrícola Comercial
agriculture, Salvadoran, 7–8, 11–12, 39–40, 44–45; and agrarian reform, 100–101, 286n23; history of, 62–73, 80–82, 85, 88, 92, 116, 140, 163; and image on one-colon note, 67–71, *68;* and Raúl's family, 198–99, 201–2, 206. *See also* agro-exports
agro-exports, 32, 44–45, *44, 45,* 50. *See also* coffee production and export; cotton production and export; sugar production and export
Aigner-Clark, Julie, 252, *252*
Air Force, US, 77–79, 82, 105–6, 286n28
Akron (Ohio), 209–11
Algerian revolution (1954–62), 135–36
Alliance for Progress, 90, 209
ambassadors, Salvadoran, 175

ambassadors, US, 41–42, 177, 183–87, 194, 197, 215
American Dream, 8, 12, 85, 148, 174, 176
"Model for the Analysis of Insurgencies, A" (BDM), 135–37, 142–43, 290n35
Amoroso, David, 42
Annan, Kofi, 254, 256–57, 259–260
ANSESAL (Salvadoran National Security Association), 90
ARC (Atlantic Research Corporation), 107
ARENA *(Alianza Republicana Naciona- lista),* 30–31, *31,* 42, 48, 192–94, 197, 203–4, 207, 213
Argueta, Manlio, 84–88, 95, 218
Arias, Maximiliano, 149
Arias family, 89
Arkin, William, 290n30
Army, Salvadoran. *See* military, Salvadoran
Army, US. *See* military, US
Army War College, US, Strategic Studies Institute, 135–36
Arnold & Porter (law firm), 176
Aronson, Cynthia, 127
Artiga, Manuel, 285n3
Asociacion Cafetalera, 73
assassinations. *See* killings
Atchison, Dean, 76
automobiles, 11, 89, 97, 199; of migrants, 6, 19, 61, 93–94, 102, 154, 165; parts for, 56

Badiou, Alain, 23, 277n51
Banco Agrícola Comercial, 187, 197, 213–15; and *ladrones* ("thieves"),

Banco Agrícola Comercial (*cont.*)
213–15; savings accounts in, 214; secret
passageway in, 213–14
Banco Cuscatlán, 99, 170, 173
banks, Salvadoran, 42, 45, 50, 67, 73, 76, 93,
97, 99–100, 127, 163–64, 198, 286n23. *See
also names of Salvadoran banks*
banks, US, 75, 79, 114, 121, 123; and Banquito (Little Bank), 167–175, 178; and
S&L failures, 174–75. *See also names of
US banks*
Banquito (Little Bank), 167–178, 184–85,
198, 213–16; collapse of, 168, 174–78,
185, 187, 194, 197, 203–4, 214; and
ladrones ("thieves"), 168, 213–14; and
Salinas, Hugo, 196–97, 293n2; savings
accounts in, 167, 171–72, 174–76, 214
Barry, John, 238
Bay of Pigs invasion (Cuba), 90
BBC (London), 40–41, 279n16
BCR (Salvadoran Central Reserve Bank),
45, 67, 73, 100, 127
BDM International, 113–14, 124–27, 134–37,
142, 241, 245–46, 288n63; Management
Services, 134; "Model for the Analysis
of Insurgencies, A," 135–37, 142–43,
290n35
Beckhorn, Duane W., 126
Bencastro, Mario, 42–43
Benjamin (pseud.), 91, 94
Benjamin, Walter, 53–54
Bennett, William, 157
Berg, Elliott, 255–56, 295n32
Bhaskar, Roy, 117
Bilbo, Theodore, 79
Billy (pseud.), 151–53, 155–56, 159, 166
"birds of passage," 148
Bjork, Schel, 98
Black, Robert P., 123
"blacks," 63, 102. *See also* African
Americans
Black Swan, The (Taleb), 248–49
Blanco family, 89
Boletín del Ejército (magazine), 80–81,
285n45
Bolivia, 155–56
Booz Allen Hamilton (consulting firm), 135
bordellos, 91–92, 97, 128, 199–202, 227
Borden's coffee, 76–77
Borges, Jorge Luis, 23, 277n51

Bosnian war, 256
Braddock, Joseph, 113–14
Brittle, Waverly L., 111
Brooks, David, 237
Browning, David, 281n13
bruja (witch), 229
Bush, George H. W., 30, 39, 246
Bush, George W., 157, 236, 238, 240, 293n3,
293n7; and polls, 250, 294n27; State of
the Union address, 250–53, 252, 255,
257, 260
Bush, Laura, 252–53, 252

Caballo de Troya (Trojan Horse), 164–65
caciques (chiefs or political bosses), 65
Calderon, Vilma, 163–64
Calderón Sol, Armando, 27, 42, 191–94, 202,
204, 207–10, 215–16
Calvino, Italo, 3, 19, 22, 26, 261
campesinos. *See* peasants
Cantor, Georg, 22–23, 277n51
Capital (Marx), 18
Capital Holding Corporation (Louisville,
Ky.), 107–8
capitalism, 7–8, 12, 16–19, 32, 208, 265,
275n37, 275n40, 280n25; and Banco
Agrícola Comercial, 213; and Banquito
(Little Bank), 172, 175–76; and Chávez,
Sigfredo, 65; and coffee production/ex-
port, 57, 75–78, 82, 206
Caribbean Basin Initiative, 162
Carlyle Group, 241
Carter, Jimmy, 38, 100, 120
Casítas, 141
Castañeda Castro, Salvador, 66, 79
Catholicism, 71, 90–91, 176, 209–12; Catho-
lic Diocese of Cleveland (Ohio), 90–91,
209; liberal theology, 95. *See also* Jesuit
priests
Caulotio, 64–65, 72, 101, 195
causal powers, 12–19, 23, 28, 61, 87, 250, 265
"Caveman." *See* Chávez, Marvin
CDC (Control Data Corporation), 109–10,
126, 287n45
CEL (Comision Ejecutiva Hidroelectrica
del Rio Lempa), 81
CEMFA *(Centro de Entrenamiento Militar
de la Fuerza Armada)*, 243–47, 250
"Central America and the Politicization of
US Immigration Policy" (Schoultz), 5

Central Reserve Bank. *See* BCR (Salvadoran Central Reserve Bank)

CEPAL (Economic Commission for Latin America and the Caribbean), 48

Chakrabarty, Dipesh, 275n40

Chaletenango, 84–85, 95

chance, 247–250

Chaney, Clarence A., 104

Chaparrastique (volcano), 58

Chávez, Marvin, 59, 63; arrest of, 158, 160, 166; and Coca-Cola distribution, 159–163, 224–25; and drug trade, 152–160, 165–66, 225; education of, 39, 96, 101, 118–19, 130, 150; in Gruson's *New York Times* article, 33, 35–40, *35*, *36*, 43, 51, 147, 165, 253, 278n11; and Intipucá–DC connection story, 33, 36–40, 96, 101, 118–121, 130–32, 147, 149–160, 165, 200; and Intipucá park activities, 214–16; motorboat of, 150–51; motorcycle of, 33, *35*, 36–37, *36*, 40, 51, 147, 149–151, 154, 165–66, 265; and "Playboy" underwear, 162–63; and Roberto (pseud.), 91–92

Chávez, Serapio, 281n11

Chávez, Sigfredo, 40; education of, 64–65, 82, 89; as farm manager, 65, 67, 76, 101–3, 119; as "field hand," 61–62, 65, 281n10; in Gruson's *New York Times* article, 37, 51; and Intipucá–DC connection story, 59–61, 65–67, 70, 79–81, 93, 96, 102–3, 119, 196, 223–24, 263, 281n8; narrative of, 55–57, 59–67, 70, 81, 94, 102–3, 197, 281n8, 286n24; new car of, 6, 19, 61, 93–94, 102, 165

Chávez family, 89

Cheney, Dick, 237–38

Chicago Daily News, 76

Chichipate, 39, 62, 218

Chirilagua, 66, 89, 91, 101, 163, 209, 214, 282n19

CIA (US Central Intelligence Agency), 39, 90, 131, 136, 238, 290n20

Cinco de Mayo celebration, 178–79

Citicorp (N.Y.), 168, 170

citizenship, US, 40, 118–120, 138, 171, 183, 230–31, 253

civilization, 55–61, 66, 81–82

civil rights movement, 183

civil war, Salvadoran (1980–1992), 5, 8, 12, 26–27, 29–33, 35–40, 51, 86, 278n6; and

Banquito (Little Bank), 175–76, 178; and Coca-Cola distribution, 159–161; end of, 183, 203, 290n35; and Gruson's *New York Times* article, 35–38, 40, 148; and Intipucá, 128–130, *129*, 132, 289n18; Iraq war compared to, 237–39, 241–42; migration due to, 12, 32–33, 36, 99, 115, 119, 131, 138–140, 148, 154, 262; stalemate in, 245; US involvement in, 116–120, 127, 129–135, 137, 141–43, 162, 175–76, 183, 217, 237–39, 241–46, 250, 288n5; and Wood's charts, 44–46, *44*, *45*, 279n24, 280n25

Clark, A. James, 289n14

Clark, William E., 252

Clark Enterprises, 289n14

Clash of Civilizations (Huntington), 4

class, 35, 37, 57, 63, 85–86, 102–3, 216, 263, 280n25, 286n24

Clinton, Bill, 42, 192–93, 207–8, 256, 259

Coca-Cola bottling factory and distribution, 159–163, 224–25

cocaine, 152–160, 165–66, 201, 225

coffee production and export, 11–12, 17–20, 24, 26, 32, 44, 51, 274n27, 279n16; *el Grano de Oro* (the Golden Grain), 11–12, 18, 24, 56, 69; "Gift of God," 69; history of, 26, 56–59, 62, 67–77, 80–82, 84, 86, 89, 100–102, 116, 118, 132, 168, 206, 263, 281n2, 283nn30–31, 286n23; nationalization of, 100–102, 286n23; taxes on, 73–74

cognition, 54, 280n1

COIN. *See* counterinsurgency, US

Cold War, 39, 76, 187, 263

Coleman, J. Marshall, 125

Colombia, 55, 58, 76, 155–56, 247

colones, Salvadoran, 42, 60, 64, 66–71, 88, 160; and Banquito (Little Bank), 167, 169–170; exchange rates, 67, 73, 100, 127, 167, 169–170, 198; fees in, 90; one-colon note, 67–71, *68*, 84; 25-colon note, 127, 132

Columbia Heights, 174

Comercio ABY (general store), 195–96

Commerce Department, US, 283n30

commodities, 16–19, 24, 41, 46–47, 149, 207; history of, 58, 61, 74–75, 156; and inflation, 122; taxes on, 74. *See also* consumer goods

communism, 63, 80, 85, 95–96, 117, 120, 131, 143
Community Humanities Council (Washington, DC), 5–6, 15, 272nn12–13
Compaña Salvadoreño del Café, 73–75
Conchagua, 70–74, 81, 88, 90, 282n22
Congo, 252–53, 255, 260
Congress, US, 77, 79, 92, 107, 122; House; H.R. 4437, 4; and Iraq war, 242; and Salvadoran civil war (1980–1992), 127, 130–31, 139, 237–39; Senate Armed Services Committee, 120, 126; and TACA (Central American airline), 186
Constancia brewery, 207
construction workers, 37–38, 97, 126, 130, 149, 186, 223, 227, 289n19
consumer goods, 41, 48, 50, 56, 148–150, 165, 196, 206, 244, 279n16
corn production, 11, 39, 64–67, 70–71, 74, 76, 82, 88–90, 92, 128, 217, 263
Coronil, Fernando, 47, 53–54
cotton production and export, 26, 44, 204; and civil war, 128, 132; history of, 58, 82–83, 87–94, 98, 115–16, 118, 127–28, 132, 162, 168, 263, 283nn25–26; in *Un Dia en la Vida* (Argueta), 87–88
counterinsurgency, US, 8, 27, 132–37, 141, 143, 242–48, 250; in Iraq, 235–241, 247–48, 250, 293n1; and "War on Drugs," 246–47
coups d'etat, Salvadoran, 57, 79–82, 90, 99–102
CREMS (US Regional Military Training Center), 243
Cristiani, Alfredo, 30–31, *31*, 32, 35, 38, 48, 50, 192, 206, 278n6
Cristiani-Burkhardt family, 88
Cuban revolution, 83, 90
Cuco, 97, 99, 101, 150, 163, 214
"cultural," the, 83, 86, 115, 148
Cuscatlán Bridge, 93, 127, 132
Cutuco (port), 74

dairy farming, 11, 39, 78, 101–2, 128, 198–99, 263. *See also* livestock
Daisy (pseud.), 218–222
Dalton, John N., 111–12, 124–26
Dalton, Roque, 285n2
Daniel (pseud.), 88–89, 92, 94–96, 160, 285n3

Daniel, E. Valentine, 274n31
Darío, Rubén, 57
D'Aubuisson, Robert, 31
DCM Group (Arlington, Va.), 124
DEA (Drug Enforcement Agency, US), 157–58, 166
Deale, Melvin J., 112
death squads, 31, 84–85, 95, 101, 238–39
de Dios Blanco, Juan, 197, 203–4, 206
Deering, Richard, 176
Defense Department, US, 239, 246–48, 250. *See also* Pentagon
deindustrialization, U.S., 86, 276n47
Delgado, Pedro Abelardo, 163–64
Del Valle, Girsel, 179
democracy, 113, 118, 131, 237–240
Democratic Christian Party. *See* PDC (Democratic Christian Party)
Department of Highways (Va.), 112–13
depression, economic, 67, 73
Derrida, Jacques, 23
Descartes, 271n1
development, 8, 11; and Banquito (Little Bank), 169, 174–75; coffee-led, 84; export-led, 86; and immigrant entrepreneurs, 235, 251–260, 262; remittance-led, 8, 22, 27, 29, 41, 50, 129, 161, 164, 194, 203–4, 207, 213, 219, 279n16; sign-in-development, 18; state-led, 41, 81, 90, 93, 127; in Washington, DC, metropolitan area, 107–13, 117, 122–27, 142–43, 169
DeYoung, Karen, 6, 84–87
Dickey, Christopher, 6, 84–87
DI Design and Development (Toronto), 126
DiRita, Lawrence, 239
divorce, 202
Dixon, Sharon Pratt, 181–82
dollars, US: and Banco Agrícola Comercial, 214; and Banquito (Little Bank), 167–170; and coffee production/export, 73, 75, 100; dollarization, 42, 196, 279nn21–22; and drug trade, 152–59; exchange rates, 60, 66–67, 73, 100, 121–22, 124, 167, 169–170, 198, 214; "hardened," 122, 124; printing of, 282n21; as remittances, 42, 44, *45*, 50, 58, 118, 148–49, 157, 163–64; as US government aid, 44, *45*, 81
Dominican Republic, 153–55
Donovan, Jean, 209

Draper, William, 76
"Drug Czar," 157
drug trade, 152–55, 157–160, 165–66, 201,
    225, 229
Duarte, José Napoleon, 30–31, 131–32,
    138–141, 143, 200, 204, 237, 290n20,
    290n36, 291n38, 291n41
Duke, Armando, 281n2
Dulles, Eleanor, 79
Dulles International Airport, 39, 123, 185;
    access roads, 108–9
Dunn, Bernard, 114
"Dutch disease" phenomenon, 47–48, 255
Dynamic Hedging (Taleb), 248

earthquakes, 138
ECLA. See CEPAL (Economic Commis-
    sion for Latin America and the Carib-
    bean)
"economic," the, 83, 86, 115
Economic and Social Bulletin (FUSADES),
    48
"economic migrants," 85–86, 139
Economist, 256
Edwards, John, 237
Eisenhower, Dwight D., 90
Eladio, 83, 285n2
El Banco Hipotecario de El Salvador, 73
El Delirio, 72, 81, 161, 283n25
elections, Afghan, 237–38
elections, Iraqi, 237–39
elections, Salvadoran, 30–33, 31, 90, 95, 131,
    192, 204, 206, 237–38, 245, 290n20
electricity, 56, 61, 225, 263; and diesel gener-
    ator, 92–93, 97, 215; in Iraq, 240; rural
    electrification, 81, 89, 92
elites, African American, 169
elites, Salvadoran, 12–13, 17–18, 73, 93; and
    Banco Agrícola Comercial, 213, 215–16;
    and Banquito (Little Bank), 185, 187,
    194; and Calderón Sol, 207–8; and Inti-
    pucá's road sign, 196; and remittances,
    31–32, 278n6; violence against, 98–99.
    See also landowners, Salvadoran
El Latino (Spanish-language publication),
    172–73
El Mozote massacre, 199
El Papalón, 89, 91
El Salvador, 7–11, 13, 18–20, 26, 274n27;
    climate of, 68–69, 74; Interior Ministry,

66; map of, 34; "puertoricanization"
    of, 279n22; Salvador Option, 238–39,
    241–42, 245, 247, 250, 260
El Salvador at War: An Oral History of
    Conflict from the 1979 Insurrection to the
    Present (Manwaring and Prisk), 135–37
"El Salvador: International Remittances
    and Family Economics" (CEPAL), 48
Elson, Diane, 275n37
embassy, Salvadoran, 175
embassy, US, 37, 60, 177, 238, 244, 279n21
embezzlement, 213
"Emigrants Feather Their Old Nests with
    Dollars" (Gruson), 35–43, 36, 51, 147–49,
    156–57, 165–66, 197, 253, 257, 265,
    278nn11–12
Empirica Capital, 248
empiricism, 141–42, 249–250, 254, 257, 265
English language, 41, 119, 132, 135, 140,
    171–72, 175, 199, 225–26, 236, 244; and
    Intipucá's road sign, 195–96
Enquiry Concerning Human Understanding
    (Hume), 248–49
Enron Corporation, 240
entrepreneurs, immigrant, 7–8, 12, 22, 27,
    41, 273n21; and Banquito (Little Bank),
    173–76; and development, 251–260, 262;
    and Intipucá–DC connection story,
    164–65, 208, 235
ERP (People's Revolutionary Army), 97,
    285n2
ERU (Emergency Response Unit), 240–41
Escobar, Gabriel, 55–56, 61–62, 65, 280n1,
    281n10
Escobar, Pablo, 155
evangelicals, Protestant, 210, 219, 251
EVD (Extended Voluntary Departure,
    US), 139
Ewing, Charles B. Jr., 287n35
exploitation, 27, 85, 143, 206, 208, 216, 263
"Export Processing Zones," 162–63

factories, Salvadoran, 89, 159–163
Fairfax County (Va.), 107–13, 117, 124;
    Board of Supervisors, 111–13, 126;
    Board of Zoning Appeals, 109; Cham-
    ber of Commerce, 124, 126
Fairfax Parkway Coalition, 124, 126
Fairlakes Center, 126
Falls Church (Va.), 78

falsification, 249
family consumption, 48, 50
farms and farmers. *See* agriculture, Salvadoran
farm workers, 62, 64, 68–69, 97–98, 171, 198, 204–5, 216–17, 262. *See also* tenant farmers
FECCAS (Christian Federation of Salvadoran Peasants), 95
Federal Highways Administration, US, 111–12
Federal Reserve, US, 121–23; Richmond Federal Reserve Bank (Va.), 123
FENASTRAS *(Federación Nacional Sindical de Trabajadores Salvadoreños)*, 38
Fernandez, Manola, 61, 94
fincas, 11, 57, 70, 73
firearms, 61, 80–81, 153, 199, 205; Uzi machine gun, 97
Firestone Tires, 209
fishing, 63, 71, 150, 217–223
Flores, Francisco, 42
FMLN *(Frente Farabundo Marti para la Liberacion Nacional)*, 30–32, 38–39, 127–130, 132–34, 137, 242–45; and CEMFA, 243–45; and Coca-Cola distribution, 159–161; Final Offensive, 119, 127, 178; as political party, 245, 290n35; rear guard of, 199
Folgers, 75, 283n30
Fonseca, Gulf of, 62, 74
Fooled by Randomness (Taleb), 247–48
Ford Foundation, 175
foreign exchange inflows, 45–47, 45, 73–74, 100, 156
Foreign Policy, 271n2
foreign policy, U.S., 5, 235, 250–51, 272n10. *See also* counterinsurgency, U.S.; entrepreneurs, immigrant
Forestall, James, 76
Forolo. *See* Miguel (pseud.)
Four Seasons Restaurant, 131–32, 200
Franklin, Benjamin, 80
FUNDE (Fundación Nacional para el Desarrollo), 164–65
Funes, Mauricio, 245
FUSADES *(Fundacion Salvadoreña para el Desarollo Economico y Social)*, 32, 35, 48, 50, 163–65
future, 8–9, 11, 21, 27

Galdámez, Romeo, 258, 295n34
Gallo family, 62, 88
Galvin, John R., 132–35, 141, 290n22, 290n35
gambling, 225, 228, 247–48
"Gambling with the Wrong Dice" (Taleb), 248
García, Juan José, 48–50, 140–41
Garner, Jay, 240
Garreau, Joel, 117
Gavidia, Francisco, 57–59, 84, 281n3
Gavilan Express (DC store), 195–96
GCIM (Global Commission on International Migration), 254
GDP (gross domestic product), 11, 44–46, 44, 47–48, 100; calculation of, 45–46
General Foods, 75, 283n30
George Hyman Construction Company, 289n14
Gerson, Michael, 251
Global Development Finance (World Bank), 253
"Global Economic Prospects" (World Bank), 254
globalization, 46–47, 50
Gomez, Daniel, 178–182
government aid, US, 26, 32, 35, 44, 45, 100–101, 116, 127, 132, 139–140, 254. *See also* military, US
Grant, Elaine, 176
Green Berets, 244
Greider, William, 122
Gruson, Lindsey, 35–43, 36, 51, 147–49, 156–57, 165–66, 197, 253, 257, 265, 278nn11–12
Guardia (National Guard), 61, 80, 85, 93, 95–97, 101, 141, 150, 205, 209–10
Guatemala, 66–67, 81, 179, 240
Guerrero, Jorge, 175–76
guerrillas, Iraqi, 236
guerrillas, Salvadoran, 97, 99, 127–29, 133–34, 159–161, 219, 237, 242–45. *See also* FMLN
Guillermo (pseud.), 161, 163

Hacienda Police, 205
haciendas, 62, 80–81, 88–89, 101, 198, 204–5. *See also* agriculture, Salvadoran; landowners, Salvadoran
Hailes, Edward, 106

Halpin, Gerald T., 107–9, 126, 287n35, 287n40
Harriman, W. Averill, 76
Harris, Andrew, 279n15
Harris, Irwin, 179
Harrison, Stanley E., 127
Harvey, David, 277n51
Harza Engineering Company, 81
Hazel, John Tilman ("Til"), 108–13, 124–26, 216, 287n41
Hazel/Peterson Company, 109–10, 289n15
Hegel, 278n3
Heidegger, 275n40
Heineken beer, 207
Hellmuth, Obata, and Kassabaum (architectural firm), 126
Helms, Jesse, 290n20
Henson, Jim, 283n31
Hernández family, 59
Herrity, John F., 111–12, 126
Hersh, Seymour, 238–39
hierarchy, relational, 10–13, 22
Highlands Forum, 247–48
high-tech corporations, 20, 109, 113–14, 123–24, 127, 134, 155, 288n60. *See also names of corporations*
Hirsch, Leon, 283n25
Hirsh, Michael, 238
"Hispanics," 119, 152, 154, 181, 224
Historia Moderna de El Salvador (Gavidia), 58
Hodson, William K., 114
Holbrooke, Richard, 259
"hometown associations," 41, 192, 262
Honduras, 200, 243
Hoover, Herbert, 76
Horwatt, Michael, 111
Hughes, James C., 126
human capital, 254
Hume, David, 248–49
Huntington, Samuel P., 4–5, 7–10, 15–16, 18, 24–25, 46, 271n2, 272n10
Hussein, Saddam, 236, 240–41
hydroelectric dams, 81, 127; "Sept. 15 Hydroelectric Dam," 127

IACA (Inter American Coffee Agreement), 75
IBM, 247
Icacal beach, 159

illegals, 85, 94, 116–19, 138–142, 262. *See also* undocumented migrants
IMF (International Monetary Fund), 8, 22, 41, 127, 156
immigration law, US, 4, 178, 203
imperialism, US, 235
INCAFE (Instituto Nacional del Café), 100
indigo trade, 57–58, 89, 281n2
indios (indigenous population), 62–63, 65, 161, 170, 282n14
individuated parts, 22–23, 25
induction, 248–250
infinite whole, 22–23
inflation, 47, 120–23
Informe sobre Desarrollo Humano 2005 (UNDP–El Salvador), 257–58, *259*, 273n19, 295n34
infrastructure, Salvadoran, 56, 65, 80–82, 88–89, 93–94, 127, 185, 203
INS (Immigration and Naturalization Service, US), 138, 171
Institute for International Economics, 256
"Insurgency Buster, The" (Brooks), 237
interest-bearing capital, 25, 29, 46, 50, 122–23, 198; and Banquito (Little Bank), 171–72, 175
International Bank for Reconstruction and Development. *See* World Bank
"International Conference on Migrant Remittances" (World Bank conference), 253–54
International Crisis Group, 256–57
International Railway of Central America, 66–67, 74
interpretant, 14–15, 289n18
Intipucá, 3, 5–12, 18, 27, 262–64, 273n15; and agrarian reform, 101; Agrícola office in, 187, 197, 213–15; Americanization of, 184; and Banquito (Little Bank), 167–68, 170, 172–77, 184, 187, 194, 215; Calderón Sol's visit to, 27, 42, 191–94, 202, 204, 207–8, 215–16; and Catholic missionaries, 91, 209–12; and CEMFA, 243–45, 250; chalet operators in, 212–17, 223–27, 231; and Chávez, Marvin, 33, *35*, 36, *36*, 39–40, 43, 59, 63, 96, 101, 118–19, 132, 147, 149–150, 154, 158–163, 165–66, 214–16; and Chávez, Sigfredo, 55–57, 59–62, 64–67, 70, 80–81, 94, 96, 119, 281n8, 281nn12–13; and Chirilagua

Intipucá (*cont.*)
  boundary dispute, 66, 282n19; and civil war, 128–130, *129*, 132, 243–45, 250, 289n18; and Coca-Cola distribution, 160–61; and coffee production/export, 56–57, 70–72; and cotton production/export, 88–94; and dead US soldier, 244–45, 250; and dollarization, 42, 279nn21–22; elections in, 33, 192, 203–4, 206; festival in, 33, 197, 226–27; *Guardia* (National Guard) in, 61, 80, 93, 95–97, 141, 150; as Intipucá City, 195, 258, 295n34; map of, *34*, 197; mayors of, 33, 60, 64–66, 70, 93, 97, 141, 154, 183, 192–97, 203–6, 212–13; Montes' research on, 141, 147, 175–76; *New York Times* article on, 35–43, *36*, 51, 55, 147–49, 165–66, 197, 253, 278nn11–12; park activities in, 212–17, 223–27, 231; patron saint of, 33, 197, 226–27; Public Radio International report on, 40–41, 279n16; and Raul's family, 198–202, 204–6; road sign for, *49*, 194–96, *195*, 258; and soccer stadium, 193, 204, 213; and taxes, 203; three women in, 9–10, 13, 15–18, 24–25, 46, 235, 265; US-style food in, 224–28; violence in, 95–97, 99, 128–29, *129*; Walker's visit to, 41–42, 183–87, 194, 197, 203. *See also* Intipucá–DC connection story
Intipucá (magazine), 196–97, 203–4, 281n12
Intipucá City (club), 5
Intipucá–DC connection story, 6–9, 10, 20, 26–27, 53, 261–63, 273n17; and African American soldier, 244; and Banquito (Little Bank), 168, 170, 174, 178; and Calderón Sol, 191–93, 208; and Chávez, Marvin, 33, 36–40, 96, 101, 118–121, 130–32, 147, 149–160, 200; and Chávez, Sigfredo, 59–61, 65–67, 70, 79–81, 93, 96, 102–3, 119, 223–24, 281n8; and coffee production/export, 19, 77, 82; and cotton production/export, 92–94; and drug trade, 152–57; in Gruson's *New York Times* article, 35–43, *36*, 51, 147–49, 156–57, 278nn11–12; and immigrant entrepreneurs, 164–65, 208, 235; and *Intipucá* (magazine), 196–97, 203–4, 281n12; and Intipucá's road sign, 194–96, *195*; and Manuel (pseud.), 38–40, 51, 130, 242, 250; and remittances, 22,

25, 40–43, 50–51, 147, 211, 213–14, 219, 223–26, 231, 256, 258, 260; and storytelling, 17; and Tommy (pseud.), 200–201; and USAID, 183–85, 203; and Walker, William, 41–42, 177, 183–87, 194, 197; in *Washington Post* articles, 6–7, 12, 15–16, 19, 40, 84–87, 94–95, 148. *See also* migrants and migration
Intipucá III (painting), 42
investments, 47, 198, 203; and Banquito (Little Bank), 167–69, 172–75, 177, 187, 197; and Calderón Sol, 192–93; investment savvy, 7, 41; remittance-led, 164–65; in Washington, DC, suburbs, 75–76, 79, 104, 107–8, 114
Iranian hostage crisis, 140
Iraq war, 8, 27, 235–241, 245, 247–48, 250, 293n7; Iraqi Electricity Commission, 240; Iraqi Security Forces, 236; and "Mission Accomplished," 236, 240, 293n3; National Iraqi Police Service Emergency Response Unit, 240–41; and "Oil for Food" program, 260; Republican Guard, 241; Salvadoran civil war as model for, 237–39, 241–42; Special Police Commandos, 241; and US "surge," 242
IRCA (Immigration Reform and Control Act, US; 1986), 138–140, 291n41
ISI (import substitution industrialization), 91

Jacinto (pseud.), 207
J. A. Folger & Co., 75, 283n30
Jamaicans, 216
Japanese, 98, 162, 292n5
Jarvis, Charlene Drew, 168–69, 173, 177
Jesuit priests, 38, 49, 84–85, 95, 101, 140, 178
Jesus, parables of, 251
Jewell, Angela, 179–181
"Jhoon Rhee Self Defense" commercial, 40, 279n15
Johnson, George W., 124
Johnson, Walter, 289n19
Joint Coffee Publicity Committee, 75
Joint Task Forces, 246; Joint Task Force Six (JTF-6), 246
Jonas, Jeff, 247
Jorge (pseud.), 159–161, 163, 224–25
Justice Department, US, 140, 246

Kappeler, Victor, 246
Kennedy, John F., 90
Kermit Roosevelt Lecture (UK), 132–35
kidnappings, 98–99
killings, 30, 38, 49, 65–66, 96, 98, 101, 175, 178, 239
King, Harold C., 124–25
King, John ("Padre Juan"), 209–12
Kirkpatrick, Jeanne, 120
Kissinger Commission, 131
"K-Mart look," 186–87
Knox, Frank, 76
Kraska, Peter, 246

L&L Construction (Washington, DC), 172, 176, 187
labor organizers, 84–85, 95
labor-power, 16–18, 24, 82, 84, 263
La Leona, 223–24, 227, 244–45
La Libertad, 209
La Matanza (1931–32), 63, 68, 101
landowners, Salvadoran, 11–12, 18, 32, 39–40, 263; and Calderón Sol, 192; and Chávez, Sigfredo, 59, 62–66, 102–3, 281nn10–11; and coffee production/ export, 71, 100–102; and cotton production/export, 88–89, 92–94; and firearms, 80, 97, 205; Omar (pseud.) as, 225–26; and one-colon note, 68, 71; and Raul's family, 197–202, 204–5; violence against, 97–99, 101–2, 244. See also elites, Salvadoran
Lane, Charles, 37, 173–74, 278n12
La Peña community center, 176
La Prensa Grafica (newspaper), 258
Latino Civil Rights Task Force, 183
"Latino National Conversation, A" (Great Books Foundation), 42
La Union, 64, 66, 70–71, 74, 81, 88, 90, 209, 242–43, 246, 282n22
Law of the Defense and Guarantee of Public Order (1977), 95–96
Lazo family, 89
Lefebvre, Henri, 23
Leitch, Brian, 176
Leith, William T., 107–8, 287n38
Leiva, Manuel, 172, 176, 186–87
Lempa River, 81
Lemus, Jose Maria, 90
Lenca settlements, 282n14

Leonzo, Fernando, 167, 170–74, 176–77, 216; bankruptcy of, 176–77
Leonzo, Manuel, 281n11
Ley Moratoria, 67, 73
"Library of Babel" (Borges), 277n51
LIC (Latin Investment Corporation), 171–77; Depositors Committee, 175–76
Liebes, Ernesto, 98–99
Littoral highway, 72, 81–82, 161–62, 194, 218, 258, 292n5
livestock, 11, 39–40, 70–71, 90, 101, 128, 130. See also dairy farming
Llerena, Juan, 179
Lloyd, David, 275n37
London Times, 238
Los Angeles (Calif.), 97; uprisings, 105, 183
Los Laureles (Intipucá), 59, 281n6
Los Morenos, 205
Los Morenos (hacienda), 204–5
Lowe, Lisa, 275n37
Lubbock, Robin, 30–33, 31, 35–36, 35, 36, 40, 43, 46, 147, 265, 278n11
Lupe (in Un Dia en la Vida), 84, 87–88, 95

Maas, Peter, 241
machetes, 70, 80, 92–93, 98
maguey plant (sisal), 72, 161. See also sisal production
Maimbo, Samuel Munzele, 254
malaria, 283n25
Malloch-Brown, Mark, 256–58, 260, 295n32
Manlio (pseud.), 217–223, 231; and self-discipline, 222–23
Manuel (pseud.), 38–40, 51, 130, 242, 250
Manufacturers Hanover Trust Company, 114, 288n63
manufacturing, Salvadoran, 44, 44
manufacturing, US, 8, 20, 58
Manwaring, Maxwell G., 134–37, 245, 247, 249–250
Maria (pseud.), 226–231
Márquez, Elsy, 170
Márquez, Ursulo, 167, 170, 172–73, 198
Marshall Plan, 77
Martí, José, 57
Martínez, Maximiliano Hernández, 67, 72–73, 75, 283n26
Marx, Karl, 16–18, 265, 275n37, 275n40, 277n51
masculinity, 223

massacres: El Mozote massacre, 199; in San
    Salvador (1977), 95; "San Sebastian mas-
    sacre," 30, 38, 278n5; in *Un Dia en la Vida*
    (Argueta), 95
mass media: and Intipucá–DC connection
    story, 7, 40–41, 273n17; rhetorical logic
    of, 279n17; and Salvador Option, 238–
    39, 241–42. *See also names of radio, print,
    and television outlets*
Matamoros, Cesar, 60, 80
Matsumoto, Fugio, 98
Max (pseud.), 204
Max Hernandez Brigade, 101
McChrystal, Stanley A., 293n1
McCloy, John J., 76
McDonald, Daniel, 114
McDonald's, 40, 43
McLaughlin, George, 76
McLean (Va.), 109–11, 114; McLean Citi-
    zens Association, 109–11
McNamara, Robert, 114, 255
Meanguera (island), 62, 74
Measure, 29, 278n3
Meeting the Challenge of Globalization
    (World Bank), 46–48, 50–51
"Meet the Press" (US television show), 237
Meloy, Thomas, 78
Melpar, 78–79, 107, 113
Mendez Novoa, Luis, 98
mestizos, 11, 63, 186
metamodels, future, 8, 274n23
Metropolitan Life Insurance Company,
    289n15
Mexico/Mexicans, 4, 160, 230
middle class, Salvadoran, 31, 90, 140–41, 187
migrants and migration, 12–13, 24, 26, 262–
    65; and Banquito (Little Bank), 168, 171,
    174, 177; civil war as cause of, 12, 32–33,
    36, 99, 115, 119, 130–31, 138–140, 148,
    154, 262; Duarte's letter concerning,
    138–141, 143, 290n36; "economic mi-
    grants," 85–86, 139; in Gruson's *New
    York Times* article, 35–43, 36, 147–48,
    278nn11–12; Huntington's views on, 4–5,
    7, 271n2; migrant entrepreneurs, 7–8,
    12, 22, 27, 41, 164–65, 173–76, 208, 235,
    251–260, 262, 273n21; migration studies,
    21, 141–42, 271n7, 276n47; in *Odisea del
    Norte* (Bencastro), 42; political asylum
    for, 139, 291n37; and return migration,

203; violence as cause of, 84–87, 95–97,
    99, 101, 115, 148, 159. *See also* Intipucá–
    DC connection story; remittances; *names
    of migrants*
"Migration in an Interconnected World"
    (GCIM), 254
Miguel (pseud.), 70–73, 75–76, 81, 88, 94,
    130, 282nn22–23
military, Salvadoran, 93; *Boletín del Ejército*
    (magazine), 80–81, 285n45; and Coca-
    Cola distribution, 160–61; conscription
    into, 130, 217–19; coups d'etat, 57, 79–
    82, 90, 99–102; Fifth Brigade's *Batallón
    Jiboa*, 30, 38, 278n5; *Guardia* (National
    Guard), 61, 80, 85, 93, 95–97, 101, 150,
    209–10; and Iraq war, 238; phenotypic
    records kept by, 63; and "San Sebastian
    massacre," 30, 38, 278n5; 3rd Brigade,
    199; US support for, 5, 30, 84, 90, 100,
    117–18, 127, 129, 132–35, 137, 141–43,
    183–84, 238–246; and violence, 30–31,
    38, 49, 86, 95, 98–99. *See also* civil war,
    Salvadoran (1980–1992)
military, US, 5, 38–39, 57, 77–79, 82, 90; Army
    Rangers, 246; and Chávez, Marvin, 150,
    159; and counterinsurgency, 8, 27, 132–37,
    141, 143, 235, 237–248, 250, 293n1; and
    defense budget, 120–22, 124–26, 187, 263;
    and high-tech corporations, 113–14, 123–
    24, 127, 134, 155, 288n60; and Iraq war, 8,
    27, 235–242, 245, 247–48, 250, 260, 293n3,
    293n7; Joint Task Forces, 246; Navy
    SEALS, 246; and Salvadoran civil war
    (1980–1992), 116–120, 127, 129–135, 137,
    141–43, 162, 175–76, 183, 217, 237–246,
    250, 288n5; Southern Command, 132,
    134–36; Special Forces advisors, 84, 238–
    246; and "uncomfortable wars," 116–18,
    132–37, 142–43, 290n22; USMILGP
    (US Military Group), 242; and "War on
    Drugs," 246–47
Military Review, 247, 294n23
Miller & Long (construction company), 130,
    289n19
Miss Canada, 152, 155
missionaries, 90–91, 209–11
Mitchell, Christopher, 5
Mobil Oil Company, 126
monopolies, state, 73, 100
Montes, Segundo, 49–50, *49*, 140–43, 175–76

Moore, Audry, 112
Morazán, 64
Mortenson, Greg, 235, 293n1
motorcycles, 33, 35, 36–37, 36, 40, 51, 97,
    147, 149–151, 154, 165–66, 265
Mount Pleasant, 6, 37, 39, 42, 61, 96, 118,
    121, 130, 152, 156–58, 200, 216, 229,
    273n14; and Banquito (Little Bank),
    170, 174, 176, 178; and Intipucá's
    road sign, 196; riots in (1965), 104–7,
    286nn27–28; riots in (1991), 178–184
Mr. Palomar (Calvino), 261
"multiculturalism," 183
Muppets, 283n31
murder. See killings
Musavizadeh, Nader, 260
Mutombo, Dikembe, 252–53, 252, 255, 257,
    260

NAACP, 106
Napito (pseud.), 219–221
"Narco-Enforcement Complex," 246
narcotics trafficking, 8, 246–47. See also
    drug trade
National Airport (Washington, DC), 123
National Capital Beltway (Washington,
    DC), 108–13; bypass, 110–13, 124–26
National Coffee Association, 75
National Committee on Segregation in the
    Nation's Capital, 79
nationalism, Salvadoran, 172, 207, 264
National Mall (Washington, DC), 113
national security, US, 108, 143, 247, 253
Nature Channel (cable TV), 119
Naval War College, US, 184
NBA basketball players, 252–53, 252
neoconservatism, 239–240, 260
neoliberalism, 8, 27, 31, 42, 48, 127, 140, 163,
    165, 192, 206, 241, 255–56, 260
New Deal, 75–76, 79, 81
New Republic, 260
Newsweek, 37, 119–120, 173, 238
New York Coffee and Sugar Exchange, 58,
    74
New Yorker, 238–39
New York Stock Exchange, 114
New York Times, 33; Duarte's letter, 138–39,
    290n36, 291n38; "Emigrants Feather
    Their Old Nests with Dollars" (Gruson),
    35–43, 36, 51, 147–49, 156–57, 165–66,

197, 253, 257, 265, 278nn11–12; "The
    Insurgency Buster" (Brooks), 237
New York Times Magazine, 241
Nicaragua, 57, 62, 74, 200; revolution in, 119,
    130–31
Nicholson, Thomas F., 287n35
9/11 terrorist attacks, 4, 250
Nitz, Paul, 76
nongovernmental organizations (NGOs),
    27, 41. See also names of NGOs
Noriega, Manuel, 38
Norman, Ellen, 106
Norman, Michael, 105–6

Odisea del Norte (Bencastro), 42–43
oligarchy, 32, 90, 95, 281n2
Ollman, Bertell, 277n51
Olomega, Lake, 66, 217–18
Omar (pseud.), 225, 227–28, 231
Omni Construction Company, 126, 130,
    289n14, 289n19
O'Neil, Richard P., 247
open holism, 20–23
oppositional co-inclusion, 53–54
options, 236, 238–39, 248, 293n2; Salvador
    Option, 238–39, 241–42, 245, 247, 250,
    260
ORDEN (network of informants/paramili-
    tary groups), 90
Oriente (eastern El Salvador), 58, 88–89, 93,
    171, 177
Orr, Robert, 260
Oscar (pseud.), 192–93, 203–6
Osmine (pseud.), 191
Osorio, Oscar, 79, 81
Otis McAllister, 283n30

Pacific Ocean, 70–71, 88, 91, 128, 150, 217
Padre Juan. See King, John ("Padre Juan")
Paige, Jeff, 278n6, 280n25, 286n23
Panama, 38–39, 131–32, 135
Pan-American Coffee Bureau, 75
Pan-American Highway, 91, 199; El Tri-
    angulo intersection, 199; Ruta Militar
    (Military Route), 199
paramilitary forces, Salvadoran, 31, 38, 90,
    95, 210, 238–39
Parks, Joseph, 78
PDC (Democratic Christian Party), 30–31,
    192, 204

Peace Corps, US, 90, 209

Pear, Robert, 138, 290n36

peasants, 12–13, 18, 63, 67–71, 84–86, 102–3, 208, 262, 283n26; and one-colon note, 67–71, *68*, 84; organizing of, 95

Pedro (pseud.), 61, 64, 93, 96, 281n9

Peeters, Marisa, 295m2

Peirce, Charles S., 13–15, 18, 23, 274n31, 275n33, 289n18

Pennino, Martha V., 111

Pentagon, 32, 107, 114, 120, 238–39

Peoples Life Insurance Company (Washington, DC), 107–8, 287nn38–39

Peralta, Ricardo Acevedo, 291n37

Perpetual Savings and Loan (Washington, DC), 171, 175

Pessar, Patricia, 291n41

pesticides, 89, 91, 283n25; DDT, 89

Peterson, Milton, 78–79, 109–13, 117–18, 122–26, 287n42

Phillips Corporation, 98

Pilsner beer, 207

pirates, British, 62, 74

"Playboy" underwear, 162–63

Pleitez, William, 257–58

Plicom Investments, 108

police: in DC parks, 130; and DC riots (1965), 104–7, 286nn27–28; and DC riots (1991), 178–183; and drug trade, 153, 156, 229; "Riot Squad," 105–6; and Roberto (pseud.), 224–25

"political," the, 83, 85–86, 115

political prisoners, 98

pool halls, 33, 39, 130, 196

Popper, Karl, 248–49

Portugal, 163

positivism, 141, 249

Potomac (Md.), 151–52, 156

poverty, 37, 178, 214–16; reduction of, 254–57

PRC (Planning Research Corporation), 114, 125–26, 289n15

pressing out, 23–25, 29

Prince, Tymia, 179

Prisk, Courtney, 135

privatization, Salvadoran, 32, 127, 192, 255

"Proclamation of the Armed Forces of the Republic of El Salvador, 15 October 1979," 100

progress, 55–56, 58, 116, 207, 213

public drinking, 178–79, 181

Public Order Law (1977), 95–96

Public Radio International, 40–41, 279n16

public spaces, 65, 104, 106

Pueblo Viejo, 281n13

Puente de Oro Bridge, 161–62, 292n5

"Puerto Rican, The," 128–29, 289n17

Puerto Viejo, 218, 221

Pyles, Raymond S., 105

quantity-to-quality transformation, 28–29, 50–51, 277n2

Quayle, Dan, 30, 278n5

race, 37, 63, 65, 102–4, 183, 193, 286n24

rape, 93

Ratha, Dilip, 253–54, 257

Raul (pseud.), 95, 99, 197–202, 204–6

Reagan, Ronald, 31–32, 38, 118–122, 125; discretionary funds used by, 127; Duarte's letter to, 138–141, 143, 290n36, 291n41; and Salvadoran civil war (1980–1992), 127, 130–32; and Strategic Defense Initiative, 155; and "structural adjustment," 255

real estate market collapse, 174, 187, 263

recession, US, 167

Refugees International, 256

Regardie's Magazine, 37, 173–74, 278n12

Regelado family, 62–63, 216

regulation, governmental, 167, 169–170, 172–73

remittances, 7–8, 20, 22, 25–51, 207–8, 211, 213–14, 262–65; and Banco Agrícola Comercial, 213–14; and Banquito (Little Bank), 168–170, 174–76; and Calderón Sol, 193–94, 202; and dollarization, 42, 279nn21–22; Duarte's letter concerning, 138–141, 143, 290n36, 291n41; "family remittances," 118, 163–64; and Gruson's *New York Times* article, 33, 35–43, *36*, 51, 148–49, 156–57, 165–66, 278nn11–12; history of, 53, 56–60, 82, 85–86, 115–18; and *illegals*, 138–143; and immigrant entrepreneurs, 253–55; and Lubbock's photographs, 30–33, *31*, 35–36, *35*, *36*, 40, 43, 46, 278n11; and Public Radio International report, 40–41, 279n16; remittance-led development, 22, 27, 29, 41, 50, 129, 161, 164, 194, 203–4, 207, 213, 219, 279n16; Siri's views on, 163–64; and Wood's charts, 43–46, *44*, *45*, 279n24,

280n25; and World Bank report, 29, 32, 41, 46–48, 50–51
respect, 56, 58–59, 61
retroduction, 24–25
Richard (pseud.), 154–55, 157–58
Riggs National Bank (Washington, DC), 171, 173, 175–76
ripple effect, 145
"Risk in a Networked Environment" (Highlands Forum conference), 247–48
Risse, Edward M., 124
Rivas, Juan Bautista, 62, 64–65, 281n11
Rivera, Julio, 90
RN *(Resistencia Nacional)*, 98–99, 285n2
roadmap metaphor, 25, 29, *49*, 50
Robb, Charles ("Chuck"), 125
Roberto (pseud.), 91–92, 94, 128, 223–28, 231; arrest of, 224; as soccer player, 223–24
Robinson, William, 277n49
Rolling Stone (magazine), 122
Rome, Benjamin, 289n14
Romero, Carlos, 95, 99–100
Rooney, Matthew, 279n21
Roosevelt, Franklin Delano, 75–76, 81
Rosa (pseud.), 62–64, 66–67, 70, 74, 76, 82, 89, 96, 101–3, 195, 198, 281n11, 282n17
Rosello, Victor, 247
Rourke, Walter G., 105
Ruggie, John, 260
Rumsfeld, Donald, 238, 250, 293n7
Russert, Tim, 237

Sahlins, Marshall, 295m1
Salavan, J., 136
Salinas, Hugo, 196–97, 203–4, 281n12, 293n2
Salinas, Leonel, 167, 170
"Salvadoran Emigration and Its Economic and Social Impact" (FUSADES), 48
"Salvadorization of Iraq?, The" (Maas), 241
Salvador Option, 238–39, 241–42, 245, 247, 250, 260
San Bartolo (Export Processing Zone), 162–63
Sandoval, Mena, 99
Sandra (pseud.), 227–28, 231
San Francisco Gotera, 64–65, 89
San Miguel, 32, 263; and Argueta, Manlio, 84; and Banquito (Little Bank), 167, 170, 172; bordellos in, 199–202; and bound-

ary struggle, 66; and Catholic missionaries, 209; and Chávez, Sigfredo, 60, 62, 64, 93; and civil war (1980–1992), 38–39; and corn production, 66–67, 74, 76, 82; and cotton production/export, 58, 89–91; and Duke, Armando, 281n2; El Gran Tejano (restaurant) in, 172, 198; El Papalón in, 89, 91; and Gavidia, Francisco, 57–58, 84; hospital in, 228–29; and Manlio (pseud.), 217–18; National University in, 95, 101; and Raúl's family, 198–202
San Ramón (hacienda), 88
San Salvador, 12, 32, 38, 42, 60, 66, 72, 80–81, 101, 178, 279n21; and Calderón Sol, 191–92, 205; Coca-Cola bottling factory in, 159–163; massacre of demonstrators in (1977), 95; mayor of, 192
"San Sebastian massacre," 30, 38, 278n5
Santa Ana, 58
Santa Juliana, 59, 217
San Vicente, 128
Sawyer-Miller group, 256
Schoultz, Lars, 5, 7, 15–16, 272n10, 272n13
seasonal laborers, 12, 18, 69–73
SEC (US Securities and Exchange Commission), 173, 176–77
Seeley, Rudolph G., 107–8, 287n35
self-discipline, 222–23
semeiosis, 13–16, *14*, 18–19, 25–26, 274n31, 275n33
service workers, 86, 262; and Banquito (Little Bank), 171; Chávez, Marvin, as, 130–32, 150–52, 156, 200; and Intipucá–DC connection story, 7, 12, 20, 22, 37, 79, 115, 142, 149, 155–56, 186, 201, 206, 216–17, 223–24
Sesori, 216, 226
SETA (Systems Engineering and Technical Assistance), 113, 288n60
set theory, 23, 277n51
Sewell, William, 275n32
sex workers, 199–202, 227
sharecropping, 11, 64, 90, 98, 101, 215
sign, 13–16, 18–19, 24–26, 274n31, 275n33; Intipucá–DC connection story as, 43; and Salvadoran civil war (1980–1992), 289n18; sign-in-development, 18
Singer, Milton, 274n31
Siri, Gabriel, 163–64, 292n6
sisal production, 72–73, 161, 283nn25–26
skin color, 63, 65, 102, 193

small businesses, 7–8, 12, 167, 256. *See also names of small businesses*
Smallwood, Ronald, 105–6
Smith, Reginald, 181
Smith Jr., Frank, 181
Smithsonian Institution, Air and Space Museum, 126
soccer stadium (Intipucá), 193, 204, 213
social abstraction, 10–13, 19
social security, US, 60
Sol Meza, Ernesto, 98
Sonsonate, 203
Sonya (pseud.), 216–18, 223, 226, 231
Soros, George, 256
Spanish colonial ancestry, 39, 56, 62
Spanish language, 9, 28, 61, 102, 119, 135, 162, 217; and Banquito (Little Bank), 171–74, 177; and DC riots (1991), 179–181; and Intipucá's road sign, 195
spatial scales of analysis, 20–26, 191
Spies, James, 293n1
Standard Brands, 75
Stasch, Rupert, 279n17
State Department, US, 32, 131, 133, 140, 162, 175, 248; Bureau for Refugee Programs, 140
State Highway Commission (Va.), 112, 124–25
"steak and cheese" sandwiches, 224–28
Steele, Jim, 240–42, 247–48
stewardship, 251–53
Stimson, Harry, 76, 78
storytelling, 9–10, 13–19, 274n25, 275n34
Strategic Defense Initiative, US, 155
structural adjustment, 255–56
students, Salvadoran, 95–96, 101, 141
sugar production and export, 44, 127–28, 279n16
Sullivan, John L. C., 106
Superior Court, DC, 176
Suster family, 72
SWORD (Small Wars Operations Research Directorate), 135–36, 290n35
"SWORD Paper" (US Army), 137

TACA (Central American airline), 39, 185–87
Taleb, Naseem, 247–49
"techno" music, 199
temporal scales of analysis, 21–26, 191

tenant farmers, 11, 18, 62, 64–65, 68–69, 76, 91, 198, 217, 263. *See also* farm workers
terrorists, 117, 238–39, 245, 247
testimonio, 42, 84–85, 87–88
"Theses on the Concept of History" (Benjamin), 53
Thompson, John, 252
Thompson, Robert, Sir, 136
Three Cups of Tea (Mortenson), 235
Tierra Blanca, 64, 71, 217–18
time, telling of, 217–18
TM Power Ventures (Houston, Tex.), 240
Tolentíno, Nicolas, San, 33, 197
Tommy (pseud.), 200–202
Tony's (bordello), 199–202
Torres, Eberth, 167, 170, 173
Toupes, John M., 114, 288n65
transvaluation, 17, 24–25, 54, 264–65
Travesky, Marie B., 111
Treasury Department, US, 246
TRW, 113, 126
Tuchman, Barbara, 288n5
Tuco y Tico (propane distributorship), 197–98
20 percent measure, 5–7, 9, 15–16, 20
Tyson-McLean Joint Venture, 126, 289n15

"uncomfortable wars," 116–18, 132–37, 142–43, 290n22
Un Dia en la Vida (Argueta), 84–88, 218
undocumented migrants, 4, 37–38, 40, 97, 99, 117, 130, 138–39, 230–31; and Banquito (Little Bank), 167, 171, 178; and deportation, 138–39, 171, 178, 193, 224–25, 231; and Walker, William, 186. *See also illegals*
UNDP (UN Development Programme), 257–58; UNDP–El Salvador, 257–58, 259, 295n34
unemployment, 85, 103
Unidos por Intipucá, 192–94, 203–4, 207, 213, 215
United Nations (UN), 8, 74, 120, 245, 255–260; Development Programme, 257–58, 259, 295n34; GCIM (Global Commission on International Migration), 254; High Commission for Refugees, 256
Universidad Tecnologica, 42
University of Central America, 38, 178
unpaid labor, 178, 280n28

UPS delivery truck, 160–63
Urizar, Jorge, 179–180, 182
Ursulo (pseud.), 204–6
USAID (US Agency for International De-
    velopment), 32, 48, 164, 183–85; MEA
    (Municipios en Accion), 183–85, 203
USIS (US Investigations Service), 241
US-Mexico border regions, 4, 131, 138, 230,
    246
*Uso Productivo de las Remesas Familiares
    en El Salvador* (Siri, Delgado, and
    Calderon), 163–64
Usulután, 81, 128, 161
Utfelder family, 107, 287n36

Valenzuela, Alfred, 247
value, 13, 265; and remittances, 36–37;
    as representational tendency, 16–19,
    275n37, 275n40
"Vietnam Syndrome," 120, 288n5
Vietnam War, 120, 132–33, 138, 140, 143,
    242–43, 288n5, 290n22
vigilante groups, 4
Villatoro brothers, 89–90, 93, 99
violence, 83, 85; and cotton production/ex-
    port, 98; death threats, 128; extortion,
    128; and *Guardia* (National Guard), 93,
    95–97, 209–10; kidnappings, 98–99; kill-
    ings, 30, 38, 49, 65–66, 96, 98, 101, 175,
    178, 199, 209–10, 239; massacres, 30, 38,
    95, 199, 278n5; migration due to, 84–87,
    95–97, 99, 101, 115, 130, 159; rape, 93;
    against students, 95–96; torture, 97; in
    Un Dia en la Vida (Argueta), 84; war-
    time, 30, 35–36, 38, 119–120, 128–130,
    129, 131, 139–140, 143, 148, 239, 244,
    278n5; in Washington, DC, 104–7,
    178–183, 286nn27–28
visas, 39, 60, 101, 130
Volker, Paul, 121, 123

Walker, Greg, 243–44
Walker, William, 41–42, 177, 183–87, 194,
    197, 203; Calle Central William Walker,
    185, 187, 215; and "K-Mart look,"
    186–87
Warner, John, 124–26
"War on Drugs," 157, 246–47
Washington, DC, 3, 5–10, 12–13, 25, 27;
    Banking Office, 169–170, 173, 177;
Banking Superintendent, 169; and Ban-
    quito (Little Bank), 167–178; Board of
    Trade, 79; City Council, 168; and coffee
    production/export, 56–57, 75–77; Com-
    mittee of Housing and Economic Devel-
    opment, 168; Corporation Council, 173;
    demographics of, 103; drug trade in, 152–
    160, 165–66, 201, 225, 229; mayor of, 181–
    82; Office of Comptroller of Currency,
    173; Real Estate Board, 79; riots in (1965),
    104–7, 286nn27–28; riots in (1991), 178–
    184; suburbs of, 26, 33, 57, 78–79, 82–83,
    103–4, 107–15, 117, 122–27, 130, 142–43,
    151–56, 178, 287n40; taxes in, 169; Ward
    1, 181; Ward 4, 168–69; zoning of sub-
    urbs, 108–13, 126. *See also* Intipucá–DC
    connection story; *names of suburban
    areas*
Washington, DC, Afro American (newspa-
    per), 106–7
Washington, George, 80
"Washington Consensus," 255–56
"Washington homes," 219
Washington Hospital Center, 179–180
Washington Post: on Banquito (Little
    Bank), 176–77; on DC riots (1965),
    104–6, 286nn27–28; on DC riots (1991),
    181–83; and Escobar, Gabriel, 61–62,
    65, 280n1; and Intipucá–DC connec-
    tion story, 6–7, 12, 15–16, 19, 40, 84–87,
    94–95, 148; Peterson interview, 117
Washington Senators (baseball team),
    289n19
watermelons, 92, 128, 160, 191
Watts Rebellion (Los Angeles), 105, 183
wave-water metaphor, 3–4, 19, 22, 26, 32,
    261–64, 271n2
wealth, Salvadoran, 7–12, 17–19, 27; and
    agrarian reform, 100–101; and Banquito
    (Little Bank), 174, 176, 213; and Chávez,
    Sigfredo, 57, 61–62, 65; and coffee prod-
    uction/export, 69, 72–74, 76, 82, 116, 132,
    263, 281n2; and cotton production ex-
    port, 92, 94, 116, 132, 215; in and im-
    ported beer, 207; and Intipucá's road
    sign, 196; and one-colon note, 68–70;
    and Raúl's family, 198–202; and remit-
    tances, 29, 33, 35–36, 40–41, 44, *45*, 47–
    48, 50, 116, 129, 132, 138–140, 148–49,
    157, 165–66, 202, 254, 262, 265,

wealth, Salvadoran (*cont.*)
279n16; *Un Dia en la Vida* (Argueta),
84–86; and US government aid, 35, 44,
45, 100–101, 116, 132, 139–140, 254; and
violence, 98–101. *See also* elites, Salva-
doran; landowners, Salvadoran
wealth, suburban, 150, 153–56, 159
Weinberger, Casper, 120–21
*Western Hemispheric Immigration and US
Foreign Policy* (Mitchell), 5
Westgate Corporation, 107–8, 287nn35–36
West Group, 107, 126
Westinghouse Air Brake Company, 78
Westpark Associates, 108, 287n40
West Park Office Complex, 126, 289n16
WGBH (Boston), 40–41, 279n16
whites and whiteness, 65, 102–3, 152–54,
169
"White Warriors Union," 95
*Who Are We? The Challenges to America's
National Identity* (Huntington), 4–5,
271n2
Wilkins Coffee (Washington, DC), 75–76,
283n31

Williams, Earle, 114, 124–26
Williamson, John, 256
Wilson, Jackie, 104
Wilson Community Center (Northwest
DC), 176
WMDO (Radio Mundo), 174
Woemer Report, 127
Wolfensohn, James, 256–57
Wolfowitz, Paul, 239–242, 248, 250–51
Wolf Trap National Park for the Performing
Arts (Va.), 126
Wollard, Kit, 275n34
"Woman's Voluntary Committee for the
Improvement of Intipucá," 194
Wood, Elizabeth, 43–46, *44*, *45*, 279n24,
280n25
Woodrow Wilson High School, 118–19
World Bank, 8, 22, 29, 32, 41, 46–48, 50–51,
81, 163, 250–51, 253–59, 292n6; Develop-
ment Report (1987), 256; *Global Devel-
opment Finance*, 253; "Global Economic
Prospects," 254; "International Confer-
ence on Migrant Remittances," 253–54
Wrench, William B., 112, 124–25